P9-BJC-537

THE AMZALAK FAMILY

SEPHARDI ENTREPRENEURS IN ERETZ ISRAEL
THE AMZALAK FAMILY 1816–1918

by

JOSEPH B. GLASS & RUTH KARK

JERUSALEM 1991
THE MAGNES PRESS, THE HEBREW UNIVERSITY

©
By The Magnes Press
The Hebrew University
Jerusalem 1991

ISBN 965-223-751-5
Printed in Israel
Typeset by Keterpress Enterprises, Jerusalem

CONTENTS

LIST OF FIGURES

LIST OF PLATES

ABBREVIATIONS OF ARCHIVES

AFP   Simon Amzalak Family Papers, Jerusalem
ANTT   Arquivo Nacional da Torre do Tombo, Lisbon
BHMA   Beit HaGdudim Museum Archives, Avihail
CZA   Central Zionist Archives, Jerusalem
CFA   Chelouche Family Archives, Tel Aviv
GGA   Gibraltar Govenment Archives, Gibraltar
HATAJM   Historical Archives of the Tel Aviv-Jaffa Municipality, Tel Aviv
ISA   Israel State Archives, Jerusalem
JMA   Jerusalem Municipal Archives, Jerusalem
JSTA   Jewish Theological Seminary Archives, New York
NLA   National Library Archives, Jerusalem
PMFAA   Portuguese Ministry of Foreign Affairs Archives, Lisbon
PPJA   Private Papers of James Amzalak, Jerusalem
PRO F.O.   Great Britain, Public Record Office, Foreign Office, London
TAJMA   Tel Aviv-Jaffa Municipal Archives, Tel Aviv
USNA   United States National Archives, Washington
YIBZA   Yad Itzhak Ben Zvi Archives, Jerusaelm

PREFACE

This study of the Amzalak family in Palestine during the late Ottoman period focuses upon its prominent members, their activities within the Jewish community and their contribution to the economic development of Palestine. Four generations of the Amzalak family lived in Palestine, from 1816, when Joseph Amzalak immigrated from Gibraltar, until the outbreak of World War I in 1914, when the family at large left the area so as to avoid becoming Ottoman citizens. Part of the family returned to Palestine, while other family members later became dispersed in Europe and the United States.

This study constitutes the first comprehensive work of the family's activities. Earlier articles and books have made mention of different family members in connection with many projects in Palestine, but none have attempted to study the family as a unit.

The family history is viewed against the background of the political, administrative, legal, economic, urban and rural changes in Palestine between the years 1799 to 1917. It is examined in the context of two central themes: the development of the local entrepreneur class in Palestine on the one hand and the Sephardi Jewish elite and its contribution to the process of change and modernization in the region on the other hand.

Our research drew mainly upon archival sources: the Amzalak family archives as well as those of the Navon, Chelouche, Eliachar and Yellin families, and the Archives of the British, American and German Consulates in Jerusalem as well as archives abroad — the Portuguese National Archives and the Portuguese Ministry of Foreign Affairs Archives in Lisbon and the Gibraltar Government Archives in Gibraltar.

Special attention was given to primary sources, such as correspondence and diaries found in archives, as well as contemporary accounts in newspapers, etc. These were combined with an analysis of maps, engravings and photographs of the sites mentioned in the book, and the conclusions drawn from field work conducted in these places. In addition, studies such as those of Bartal, Ben-Arieh, Kaniel, Parfitt, Sharabi and others were not ignored. One important study which has contributed to the understanding of activities of Joseph

11

Amzalak is that of Morgenstern. Also worthy of mention are the research papers describing the activities of the Amzalak family in nineteenth century Palestine by undergraduate students Ilona Winkler, Riki Sade-Rave and Eva Atia, written under the guidance of one of us (R.K.) at the Department of Geography of the Hebrew University of Jerusalem.

The book is divided into six chapters. Chapter one describes the political and legislative changes in the Ottoman Empire, especially in Palestine. The following chapters deal specifically with the Amzalaks: either a particular individual or a generation. The second chapter describes Joseph Amzalak, the founder of the family in Palestine, and the third, the generation of his children in Jerusalem. The fourth focuses upon Haim Amzalak's life in Jaffa. The fifth chapter deals with the third generation in Palestine, while concentrating on three individuals: Ben-Zion Amzalak, Joseph Amzalak and Joseph Navon Bey. The final chapter discusses the fourth generation, and the exodus of the family from Palestine in 1914.

Terms of Hebrew, Arabic or Turkish origin which are included in Webster's International Dictionary, e.g. Sephardim, Hasidim, pasha, are not printed in italics. The transliteration of foreign words is based on the rules of *Encyclopedia Judaica*, Jerusalem 1973, 1, pp. 90–92. However, diacritical marks under the letters have been omitted.

Finally, we wish to express our thanks to James Amzalak, grandson of Haim, the British vice-consul in Jaffa, and to Golda Amzalak, wife of Simon Mark Amzalak, another grandson of Haim, both of whom graciously provided us with numerous documents and an oral history of the family. Others helped us in the different stages of the research, including Yael Amzalak, Yehudit Avraham, Messod Belilo, Gila Brand, Sarit Danziger, Oodie Eilat, Maria Isabel Fevereiro, Michael Gordon, Daniel Halutzi, Gideon Hermel, Isaac Amzalak-Levi, Ephraim Levi, Mazal Linenberg-Navon, Marlis Roth and Rehav Rubin — to whom we owe our thanks. Tamar Soffer, Michal Kidron and Anath Altman-Bloch have skillfully drafted the maps and family trees.

Ruth Kark and Joseph Glass
Jerusalem, August 1990

INTRODUCTION

The nineteenth century marked a new era in the sphere of economic development in Palestine. This development was precipitated by both external and internal factors, including the improvement of institutional, political and security conditions. Two distinct population groups were involved in this process, namely new elements that came from abroad and members of the indigenous population.[1] Among the latter it was specifically the entrepreneur class — definable as those who organize and direct business undertaking while assuming the risk for the sake of profit[2] — that set this process in motion. Their economic activities influenced not only the economy, but also the landscape and settlement pattern of the region.

One approach in the historiography of the development of Palestine, as expressed in the works of Eliav, Kolat, Margalit and Szereszewski[3] has emphasized the contribution of the first group — foreign consuls, missionaries, philanthropists, and European and mainly Jewish settlers — while ignoring that of the second group, consisting of Arabs, Sephardi Jews and Levantines, mainly of Italian, Greek and Armenian origin. This school posits the existence of an "economically stagnating, unproductive and neglected Palestine before 1882 (that is, before the beginnings of foreign colonization)," with all its ideological implications.[4]

The separation of the two forementioned groups encouraged the idea of a dual economy, as asserted by Robert Szereszewski. He emphasizes that the Jewish

1   Nahum Gross, "Changes in Eretz-Israel at the End of the Ottoman Period," *Cathedra*, 2 (November 1976), p. 124 (Hebrew).
2   Jean L. McKechnie, *Webster's New Twentieth Century Dictionary of the English Language*, 1, Cleveland and New York 1969, p. 608.
3   Mordechai Eliav, "The Jewish Yishuv: the Determining Factor in the Economic Development of Eretz Israel," *Cathedra*, 2 (November 1976), pp. 126-127 (Hebrew); Israel Margalit, "The Contributions of the Baron to the Economic Development," *Cathedra*, 2 (November 1976), p. 132 (Hebrew); Robert Szereszewski, *Essays on the Structure of the Jewish Economy in Palestine and Israel*, Jerusalem 1968, pp. 92-96.
4   Alexander Schölch, "The Economic Development of Palestine, 1856-1882," *Journal of Palestine Studies*, vol. 10, no. 3 (Spring 1981), pp. 35-36.

13

economy had consisted of "a set of separate and fragmented enclaves which, under the impact of a large inflow of people and capital and of the strategy of the Zionist movement and the pressure of external events, congealed into a definable economic organization."[5] Mordechai Eliav even sees the need

> to place greater emphasis on the Jewish initiative and the role of the *yishuv* [the Jewish community of Eretz Israel in the pre-State period] in the economic development of Eretz Israel. This is prominent principally during the ten years between the founding of the Anglo-Palestine Bank and the outbreak of World War I. There is no doubt in the fact that the Zionist foundation, represented by its institutions and the whole *yishuv*, was the most dynamic factor in the economic development.[6]

According to Eliav, the influence of the foreign consuls was mainly expressed through their defending the interests of their protegés, the majority of whom were Jews.[7] Israel Margalit stresses the contribution of the foremost philanthropist, the Baron Edmond de Rothschild. His investment of over 40 million francs [£1,600,000] up to 1900, according to Margalit, greatly influenced not only the Jewish agricultural settlements but the whole economy of Palestine.[8]

However, other researchers, such as Chevallier, Gross, Issawi, Kark, Owen and Schölch,[9] trace the origins of Palestine's economic development to the period of Egyptian rule, and later in the mid-nineteenth century. Charles Issawi writes:

> the Egyptian occupation (1831-1840) saw an interruption of this stagnation. Ibrahim Pasha both enforced order and tried to promote development. Agriculture expanded and trade increased. However, the Egyptian withdrawal was followed by renewed deterioration.

5   Roger Owen, "Introduction," Roger Owen (ed.), *Studies in the Economic and Social History of Palestine in the Nineteenth and Twentieth Centuries*, Oxford 1982, p. 5.
6   Eliav (supra n. 3), p. 127.
7   Mordechai Eliav, "The Relation Between the Sectors," *Cathedra*, 2 (November 1976), p. 135 (Hebrew).
8   Margalit (supra n. 3), p. 132.
9   Gross (supra n. 1), pp. 111-125; Charles Issawi, *The Fertile Crescent 1800-1914*, New York 1988, pp. 9-30; Owen (supra n. 5); Schölch (supra n. 4), pp. 35-58; Dominique Chevallier, "Western Development and Eastern Crisis in the Mid-Nineteenth Century: Syria Confronted with the European Economy," William R. Polk, and Richard L. Chambers (eds.), *Beginnings of Modernization in the Middle East*, Chicago 1975, pp. 205-222.

Concurrently, European competition was forcing many craftsmen out of business.[10]

Issawi proceeds to assert that Palestine's economic recovery began in the mid-nineteenth century. Alexander Schölch elaborates upon this further in his work on Palestine between the years 1856-1882:

> Palestine produced a relatively large agricultural surplus which was marketed in neighbouring countries, such as Egypt or Lebanon, and increasingly exported to Europe. The transmission links between European demand and the adjustment of production to the requirements of the European market after 1850 were European consular agents (the majority of whom were themselves merchants, entrepreneurs, landowners, and even tax-farmers), the representatives of European commercial houses in the ports, and their partners and middlemen in the interior of the country.[11]

The initiators of economic transformation came from the local and foreign populations. The latter, according to Nahum Gross, contributed in various manners. Growing numbers of tourists increased demands for tourism-related services, new construction and to a limited extent, local produce. Missionaries contributed to improved social services — health, education and welfare. The presence of foreign consuls led to improvements in the judicial system, public order, security of life and property as well as the postal service. The investment of foreign capital towards the end of the century fostered additional economic growth. Gross views the economic leap forward after 1900 as an acceleration of earlier activities and the hastened imperialistic competition over the Palestine market. A second factor was the influence of the Second Aliyah [the wave of Jewish immigration to Palestine between 1904 and the outbreak of World War I], with the attendant increased import of capital.[12]

The following two sections elaborate upon two aspects of Palestine's society in the late Ottoman period. Firstly, the emergence of the entrepreneur class from the beginning of the nineteenth century is discussed. The development of this class up to World War I is on the one hand an indication of change in society and economy, and on the other hand a factor in it. This development is analyzed in the economic framework of the period; various statistics, especially trade figures, are emphasized as an index of change. Secondly, the Sephardi elite in

10 Issawi (supra n. 9), p. 10.
11 Schölch (supra n. 4), p. 36.
12 Gross (supra n. 1), pp. 114-120.

Palestine, one of the components of this entrepreneur class, is described at length. The information presented in both of these sections is supplemented and contextualized in Chapter One; it expands upon changes in political, administrative and security conditions, which weighed heavily on the aforementioned economic developments.

The Development of the Local Entrepreneur Class in the Light of Economic Changes in the Levant

At the beginning of the nineteenth century, the Middle Eastern economy, which was based on agriculture for local consumption, small-scale crafts and trade on regional and international levels, was stagnant.[13] It was at this time that the Industrial Revolution, which had gained momentum in Britain at the turn of the eighteenth century, and later in America and Europe, influenced the development of the Middle East. This industrialization was reflected in the quantity of output and, in mechanization and the use of steam power. It was followed by a revival of overseas trade and mercantilism. The Middle East became an important market for cheap British and European manufactured goods, and a source for food products and raw material. The roots of the local entrepreneur class lie in these developments.[14]

In addition, the Middle East was a middleman for international trade; goods from India and Persia were forwarded via Aleppo, goods from Africa via Alexandria, and goods from the Caucasus via Istanbul. A small merchant class existed, but with little liquid capital and little reason to invest in the region.[15] [see Figure 1]

---

13   Amnon Cohen, *Palestine in the 18th Century*, Jerusalem 1973, pp. 311-328; E.R.J. Owen, *The Middle East in the World Economy*, London 1981, pp. 1-56; Owen states in his conclusion to the chapter on the Middle Eastern economy in 1800 on page 65: "If a single word is needed to describe the general state of the Middle East economy as it existed in this period, it would have to be 'stagnant' whether in terms of income and investment, techniques and methods or organization, or simple facets of population. On the other hand easily cultivable land which required only minimal attention to questions of security, better transport, in some districts improvements in the system of irrigation to put them to productive use."

14   Charles Issawi, *The Economic History of the Middle East and North Africa*, New York 1982, pp. 150-159; Ruth Kark, "The Decline and Rise of the Coastal Towns in Palestine, 1800-1914," G. G. Gilbar (ed.), *Ottoman Palestine 1800–1914, Studies in Economic and Social History*, Leiden 1990, pp. 69–90; Owen (supra n. 13), pp. 83-99; William R. Polk and Richard L. Chambers, "Introduction," William R. Polk and Richard L. Chambers (eds.), *Beginnings of Modernization in the Middle East*, Chicago 1975, p. 4.

15   Owen (supra n. 13), pp. 50-56.

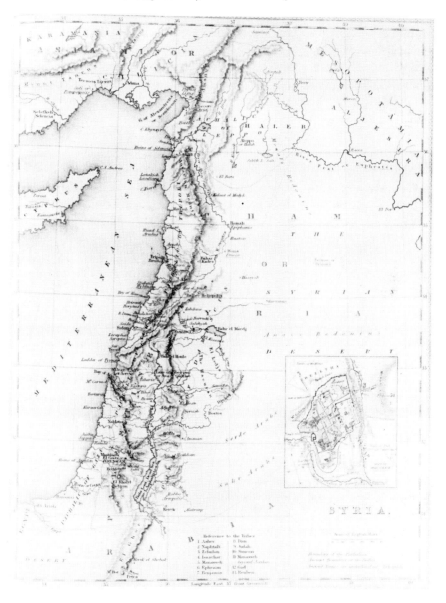

Figure 1: Eastern Mediterranean Sea,circa 1835
(Source: John Carne, *Syria, the Holy Land, Asia Minor etc.*, London 1835,
op. frontispiece)

Europe saw the Ottoman Empire as an untapped market, ripe for conquering. The number of European commercial houses found in the Middle Eastern ports increased rapidly during the first half of the century. The quantity of exports to the Ottoman Empire rose at a swift pace. England exported £154,000 worth of merchandise in 1814, a sum which increased almost sixteenfold to £7,468,000 in 1850. France exported commodities totaling 11,000,000 francs [£440,000] in 1816-1817, a figure which increased almost threefold by 1850. Trade also grew with other countries: Russia, Belgium, Holland, the United States, Italy and Austria. An important factor which led to this development was the inauguration of rapid and regular steam navigation from England, France and Austria to the eastern Mediterranean basin in the late 1830s. At first freightage was expensive and limited to travelers, mail and luxury goods. Technical improvements led to the lowering of costs, and steam ships were employed for the transportation of the entire range of merchandise. By the 1860s the majority of goods were shipped by steamers.[16]

During this period of commercial growth, certain difficulties, arising mainly from security problems, impeded trade with the interior. Thus a body of local intermediaries emerged, who served as middlemen between inland centers and European merchants located in the coastal towns. Slowly the local population took on the duties of the foreign merchants and partially replaced them. In parallel, there developed a local merchant class in the larger ports of Alexandretta, Beirut and Alexandria, as well as in the smaller ports of Palestine — Jaffa and Haifa. The shifting of trade centers from the interior to the Mediterranean led to the decline of Damascus and Aleppo, cities oriented toward the desert and traditional overland routes.

Beirut's rapid growth during the first half of the nineteenth century stemmed largely from the fact that its harbor could accommodate ships with deeper drafts than could Sidon's harbor, which was silting up at the time. Between 1833 and 1871-1873, Beirut's imports increased at a rate of 2.7 percent per annum, and its exports at a rate of 2.5 percent. The opening of the Beirut-Damascus carriage road in 1863 facilitated accessibility with the port's hinterland and contributed to the growth in trade. During the period from 1871-1873 to 1910-1912, the growth rate of trade in Beirut slowed; imports rose 1.1 percent annually while exports increased by 0.1 percent. This period witnessed further improvements in transportational infrastructure; the Beirut-Damascus-Hauran railroad was completed in 1895, with later extensions to Hama in 1903, Aleppo in 1908, and Tripoli in 1911. Despite these ameliorations, the expansion in Beirut's trade

---

16   Owen (supra n. 13), pp. 72-75; Chevallier (supra n. 9), pp. 205-209, 215-216.

Plate 1: Beirut, 1835
(Source: John Carne, *Syria, the Holy Land, Asia Minor etc.*, London 1835, I, p. 48)

slowed, partly due to the increased trade of Alexandretta and Jaffa. Nevertheless, Beirut remained the principal distribution center for the whole district.[17] [see Plate 1]

The volume of Alexandretta's trade reflected the vicissitudes of conditions in Aleppo, the center of a large agricultural hinterland and transit trade with Mesopotamia and Persia. Between 1833 and 1871-1873, Alexandretta's imports rose at a compound annual rate of 5.7 percent, and its exports 6.0 percent. Between 1871-1873 and 1906-1908, the increase slowed to 2.2 and 2.0 percent respectively.[18]

Jaffa's trade expanded rapidly between 1825 and 1871-1873: imports rose at a rate of 6.6 percent a year, and exports 8.7 percent. The following period, 1871-1873 to 1910-1912, also reflected the rapid growth of exports, the result of amplified shipments of grain, olive oil, soap and, increasingly, oranges. This trend was enhanced by road development in the region and the opening of a railway line from Jaffa to Jerusalem in 1892, which served to expand Jaffa's hinterland in the center of Palestine. Imports multiplied, mainly as a result of the development of Jerusalem, increased immigration and an expanding tourist

17   Issawi (supra n. 9), pp. 137-138; Polk (supra n. 14), p. 16.
18   Issawi (supra n. 9), pp. 138-139.

Plate 2: Jaffa from the north, 1859
(Source: William M. Thomson, *The Land and the Book*, New York 1859, II, p. 271)

trade. Imports for the forementioned period expanded yearly by 5.4 percent, while exports grew by 2.7 percent.[19] [see Plate 2]

Haifa, whose trade developed rapidly during the last two decades of Ottoman rule, eclipsed Acre as the main port of northern Palestine. Improved inland communications — the opening of a branch line of the Hejaz railway in 1905, and the development of its natural port, which was particularly suitable for the anchoring of steamships, contributed to its success. Imports rose by 6.3 percent per annum and exports by 12.0 percent between 1895-1908 and 1910-1912.[20]

Resident in these port cities were both the intermediaries and the local merchants who came from the minority populations: Armenian- and Greek-Christians, and Jews. They had the advantage over the Muslim population of enjoying the protection of foreign consuls, and of knowing both European and local languages.[21]

19 Issawi (supra n. 9), p. 139; Kark (supra n. 14).
20 Issawi (supra n. 9), p. 139; Kark (supra n. 14).
21 Alexander Schölch, "European Penetration and the Economic Development of Palestine 1856-1882," Roger Owen (ed.), *Studies in the Economic and Social History of Palestine in the Nineteenth and Twentieth Centuries*, Oxford 1982, p. 12; Leila Tarazi Fawaz, *Merchants and Migrants in Nineteenth Century Beirut*, Cambridge, Mass. 1983, p. 85; Owen (supra n. 13), pp. 72-81.

The local entrepreneurs provided the Europeans with services that were indispensable to the conduct of business. Hence they were exempted from certain taxes levied by the Ottoman government, and became eligible for the same judicial, financial and economic privileges granted to Europeans; this, in turn, advanced their business undertakings. Many of these local entrepreneurs offered their services, sometimes free of charge, to the consuls to gain protection and the accompanying advantages. Sometimes they themselves served as consular agents, which strengthened their social and economic status.[22]

They found themselves in a variety of roles: as intermediaries between European wholesalers and local retailers, and between European merchants and cultivators of crops; as partners with Europeans in land ownership during the period of restrictions; as money lenders to cultivators at exorbitant rates; and as middlemen for manufacturers.[23]

The result of all these activities was the accumulation of capital and the development of close connections with European financial institutions. The trend was toward reinvestment in one or more other areas of the business world. These areas of reinvestment fall into five categories: 1) land, for speculation and development; 2) industry; 3) natural resources; 4) banking and 5) public works.[24]

Land was regarded as a sound investment during a period of rapidly-rising prices and heightened agricultural development. Between the 1850s and 1880s factors such as increased security, rising population pressure, changes in the Land Code, increasing interest by city capitalists, growing world demand for agricultural produce and better communications combined to expand agricultural settlement. Grain production markedly increased; however, the condition of the peasantry remained unchanged. In the 1870s a combination of poor harvests, conscription and debt brought large tracts under the ownership of urban capitalists. According to Claude Reiner Conder, the coastal plain around Jaffa was bought up by Jewish, Greek and Maronite capitalists.[25]

22 Fawaz (supra n. 21), p. 86; Owen (supra n. 13), pp. 86-88.
23 Owen (supra n. 13), pp. 88-89; Fawaz (supra n. 21), pp. 87-88.
24 This division is based on an earlier study: Joseph Glass, *Joseph Navon Bey (1858-1934): A Local Entrepreneur and his Contribution to the Changing Landscape of Eretz Yisrael in the Late 19th Century*, M.A. Thesis, Hebrew University of Jerusalem, Jerusalem 1988; Joseph Glass, "The Biography in Historical-Geographical Research: Joseph Navon Bey — A Case Study," Ruth Kark (ed.), *The Land that Became Israel — Studies in Historical Geography*, New Haven 1990, pp. 77-89.
25 Claude Reiner Conder, *Heth and Moab, Explorations in Syria in 1881 and 1882*, London 1886, p. 368.

The Sursuks of Beirut purchased 181 square kilometers in the Jezreel Valley (Marj Ibn 'Āmir) in the north of Palestine, and the Bustroses of Beirut owned real-estate in Syria, Palestine and Egypt. In addition, the Sursuks attempted to exploit their land through its cultivation by tenants, providing the latter with approximately one-fifth of the produce. Thus the Sursuks, who also obtained the tax-farming rights to these lands, practically monopolized the agricultural surplus in the Jezreel Valley.[26]

Industry also became a new area in which the local entrepreneurs could increase their wealth, but only to a limited extent. Attempts at industrialization were handicapped by the small local market, shifting demand for foreign goods, expensive fuel, the lack of raw material, costly transportation, expensive and almost unavailable skilled labor, limited capital and almost no government support. However, in Lebanon the silk industry became an avenue for investment. Between 1862 and 1880 the number of silk-reeling factories there increased from 33 to 100, with no growth in the number of foreign-owned factories. In Palestine, there are very few examples of this type of investment by the local entrepreneur class.[27]

Areas rich in natural resources, particularly in Asia Minor, were exploited by the local entrepreneurs. An indication of this trend can be seen through the following two examples: in the Amasiya region, two coal mines were owned by Greeks and one by a Turk, and in Trabzon the copper mines were controlled by one German, one Greek, one Armenian and two Turks, while the zinc mines were controlled by a Greek, a Turk and a German.[28] The limited natural resources of Palestine and Syria were not considered exploitable during the late Ottoman period.[29]

Banks sprouted throughout the Ottoman Empire. During the 1830s and 1840s there were a number of private bankers who began to establish themselves in various port cities. Family-owned banks, some of them small, with connections with larger European commercial banks, organized through joint stocks with European interests. The overwhelming majority of local bankers came from foreign and minority communities. In Palestine, local Jews and

26 Owen (supra n. 13), p. 175; Issawi (supra n. 9), pp. 270-271; Ruth Kark, "Changing Patterns of Land Ownership in Nineteenth Century Palestine: The European Influence," *Journal of Historical Geography*, vol. 10, no. 4 (1984) pp. 357-368; Glass (supra n. 24), pp. 101-105; Haim Gerber, *The Social Origins of the Modern Middle East*, London 1987.

27 Owen (supra n. 13), p. 157; Issawi (supra n. 9), pp. 378-380.

28 Charles P. Issawi, *The Economic History of Turkey 1800-1914*, Chicago 1980, pp. 291-298.

29 Issawi (supra n. 9), pp. 367-368.

Christians dominated the field, some examples being the Valero, Bergheim, Spittler (later Frutiger & Co.) and Hamburger Banks in Jerusalem.[30]

Public works projects were another area for investment. According to David Landes, "the real stakes lay in contracts and concessions for the construction of public works and the creation of public services." His comments on the situation in Egypt can be applied to the entire Ottoman Empire:

> All were designed to exploit the needs of Egypt and the weakness and ignorance of the Egyptian government. All aimed at making the most of a good thing, imposing one-sided conditions and charging exorbitant fees. All were intended to yield exceptional, even fabulous profits although it must be admitted that results did not always meet expectations and it goes without saying that none was expected to show a loss. Those who invested in Egyptian ventures had no intention of venturing his money and where the normal returns were not sufficient there were always ways to convince the Viceroy that he owed it to his credit, to his people and to fair play to save the skin of his guests.[31]

In Palestine, one of the more notable figures in this field was Joseph Navon Bey, the grandson of Joseph Amzalak. He received the concession for the first railroad actually built in Palestine, the Jaffa-Jerusalem line, inaugurated in 1892. In addition, he received the concessions for the port of Jaffa and the intensive exploitation of the Yarkon River waters.[32]

Local entrepreneurs found diverse areas in which to invest their newly amassed wealth. Starting as middlemen for foreign merchants at the beginning of the nineteenth century, they developed into a wealthy class engaging in commerce, finance, industry and development. These Arabs, Sephardi Jews and Levantines, mainly of Italian, Greek and Armenian origin, became a dominant force in the economy of Palestine and the Middle East as a whole, and brought about changes in the landscape of the region.

---

30 David S. Landes, *Bankers and Pashas — International Finance and Economic Imperialism in Egypt*, London 1958, pp. 61-63; Glass (supra n. 24), pp. 106-109; Yehoshua Ben-Arieh, *Jerusalem in the 19th Century, The Emergence of the New City*, Jerusalem 1986, pp. 378–382; Kurt Grunwald, "Banking in Jerusalem during the Ottoman Period," *Economics Quarterly*, vol. 24, nos. 92-93 (1977), pp. 117-120 (Hebrew).

31 Landes (supra n. 30), p. 98; Glass (supra n. 24), pp. 101-126.

32 Glass (supra n. 24) for Navon's involvement in public works projects, see pp. 81-100.

The Sephardi Elite in Palestine

The Jewish population of Palestine at the beginning of the nineteenth century totaled about 5,000-6,000. The majority were Sephardim — literally the descendants of Iberian Jewries wherever resident but also members of Oriental communities in the Ottoman Empire and North Africa — and from ancient local families; they were mainly Ottoman subjects. The remainder, a few hundred families, were Ashkenazim — Jews of Eastern- and Central- European origin. The Ashkenazim had immigrated to Palestine throughout the Ottoman period, and most retained their former citizenships. The vast majority of Jewry in Palestine resided in the four holy cities: Jerusalem, Safed, Tiberias and Hebron.[33]

In the early decades of the nineteenth century, the Ashkenazi community began to increase in number and strength. The Prushim (the disciples of Rabbi Elijah the *gaon* of Vilna, and who opposed the Hasidim) began to immigrate to Safed, and from 1816 some of them made their way to Jerusalem, renewing the Ashkenazi presence there. Similarly, at first the Hasidim (the disciples of Israel ben Eliezer Baal Shem-Tov) settled in Safed, Tiberias and Hebron, but by the 1840s they too had established themselves in Jerusalem.

By 1875 the Jewish community in Palestine had increased to 23,000, and the proportion of the Ashkenazim rose to half. Towards the end of Ottoman rule in Palestine, the Jewish community numbered approximately 80,000, over two-thirds Ashkenazi.[34]

Great differences between the two communities existed in nearly all areas of life. The Ashkenazim and Sephardim were very distant from each other in mentality, folklore and customs. Their religious traditions, particularly the form of prayer and ritual slaughter, also expressed differences. They had dissimilar social and educational concepts. The Sephardim spoke Ladino and Arabic, while the Ashkenazim spoke Yiddish. Hebrew was used for official communication between the communities, although only their respective

---

33 Moshe Maoz, "Changing in the Position of the Jewish Communities of Palestine and Syria in Mid-Nineteenth Century," Moshe Maoz (ed.), *Studies on Palestine during the Ottoman Period*, Jerusalem 1975, p. 143.

34 Mordechai Eliav, "Intercommunal Relations within the Yishuv at the end of the Ottoman Period," *Offprint from the International Conference on Jewish Communities In Muslim Lands*, Hebrew University of Jerusalem, Jerusalem 1973, p. 8 (Hebrew); Yehoshua Kaniel, *Continuity and Change: Old Yishuv and New Yishuv During the First and Second Aliyah*, Jerusalem 1981, p. 4 (Hebrew); this work provides a slightly higher figure of 85,000 Jews in Palestine at the end of the period of Ottoman rule; Owen (supra n. 13), p. 264 gives a lower figure of 50,000.

leaders had some command of the language. The origins of the two groups affected their dress, housing and cuisine; the Ashkenazim had imported their European ways from the Christian world, while the Sephardim were influenced by the Orient and Islam. The attitudes of each group towards productivity and manual labor differed, as their respective *halukkah* (charity distribution) systems attest. The Sephardi communal funds were allotted as follows: one-third for payment of taxes, debt and maintenance of institutions; one-third for *Talmidei Hachamim* (scholars) and one-third for the needy. As the majority of the Sephardi population were neither *Talmidei Hachamim* nor indigent, they did not directly benefit from this system, and were encouraged to earn a living in trade, crafts and brokerage. On the other hand, the Ashkenazi *halukkah* system allotted sums to all the members of its community, in accordance with set criteria.

The contrast between the communities was visible to outside observers, as discussed by Israel Bartal:

> A striking illustration of the power of preconceptions is the difference in attitude towards Sephardi and Ashkenazi communities. Most of the British travellers tended to lavish more praise on the Sepharadim than on the Ashkenazim, from the standpoint of physical appearance and lifestyle as well as of ideology and moral fiber. On the whole, Sepharadim (often called "Portuguese") were portrayed much more favourably than their East-European and German counterparts. Their superior image among the Europeans of the seventeenth-nineteenth centuries may derive from the traces of oriental exoticism discernable in them, and in the impression they gave of being relatively more open to cultural change — an openness that was praised even when the observer did not comprehend the reasons for it. On the other hand, East European Jews, who were more familiar with traditional society, viewed some of the same Sephardi characteristics negatively, and related more positively to the Ashkenazim.[35]

Sephardi Jews, unlike their Ashkenazi counterparts, were encouraged to enter into various branches of the local economy. The lengthy Sephardi presence in the region provided these people with an understanding of the ways and customs of the Imperial government, its local representatives and the non-Jewish inhabitants of Palestine. It facilitated their integration into the fields of

35   Israel Bartal, "'Old Yishuv' and 'New Yishuv' Image and Reality," Lee I. Levine (ed.), *The Jerusalem Cathedra*, 1, Jerusalem 1981, pp. 218-219.

commerce and early modern banking. Together with North African immigrants, the Sephardim were instrumental in the development of the coastal cities of Jaffa and Haifa. They played an important role in the modernization of the economy and the assimilation of Western influences.

The historiography of Palestine places little emphasis on the actions of the Sephardi sector as a separate entity. Instead, the Jewish population was viewed as being divided into the Old *Yishuv* and New *Yishuv*, with their conflicting concepts. Yehoshua Kaniel, in his discussion of the problematic definition of these two groups, attempts to place the Sephardi population within the framework of one or the other:

> We have seen how the term Old *Yishuv* was usually applied to the Ashkenazi Jews. But what about those Sepharadim who, on the whole, were self-supporting? Not receiving *halukka* money, they joined or worked in the new settlements, and generally supported the nationalist aspirations of the New *Yishuv*. Were they part of the New *Yishuv* or not? Clearly it is necessary to examine each individual incident or statement under consideration in order to decide.[36]

Kaniel, in the summation of his study, divides the Jewish population of Palestine into three groups: 1) those who met all the criteria for membership in the Old *Yishuv*; 2) those belonging organically to the Sephardi community; and 3) members of the New *Yishuv* including all ethnic groups within the Jewish population of Palestine.[37]

Yisrael Bartal, in his definition of these terms, integrates the Sephardi community into the New *Yishuv*. He sees their involvement in the new and modern economic processes, and their possession of certain values similar to those of the New *Yishuv*, as criteria for their inclusion. Bartal explains the lack of attention to the Sephardi community in the historiography:

> The participation [of the Sephardim] was relegated to the sidelines, because the changeover to the "new" society was conceived mainly in terms of agricultural development. Thus, for example, greater importance was ascribed to a Jew contemplating purchase of land in an Arab village (while attributing to him intentions that had never crossed his mind nor been hinted at in his actions), than to the description of urban development that really existed....Because of preoccupation with

36   Yehoshua Kaniel, "The Terms 'Old Yishuv' and 'New Yishuv': Problems of Definition," Lee I. Levine (ed.), *The Jerusalem Cathedra*, 1, Jerusalem 1981, p. 244.
37   Kaniel (supra n. 36), p. 245.

dominant social groups which were actually ideology-oriented elites in both the "old" and "new" communities, inadequate attention was paid to the integration of certain sectors of the Sephardi population into the socio-economic fabric of Palestine.[38]

Nevertheless, from the ranks of the Sephardi community a number of individuals and families stood out as an elite group, and did receive some attention in the historiography of Palestine during the late Ottoman period. Their position within the Sephardi community, the total Jewish community and the general population of Palestine was one of prominence based on power and wealth. One source of power was their involvement in various religious institutions, which placed them in a position of control, allowing them to be part of the decision-making process regarding the future of the community and its financial resources. The most important position was that of Chief Rabbi. His role was that of leader of the Jewish community and its representative vis-à-vis the other religious communities and the Ottoman government. Another basis of power was material wealth, either accumulated earlier or based on ongoing commercial activities. In many cases there was an overlapping of wealth and prominence, and at times a merging of the two through connections of marriage. Families such as the Amzalaks, Eliachars, Meuchases, Navons and Valeros stood out in Jerusalem, as the Moyals and Chelouches did in Jaffa.

With the opening up of possibilities of serving on Ottoman local councils or being employed within the ranks of the Ottoman administration, these elite families took an active role in local government. At the same time, they found themselves in the service of foreign governments and their representatives in Palestine. Both these developments further enhanced their elite status and broadened their base of influence.

The Sephardi elite played a prominent role in the development and modernization of Palestine during the late Ottoman period. They were a separate entity, one that rose above the differences of the Old *Yishuv* and New *Yishuv*, at times bridging the differences between the two.

Many members of the Sephardi elite were harbingers of change not only within the Jewish community, but within the population of Palestine on the whole. Before the schism emerged in the Ashkenazi community between the Old *Yishuv* and the New *Yishuv* with regard to modernization and productivization, they were already involved in these processes. After the appearance of this rift, they were relegated to the sidelines by historiographers, while the processes they had set in motion were attributed to others.

38 Bartal (supra n. 35), pp. 216, 224-225.

This study depicts the Amzalak family in the light of the developments of the period — as does an earlier study of Joseph Navon Bey. The present study differs from others, such as those by Gaon, Ben-Ya'akov and Efrati,[39] in that it describes the distinct role of Sephardi elite families not only within the context of the Jewish community, but also within that of the general population of the region.

---

39   Moshe David Gaon, *The Jews of the East in the Past and Present*, 1, Jerusalem 1928, p. 131 (Hebrew); Abraham Ben-Ya'akov, *Jerusalem within its Walls: the History of the Meyuhas Family*, Jerusalem 1976 (Hebrew); Nathan Efrati, *The Role of the Eliachar Family in Jerusalem*, Jerusalem 1975 (Hebrew).

CHAPTER ONE

THE POLITICAL BACKGROUND 1799-1917

A complete understanding of the history of the Amzalak family in Palestine would be difficult without the background covering the political affairs of the time and the administrative orders then effective in Palestine. The year 1799, when Napoleon Bonaparte's army invaded Palestine, shall serve as our starting point. What ensued was a new era in the history of Palestine. From a forsaken province, it became the focal point in a tug-of-war between the European powers competing for influence in the Middle East.

From a political perspective, this period in the history of Palestine could be divided into four sub-periods: a) the rule of pashas and local leaders (1799-1831), which had begun earlier in the eighteenth century; b) the conquest of Syria and Palestine by Egyptian ruler Muhammad Ali via his adopted son, Ibrahim Pasha (1831-1841) — a pivotal period which, despite its brevity, was marked by numerous changes in government and other spheres; c) the period of reforms (1841-1876), when the Ottomans, having regained power, attempted to institute new patterns of government; d) the end of the Ottoman period (1877-1917). The first and larger part of this final sub-period was that of the centralized rule of Sultan Abdul Hamid II; then came the rise of the Young Turks, who staged a revolution in 1908 and remained in power until the British occupation of Palestine in 1917-1918.[40]

At the Turn of the Nineteenth Century

During Turkey's golden age in the sixteenth century, it was one of the largest empires in the world. By the late eighteenth and early nineteenth century it had declined to a nadir in its history.[41] True, Sultan Selim III (1789-1807) attempted

40 This chapter is an updating of an earlier study: Ruth Kark, *The Development of the Cities Jerusalem and Jaffa — 1840 up to the First World War, a Study in Historical Geography*, Ph.D. Thesis, Hebrew University of Jerusalem, Jerusalem 1976, pp. 1-40 (Hebrew).
41 Uriel Heyd, *Westernization and Modernization in the Ottoman Empire*, Jerusalem 1963 (Hebrew); Bernard Lewis, *The Emergence of Modern Turkey*, London 1968, pp. 21-39.

to introduce military and administrative reforms, emulating the nations of Europe (France in particular), but he was unsuccessful, and in the end was assassinated by opponents. Repeated defeats abroad and dangerous revolts at home had sapped the empire's strength. Moreover, the reforms were opposed by the Janissaries, the *'ulema* (religious leaders), the feudal lords and the general population — the last group primarily because they were heavily taxed to finance these measures.[42]

Selim's successor, Sultan Mahmud II (1808-1839), introduced a series of new reforms in 1826, after systematically liquidating the Janissary corps and weakening the *'ulema*. Mahmud II knew that military reforms were insufficient; he endeavored to reorganize the administration, strengthen centralized rule, and introduce direct supervision of the empire's provinces. He reduced the authority of the Grand Vizier, set up ministries and councils, paid officials large salaries, revised inheritance laws to make life and property more secure, and published a newspaper. Economic development may have been overlooked to some extent, but some scholars point out that in both Selim III's and Mahmud II's time, industrialization was beginning to make its appearance, mainly for the benefit of the military and the royal court.[43]

Nevertheless, the important reforms introduced by Mahmud II with the assistance of Mustafa Rashid Pasha could not keep the empire from crumbling. During his rule, strategic regions were lost by the Ottomans: Greece, Bessarabia, the Circassian coast on the northeastern Black Sea and several Armenian districts. The Ottomans also lost direct control over Serbia, Algeria, Egypt, Syria, Palestine and the district of Adana, which remained part of the empire in theory, but in practice were governed by autonomous rulers.[44] It should be remembered that even where the Ottoman government presided, only that part of the permanent population residing in or near the towns and villages was under its jurisdiction; these areas were only narrow strips within the territory controlled by Bedouin.[45]

Palestine as a Forsaken District
The reforms instituted at the center of the Ottoman Empire hardly reached the periphery; Palestine in those days remained a forsaken district in a crumbling empire. In 1800, the population totaled 300,000. The country was split between

42   Lewis (supra n. 41), pp. 21-39.
43   E.C. Clark, "The Ottoman Industrial Revolution," *International Journal of Middle East Studies*, vol. 5, no. 1 (1974), pp. 65-76.
44   Heyd (supra n. 41); Lewis (supra n. 41), pp. 76-106.
45   Izhak Ben-Zvi, *Eretz-Israel under Ottoman Rule*, Jerusalem 1955, p. 79 (Hebrew).

two *eyālets* (provinces) whose borders changed from time to time in keeping with the military might of their governors. In general, however, the central mountain region from Nablus to Hebron (Jerusalem included) belonged to the province of Damascus, and the Galilee and the coastal plain up to Khan Yunis to the province of Acre (or Sidon). The Negev was largely outside the jurisdiction of the Ottomans at this time.[46]

In Palestine and other Muslim-Arab regions of Asia, local traditions and leadership were still much respected, as were the heads of the religious communities. The Ottomans merely added an upper echelon — military garrisons and governors — to the existing hierarchy in non-ethnic Turkish areas.[47]

At the end of the eighteenth century, the pashas of the Syrian-Palestine region functioned as autonomous rulers. They remained in power as long as they were able to overcome the obstacles set in their path by the imperial authorities. All local leaders recognized the sovereignty of the Sultan, sometimes ex post facto.[48]

This form of government, with slight modifications, persisted throughout the first thirty years of the nineteenth century. Ahmad al-Jazzar ("the Butcher") held power until 1804, and was succeeded by Suleiman Pasha, who ruled until 1818. His successor, 'Abdallah Pasha (1818-1831), broadened his authority to incorporate subdistricts outside the province of Sidon (Acre): Jerusalem, Gaza, Jaffa and Nablus.[49] Although these pashas remained affiliated with the Sublime Porte and regularly paid it taxes, in the provinces they acted as sovereign rulers, establishing private armies, imposing taxes and surcharges at whim, and governing to suit themselves. The welfare of the people was of no interest to them. However, these practices drew them into frequent disputes with the subdistrict governors, who tried to follow the same model and establish their own private princedoms.[50] [see Plate 3]

The pashas saw their major mission as the collection of taxes. There were three sources of revenue: the *miri* or land tax on Muslims, the *kharaj*, a military exemption fee paid by Christians and Jews, and customs duties. From time to time, various city taxes were imposed arbitrarily. The pasha's army served not

46 J.C. Hurewitz, "Eretz Israel, History 1800-1882," *Encyclopaedia Hebraica*, 6, Ramat Gan 1970, pp. 498-500 (Hebrew).

47 James Finn, *Stirring Times*, 1, London 1878, pp. 109-118.

48 Great Britian Foreign Office, *Syria and Palestine*, London 1920, p. 21.

49 Uriel Heyd, *Eretz-Israel during the Period of Ottoman Rule*, Jerusalem 1972, p. 76 (Hebrew); Ulrich Jasper Seetzen, *Reisen durch Syrien, Palästina Phoenicien, die Tranjordenlander, Arabia Petraea und Unteraegypten*, 2, Berlin 1854-1859, p. 69.

50 Hurewitz (supra n. 46).

Plate 3: St. Jean d'Acre with Mount Carmel in the distance, 1840
(Source: C. Pellé and L. Galibert, *Voyage en Syrie et dans L'Asie Mineure*,
Paris 1843, p. 67)

so much to keep the peace as to terrorize the population into paying these taxes.[51] The insecurity was such that the Bedouin would raid populated areas and the fellahin attack neighboring villages. Danger and lawlessness ruled the roads, too.

The ones who suffered from this state of affairs were the Ottoman subjects of Palestine, Muslim and non-Muslim alike. The latter were in an even worse position, as they were considered second-class citizens by the government and the Muslim community. Non-Muslims were required to wear special clothing and pay additional taxes (*jizya*), and their testimony was invalid in a court of law. There were additional restrictions which varied from town to town, and they were subject to persecution and violence.[52]

The Period of Ibrahim Pasha: 1831-1840

Methodologically, it appears that this period in Ottoman history should be studied together with the previous one; practically speaking, it was a

---

51 Ze'ev Vilnay, *Jerusalem the Capital of Israel — The Old City and Its Environs*, 2, Jerusalem 1972, pp. 225-233 (Hebrew).

52 Moshe Maoz, *Ottoman Reform in Syria and Palestine 1840-1861*, London 1968, p. 10.

continuation of the rule and policies of Sultan Mahmud II. However, in Palestine and Syria, it was a period unto itself. In November 1839, an important event took place in Turkey: the issuance of the *Khatt-i Sheriff* of Gul Khane (the Rose Law or the Rescript of the Rose Chamber) following the rise of Abdul Majid (1839-1861). This edict marked the official commencement of a new period, the *Tanzimat* or period of reforms, and laid the foundations for future legislation. It dealt with civil rights and various administrative reforms in an attempt to protect the lives, property and dignity of all subjects, regardless of religion and ethnic affiliation. It called for fairer taxation and the abolishment of the *iltizām* (right to levy taxes). In order to put an end to the widespread bribery, government officials were now to be salaried. Changes were also introduced in the military draft and the duration of service.[53]

In 1840, the first of the promised regulations went into effect: a new criminal law. Administrative and fiscal reforms were instituted as well. That year, steps were taken to reform the monetary system through the establishment of banks and financial institutions. A *firman* (imperial edict) was issued for the founding of a European-style Ottoman bank, and for the first time paper money was circulated in addition to coins.

On the whole, public opinion in Istanbul and other cities was hostile to these reforms, which were also opposed by landowners and the *'ulema*, who felt their interests were being harmed. However, the edict was welcomed by Western powers, and as a result England, Austria, Prussia and Russia agreed to vouch for the territorial sovereignty of the Ottoman Empire.[54]

In Palestine

In Palestine, provincial government was at its peak. Muhammad Ali, for all intents and purposes an autonomous ruler, rebelled against the Sublime Porte. His stepson, Ibrahim Pasha, conquered territory from the other pashas and forced the Sultan to acknowledge the "legality" of his actions. Nevertheless, after fortifying his position in 1834, Ibrahim Pasha agreed to pay the Sultan "the usual share of taxes."[55] Ibrahim created a strong centralized government in Palestine and Syria by almost entirely removing the feudal lords and setting up a modern, multi-branched administration. He diminished the power of the religious judges, transferring authority over criminal courts to the governor, and over the civil courts to the *majlis al-shūrā* (advisory councils) established in

53   Heyd (supra n. 41); Lewis (supra n. 41), pp. 106-155.
54   Hurewitz (supra n. 46), pp. 500-501.
55   Yitzhak Hoffman, *Muhammad Ali, Khedive of Egypt 1769-1849*, Ph.D. thesis, Hebrew University of Jerusalem, Jerusalem 1973, pp. 1-63 (Hebrew).

Plate 4: Jerusalem from the Mount of Olives, 1840
(Source: C. Pellé and L. Galibert, *Voyage en Syrie et dans L'Asie Mineure*,
Paris 1843, p. 36)

each city of over 2,000 inhabitants. He was tolerant towards Christians and Jews, and abolished discriminatory practices common in the past.[56] Changes in the status of Christians were introduced both for economic reasons and to please the Great Powers, France and Britain. The same considerations motivated him to allow the opening of consulates in Damascus and Jerusalem, and to permit the missionary societies to pursue their activities among non-Muslims freely. These actions were unprecedented in the history of Ottoman Palestine, and exposed the region for the first time to Western influence and a new era of modernization.[57] [see Plate 4]

Also conspicuous was the improvement in domestic security. With the help of a large army, banditry was wiped out and the stronger Bedouin tribes were held in check and encouraged to settle down. The enhanced security in rural areas and on the roads was a boon to agriculture, which the authorities actively

56   Heyd (supra n. 41), pp. 48-51.
57   Derek Hopewood, *The Russian Presence in Syria and Palestine 1843-1914, Church and Politics in the Near East*, Oxford 1969, p. 9; Maoz (supra n. 52), p. 19; Shimon Shamir, "Egyptian Rule (1832-1840) and the Beginning of the Modern Period in the History of Palestine"; Amnon Cohen and Gabriel Baer (eds.), *Egypt and Palestine: A Millennium of Association (1868-1948)*, Jerusalem and New York 1984, pp. 214-231.

sought to develop in an effort to supply the needs of the Egyptian army. Public buildings and fortresses were built, as well as quarantine housing to prevent the spread of epidemics. The Egyptian government also controlled the currency and kept it from devaluating.[58]

However, the draft, taxation, *angaria* (forced labor), monopolies, secularism, equality for non-Muslims and, finally, the European presence, all greatly angered the Muslim population and set off a series of uprisings against the government in various parts of Palestine and Syria. These revolts, some incited by agents of the Sublime Porte, were harshly suppressed. Ibrahim Pasha even succeeded in defeating the Ottoman army, which tried to oppose him in 1839. Only after the intervention of the European powers at the end of 1840 and the beginning of 1841 was he forced to surrender and relinquish his claim over Palestine and Syria.

The Period of Reforms, 1841-1876

In 1841, Mustafa Rashid, vizier in charge of the reform, was temporarily dismissed. Conservative officials rose in his stead, concerned mainly with improving administrative efficiency. At the time, the British ambassador to Istanbul, Sir Stratford Canning, a supporter of the reforms and the integrity of the Ottoman Empire, was becoming increasingly influential in the royal court. It was Mustafa Rashid and Canning who stood behind some of the important reforms instituted between 1845-1852. Advisory councils were established to run the districts, mixed courts for lawsuits between Ottomans and non-Ottomans were created, a modern commercial code was promulgated, secular high schools were opened and a school system was planned. An attempt was made to abolish the slave trade and grant the status of *millet* (recognized religious group) to Protestants. Due to a series of abortive coups in Europe in 1848 and the slackening of Rashid Pasha's activity, the pace of the reforms began to slow down in the late 1840s. The economic situation of the empire continued to deteriorate, and in 1853 the Crimean War broke out.[59]

Turkey continued to promulgate important reforms even during the war, largely to curry favor among its allies. May 1855 saw the abolishment of the *jizya*, the tax on non-Muslims, who were given the choice of enlisting in the army or paying the *bedel* (exemption fee).

---

58   A.J. Rustum, *The Archives of the Royal Egyptian Expedition to the Levant (1831-1840)*, 3, Damascus 1936, pp. 257-265 (Arabic).

59   Heyd (supra n. 41); Lewis (supra n. 41), pp. 110-119; Moaz (supra n. 52), pp. 21-30.

On the eve of the peace conference in Paris, the Sultan issued the *Khatt-i Humayun* (the Imperial Rescript), chiefly to grant equality to non-Muslims and to safeguard the lives, property and religious liberty of all Ottoman subjects.[60]

The Rescript allowed for the repair and renovation of religious institutions, and opened up official and military posts, state schools and military academies to all Ottoman subjects. Non-Muslims could now serve on local and district councils, and in the courts. This charter authorized mixed criminal and commercial courts, and validated the testimony of non-Muslims. It called for reorganization and tighter control over the *millet* system, and even permitted foreign nationals to purchase Ottoman land. Aside from this, it reaffirmed the abolishment of the *iltizām* (the right to collect taxes), promised to eradicate bribery, reinstituted prisons and police, and called for the cessation of inhumane punishment. The Rescript also recommended the publication of an annual budget, the establishment of banks and the development of a transportation system.[61]

At the signing of the Paris Treaty in 1856, the *Khatt-i Humayun* was greeted with satisfaction by France and England; that year Turkey had been accepted into the European Concert and its territorial sovereignty had been assured. However, the implementation of these reforms was acceptable to but a few: Muslim public opinion was opposed, the Christians and Jews had little faith in the promises, and an infrastructure of educated, tolerant officials was lacking. The financial state of the empire, which took a turn for the worse in the 1850s and 1860s, was another excuse for increased hatred of foreigners, of the Great Powers, and indirectly, of all the reforms that had been or were about to be implemented at the initiative or insistence of the Powers.[62]

A commercial code advanced by Rashid Pasha and the Grand Vizier was

60   Hurewitz (supra n. 46), pp. 149-153.
61   Hurewitz (supra n. 46), pp. 149-153.
62   Opinions are divided about the motives for the reforms. Some believe that domestic reasons and structural change were chiefly responsible, and that centralized rule, bureaucracy, Western influence, urbanization and better communications only served as catalyzers; see: K.H. Karpat, "The Transformation of the Ottoman State 1789-1908," *International Journal of Middle East Studies*, 3 (1972) pp. 243-270. Others emphasize foreign influence, arguing that the political and economic involvement of the Western Powers was the motive for change; see Shimon Shamir, "The Modernization of Syria: Problems and Solutions in the Early Period of Abdulhamid," W.R. Polk and R.I. Chambers (eds.), *Beginnings of Modernization in the Middle East*, Chicago 1968, p. 381 and Hopewood (supra n. 57), p. 62. On the question of whether these were only "paper reforms" and no more than lip service to the West, see: Lewis (supra n. 41), pp. 170-171, 480.

issued in 1850, followed by a new penal code in 1858, based on the French model. The new land law that same year gave leaseholders full possession rights but ended up unintentionally strengthening the *effendis* (landowners).[63] The Law of *Vilayets* of 1864 reorganized the administration of the provinces and non-Muslim participation in local councils.

In 1861, the throne was assumed by Abdul Aziz (1861-1876), who was less enthusiastic about the reforms than his predecessor had been. Under French pressure, however, the reforms were resumed. Work began on the publication of the *Mejelle* (a collection of judicial laws of the *sharī'a*), which continued until 1876.[64]

The Franco-Russian war was followed by increasing opposition to Westernized reforms and the Capitulations (special privileges granted to foreigners and Christians), and a growing sense of Ottoman patriotism. During the 1860s and 1870s, Serbia, Egypt and Khartoum rapidly approached independence. Sultan Abdul Aziz was overthrown in May 1876, with Murad V succeeding him for a short period, followed by the rule of Abdul Hamid II. During the reign of the latter, the Grand Vizierate fell into the hands of Midhat Pasha, later the leader of the Young Ottomans, who desired a liberal, constitutional state modeled after the nations of Europe. When the Great Powers convened in Istanbul in 1876 to decide the fate of the Balkans after the Serbia-Montenegro war, the Sultan proclaimed a new Turkish constitution that would guarantee equality and constitutional liberties to all inhabitants of the empire. This time it was not just acquiescence to Western pressure, but an articulation of the desire of a broad class of educated people to curb the despotism of the Sultan.[65]

In Palestine

Basically, the Ottoman government's policy in Palestine and Syria during the *Tanzimat* was no different from that of Ibrahim Pasha. It was a reformist policy seeking to implement the new laws promulgated by Abdul Majid in the *Khatt-i Sheriff* of 1839 and the *Khatt-i Humayun*. The Ottomans could not accomplish this fully because of the opposition of the local inhabitants, administrative ineptitude, and the weakness of the new bureaucratic and government networks in the Syrian provinces.[66]

---

63 Heyd (supra n. 41); Issawi (supra n. 9) pp. 3-39.
64 Lewis (supra n. 41), pp. 120-124.
65 Heyd (supra n. 41).
66 Heyd (supra n. 49), p. 52; on the opposition of the local populace to the reforms, see: Finn (supra n. 47), pp. 566-572 and Maoz (supra n. 52), p. 230.

All of Palestine, with the exception of Transjordan, belonged to the *eyālet* (province or *vilayet*, after the 1864 Law of *Vilayets*) of Sidon, whose capital was Beirut. The *sanjak* (district) of Jerusalem, which included Nablus and Gaza, was a separate administrative unit within the *eyālet* of Sidon, called the *mutasariflik* of Jerusalem. The ruler of this district was subordinate sometimes to the Sublime Porte and sometimes to the *vālī* (governor) of Sidon.[67] In 1873 the *mutasariflik* of Jerusalem attained the status of *iyāla*, and was governed directly by Istanbul.[68]

The Ottoman government introduced more and more Turkish elements into the local administration and revoked its semi-independent status. The new administration was founded on tight centralization, and officials were replaced every year. There was a rigid hierarchy of Turkish functionaries subordinate to superintendents in different spheres, while the *vālī* was responsible to the Ministry of Interior in Istanbul. At each level, the Turkish official heading an administrative division was assisted by the *majlis*, which represented all sectors of the Muslim population. This form of rule did not stifle all corruption and misuse of power or produce an electoral government, but it did curb arbitrary actions on the part of the governors.[69]

The new controls on the pashas and the removal of many of their military and financial powers made it difficult for them to carry out the reforms. Further obstacles were the inefficient and corrupt bureaucracy, unreliable police force and gendarmerie, and chronic shortage of funds. This state of affairs led to concessions, compromises, delays and distortions in the implementation of the reforms in Palestine. Nonetheless, there was an atmosphere of greater liberality, and a considerable improvement in personal safety and the administration of justice. The Ottoman army controlled the district centers, and the power struggles once waged through military channels were relegated to the *majlis*.[70]

The Ottomans took steps in the 1850s to suppress the mountain dwellers, institute direct rule and keep the Bedouin at bay. Efforts were made to settle nomadic tribes, but these had little impact. Fearing the Bedouin and tax extortion, the farmers either abandoned their lands and villages in the coastal region or transferred farming and ownership rights to the tax collector or a city-dwelling strongman, thus becoming tenant farmers. In this way, large amounts

---

67 Maoz (supra n. 52), pp. 32–34.
68 Vital Cuinet, *Syrie, Liban et Palestine, Geographie Administrative Statistique, Descriptive et Raisonée*, Paris 1896, p. 513; Maoz, (supra n. 52), p. 230.
69 Hurewitz (supra n. 46), pp. 501–502.
70 Finn (supra n. 47), pp. 97–121; he devotes an entire chapter to the subject of the Turkish government; Heyd (supra n. 49), p. 53.

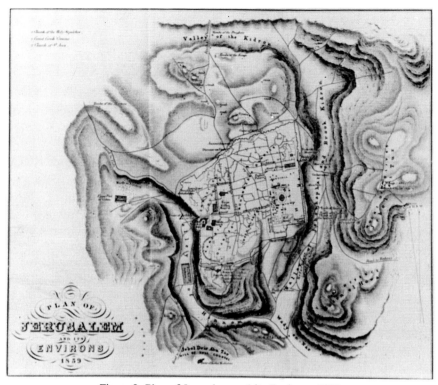

Figure 2: Plan of Jerusalem and its Environs, 1859
(Source: W.M. Thomson, *The Land and the Book or Biblical Illustrations drawn from
the Manners and Customs, the Scenes and the Scenery of the Holy Land*, II,
New York 1859, p. 602)

of land fell into the hands of an isolated few, and the socioeconomic gaps widened.[71] This is one of the reasons for the increasing strength of urban families — particularly in Jaffa and Jerusalem. [see Figure 2]

The Great Powers were becoming very active in the region. England and France were the most visible in Palestine and Syria until the 1860s; aside from protecting various religious communities (England protected the Protestants, Druze and Jews, and France the Catholics), their representatives exerted an influence among the notables and frequently intervened in local matters.[72] The Russian government's involvement commenced toward the end of the 1850s,

71 Heyd (supra n. 49), pp. 54-58; Kark (supra n. 26) pp. 357-368.
72 Heyd (supra n. 49), pp. 54-58.

when the Greek Orthodox Arabs came under its wing. Most of its activities were in the sphere of education. However, after the Crimean War, Russia became convinced of the need to establish a presence in the Middle East, including Palestine, through the church. Large sums of money were mobilized to purchase real estate and finance building activities in Palestine. The most important of these transactions was the purchase of land in Jerusalem which was to become the Russian Compound.[73] Germany stepped up its involvement only at the end of the nineteenth century, extending patronage to Muslims. In many cases, Austria was supportive of the Jews, and not only those with Austrian citizenship.

Missionary institutions began to multiply in the country during the period of Ibrahim Pasha, when missionaries were permitted not only to proselytize non-Muslims, but also to open schools, hospitals and charitable institutions. Most of this activity was centered in Jerusalem, but it had repercussions in Jaffa and elsewhere. The leaders in missionary work were the Protestants. In later years other Christian denominations built charitable institutions of a similar nature, as did the Jews and the Turkish government.[74] While pursuing religious activities, the churches acquired large tracts of land, especially after foreign residents were allowed to purchase real estate, legally in 1856 and in practice in 1867. This privilege was also extremely important for the continuation of Jewish settlement and urban development in Palestine.[75] This period marked the opening of many consulates, vice consulates and consular agencies all over Palestine.

The End of the Ottoman Period: 1877-1917

Throughout most of this period (1876-1909), the sultanate was in the hands of Abdul Hamid II. The constitution proclaimed in 1876 may have inspired hope, but Abdul Hamid II had no intention of implementing it. In 1877, he dismissed Midhat Pasha, sending him into exile. The following year he dispersed the Parliament, which was to be reconvened only thirty years later.

Great changes were taking place in Turkey's foreign relations with France and England, which for many years had presided over the reforms and served as a

---

73 Hopewood (supra n. 57) pp. 51, 62; Alex Carmel, "Russian Activity in Palestine during the Late Ottoman Period," E. Shaltiel (ed.), *Jerusalem in the Modern Period*, Jerusalem 1981, pp. 97-102 (Hebrew).

74 Hurewitz (supra n. 46), p. 502.

75 Hopewood (supra n. 57), pp. 61-71, 88-93; Maoz (supra n. 52), pp. 194-195; Elizabeth Anne Finn, *Reminiscences of Mrs. Finn*, London 1929, pp. 105, 174.

political and military buttress for the empire. After the Berlin Congress (1878), they relinquished their policy of safeguarding the integrity of the empire, and began to annex portions of it themselves (Cyprus, Egypt and Tunisia). In their stead, the Ottomans gained a new ally: Germany, which sent officers to train the Turkish army and secured various concessions from the Ottomans.[76]

During Abdul Hamid II's reign, no reforms were introduced in legislature or political life. On the other hand, he did inaugurate reforms and make headway in the spheres of education, law, finance, transportation and mining. During his first decades in power, the *Tanzimat* reached a peak insofar as administration, jurisprudence and education were concerned.[77]

Abdul Hamid II favored an Imperial policy and tried to achieve genuine rule in all areas designated on his map as Ottoman. Contrary to his predecessors, he attached importance to the Asiatic territories. Asia Minor had already taken shape; it was necessary to pursue Kurdistan, Mesopotamia, the Hijaz and especially Syria and Palestine. He resettled Circassian and Turkoman refugees in Transjordan. Bedouin in the Syrian Desert and Transjordan were offered incentives to settle down permanently as farmers. In 1900, an urban administrative center, Beersheba, was established in southern Palestine and a court was opened there to settle tribal disputes. The Ottomans re-established settlements at Jarash, Rabbat Ammon, Beit She'an and Caesaria. During the 1880s troops in northern Syria and southern Palestine were doubled to enhance security. Improvements in communication and transportation, the opening of the Hijaz railway in 1908 for example, contributed to better control of distant regions.[78]

The revolution of the Young Turks in 1908 stirred up great hopes and expectations. The constitution was reissued and a House of Representatives was established in Istanbul with delegates from all the peoples and nationalities in the empire. There were four Jews, but none from Palestine.[79] Abdul Hamid II was deposed in 1909 and the reforms were to be resumed in the spirit of growing

---

76 Lewis (supra n. 41), pp. 178-194; Heyd (supra n. 41).

77 Lewis, (supra n. 41), pp. 178-194; R.H. Davidson, *Reform in the Ottoman Empire, 1856-1876*, Princeton 1963, pp. 402-403. According to one source, a medical school was founded in Syria in 1903 after the earlier establishment of such a school in Constantinople. The project entailed an expenditure of 200,000 francs; see: Avraham Moshe Luncz, *Eretz Israel Almanac*, 9, Jerusalem 1904, p. 187 (Hebrew).

78 Great Britian Foreign Office, *Syria and Palestine*, London 1920, vol. 10, no. 58, pp. 9-10 and no. 60, pp. 39-41. On the new settlements, see: Yeshayahu Press, *Eretz Israel and Southern Syria*, Jerusalem 1921, p. 85 (Hebrew).

79 Avraham Moshe Luncz, *Eretz Israel Almanac*, 19, Jerusalem 1914, p. 10 (Hebrew).

Turkish nationalism and zealous preservation of the empire. The Young Turk regime was a source of disappointment throughout the empire, and was much criticized for violence, repression, terrorism and military involvement in politics. Nevertheless, there were successes in the field of education.[80]

In Palestine

Abdul Hamid II's policy in Palestine left its imprint on the big cities. New office buildings, mosques and other edifices sprouted as symbols of Imperial authority and the patronage of the Sultan.[81] His policy led to considerable development in the area, and it was not only Western activity that had an impact, as is commonly believed:

> When it is remembered, further, that such harbour structures as exist in Syria, and the equipment of principal cities like Aleppo, Damascus, Beirut and Jerusalem, with broad ways, modern buildings, electric lighting, tramways, and other convenient apparatus, are also of Abdul Hamid's time, one is bound to admit that a great deal of beneficent construction — almost all that makes Syria as a whole the most civilized province of Turkey at this day — stands to the credit of a Sultan whose energies are popularly supposed to have been uniformly destructive and sinister.[82]

The time of Abdul Hamid II may certainly be considered one of progress in Palestine, in certain spheres surpassing that in other parts of Turkey. True, the evidence of persecution was not lacking and fear of foreign penetration resulted in a restricted approach to coastal regions and repeated bans on Jewish immigration. However, the general feeling was not one of oppression and terror.[83] From the writings of David Yellin, one learns that the Jewish community and other minorities had a sense of greater equality and participation.[84]

---

80   Lewis (supra n. 41), pp. 207-238, 482.
81   Great Britian Foreign Office, *Syria and Palestine*, London 1920, vol. 10, no. 58, pp. 9-10.
82   *Ibid.*
83   One source attributes these prohibitions to the complaints of the Jewish community regarding the large numbers of poor immigrants, who were causing housing shortages and a rise in the price of foodstuffs. The restrictions were imposed in 1882 and 1891; see: Z. Smilansky, "The Jewish Population in Jaffa According to Statistics Collected in 1905," *Ha'Omer Supplement*, vol. 1, no. 1 (1907), p. 10 (Hebrew).
84   David Yellin, *The Writings of David Yellin: The Jerusalem of Yesterday (Letters from Jerusalem to "Hamelitz" 1896-1904)*, 1, Jerusalem 1972, p. 99.

In the early twentieth century, Yellin writes, steps were taken "to found an organization responsible for all Jewish community affairs in Palestine, whose members would be from all the different parties and *'edot* (ethnic communities)." A general meeting was called to discuss its establishment and its relationship with overseas institutions, to settle public matters, and "to investigate how to employ the rights the government has given all the Jews in the country." Yellin went on to say: "Our government has bestowed upon us many rights which, if we know how to use them, would change the face of our settlement, and the respectability of our people in general..."[85]

There was a constant increase in population. In 1800, only 300,000 persons lived in Palestine. By 1882, there were 450,000, and during World War One (1916), 700,000.[86]

While Abdul Hamid II was in power, Palestine was part of two administrative divisions, the *vilayet* of Beirut, which included the *sanjaks* of Nablus and Acre, and the *mutastariflik* of Jerusalem. The three *aqadiya* (plural of *qada'*) — Jaffa, Gaza and Hebron — were part of the province of Jerusalem, and in 1908 the territory south of Beersheba was declared a separate district affiliated with the *mutastariflik* of Jerusalem. A *mutassarrif* ruled the province, and three *kaymakams* ruled the *aqadiya*.[87] [see Figure 3]

During this period, the Ottoman government was active in Palestine in the spheres of transportation, public health, communication and education. City schools were opened, as well as village schools funded by agricultural taxes. An antiquities museum was founded in Jerusalem in 1901; a theatre was built outside Jaffa Gate in 1904.[88] [see Plate 5]

Citizen participation in local government increased, and public opinion was sometimes influential even in the appointment and dismissal of pashas.[89] The authorities' concern about the people is evident from the fact that during the 1902 cholera epidemic in Palestine, which led to food shortages and famine, wheat was brought from Turkey "so the inhabitants would have enough to live on."[90] That year the government decided to dry out the swamps on state lands owned by the Sultan in the Hula Valley in order to plant winter wheat.[91] In 1904,

85 Yellin (supra n. 84), pp. 403-404.
86 Hurewitz (supra n. 46), pp. 498, 503.
87 Great Britian Foreign Office, *Syria and Palestine*, London 1920, vol. 10, no. 60, p. 3; Hurewitz (supra n. 46), pp. 500-510; A.L. Tibawi, *A Modern History of Syria including Lebanon and Palestine*, London 1969, pp. 180-181; Cuinet (supra n. 68), pp. 514-515.
88 Yellin (supra n. 84), pp. 62, 242, 388-389.
89 Avraham Moshe Luncz, *Yerushalayim*, 3 (1889), p. 203 (Hebrew).
90 Avraham Moshe Luncz, *Eretz Israel Almanac*, 9, Jerusalem 1904, p. 173 (Hebrew).
91 Avraham Moshe Luncz, *Yerushalayim*, 6 (1903), p. 166 (Hebrew).

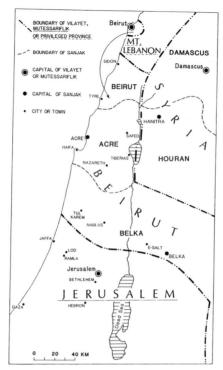

Figure 3: Administrative Divisions of Palestine and Southern Syria for 1890
(Based on: Vital Cuinet, *La Turquie D'Asie, Géographie Administrative, Statistique,
Descriptive et Raisonee de Chaque Province de L'Asie Mineure*, I, Paris 1892,
op. frontispiece)

the government began to put out an official newspaper called *Quds el-Sharif* in
Arabic and Turkish for the residents of the Galilee and Jerusalem.[92] That year,
it waged an extremely important campaign to save Palestine's forests, which
were being destroyed. Afforestation was accompanied by the designation of
specific locations for storing firewood (near Jericho).[93]

   This is not to say that everything being done in Palestine at the time was
positive, and that development and progress were visible in all spheres of life.
A more balanced portrayal can be obtained by citing Arthur Ruppin on Hebron,
Safed and Tiberias in 1907: "Hence these cities present to European eyes a
wretched picture of cultural and economic stagnation. There is no connection

92   Avraham Moshe Luncz, *Yerushalayim*, 5 (1904), p. 221 (Hebrew).
93   Avraham Moshe Luncz, *Eretz Israel Almanac*, 10, Jerusalem 1905, pp. 165-166 (Hebrew).

Plate 5: Approach to Jaffa Gate from the railroad station, Jerusalem, circa 1900
(Source: Central Zionist Archives, Jerusalem)

with the outside world, newspapers and modern books are unknown in these places and life goes on as it did a hundred years ago."[94]

As seen from Luncz, the rise of the Young Turks engendered the enthusiasm of the inhabitants of Palestine, who looked forward to the change it would bring: "The great change in Turkey as a whole has breathed life and action into our country too, and even if no great deeds have yet been accomplished, the hearts of the inhabitants are filled with hope that little by little, employment, industry and commerce will expand and any man wishing to work will be able to earn a living. And the second thing which has already taken effect since the political change is the requirement that non-Muslims serve in the army...."[95]

However, the policies of the Young Turks eventually led to disappointment because of their radical nationalism, which reached a peak in Palestine with Jamal Pasha's actions against foreigners, Jews and local Arabs. One of the explanations given for the disappointing results was the remoteness of Palestine from the center of things: "We had hoped for much good from this change, but political events prevented the general government from concerning itself with any districts smaller than the capital city or introducing in them the desired reforms, and all remained as before...."[96]

94 Arthur Ruppin, *Three Decades of Palestine*, Jerusalem 1936, p. 3.
95 Avraham Moshe Luncz, *Eretz Israel Almanac*, 15, Jerusalem 1910, pp. 160-161 (Hebrew).
96 Avraham Moshe Luncz, *Eretz Israel Almanac*, 19, Jerusalem 1914, p. 10 (Hebrew).

CHAPTER TWO

THE AMZALAKS — FIRST GENERATION IN JERUSALEM

The history of the Amzalak family in Palestine began with two brothers, Joseph Amzalak (1779–1845) and Moses Amzalak (1767–1858), who settled in Jerusalem during the early nineteenth century. Of the two, Joseph was the first to arrive, settling in Acre in 1816. He later settled in Jerusalem, only to be joined by his elder brother, Moses. Joseph Amzalak became a prominent figure in Jerusalem. He was known for his affluence and influence, his hospitality and generosity, and his devotion as a Jew. Joseph Amzalak was a famous personality in the city, well known to its residents and visitors alike. There exist many accounts of his life and activities in letters, journals and travelers' memoirs. Unlike Joseph, Moses was relatively unknown in Jerusalem, having moved there to live out his last days without his children. Few accounts of his activities remain, except those of the occasional traveler and those of the British consul, James Finn, which provided limited information.

Before Joseph Amzalak's Arrival in Jerusalem

The years before Joseph Amzalak's arrival in Jerusalem remain somewhat of a mystery; nevertheless, a few fragments of information provided by Amzalak himself have come down to us through his contemporaries in Jerusalem. This section will briefly piece together Joseph's life prior to his arrival in Palestine, while mainly focusing on his life in Jerusalem.

Joseph Amzalak was born in the British colony of Gibraltar in 1779.[97] His ancestors originally hailed from Spain or Portugal whose Jewries were expelled

---

97   NLA 4°1613/2, Amzalak Family Archives, Laissez-Passer January 17, 1799. The document states that Amzalak was 21 years old; it is more probable that he was born between 18.1.1779 and 31.12.1779, although it is possible that he was born between 1.1.1778 and 17.1.1778.

in 1492 and 1497 respectively. These once illustrious Jewish communities wandered to North Africa and the areas on the northern coast of the Mediterranean as far east as Turkey and Palestine. It would appear that the ancestors of the Amzalak family had settled in Morocco during the sixteenth to eighteenth centuries before returning to the Iberian Peninsula and taking up residence on its southern tip, Gibraltar.

Two individuals bearing the family name are mentioned in sources from the seventeenth and eighteenth centuries. The first is Moshe Amzalak, a rabbi from Fez, who died in 1621. The second, is Haim Yehuda Amzalak, who immigrated to Jerusalem with Rabbi Haim ben Attar in 1742. Haim Yehuda Amzalak's signature and a Hebrew abbreviation denoting his recent death are found at the end of the preface to Rabbi Haim ben Attar's work, *Sefer Rishon LeZion* "Premier in Zion Book", published in Constantinople in 1750.[98]

The name Amzalak may have been derived from the Berber word meaning ropemaker or maker of chains, or from the Arabic "Al Amzalaq" — one with shining skin or one who is bald. Its origin could equally be from the Zalag tribe in the environs of Fez, Morocco.[99]

It appears that the family had emigrated from Morocco to Gibraltar during the years of peace and prosperity in this colony (1755-1777). During this period the Jewish population at Gibraltar increased from 572 to 863. The family may even have taken up the trade which the Berber meaning of their name alludes to, ropemaking, which in Gibraltar was mainly practiced by emigrant Jews. Joseph Amzalak's family appears to have been unknown in the historiography of Gibraltar Jewry, and of little social importance, probably living in abject poverty. A possible reference to the family can be found in the *List of Inhabitants of Gibraltar* from 1777. Mentioned are Haim Anralack (or Anraleck) aged 53, Sarah Anralack aged 41, and Abram Anralack aged 17, all reported to have been born in Gibraltar. The name Anralack may be, in fact, Amzalak, registered by a British official who had transcribed what he had thought he had heard. If so, Haim and Sarah would have been Joseph Amzalak's

98 Abraham I. Laredo, *Les Noms des Juifs du Maroc*, Madrid 1978, pp. 333-334. It is likely that the Amzalaks reached Gibraltar via North Africa. George Borrow, the author of *The Bible in Spain*, London 1906, in a letter to James Finn, wrote, "There are no Spanish Jews at Gibraltar. Those of the place are from Barbary...their priest is from Fez...," as quoted by Beth-Zion Lask Abrahams, "James Finn: Her Britannic Majesty's Consul at Jerusalem Between 1846 and 1863," *Transactions of the Jewish Historical Society of England*, vol. XXVII, and misc. part XII (1982), p. 41; Haim Ben Attar, *Sefer Rishon LeZion*, Constantinople 1850, preface, (Hebrew).

99 Laredo (supra n. 98), p. 333.

parents and Abram his brother. The naming of Joseph's son Haim, following the Sephardi tradition of giving one's son his father's name, could attest to the forementioned relationship. The family name is not mentioned in any of the lists of Jews living in Gibraltar from 1783 to 1814, nor in other documents detailing the Jews of Gibraltar. A possible explanation for this could be that during the Great Siege of Gibraltar by the Spanish from 1779 to 1783, many of the inhabitants left, some taking refuge in England. The Amzalaks (Anralacks) may have been among this group, possibly never returning to Gibraltar and perhaps permanently settling in England.[100] [see Plate 6]

The genealogy of the Lisbon branch of the Amzalak family presents another possible origin of the Amzalak family. This record begins with Isaac Amzalak, born around the year 1750. Isaac was described as a humble and righteous rabbi. His son Moses arrived in Lisbon from North Africa via Gibraltar. Moses later established himself in Jerusalem. From other sources it is known that Joseph was Moses' brother. Therefore this genealogy would point to Isaac Amzalak as being Joseph's father. The naming of Joseph's son Isaac, following the Sephardi tradition of giving one's son his father's name, could attest to this relationship.[101]

Gibraltar was a center of opportunity for both native residents and immigrants. As a port between the Atlantic Ocean and the Mediterranean Sea it offered merchants diverse opportunities in international trade, and in outfitting and supplying vessels sailing through the adjacent straits. In addition, even greater profits were made through smuggling contraband and duty-free goods to nearby Spain.

Joseph Amzalak, through financial ingenuity, business acumen and good fortune, rose from the ranks of poverty to wealth. John Lloyd Stephens, an

---

100 GGA, List of Inhabitants of Gibraltar 1777, List of Jews in Town Gibraltar, January 16, 1784, Census of 1791. We would like to thank Messod Belilo, Honourary Registrar of the Jewish Community of Gibraltar, for providing these documents and for his other assistance. See also Abraham B.M. Sefarty, *The Jews of Gibraltar under British Rule*, Gibraltar 1933, and Messod Benady, "The Settlement of Jews in Gibraltar, 1704-1783," *Transactions of the Jewish Historical Society of England*, XXVI (1979) pp. 87-110; Jean-Louis Miège, "Les Juifs de Gibraltar au XIXe Siècle," *Les Relations Intercommunautaires Juivres en Méditerranée Occidentale XIIe-XXe Siècles*, Paris 1984, pp. 99-118; Magali Morsy, "Les Juifs Marocains à Gibraltar au XVIIIe Siècle: Histoire d'une Minorité Manipulée" *Pluriel Débats*, 6 (1976), pp. 47-60; none of these sources make mention of the Amzalak family.

101 Jose Maria Abecassis, *Genealogy of Some Jewish Families in Portugal*, Lisbon 1976, (unpublished manuscript).

Plate 6: Rock of Gibraltar, Devil's Tongue Battery, 1804
This painting relates directly to a segment of the Henry Aston Barker's 'Panorama of Gibraltar', exhibited in the Large Circle at the Leicester Square Panorama from May 13, 1805- May 3, 1806. To make his drawing Barker sailed to Gibraltar in September 1804 on H.M.S. Hyra. Fears of a French attack on Gibraltar dictated Barker's choice of subject and ensured the panorama's popularity
(Source: Ralph Hyde, *Panoramania, the Art and Entertainment of the 'All-Embracing' View*, London 1988, p. 73)

American traveler who visited Jerusalem in the spring of 1836, wrote the following account based on his meetings with Joseph Amzalak:

> ...born in Gibraltar to the same abject poverty which is the lot of most of his nation. In his youth he had been fortunate in his little dealings and had been what we call an enterprising man, for he had twice made a

voyage to England, and was so successful and liked the country so much that he always called himself an Englishman.[102]

One such voyage to England was made in 1799, as a laissez-passer issued by the Duke of Portland attests, and the second in 1808, when he was wed for the first time. Joseph Amzalak may have resided in England for extended periods during these visits and may have made additional trips there.[103] [see Plate 7]

A later traveler, John P. Durbin, provided further details of how Joseph Amzalak had amassed his fortune. According to Durbin, he had spent a number of years trading in the West Indies, where he prospered in his business undertakings. The large fortune that he had accumulated was invested upon his return to London in stocks of the Bank of England. With the threat of an invasion of England by Napoleon Bonaparte in 1805, Joseph Amzalak grew anxious and sold his stocks at a great loss.[104]

Part of Durbin's account can be confirmed by a laissez-passer issued on January 17, 1799 to Joseph Amzalak by William Henry Cavendish, Duke of Portland, "one of His Majesty's most honourable privy council, and principal secretary of state." It stipulated the following:

> To all concerned, Admirals, Vice Admirals, Captains, Commanders of His Majesty's Ships of War or, Privateers, Governors, Mayors, Sheriffs, Justices of the Peace, Constables, Customers, Controllers, Searchers and all others to whom it may concern, Greetings: These are, in His Majesty's Name to will and require you to permit and suffer the Bearer hereof Joseph Amzalac [sic], 21 years of age, 5 feet, 5 inches, dark hair, native

---

102 John Lloyd Stephens, *Incidents of Travel in Egypt, Arabia and the Holy Land*, New York 1837, (reprint, Norman, Oklahoma 1979), p. 371. Stephens was a lawyer whose extensive travels took him through many parts of the world, including the Middle East and Central America. He was a self-acknowledged tourist who described his journey to the Holy Land in a lively narrative style. His work quickly became popular and was reprinted many times. See: Yehoshua Ben-Arieh, *The Rediscovery of the Holy Land in the Nineteenth Century*, Jerusalem 1983, p. 84.

103 NLA 4°1613/2; Lionel D. Barnett (ed.), *Bevis Marks Records*, Oxford 1940, II, p. 116.

104 John P. Durbin, *Observations in the East, Chiefly in Egypt, Palestine, Syria and Asia Minor*, I, New York 1845, pp. 253-255. We would like to thank Dr. Gideon Hermel for placing this rare text at our disposal. Durbin was a doctor of theology and a central figure in the Methodist Church in the United States. He visited Palestine in 1843; see also: William Henry Bartlett, *Walks about the City and Environs of Jerusalem*, London 1844, p. 191: Bartlett wrote, "...in his youth he had been a wanderer under the burning tropics, as well as in England and in Spain, by various means having accumulated a sum sufficient to render him the envy of his poor abject brethren..."

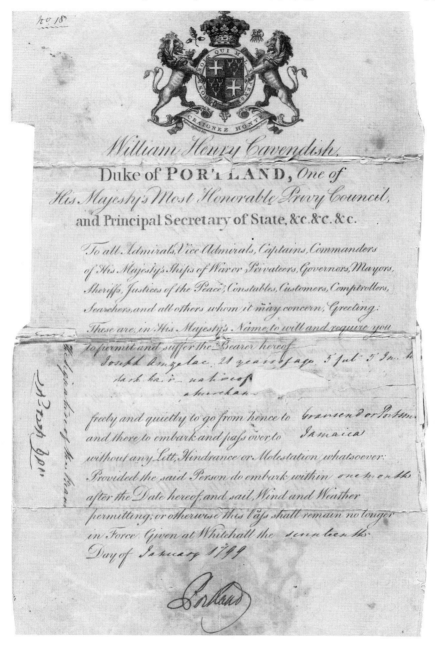

Plate 7: Laissez-Passer from the Duke of Portland given to Joseph Amzalak, January 17, 1799
(Source: Amzalak Family Archives, National Library Archives, Jerusalem, 4°1613/2)

of [erased] a merchant, freely and quietly to go hence to Gransend or Portsmouth and there to embark and pass to Jamaica without any Lett, Hindrance or Molestation whatsoever: Provided the said person do embark within one month after the date hereof, and sail, Wind and Weather permitting; or otherwise this Pass shall remain no longer in Force. Given at Whitehall the seventeenth Day of January 1799.

[signed] Portland[105]

Joseph Amzalak's great grandson, Meir Henry Amzalak, basing his assessment on information handed down through the generations, stated that the elder Amzalak had been "a sailing-ships owner, plying between Spain, Portugal, North and East Africa, and the Caribbean Islands."[106]

This background offers no clear explanation as to when and why Joseph Amzalak settled in Jerusalem. Captain Henry Light of the British Royal Artillery, who visited Palestine in the summer of 1814, analyzed the phenomenon of Jewish immigration to Palestine at the beginning of nineteenth century: "...to sleep in Abraham's bosom is the wish of the old: the young visit in the hopes of the coming of the Messiah: some are content to remain for the commerce they carry on."[107]

Another underlying reason for immigration to Palestine was the mystic Jewish belief of the transmigration of the soul, or reincarnation. In order to avoid the torments of *gilgul* (the rolling of the soul under ground until it reaches the Holy Land) and *hibbut hakever* (the beating by heavenly spirits of bodies buried outside the Holy Land) these immigrants desired to be buried in Palestine.[108]

John Lloyd Stephens suggests the following reason for Joseph Amzalak's immigration to Palestine:

> Having accumulated a little property or, as he expressed it, having become very rich, he gratified the daring wish of his heart by coming to Jerusalem, to die and be buried with his fathers in the Valley of Jehoshaphat. But this holy purpose in regard to his death and burial did

105 NLA 4°1613/2.
106 PPJA, M.H. Amzalak to James Amzalak, January 23, 1963.
107 Henry Light, *Travels in Egypt, Nubia, Holy Land, Mount Libanon and Cyprus*, London 1818, p. 184.
108 Tudor Parfitt, *The Jews in Palestine 1800-1882*, Woodbridge, Suffolk 1987, pp. 119-120; see pp. 119-126 for a discussion of the various reasons for Jewish immigration to Palestine during the first eighty years of the nineteenth century.

not make him undervalue the importance of life and the advantages of being a great man now.[109]

This same motivation is also cited in an account by Dr. Richard Madden, who stated that in order to die in Jerusalem and to be buried beside its holy walls, Amzalak abandoned his spacious home in Europe and literally dug his own grave. Madden was even shown by Amzalak the site of the tomb where the latter would be buried.[110]

According to John Durbin, Amzalak at first settled in Malta, but with the outbreak of a plague there he fled to Jerusalem. Only then did he decide to take up permanent residence in Jerusalem.[111]

Arieh Morgenstern's article on Joseph Amzalak elaborates on Durbin's account by describing the severity of the plague in Malta, which took the lives of 5,000 people in 1813 over a period of ten months. Morgenstern surmises that Amzalak had sworn a solemn oath to settle in the Holy Land if he were to survive the plague.[112]

These accounts apparently present only part of the picture. Hearsay in the Amzalak family tells that Joseph Amzalak was a slave trader, transporting blacks from Africa to the West Indies. It also expands upon the incident in Malta. These rumors claim that a rabbi there cautioned him that the plague was a warning from God and that he must repent for his commerce in human beings. The rabbi told him to settle in Jerusalem and to carry out acts of charity, which Joseph Amzalak did.

In 1813, Joseph Amzalak reached Constantinople, where he received a *firman* (Imperial Edict) from the Ottoman Sultan, Mahmud II (1808-1839). This *firman* was received with the help of the British ambassador to Constantinople, Bartholomew Ferere. It allowed Joseph Amzalak and two of his companions, with no mention of Joseph's family, to travel as tourists by sea

---

109 Stephens (supra n. 102), p. 371; Bartlett (supra n. 104), p. 191 also cites the same reason for their coming to Palestine.

110 Richard R. Madden, *Travels in Turkey, Egypt, Nubia and Palestine in the Years 1824-1827*, London 1829, translated into Hebrew by Michael Ish-Shalom, *Christian Travels in the Holy Land, Description and Sources on the History of Jews in Palestine*, Tel Aviv 1965, p. 439 (Hebrew). Dr. Madden was a physician who traveled in the Middle East between the 1824 and 1827. His book is a collection of letters about the customs and the people of the East. See Ben-Arieh (supra n. 102), pp. 61-62; Arieh Morgenstern, "Joseph Amazalak — His Status and Activites for the Benefit of the Jews of Jerusalem" *Asufot*, 3, Jerusalem 1989, p. 398 (Hebrew). We would like to thank Dr. Morgenstern for graciously letting us use his manuscript.

111 Durbin (supra n. 104), pp. 253-255.

112 Morgenstern (supra n. 110), p. 398.

Plate 8: Firman from Sultan Mahmoud II given to
Joseph Amzalak in 1813
(Source: Amzalak Family Archives, National Library
Archives, Jerusalem, 4°1613/3)

Plate 9: Silver Box containing the Firman given to Joseph
Amzalak
(Source: Amzalak Family Archives, National Library
Archives, Jerusalem, 4°1613/3)

from Constantinople to Jerusalem and back, via Rhodes, Cyprus and Jaffa.[113] [see plates 8 and 9]

During the early nineteenth century, travel in the Eastern Mediterranean basin was unreliable, hazardous, and expensive. No regular sailing routes existed until the mid-1830s. The vessels used were sail-driven and as such subject to contrary winds and sudden storms. Pirates cruised unchecked in the area. Furthermore, upon reaching a port, travelers were charged various taxes and bribes were elicited. The *firman* received by Amzalak states that no taxes or payments might be demanded from the bearer and that it was the duty of all to provide aid and protection. The *firman* given in 1813 suggests only a visit to Jerusalem and does not hint at long-term plans.[114] Other information indicates that Joseph Amzalak settled in Palestine only three years later. A possible explanation for this three-year interval could be that he returned to collect his family and arrange for their immigration and the transportation of their possessions.

In the spring of 1816, Joseph Amzalak visited Izmir. In the fall of that year, on a visit to Safed, Joseph Amzalak observed the desperate plight of the Jewish community there. He later carried a letter on their behalf for the collection of charity. This letter elaborated upon the famine and plague that they had endured, stating that Amzalak was well-acquainted with their predicament. Having evacuated the city until the epidemic should pass, the Jewish community left its houses and institutions unguarded. They suffered a second blow — their Beit Yosef *beit misdrash* (religious seminary) was robbed of all its holy books. The Jewish community in Safed begged those receiving the letter to have mercy upon them and send money for food and new books so that they could continue to reside in the holy city.[115] [see Plate 10]

---

113 NLA 4°1613/3, Firman from Sultan to Joseph Amzalak (Turkish and French translation); Pinhas Benzion Grayevski, *From the Archives of Jerusalem*, 1, Jerusalem 1931, pp. 30-31 (Hebrew translation).

114 Chevallier (supra n. 9), pp. 205-206; NLA 4°1613/3.

115 JTSA, Mic 3927-61, Letter from the Rabbis of Safed, Tishrei 5576 (Fall 1816), (Hebrew). We would like to thank Arieh Morgenstern for bringing this document to our attention. As the document is incomplete, the addressee is unknown. Regarding the plight of the Jews of Safed, a plague devastated the community during the years 1813-1815. For a detailed discussion on the events affecting the Jewish community in Safed see: Sherman Lieber, "The Development of the Jewish Population of Safed 1800-1839," *Cathedra*, 46 (December 1987), pp. 13-44 (Hebrew); AFP, Record of Circumcisions. In a special prayer book used by ritual circumcisers, Joseph Amzalak and his son Haim recorded the cirumcisions they performed. We hope to publish a separate paper on this source.

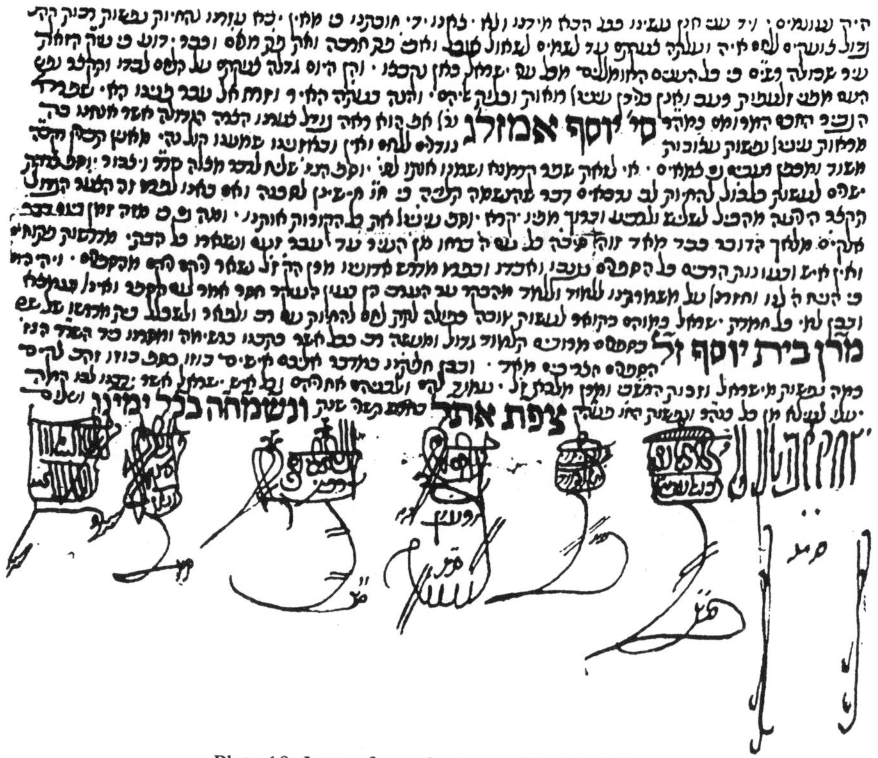
סי' יוסף אמזלג

מרן בית יוסף ז"ל

צפת אתה ונשמחה בכל ימינו

Plate 10: Letter from the Jews of Safed, 1816
(Source: Jewish Theological Seminary Archives, New York, 3927-61,
Courtesy of Arieh Morgenstern)

A later account, that of an English clergyman named John Carne, places the date of Amzalak's settlement in Palestine before 1820, but in Acre and not in Jerusalem. It is most likely that Joseph Amzalak had already settled in Acre by 1816, as indicated by the dates on his passport. A record kept of circumcisions performed by Joseph Amzalak places him in Acre in 1819.[116] This location appears to have been the most logical choice for a merchant, being the most important port in Palestine and center of administration at the time. During the first thirty years of the nineteenth century, Palestine was ruled, as mentioned above, by pashas who functioned as autonomous rulers from their capital in Acre. They remained in power in Acre as long as they were able to overcome the obstacles set in their path by the Imperial authorities. Suleiman Pasha (1804-1818) consolidated his authority and governed the region. His

116 NLA, 4°1613/4; AFP, Record of Circumcisions.

Plate 11: Haim Farhi, the Secretary and Minister of Finance of Jazzar Pasha, with his eye
missing and his nose removed, 1799
(Source: Lithograph from 1799 in Nathan Shur, "The Golden Age of Travellers'
Descriptions to Eretz Israel," *Ariel*, 47 (October 1986), p. 17. Courtesy of Eli Schiller)

successor, 'Abdallah Pasha (1818-1831), broadened his authority by
incorporating southern Palestine. Acre was the second largest city in Palestine,
after Jerusalem. It served as the port for a large agricultural hinterland which
exported produce to Beirut, and from there to Europe.[117]

John Carne recounted information provided by Joseph Amzalak, who had
been living in Acre with his family, about the death of the latter's friend and
coreligionist, Haim Selim Farhi. Farhi, scion of an ancient Jewish family from
Damascus, had served as an advisor and minister to the pashas of Acre for over
twenty years. Jazzar Pasha (1773-1804) had cut off Farhi's nose and ears but
retained him as a minister. Haim Farhi continued in this capacity and served
later pashas, but was murdered by order of 'Abdallah Pasha in 1820. [see Plate
11]

117 Ruth Kark, *Jaffa: a City in Evolution (1799-1917)*, Jerusalem 1990, pp. 13-15; Yehoshua
Ben- Arieh, "Urban Development in the Holy Land," John Patten (ed.), *The Expanding
City*, London 1983, pp. 1-39; Owen (supra n. 13), pp. 89-90.

"In those days," said Anselac [sic], the Jewish merchant, who was bewailing to us the fate of his friend [Haim Farhi], "no Turk dared to turn up his nose at a Jew in the streets of Acre, or discover the least insult in his manner; but the face of things was changed at last."

"I was returning," said Anselac [sic], "on the following evening from Sidon, and saw a body on the shore, partly out of the water; and on coming to the spot, found it was that of my friend and countryman, the minister [Haim Farhi], of whose cruel death I had not heard." This poor man [Amzalak] removed with his family to Beirout [sic], under the Consul's protection, as he thought the Pacha ['Abdallah] might take it into his head to serve him in like manner, or strip him of his property.[118]

After fleeing to Beirut for a period of time, he returned to live in Acre. Joseph Wolff, a converted Jew who carried out missionary activities in the Holy Land and other eastern countries, visited Joseph Amzalak's home in Acre twice, once on March 3, 1822 and again in 1823.[119]

By 1824, Joseph Amzalak had evidently taken up residence in Jerusalem. He had received a passport from the British consular agent at Acre, James Mc.Michael, for his family and himself to travel to Jaffa and Jerusalem, with the intent of settling in the latter location.[120] According to Amzalak's great-grandson, he packed all his belongings, his family and two black servants — one male and one female — onto two sailing vessels, and transported them to Jerusalem.[121] It is certain that he took up residence in Jerusalem by 1825, since

118 John Carne, *Letters from the East*, London 1826, II, pp. 58-60; see also: Nathan Shur, "The Death of Chaim Farhi as Reflected in Travelers' Reports," *Cathedra*, 39 (April 1986), pp. 179-191 (Hebrew).

119 Morgenstern (supra n. 110), p. 400 quoting *The Jewish Expositor*, London 1822, p. 348; see: Joseph Wolff, *Journal of the Rev. Joseph Wolff, in a series of letters to Sir Thomas Baring; containing an account of his missionary labours from the years 1827 to 1831, and from the years 1835 to 1838*, London 1839, pp. 213-214.

120 NLA, 4°1613/4; Alexander William Kinglake, a member of the British Parliament who visited Safed in 1835, mentioned in his travel account, *Eothen*, London 1876, that he was met by two leaders of the Jewish community. He referred to the second as "a Jew of Gibraltar, a tolerably well-bred person, who spoke English very fluently" (p. 337). Kinglake wrote elsewhere: "...and I was flattered too, in the point of my national vanity at the notion of the far-reaching link by which a Jew in Syria, because he had been born on the rock of Gibraltar, was able to claim me as his fellow-countryman" (p. 340). An annotated translation of Kinglake's account points to the possibility that the reference is to Joseph Amzalak: see: Michael Ish-Shalom, *Travels of Christians in Eretz Israel*, Tel Aviv 1965, p. 461, footnote 9 (Hebrew). No other information has been found as to Amzalak's having ever lived in Safed, and it appears unlikely that he ever did.

121 M.H. Amzalak to James Amzalak (supra n. 106).

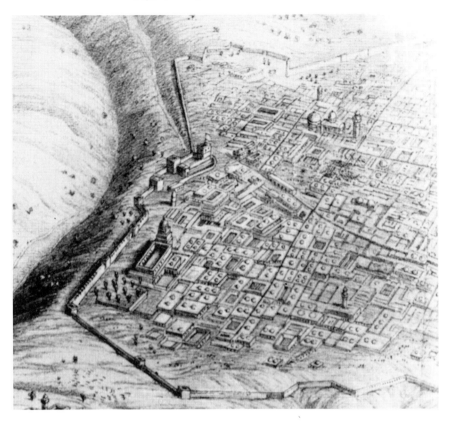

Plate 12: Mount Zion, a bird's eye view, 1846
(Source: George Williams, *The Holy City*, II, London 1846)

the English missionary Dr. Dalton reported that he had met Joseph Amzalak in his home on December 29 of that year.[122] Three years later they were well established in Jerusalem and received the Montefiores on the philanthropists' first visit to Jerusalem.[123] [see Plate 12] Joseph Amzalak was later joined in Jerusalem by his brother, Moses. Certain information points to 1841 as the date of Moses' arrival.

---

122 Morgenstern (supra n. 110), p. 400 quoting *The Jewish Expositor*, London 1827, p. 72.
123 Judith Montefiore, *Private Journal of a Visit to Egypt and Palestine*, reprint, Jerusalem 1975, pp. 192-218. The Montefiores were in Jerusalem between October 17, 1827 and October 21, 1827.

Joseph Amzalak and his Family

Few detailed descriptions exist of Joseph's physical appearance, the most elaborate one being Durbin's from 1843. Joseph would have been around 65 years old at the time:

> The old man was richly dressed in the Eastern style, and wore, in addition, a light blue pelisse faced with fur, whose ample folds enveloped his neck and shoulders, while his bushy gray beard fell in rich luxuriance upon his breast. He had a fine hazel eye, quiet and penetrating, and his conversation was lively, with an air of importance and independence.[124]

On the other hand, many verbal portraits remain of his family. It would appear that Joseph Amzalak was married three times. The first wife was Roza de Binjamin, who according to Mahamad's Records of Licences wed Joseph Amzalak on the 22 of Ab 5568 (1808).[125] Judith Montefiore, in 1827, mentioned that Amzalak's wife (the second) was not more than twenty years old, and had been married at the age of thirteen. In other words, the second wife was born around 1807 and wed around 1820. At the same time, Judith Montefiore mentions Amzalak's daughter (Esther) of a previous marriage, who was not more than fourteen. The second Mrs. Amzalak was described by Judith Montefiore as an exceedingly pretty young woman. Her manner of dress would have suited the styles fashionable at the time, described by Judith Montefiore as follows:

> The ladies in general wear a profusion of ornaments. A broad gold belt encircles the waist; but the head is simply covered by the turban, no hair being allowed to escape from its folds, which, when the features and forehead are handsome, is a becoming fashion.[126]

In 1836 another source, John Lloyd Stephens, wrote: "I must not forget the Jew's family, which consisted of a second wife [Rachel], about sixteen, already the mother of two children [Solomon, b.1832 and Raphael, b.1835] and his son [Yitzhak David, b.1825] and his son's wife, the husband twelve and the wife ten years old."[127] It appears that this "second wife" was really Amzalak's third,

---

124 Durbin (supra n. 104), pp. 68-69.
125 Montefiore (supra n. 123), p. 203; Barnett (supra n. 103), II, p. 116.
126 Montefiore (supra n. 123), pp.203-204.
127 Stephens (supra n. 102), p.372; AFP, Record of Circumcisions.

Rachel. According to Stephens' information, she would have been born before 1820 and wed around 1831.

As for Joseph Amzalak's children, he apparently had four sons, Yitzhak David, Haim Nissim [b.1828], Solomon and Raphael, and a daughter, Esther. It would appear that Esther was from the first marriage, Yitzhak David and Haim Nissim from the second marriage, and Solomon and Raphael from the third. An additional member of the Amzalak household was the orphan Rachel, whom Joseph Amzalak took in and cared for. She was the only individual residing in the Amzalak home mentioned in the Montefiore census of 1839.

Yitzhak David, the eldest son, was born in 1825 and died at an early age in 1838. The missionary John Nicolayson tells of his death on July 6 of that year:

> Poor Isaac [Yitzhak David] Amzalak died in the night & has just been carried to his grave. Soon after I called at the door to speak a word of comfort to his father; but there is but miserable comfort to be administered where the consolations of the Gospel are not admitted. Poor old man his chief comfort seems to be his belief that he did not die of plague. The quarantine authorities have most unaccountably pronounced the case no plague. May it prove so by sparing the rest of the family.[128]

This tragedy deeply affected Joseph Amzalak, perhaps reminding him of his earlier experience with the plague in Malta. Nicolayson describes his encounter with Amzalak two days following the death of the latter's son.

> This morning poor Mr. Amzalak came to my house crying like a child. His wife is almost distrached [sic] with grief at the death of her son, & is [in] danger of actually loosing [sic] her reason. She wants to run away from the country. He therefore [is] begging me to obtain permission for him from the Quarantine authorities to remove with his family to Jaffa, where if need be he can embark for some other country. I have just obtained their permission for him; & he will leave to-morrow.[129]

In memory of Amzalak's eldest son, a room in the *Talmud Torah* (school for religious studies) was dedicated to Isaac David in 1839.[130]

An important aspect of Joseph Amzalak's family life was providing for his children's education. They received a religious education in Jerusalem as well as studying Hebrew and Arabic. A letter written by Rachel Amzalak, probably to Chief Rabbi Yehuda Navon, provides information regarding the type of

128 JMA, Nicolayson Diaries, (photocopy) July 6, 1838, p. 850.
129 JMA, Nicolayson Diaries, July 8, 1838, p. 851.
130 Pinhas Benzion Grayevski, *Memories of Early Days*, Jerusalem 1928, p. 24 (Hebrew).

education given and her attitude towards it. Rachel wrote that she was upset and was unable to sleep nights since Haim wanted to stop studying. He had three or four months to complete his studies, she stated, and was throwing it all away. She appealed to the chief rabbi to intervene, and speak to Haim. She mentioned that he had thought himself capable of completing his education on his own and she hoped that if he studied with his brother-in-law (Eliyahu Navon) or took on another teacher, he would continue his studies.[131]

Joseph Amzalak intervened on behalf of his children by arranging for them to marry young. This was the norm in Jerusalem. The customary marriage age for both sexes was about fourteen or fifteen, following several years of betrothal. Joseph Amzalak arranged marriages for his children with those of prominent families in order to strengthen the bonds between his own family and these others. Esther married into the Navon family — the branch connected to Chief Rabbi Yehuda Navon (1840-1841); Raphael also married into the Navon family — the branch connected to the Chief Rabbi Yonah Moshe Navon (1836-1840); Haim married into the Levi family of Hebron — the daughter of Joseph Levi; and Solomon married into the Ashkenazi family — the daughter of Rabbi. Yehuda Shmuel Ashkenazi.[132]

Joseph's daughter Esther, not more than fourteen, lived with her husband Eliyahu Navon, who was only a year older, in her father's house. Yitzhak David was married at the age of twelve to a ten-year-old bride. John Lloyd Stephens found this situation to be quite amusing:

> The little gentleman [Yitzhak David] was at the table and behaved very well, except that his father had to check him in eating sweetmeats. The lady was playing on the floor with other children, and I did with her what I could not have done with a bigger man's wife — I took her on my knee and kissed her.[133]

---

131 NLA, Tubor Archives, V.736/7, Letter from Rachel Amzalak, Jerusalem [?], to Rabbi Yehuda Navon [?], Jerusalem [?], n.d. (Ladino). The use of certain terms in Ladino in the written appeal implies that the letter dictated by Rachel Amzalak was to the Chief Rabbi and a relation of the Amzalak family; therefore it may be assumed that the letter was to Rabbi Yehuda Navon, as such the dating of the letter would be the year 5601 [1840/1841], the year in which he served as chief rabbi. We would like to thank the translator Mazal Navon-Linenberg, who drew the connection to Rabbi Yehuda Navon.

132 Uziel Shmelz, "Some Demographic Peculiarities of the Jews of Jerusalem in the Nineteenth Century," Moshe Ma'oz (ed.), *Studies on Palestine during the Ottoman Period,* Jerusalem 1975, pp. 119-141; Montefiore (supra n. 123), p. 203.

133 Stephens (supra n. 102), pp.372-373.

Another son, Solomon or Raphael, was engaged at an extremely early age, and Stephens provides a charming description of the state of affairs at the time:

> Among the Jews, matches are made by the parents; and immediately upon the marriage, the wife is brought into the household of the husband. A young gentleman was tumbling about the floor who was engaged to the daughter of the chief rabbi. I did not ask the age of the lady, of course, but the gentleman bore the heavy burden of three years. He had not yet learned to whisper the story of his love to his blushing mistress, for in fact, he could not talk at all; he was a great bawling boy, and cared much more for his bread and butter than a wife; but his prudent father had already provided him.[134]

The Amzalak House

During Joseph Amzalak's lifetime in Jerusalem, he resided in two different houses. The first of these was described by Judith Montefiore, who had some trouble locating it upon her arrival to Jerusalem in 1827 with her husband. This is understandable since the house was located in the interior of the city, between the Armenian and Jewish Quarters. Access to the house was through a series of winding alleys. Within its walls was a private synagogue. The Montefiores found the conditions in the Amzalak house somewhat lacking, as is evident from Judith's comment about "the little rest we had been able to procure, owing to the number of insects which came forth during the night from the cushions of the divan, or sofa, that formed our bed."[135]

The exact site of the first Amzalak house has not been found. Its relative location has been identified as near John Nicolayson's residence, which later became the Bikur Holim hospital. It appears that the first Amzalak house was damaged in 1834 by a combination of natural disaster and acts of vandalism. During May 1834 a revolt broke out against the occupying Egyptian forces under Ibrahim Pasha. It was led by peasants from the mountainous districts of Hebron and Nablus, who refused to be conscripted into the Egyptian army.

---

134 Stephens (supra n. 102), p.373; The daughter of the chief rabbi being referred to is likely to be Angeline (Yael), the wife of Raphael. The chief rabbi mentioned here seems to be Rabbi Yonah Moshe Navon. That would explain why Eliyahu Navon was the executor of Raphael's will; he was concerning himself with the plight of a relative of his, Angeline Navon-Amzalak. We would like to thank Mrs. Mazal Navon-Linenberg for pointing out this possible connection.

135 Montefiore (supra n. 123), p. 203.

From the twenty-first of the month the rebels besieged Jerusalem and on the twenty-sixth, at one o'clock in the afternoon, the first shock of an earthquake shook the city.[136] No definitive information exists on the degree of damage incurred by the Amzalak house, but the journal entries of their neighbor John Nicolayson allude to some destruction there — the fate of almost all the buildings in Jerusalem:

> We had just concluded our regular divine service when on [sic] a sudden the windows began to shake terribly, and the whole house to totter....Here the scene was awful — stones falling in every direction, caused by a second shock still stronger than the first, which immediately reoccured....I brought them down to the garden, and sat there to wait the next shock, in the midst of the cries and shrieks of our neighbours round us. Mr. Amzalak, a Jew, and his family, with many more friends, came to take refuge with us, as our garden is a large open space.[137]

The shocks of the earthquake continued through the night. The residents of the city feared that the walls around Jerusalem might partially collapse, thus allowing the rebels entrance into the city, which they would in all probability plunder. Indeed, on June 2, 1834 the rebels did manage to enter Jerusalem, breaking into shops and houses. They remained until the sixth of the month, aggravating the damage which the city had incurred during the earthquake.[138] [see Figure 4]

Possibly as a result of the partial destruction of the first Amzalak house in 1834, Joseph Amzalak built a second residence closer to Jaffa Gate, at the entrance to David Street. Ferdinand Christian Ewald, a missionary to Jerusalem between 1842 and 1844, wrote during his first year in the city that Joseph Amzalak had recently built a magnificent house at a cost of £2,000. Amzalak told him that it had taken two and a half years to complete it and that it was the most beautiful building in Jerusalem. Within its walls were a

---

136 R.A. Stewart Macalister, "Gleanings from the Minute-Books of the Jerusalem Literary Society," *Palestine Exploration Fund Quarterly Statement* (1911), pp. 83-85; Macalister brought a paper on "The Revolt and Earthquake of Jerusalem in 1834," read by Miss Nicolayson at the society's meeting of March 28, 1851. Miss Nicolayson's information was taken from her father's private journal.
137 Macalister (supra n. 136), p. 85.
138 Macalister (supra n. 136), pp. 85-89.

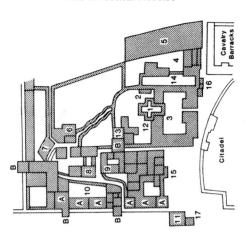

Description of Key

This Key, on an enlarged scale, represents a section of Mount Sion [sic], which embraces for the most part the premises of the London Society for Promoting Christianity among [sic] the Jews, and the British and Prussian Colony; and in tracing out most of its particular features great obligations are due to Matthew Haberhon. Esq.. Architect to the Society, who courteously and spontaneously furnished a valuable plan of the same from his own survey and drawings No.

1. Anglican Church in course of erection
2. English Church at present in use
3. Proposed Quadrangle, with intended Residence of the British and the Prussian Consul; this is at present an open space
4. Armenian Garden
5. Armenian Buildings, for the use of Pilgrims
6. Society's Hospital
7. Society's Dispensary
8. Residence of the Rev.. the Bishop's Chaplain
9. Residence of H. B. M., late Consul for Palestine, Mr Young
10. Society's Botanical Garden
11. Residence of the late Anglican Bishop Alexander
12. Old Ruined Mosque, formerly a Christian Church, dedicated to St. Thomas, or St. James the Son of Alphaeus, now in the occupation of the society
13. Mission House, occupied by the Rev. Mr. Nicolayson, the road to it is under an arched-way
14. Turk's Burying Place, with Santon
15. Turkish Custom House
16. Oil Press and Shops
17. Residence of the French Consul, adjoining that of Bishop Alexander

AAAAAA Houses in Jaffa-gate street, with Shops

BBBB Arched-ways

Figure 4: Mount Zion opposite the Citadel, Jerusalem 1846

(Source: John Blackburn, *A Handbook Round Jerusalem or Companion to the Model*, London 1846, n.p. We would like to thank Joseph Shadur for providing us with this figure)

Plate 13: Inside Jaffa Gate, including the Amzalak house, 1846
(Source: George Williams, *The Holy City*, II, London 1846, op. p. 528)

synagogue and a yeshiva. He then rented his first house to the first Protestant bishop in Jerusalem, Michael Solomon Alexander.[139] [see Plate 13]

A graphic portrait of the interior of the new house with some of its inhabitants was drawn by the renowned painter W. H. Bartlett on his visit to Palestine in the summer of 1842. It appeared as an illustration in his book *Walks in and about the City and Environs of Jerusalem*, as well as in many other travel books. [see Plate 14] Bartlett added the following written description of the house:

> On the level brow of Zion, exactly opposite the Tower of Hippicus, is the residence of the wealthiest Jew in Jerusalem. On passing through the outer door of his dwelling, we entered a small court, overshadowed by a vine-covered trellis, on one side of which are the principal apartments, which we found comfortable and in good order.[140]

Religious Observance and Belief

Joseph Amzalak was a practicing Jew, observant of the religious laws and customs. He was knowledgeable and well-versed in the Scriptures and rabbinic

139 F.C. Ewald, *Journal of Missionary Labours in the City of Jerusalem, during the years 1842-3-4*, London 1846, pp. 68-69; Muriel W. Corey, *From Rabbi to Bishop*, London n.d., p. 71.
140 Bartlett (supra n. 104), p. 191.

On entering his dwelling, we found him seated on the low divan, fondling his youngest child; and on our expressing a wish to draw the costume of the female members of his family, he commanded their attendance; but it was some time before they would come forward; when, however, they did present themselves, it was with no sort of reserve whatever. Their costume (*as represented in the vignette on the title page*) was chastely elegant. The prominent figure in the sketch is the married daughter, whose little husband, a boy of fourteen or fifteen, as he seemed, wanted nearly a head of the stature of his wife, but was already chargeable with the onerous duties of a father. An oval head-dress of peculiar shape, from which is slung a long veil of embroidered muslin, shown as hanging, in the sketch, from the back of another figure, admirably sets off the brow and eyes; the neck is ornamented with bracelets, and the bosom with a profusion of gold coins, partly concealed by folds of muslin; a graceful robe of striped silk, with long open sleeves, half-laced under the bosom, invests the whole person, over which is worn a jacket of green silk with short sleeves, leaving the white arm and braceleted hand at liberty. The elder person on the sofa is the mother, whose dress was more grave, her turban less oval, and of blue shawl, and the breast covered, entirely to the neck, with a kind of ornamented gold tissue, above which is seen a jacket of fur: she was

engaged in knitting, while her younger daughter bent over her in conversation: her dress is similar to that of her sister, but with no gold coins or tight muslin folds; and instead of large earrings, the vermilion blossom of the pomegranate formed an exquisite pendant, reflecting its glow upon the dazzling whiteness of her skin.

We were surprised at the fairness and delicacy of their complexions, and the vivacity of their manner. Unlike the wives of oriental Christians, who respectfully attend at a distance till invited to approach, these pretty Jewesses seemed on a perfect footing of equality, and chatted and laughed away without intermission.

We are happy to hear that the political position of the Jews is lately improved, owing to the interest taken in their behalf by various Christian societies, and the personal influence of distinguished English Jews.[*] It is pleasing also to reflect, as a proof of the advancement of the age, that these instances of kindness have not been without fruit. On the occasion of a recent attack upon the physician of the English mission, by some fanatic Turkish soldiers, many of the Jews who were present interfered bravely to protect him. This points out the true way, we think, to gain the best feelings, and consequently to undermine the prejudices of this interesting

[*] We cannot but allude here to the noble generosity of a Jewish citizen of London, who has sent a medical man, at his own expense, to Jerusalem, to minister to his sick and suffering brethren.

2 c

Plate 14: The Amzalak family and the description of the drawing by the artist,
William Henry Bartlett
(Source: William Henry Bartlett, *Walks about the City and Environs of Jerusalem*; London 1844, the drawing found on the title page of the book has been placed with the text of pages 192-193)

sources. Through the accounts of various travelers one can learn about various aspects of his religious observance. It appears that following his move to Jerusalem, he adhered more strictly to Jewish ritual than before. Joseph Wolff, on his third visit to Jerusalem in 1829, observed that Joseph Amzalak wore a beard, whereas six years earlier in Acre he had been clean-shaven.[141] As previously mentioned, Joseph had the desire to live out his life in Jerusalem and to be buried on the Mount of Olives.

He also practiced the daily prayer rituals, which was facilitated by the existence of a synagogue within the confines of his house. Judith Montefiore gave the following account:

> Mr. Amzlac [sic] has a synagogue in the house, and at day-break the male branch of the family assemble at prayers. Notwithstanding the earliness of the hour....Montefiore was induced, by the holy feelings so naturally excited in this place, to join them.[142]

Joseph Amzalak and his family would join the rest of the Jewish community for Sabbath and holiday prayer service in the Ben-Zakai synagogue, the largest of the Four Sephardi synagogues.[143] [see Plate 15] Judith Montefiore described her visit to synagogue on the Sabbath, accompanied by the second Mrs. Amzalak:

> At dawn of day Montefiore arose and went to synagogue, accompanied by Mr. Amzlac [sic]. An hour afterwards I repaired with Mrs. Amzlac [sic], escorted by two male attendants, to the same place of devotion. The gallery was thronged with females, all clad in deep white scarfs, which covered their head and figure. There are no seats, but two were provided for us; the other persons who were present placing their handkerchiefs on the ground, and there taking their places. We perceived, through the wooden trellis-work, that Montefiore was just called up to Sephar [Torah scrolls];[144]

Joseph Amzalak and his family celebrated the Sabbath and adhered to the commandment forbidding any work on that day. John Nicolayson "called at Mr. Amslac's [sic] soon after sunset & found him saying קדוש [kiddush] (the blessing which immediately after service on the Sabbath eve they pronounce over 12 loaves & a glass (or either cup) of wine & conclude by drinking the

141 Morgenstern (supra n. 110), p. 401 quoting *The Jewish Expositor*, London 1827, p. 357.
142 Montefiore (supra n. 123), p. 203.
143 Montefiore (supra n. 123), p. 211.
144 Montefiore (supra n. 123), p. 211.

Plate 15: Sephardi synagogue in Jerusalem
In the mid-thirties, the Jews of Jerusalem successfully appealed to Ibrahim Pasha
for permission to restore their dilapidated synagogues in the Old City. One traveler
tells us of a synagogue built of stone with a dome in the centre of its wooden roof.
Although the building could hold many people it was built in a relatively low place
for fear of angering the authorities. The description seems to fit the Sephardic
synagogue repaired in 1834. This picture did not give the name of the synagogue.
There is some ground for believing that the illustration depicts the Sephardic
synagogue immediately after its completion, at the time of an inauguration ceremony
(Source: John Carne, *Syria, the Holy Land, Asia Minor*, London 1838, III, p. 92
and the source of text: Yehoshua Ben-Arieh, *The Rediscovery of the Holy land in
the Nineteenth Century*, Jerusalem 1983, p. 108)

latter)."[145] Another gentile observer, John Lloyd Stephens, described his visit to the table of Joseph Amzalak on a Saturday:

> The command to do no work on the Sabbath day is observed by every Jew, as strictly as when the commandment was given to his fathers; and to such an extent it was obeyed in the house of my friend that it was not considered allowable to extinguish a lamp which had been lighted the night before and was now burning in broad daylight over our table. This extremely strict observance of the law at first gave me some uneasiness about my dinner; but my host, with great self-complacency, relieved me from all apprehensions by describing the admirable contrivance he had invented for reconciling appetite and duty — an oven, heated the night before to such a degree that the process of cooking was continued during the night and the dishes were ready when wanted the next day.[146]

Another aspect of his religious observance was the fulfillment of the commandment to the aid the poor and the needy. He gave charity for the benefit of the community at large as well as individuals, and took pride in this activity. Stephens wrote the following on this subject:

> My friend [Amzalak], however, did not put his own light under a bushel; for, telling me the amount he had himself contributed to the building, [of the Ben-Zakai synagogue or at least the repair of its roof], he conducted me to a room built at his own expense for a schoolroom, with a stone in the front wall recording his name and generosity.[147]

Another contribution was made toward the construction of the Talmud Torah and Yeshiva "Etz Haim" in the area of Hurvat [the Ruin of] Rabbi Judah Hasid. He financed a room known as Toldot Yitzhak, in memory of his son Yitzhak David Amzalak, who had died during Joseph's lifetime.[148]

In addition to the synagogue in his house, he also maintained a yeshiva there. Furthermore, he supported twelve Jews in a different yeshiva who studied the Mishna and read Psalms from the middle of the night until dawn.[149]

Joseph Amzalak was a patron of higher learning in Jerusalem. His financial aid allowed for the publication of *Sefer HaZohar* by Yisrael Bak in Jerusalem

145 JMA, Nicolayson Diaries, November 15, 1833. p. 432. The word קדוש which refers to the benediction over the wine and bread is found in Hebrew script using this spelling in the original text.

146 Stephens (supra n. 102), p. 372.

147 Stephens (supra n. 102), p. 371.

148 Grayevski (supra n. 130).

149 Ewald (supra n. 139), pp. 83-84. JMA, Nicolayson Diaries, January 28, 1833, p. 366.

Plate 16: Cover page and preface of Sefer HaZohar
(Source: National Library, Jerusalem)

in 5614 (1844). The preface includes words of thanks to Joseph Amzalak for his generous and gracious support.[150] [see Plate 16]

150 Shimon Bar Yoachai, *Sefer HaZohar*, Jerusalem 1844, (Hebrew) in the NLA, Rare Books Collection.

ה.ספר שיך להצבי **עץ יוסף אמזאלאן** נ״י מהל בלונדון וב[...]

בריתו של אברהם

כולל סדר ברכות מילה לכל הנימול שיהיה לחנך
פישוט · ליתום מאב · או מאם · או בשעותיהם לאם
נדול בשנים · לממזר · או סנדס בשום פנים · יבא ב
באחרונה נוסח הרחמן שאומרים בברכת המזון
בסעודה · הכל נכתב · כפי התעודרה · על יד יחזורה

בלונדון
עת
והיתה בריתי בבשרכם

**Plate 17: Cover of Joseph Amzalak's
mohel prayer book
(Source: Simon Amzalak Family
Papers, Jerusalem)**

Joseph Amzalak also distributed charity to the poor of the city on his own behalf and that of Sir Moses Montefiore. In 1827, Judith wrote that "a host of poor widows also, and others, came to ask assistance; but Montefiore had previously arranged this matter with Mr. Amzlac [sic]."[151] Again in 1839 he served as Montefiore's agent and was sent £500 for the poor of the Hebrew communities.[152]

Amzalak was a *mohel* (ritual circumcizer), having received his training in London in 5560 (1799-1800). He recorded the 118 circumcisions which he performed between 1816 and 1838.[153] [see Plate 17]

151 Montefiore (supra n. 123), p. 217.
152 Louis Loewe (ed.), *Diaries of Sir Moses and Lady Montefiore*, London 1890, 1, p. 196; Joseph Amzalak distributed the funds according to criteria established by *A Census of the Jews of Eretz Israel (1839)*. In the census there appears a letter from Joseph Amzalak to Moses Montefiore dated June 21, 1839, stating that the former had distributed the funds. Of interest is that he and his family were not listed in the census, although they were in Palestine at the time. See the introduction by H. Assouline to the reprint of the census, Jerusalem 1987, p .15.
153 AFP, Record of Circumcisions.

Plate 18: Dr. Richard R. Madden
(Source: Richard R. Madden, *Travels in Turkey, Egypt, Nubia and Palestine in the years 1824-7*, London 1829, frontispiece)

Moreover, from conversations reported by Dr. Richard Madden and other Christian informants, Joseph Amzalak appears to have been well-acquainted with Jewish thought as embodied in rabbinic literature. With great pride he showed Madden his eighteen-volume Talmud and stated that he knew every word in it. During their discussion of Christian missionary activities in the city, Amzalak pointed out that the torments of hell lasted no more than twelve months, according to Talmudic sources. He told Madden a legend from the Talmud which attested to the veracity of almost all the miracles attributed to Jesus in the New Testament. Jesus, however, had dared to do things that the religion had forbidden. Amzalak stressed that it was within his own power to perform the same supernatural feats based on the wisdom of the Kabbalah.[154] [see Plate 18]

154 Madden (supra n. 110), p. 437.

On different occasions Amzalak and John Nicolayson held lengthy conversations on the messiahship of Jesus and the differences between Judaism and Christianity.[155] At other times they sat together reading the Bible and different rabbinic commentaries. Nicolayson described one such meeting in great detail:

> Attended morning-service at Mr. Amsalac's [sic] synagogue, which he has just fitted up in his own house, & where a number of Jews from the neighbourhood attend. Afterwards read with him part of the commentary on the section (פרשה) of the day חיי שרה [The Life of Sarah, Genesis XXIII, 1 — XXV, 18]. The name of this commentary is ספר אליהו המזרחי [Sefer Eliyahu Mizrachi]. This led to much conversation on the Messiah's being צדקנו [our righteous one] & on his being one with the Father.[156]

Their conversation continued with each of them quoting different biblical passages and commentaries at great length to prove their respective opinions.

In a different discussion with Durbin, Joseph Amzalak expressed his opinion on the messiahship of Christ:

> The old man said that Jesus was a good man, but no more; that the story of his death might be true enough, but that of his resurrection was all a humbug (This English slang term was quite a favourite with him). "Who saw him? Only two or three women..." He repeatedly exclaimed with great emphasis, "There is but one God! God have a wife! Mary, the wife of God!"[157]

In a later conversation between Amzalak and Madden, the latter mentioned having been in the desert of Mount Sinai. Amzalak shook his head and said that no one knew the location of Mount Sinai. He explained that it was known that Aaron was buried in a valley between the Red Sea and Syria; the Patriarchs, Abraham, Isaac and Jacob, were entombed in Hebron only eight hours away; the tomb near Bethlehem was that of the matriarch, Rachel; the magnificent monument near the river of Siloam (Kidron Valley) had been constructed by Absalom; the distant tomb was that of Samuel; but no one knew the location of Mount Sinai or of Moses's grave.[158]

Amzalak believed in many legends connected to Jerusalem. Madden described Amzalak's account as brimming with details of miraculous

155 JMA, Nicolayson Diaries, April 10, 1833, pp. 392-393.
156 JMA, Nicolayson Diaries, November 9, 1833, pp. 427-428.
157 Durbin (supra n. 104), pp. 254-255.
158 Madden (supra n. 110), pp. 437-438.

occurrences, and including a fantastic description of the foundations of the Temple. Amzalak had emphasized that the Mosque of Omar (the Dome of the Rock), located where the Temple had once stood, was built on a large rock suspended in air. This had been a widespread legend among both Jews and Muslims during the Middle Ages. Amzalak continued by stating that beneath this unsupported rock were hidden ancient texts, the two tablets of the Ten Commandments and the golden menorah from the Second Temple.[159]

Amzalak's religious observance was tinged with superstition, as suggested by Morgenstern. On this subject, Joseph Wolff recounted an incident when Joseph Amzalak had visited the Wolff home, and they discussed Jesus. Amzalak became enraged and left abruptly when Wolff's wife burnt something in his presence. Amzalak, it was told, immediately went to the rabbi and then immersed himself in a *mikvah* (ritual bath) to ward off the influence of the witchcraft he believed to have been performed. The facts were such: Wolff's servant, Antonio, had prepared special cakes and baked them in paper. When Amzalak arrived, Wolff's wife Georgina (granddaughter of British Prime Minister Robert Walpole) offered him some cake, forgetting that he wouldn't eat food served by a Christian. Georgina sat beside the fire eating the cake and when she had finished she threw the paper into the flames, creating much smoke. This was the action that Amzalak interpreted as an act of witchcraft. Subsequently many Jews avoided Georgina Wolff, believing her to be a witch.[160] [see Plate 19]

Hospitality

Another aspect of Joseph Amzalak's life in Jerusalem, as in Acre, was the hospitality which he extended to guests. Such behavior could be regarded simply as the act of an observant Jew obeying the commandment of welcoming guests, but for Amzalak it would appear that the matter went beyond that, touching upon his sense of self-importance and pride. He was a prince among the Jews of Jerusalem and it was only fitting that important guests take up residence with him. His house was always open to Jews and non-Jews alike, because on the one hand he served as a representative of the Jewish community and spoke English well, and on the other hand he derived personal pleasure from

159 Madden (supra n. 110), p. 438; For different legends connected to a rock known as the Foundation Stone beneath the Dome of the Rock see: Ze'ev Vilnay, *Legends of Jerusalem*, Philadelphia 1980, pp. 5-36.

160 Wolff (supra n. 119), pp. 213-214.

Plate 19: Joseph Wolff
(Source: Nathan Shur, "The
Golden Age of Travellers'
Descriptions to Eretz Israel,"
Ariel, 47 (October 1986) p. 39.
Courtesy of Eli Schiller)

hosting these people. Meeting with Joseph Amzalak left a deep impression on his visitors.

He was visited in Acre by the leaders of the Hasidim in Safed, Rabbi Moshe Manarinsk and Rabbi Gershon Margoliot, together with Joseph Wolff.[161]

The Montefiores, Moses and Judith, saw Amzalak's home as the natural place to stay on their first journey to the Holy Land in 1827. At that time no modern hotels existed in Jerusalem, so travelers ordinarily stayed in the city's convents. Judith Montefiore wrote in her journal that "numbers of priests came out from the different convents, all anxious that we should take up our abode among them; but we declined their invitations, and repaired to the house of Mr. Amzlac [sic]."[162] [see Plate 20]

Had the Montefiores wanted to stay somewhere else, they would have encountered great difficulties from Amzalak. Such an action would have been considered an affront. Judith Montefiore described the situation as such:

> Having sent our letters of introduction, we had the greatest difficulty imaginable in excusing ourselves from accepting the urgent invitations of

161 Morgenstern (supra n. 110), p. 402 quoting *The Jewish Expositor*, London 1822, p. 348. The transliteration of מנארינסק and מרגליות is Rabbi Moshe Manarinsk and Rabbi Gershon Margoliot.

162 Montefiore (supra n. 123), p. 192.

Plate 20: Sir Moses and Lady Judith Montefiore at the gates of Jerusalem, 1839
(Source: Yad Yitzhak Ben Zvi Archives, Jerusalem)

the hospitable persons who had prepared rooms for us in their houses, pressed us, with most urgent invitations, to sojourn with them during our stay. One of the foremost was a relation of the late high-priest of the German congregation here, to whom the Reverend Doctor Herschel gave us a letter; but Mr. Amzlac [sic] said that it would be offering him the greatest possible affront if we left his house for that of any other friend, having stopped there on our arrival. We were therefore compelled to relinquish the obliging invitations we had received, greatly to the disappointment of those who made them.[163]

As a token of their gratitude for Amzalak's hospitality during their visit in 1839, the Montefiores sent him a silver box with a Hebrew inscription whose translation is as follows:

A memento of affection and a token of gratitude, to a distinguished friend, who does acts of charity at all times, to Joseph Amzalak forever

163 Montefiore (supra n. 123), p. 205.

in the holy city of Jerusalem, that will be rebuilt in our lifetimes, in order that my memory will never forget it, Moses Montefiore, here in London, the capital, a great day 5600 [1840] to the creation of the world.[164]

Dr. Richard Madden often dined at Joseph Amzalak's table during his stay in Jerusalem in 1827. They carried on lengthy conversations on both Jewish and Christian theology. On one occasion Amzalak took Madden to a Jewish wedding. Although it was not customary for Christians to attend such ceremonies, Amzalak's influential position in the community made this possible. Amzalak explained to Madden the intricacies of the Jewish nuptial ceremony. He also subtly touched Madden's elbow three or four times, and then whispered in his guest's ear that his staring was considered improper. Amzalak lavished much attention on his guest, making him feel welcomed and honored.[165]

Another description of Amzalak's hospitality comes from John Lloyd Stephens, from spring of 1836. At the request of the chief rabbi of Hebron, Stephens was received by the chief rabbi of Jerusalem, Rabbi Yonah Moshe Navon, and a Jew from Gibraltar who spoke English. Stephens wrote, "the friends made for me by the rabbi at Hebron were the very friends above all others whom I would have selected for myself." Being unwilling to play second fiddle and serve merely as interpreter to Stephens in his meetings with the chief rabbi of Jerusalem, Amzalak refrained from accompanying him at all.[166]

Amzalak's house was always open to John Nicolayson and his guests during the latter's years in Jerusalem. Nicolayson recorded numerous diary entries about visits to Amzalak's house. He was received by Amzalak in "his usual cordial manner."[167] Nicolayson wrote of his return to Jerusalem on May 19, 1835: "My old friend Mr. Amzalak was at the gate & followed me to the house to welcome me back."[168]

---

164 Grayevski (supra n. 130), p. 1.
165 Madden (supra n. 110), pp. 437-438.
166 Stephens (supra n. 102), pp. 367-368. Rabbi Yonah Moshe Navon was chief rabbi from 8 Shvat 5596 (January 27, 1836) until his death, 23 Tevet 5601 (January 16, 1841) see Abraham Elmaleh, *The Rishonim LeZion, their Histories and Activities*, Jerusalem 1970, pp. 172-178 (Hebrew).
167 JMA, Nicolayson Diaries, January 28, 1833, pp. 366-367. Other examples of their meetings are November 14, 1833, p. 431; November 15, 1833, p. 432; November 16, 1833, p. 432; January 23, 1834, p. 465; June 20, 1836, p. 758; July 5, 1836, p.777; April 5, 1838, p. 831.
168 JMA, Nicolayson Diaries, November 9, 1833, pp. 427-428.

Business Activities

Joseph Amzalak's main source of income during his residence in Jerusalem was moneylending. The capital that he had amassed in earlier years was reinvested in loans to residents of Jerusalem and the region, as well as visitors and travelers to the area. Detailed information on Amzalak's financial situation was provided by John Lloyd Stephens, based on a conversation with the Jewish financier:

> He told me he was rich, very rich; that he was the richest and, in fact, the only rich Jew in Jerusalem. He took me through his house, and showed me his gold and silver ornaments and talked of his money and the uses he made of it; that he lent to the Latin Convent on interest, without any security, whenever they wanted; but as for the Greeks — he laughed, laid his finger on his nose, and said he had in pledge jewels belonging to them of the value of more than twenty thousand dollars. He had had his losses too; and while we were enjoying the luxuries of his table, the leaven of his nature broke out, and he endeavored to sell me a note for fifteen hundred pounds of the Lady Esther [sic] Stanhope, which he offered at a discount of 50 per cent, a bargain which I declined, as being out of the line of my business.[169]

Lady Hester Stanhope, granddaughter of William Pitt the Elder and niece of William Pitt the Younger, traveled in the Eastern Mediterranean for six years (1810-1816), living for a number of years in Lebanon. Her limited income scarcely sufficed for her extravagant expenditures. For example, in order to fund the discovery of hidden treasures near Ashkelon, she borrowed money from Joseph Amzalak. Troubled by her debt which remained outstanding for over two years, Amzalak wrote to her with the aid of Joseph Wolff, requesting payment.[170]

Amzalak's financial dealings also played an important role in the Jewish community in Jerusalem and other cities of the Ottoman Empire. He provided financing for those in need and for important projects, including a loan of 1,000 piastre (approximately £90) to the Kolel of the Habad Hasidim in Hebron during the period of the Egyptian occupation of Palestine (1831-1841). This loan was interest-free.[171]

169 Stephens (supra n. 102), pp. 371-372.
170 Charles Lewis Meyron, *Travels of Lady Hester Stanhope*, London, 1846, 1, pp. v-xi, and vol. 3, pp. 96-97; Wolff (surpa n. 119), p. 213.
171 Austrian Consular Archives, file Jer.II/31, N.159, Letter from the leaders of the community and rabbis of the Ashkenazim in Hebron to Josef von Pizzamano, Austrian consul, Jerusalem, July-August 1849, translated into Hebrew in Mordechai Eliav, *The Austrian Consulate in Jerusalem*, Jerusalem 1986, pp. 64-65 (Hebrew).

He granted a loan, valued at 3,000 gold *adumim* (approximately £1,400) to the Prushim of the Ashkenazi community in Jerusalem in 1839, following repayment of loan to a Christian institution in the fall of 1838. This Jewish community was in financial straits and depended on contributions sent from Europe, but the flow of financial support was erratic. As collateral, Joseph Amzalak received the mortgage to the compound of Hurvat Rabbi Judah Hasid. The debt, still outstanding at the time of his death, was repaid to his heirs (see Chapter Three for a detailed discussion).[172]

Another area of financial activity was the realm of currency exchange. John Lloyd Stephens described a scene which he had stumbled across:

> Returning to the convent, and passing through one of the bazars [sic], we saw an Arab mounted on a bench and making a proclamation to the crowd around him; and my friend, the Gibraltar Jew, was immediately among them, listening earnestly. The subject was one that touched his tenderest sensibilities as a dealer in money; for the edict proclaimed was on changing the value of the current coin, reducing the tallahree or dollar from twenty-one to twenty piastres, commanding all the subjects of Mohammed Ali to take it at that value, and concluding with the usual finale of a Turkish proclamation, "Death to the offender." My Jew, as he had already told me several times, was the richest Israelite in Jerusalem, and consequently took great interest in everything that related to money. He told me that he always cultivated an intimacy with the officer of the mint, and, by giving him an occasional present, he always got intimation of any intended change in time to save himself.[173]

Amzalak's Legal Status

As a subject of the British Crown, Joseph Amzalak was afforded special rights and protection under the Capitulation laws. In order to ensure this protection, he registered important documents, such as the laissez-passer of 1799 and the 1824 passport from the consular agent in Acre with the British consul general in Beirut. Added by hand in both these documents were the words, "duly registered....at the request of Joseph Amzalak for the benefit, as may be of himself and his descendants."[174]

---

172 For a detailed discussion and description see: Morgenstern (supra n. 110), pp. 406-412 and for some of the documents, see: Grayevski (supra n. 130), pp. 4-23.
173 Stephens (supra n. 102), p. 369.
174 NLA, 4°1613/2, 4°1613/4.

With the opening of the British consulate in Jerusalem in 1839, Joseph Amzalak and his family were registered under its protection.[175] This aegis was manifested in an 1839 incident, during the Egyptian occupation. The British consul to Jerusalem, William Tanner Young (1838-1845), recorded the occurrence as follows:

> An outrage that was committed on the person of a British subject in Jerusalem named Joseph Amzalek [sic] at the time of my arrival at Jaffa. On the receipt of the annexed statement I addressed myself to Ibrahim Pacha and I required satisfaction, in having the soldier beaten on the same spot where he had beaten Mr. Amzalek.[176]

Joseph Amzalak had been beaten outside his home near the Citadel by an *euz bashi*, a captain in the Egyptian army. This act was witnessed by Amzalak's son-in-law and another British subject, Dr. Georgio Grasso. On Amzalak's behalf, Mr. Nicolayson complained to the commander of the garrison, but the latter failed to pursue the matter. The next step was to register the complaint with the British consul, but by that time the said *euz bashi* was already in Damascus. The *euz bashi*, in a statement to Ibrahim Pasha, denied having beaten Amzalak. The handling of the affair was postponed by Ibrahim Pasha who claimed that it was impossible to do anything at the time since the accused was in Damascus, so that everyone would have to wait until his return to Jerusalem.[177]

Moses Amzalak and the Lisbon Branch of the Family

The consular diaries of James Finn provide information about another Amzalak family member, Joseph's brother Moses (1767-1858). According to the Lisbon branch of the Amzalak family, he was one of the first Jews to have settled in that city with the weakening of the inquisition in Portugal by the Marquis de Pombal. Originally from North Africa, he passed through Gibraltar, there attaining English citizenship. Later he settled in Lisbon as a Jew, not having to hide this identity. Various treaties between Portugal and England permitted English citizens, including Jews, to practise their religion freely, but in privacy. Moses may have settled in Lisbon as early as 1804. A tombstone from February 26, 1804 bearing an epitaph to a child, Ioze (Joseph) Amzalaga,

---

175 PRO, F.O.78/540, List of Colonial Subjects residing in Jerusalem under British Protection, January 1, 1843.

176 PRO, F.O. 78/368, August 13, 1839 in A.M. Hyamson, *The British Consulate in Jerusalem in Relation to the Jews in Palestine 1838-1914*, 1, London 1937-1941, p. 17.

177 Hyamson (supra n. 176), pp. 17-22.

is found in the English cemetery da Estrella at Lisbon. Moses and his first wife Simy (1784-1829) had seven children. No one by the name of Joseph is mentioned among Moses's children in the Amzalak family genealogy, but this does not necessarily mean that Moses did not have a son named Joseph. After his wife's death, Moses settled in Jerusalem. He remarried two more times, according to information provided by the Portuguese branch of the family. After his immigration to Jerusalem all contact between him and the Portuguese Amzalaks ceased.[178]

Moses Amzalak and his wife Jamila are among those listed in Montefiore's census of 1855. In contrast to the account from Lisbon, this census lists Lisbon as Moses's place of birth. It cites 1841 as the year of his arrival in the Holy Land as compared to sometime after 1829, as previously mentioned. Moses was seventy-five at the time the census was taken, that is born in 1780. This information differs from the British consular records which establish his birth in 1767.[179]

Information about his later years is based upon sources from Jerusalem. James Finn described one of his meetings with him.

> Visited the other branch of the Amzalak family — being Sabath [sic] day, they could neither offer us coffee nor pipes, in obedience to Exodus XXXV. 3 — but it was strange indeed for me to hear Jews conversing in Spanish. The old gentleman and lady are healthy handsome people, and the whole family and the mansion very pleasant to visit.[180]

Moses, it appears, also received foreign visitors in his house as a representative of the prominent families of Jerusalem. During the festival of Tabernacles in October 1849, he was visited by Clorinda S. Minor, an ex-Millerite Christian from Philadelphia and a religiously motivated woman who was to work at developing farming in Palestine between 1849 and 1855. Her description sheds light on Moses's living conditions, religious observances and even his view of American tourists:

> We were invited by one of their first families to visit them, they received us with much kindness, and showed us all over their house, which this week is arranged in their best order. Their rooms were comfortable and

178 Abecassis (supra n.101); Cardozo de Bethencourt, "The Jews in Portugal from 1773 to 1902," *The Jewish Quarterly Review* (old series), no. 15 (1903) pp. 251-260, 264-268.
179 JMA, Montefiore Census of 1855 (photocopy) p. 22.
180 YIBZA, James Finn Archives, Diary 7, entry for April 25, 1846.

pleasant, with matting on the floors, divans with neat covers, beds, tables, and a few chairs, which they insisted on our using. Afterwards we sat a while with them in their tabernacle, which was enclosed at the sides with curtains, and covered above with canes, and a few pine branches, which had been brought from a great distance; a small table stood in the centre, upon which all their food must be eaten during this week of the feast; over it was suspended clusters of grapes, figs and pomegranates. The aged father [Moses], with some difficulty, expresses that from sympathy he loved the stranger, especially Americans; that *his* people were free in *their* land, and he had known them in his intercourse of trade in the Mediterranean, while he resided a long time in Gibraltar. He invited us to come often to see him, saying that "we are all united in worshipping the same God, and in looking for his kingdom." The mother and daughters were gaily dressed in English style, and served us with coffee, sweetcakes, and preserved citron, and showed us much love at parting.[181]

Finn clearly states in the entry of August 16, 1853 that Moses was Haim's uncle, or in other words, Joseph Amzalak's older brother. Other references to Moses Amzalak are contained in a contract signed between him and his nephew, Haim, and in another document of his last days. Consul Finn was given notice on October 18, 1858 that Moses Amzalak was dying and that it would be necessary to seal up his property. Moses died the following day at the age of ninety-one, and his death was recorded in the consular register. From the information in the register, one learns that he had been a merchant by profession. During the next two months Consul Finn dealt with the settlement of the estate. On a number of occasions the widow of Moses Amzalak met with the consul, who explained that he intended to satisfy both Jewish and consular law by taking inventory of all goods, reporting the same to the government and recommending that all proceeds be given to her. He also promised to write to

---

181 Clorinda S. Minor, *Meshulam! or, Tidings from Jerusalem, from a Journal of a Believer Recently Returned from the Holy Land*, Philadelphia 1851, pp. 72-73. At first it would appear that this is a description of Joseph Amzalak, but he had died in 1845, four years prior to Minor's visit. Other observations by Minor such as Moses Amzalak's difficulty in speaking and the English dress of the Amzalak women, point to her having visited a different household from that described in passages relating to Joseph Amzalak. For further information on Clorinda Minor, see: Ruth Kark, "Millenarism and Agricultural Settlement in the Holy Land in the Nineteenth Century," *Journal of Historical Geography*, vol. 9, no. 1 (1983) pp. 53-54.

her son in Lisbon.[182] (See Appendix III for the genealogy of the Lisbon branch and Appendix II for a short description of the Lisbon branch.)

Summary

Joseph Amzalak lived in Jerusalem until his death in 1845, and was buried on the Mount of Olives in fulfillment of his hopes. He was an outstanding figure in the city, known to both its residents and visitors. He developed a special relationship with the Montefiores and other honored guests of Jerusalem. He was seen by outsiders as a prince among the Jews, enjoying this special status due to his vast wealth in the impoverished city, and the protection afforded him as a British subject. This standing allowed him to acquire all the material comforts available, which he shared through philanthropic deeds with his coreligionists and other inhabitants of the city and region. This status also allowed him great leeway in meeting with whomever he wanted, including missionaries. Such behavior from other Jews would have incurred the wrath of the rabbis and the threat of excommunication. He was considered a pious and religious Jew, this too adding to the great respect given him. [see Plate 21]

With his death, he left behind heirs: his wife Rachel, his sons Haim, Solomon and Raphael, and his daughter Esther, who would all play an important role in the development of Jerusalem, Jaffa and the rest of Palestine.

---

182 Arnold Blumberg, *A View from Jerusalem 1849-1858, The Consular Diary of James and Elizabeth Ann Finn*, London-Toronto 1980, pp. 135, 300-303, entries for August 16, 1853, October 18, 1858, October 27, 1858, October 29, 1858, November 1, 1858, November 10, 1858 and November 11, 1858; PRO, F.O. 617/5, Deaths within the District of the British Consulate of Jerusalem, p. 3. We would like to thank Rhoda Cohen for providing us with this document.

Plate 21: Jewish cemetery on the Mount of Olives, Jerusalem, 1836
(Source: John Carne, *Syria, the Holy Land, Asia Minor etc.*, III, London 1836, op. p. 80)

CHAPTER THREE

THE AMZALAKS — SECOND GENERATION IN JERUSALEM

Joseph Amzalak's wife and children remained in Jerusalem after his death in 1845, with the exception of Haim, who moved to Jaffa during the late 1850s or early 1860s. This chapter focuses upon the second generation in Jerusalem; the division of Joseph's estate, including the mortgage on the Hurva Compound, among his heirs; the personal and business activities of Joseph's family in the city; and various incidents that shed light on their life style and status.

As discussed in the previous chapter, Joseph had arranged the marriages of his children. Esther was already married to Eliyahu Navon and Haim was married to Esther Levi of Hebron. The other two sons, Solomon and Raphael, were married at an early age to Bolissa and Angeline (Yael), respectively. The male members of the family brought their wives into their father's home, while Esther was taken to her husband's family's home as their responsibility.[183] (A separate section will be devoted to Esther and Eliyahu Navon and their family.)

Upon the death of Joseph Amzalak, his remaining wealth was bequeathed to his widow, Rachel, and his sons, with only a small amount being left to Esther. The best-documented portion of the Amzalak estate was the Hurva Compound, which, as mentioned, had been mortgaged by the Prushim of the Ashkenazi community as collateral on a loan received. The inheritance also consisted of the Amzalak home and of other properties, but it appears that as the years elapsed the income derived from these sources was not sufficient for the Amzalak heirs to retain the status that they had enjoyed when Joseph was alive. By the 1850s the Amzalak house was rented, and its income was used to support Rachel Amzalak and her sons. Towards the end of the decade it was necessary for Rachel to borrow jewelry. After the deaths of Solomon and Raphael in the 1870s, their respective widows encountered financial difficulties. The

183 Stephens (supra n. 102), pp. 372-373; Montefiore (supra n. 123), p. 203; David Tidhar, *Encyclopedia of the Pioneers of the Yishuv and its Builders*, 2, Jerusalem 1947, p. 816 (Hebrew).

exception to the pecuniary decline of the family was Haim, who had established himself financially in Jaffa.

Before discussing the family, an aside should be made to introduce an important figure mentioned throughout this chapter: James Finn, the British consul of Jerusalem between 1846 and 1863. Finn was born in London in 1806. His diligence and aptitude for learning attracted the attention of the Earl of Clarendon, who helped promote Finn in the latter's future endeavors. Finn took a great interest in Jews, their history and the Hebrew language. He authored two studies, *Sepharadim* and *The Jews in China*. The first of these two works embodies Finn's attitudes towards Sephardi Jews. He wrote that the Jews are entitled to Christian gratitude for preserving the written word, although they continue in their erroneous belief.[184]

James Finn was one of the more interesting and colorful figures to reside in Jerusalem. Besides his consular duties, he showed a great interest in the missionary activities in the city. He and his wife, Elizabeth Anne Finn (daughter of the missionary Alexander McCaul), were members of the 'London Society for Promoting Christianity amongst the Jews.' He was pro-Jewish in his consular duties and his private actions. He extended consular protection to British — and even non-British — Jews, helped promote their productivity and founded the Industrial Plantation for Employment of Jews in Jerusalem, in Kerem Avraham (Abraham's Vineyard). His official duties involved him in the lives of the Amzalak family, and he was present at disputes and the signing of contracts since he had judicial jurisdiction over the Amzalaks, their relationship can be traced through the British Consular Archives and the Consular Diaries, making these sources important for the study of the Amzalak family.[185] [see Plate 22]

The Hurva Courtyard

The history of the Hurva Compound dates back to the beginning of the eighteenth century, when Rabbi Judah Hasid, together with a convoy of Ashkenazim, immigrated to Jerusalem. They began the construction of a synagogue on a tract known as Deir al-Shkenaz, but the sudden death of their

184 Abrahams (supra n. 98), pp. 40-41; Ben-Arieh (supra n. 102), p. 163; Mark Tennenbaum, "The British Consulate in Jerusalem, 1858-1890," *Cathedra*, 5 (October 1977), pp. 83-108 (Hebrew); James Finn, *Sepharadim or, the History of the Jews in Spain and Portugal*, London 1841, pp. 472-476.

185 YIBZA, James Finn Archives; Blumberg (supra n. 182); Ben Arieh (supra n. 102), p. 163; Abrahams (supra n. 98), pp. 40-41.

Plate 22: James and Elizabeth Anne Finn
(Source: Yad Yitzhak Ben Zvi Archives, Jerusalem)

leader led to the disintegration of the community and the accumulation of large debts. Financial assistance did not arrive, due to political reasons unconnected with Ashkenazi Jewry. On November 8, 1720, Muslim debt-holders broke into the synagogue, setting it ablaze, and expelled the Ashkenazi community from the city. The ruined synagogue then became known as Hurvat [the Ruin of] Rabbi Judah Hasid. For almost a century after this, there was no organized Ashkenazi community in Jerusalem. The activities of individual Ashkenazim in the city had to be of a clandestine nature, and they had no place of worship of their own. Only during the second decade of the nineteenth century did a small community of Prushim start to reestablish an Ashkenazi community in Jerusalem. During the period of the Egyptian occupation, a building permit for a synagogue was obtained from Muhammad Ali by Abraham Shlomo Zalman Zoref, one of the prominent Prushim. Menahem Zion Synagogue was built to the north of the Hurva Compound and was inaugurated in 1837. The communal treasury accumulated many debts over the years, resulting from a number of projects, including the construction of the Menahem Zion Synagogue. The

Plate 23: Old German (Ashkenazi) synagogue in the Old City, Jerusalem, 1850
(Source: Joseph Schwarz, *A Descriptive Geography and Brief Historical Sketch of Palestine*, Translated by Isaac Leeser, Philadelphia 1850, p. 277)

interest payments eroded away the incoming capital from Russia, leaving insufficient funds for the support of the community in Jerusalem. That same year, an earthquake shook the Galilee, destroying much of Safed and Tiberias and taking a high death toll in the Prushim community, which outlaid the necessary funds for the burial of the victims. The coffers of the community were further taxed in order to provide loans to the survivors of the earthquake and to establish them in Jerusalem.[186] [see Plate 23]

In 1839, Joseph Amzalak lent 3,000 gold *adumim*[187] (approximately £1,400) to the Prushim Kolel, which was burdened by financial difficulties. Previously

186 Morgenstern (supra n. 110), pp. 410-412; Parfitt (supra n. 108), pp. 22, 57-70; Arieh Morgenstern, "Messianic Concepts and Settlement in the Land of Israel," Richard I. Cohen (ed.), *Vision and Conflict in the Holy Land*, Jerusalem 1985, pp. 141-162.

187 The exchange rate of 1 gold *adum* = 48 grush (piaster) is based on information found in the text of the agreement; see: Grayevski (supra n. 130), pp. 3-5, document 1: letter from the leaders of the Prushim community, Jerusalem 3 Shvat 5590 (January 8, 1840), (Hebrew); document 2: letter from Joseph Amzalak, Jerusalem, 1 Adar 5590 (February 5, 1840), (Hebrew); The exchange rate of 1 English pound = 110 piaster for the year 1851 is based on Ben-Zion Gat, *The Jewish Settlement in Eretz Israel in the years 5600-5641 (1840-1881)*, Jerusalem 1973, pp. 53 (Hebrew).

the Prushim Kolel had taken various loans with interest of up to 30 percent, but Amzalak provided financing at 9 percent, well below the market rate. In order to circumvent the halakhic [rabbinic law] prohibition against loans with interest, the compound was transferred to Joseph Amzalak and repayment of the loan took the form of rent for the premises. The annual payment was 270 gold *adumim* (approximately £126).[188]

In June 1849, Rachel Amzalak began negotiations with the Prushim community in an attempt to reach an agreement regarding the repayment of the outstanding loan. It appears that the Amzalaks were under financial pressure then since the liquid capital they had at their disposal had dwindled measurably. They were willing to make concessions and forgo part of the interest in order to regain the principal of the loan.

Rachel Amzalak brought the affair before Sir Moses Montefiore on July 27, 1849, during his third visit to Jerusalem, in the presence of the British Consul Finn. The consul played an important role in these negotiations as the representative of the Amzalak family. In the archives of the consulate were documents relating to the original agreement, so that the consul was able to verify the authenticity of papers produced before him.[189] Two sets of documents were presented by the Amzalaks, and Consul Finn made the following ruling:

> After several days consideration of matter between the Amzalag [sic] and Ashkenaz [sic] Community — namely the instituting of a new Contract about the Khorbah [sic] property by invalidating the documents registered in the Consulate by means of a previously unheard of set of documents on the subject, not sealed by the Consulate — the consul said that he could only recognize those which had been registered & sealed by Mr. Consul Young — Consequently all the new transactions fell to the ground.[190]

On December 5, 1849 a new agreement was concluded and the subsequent documents were signed between the Amzalak family and the Prushim Community before the British consul. It stipulated a lowering of the interest rate to 6 percent, which brought the annual payment down to 180 *adumim* (approximately £84), and fulfilled the will of Joseph Amzalak, which allocated

---

188 Morgenstern (supra n. 110), pp. 408-412; Grayevski (supra n. 130), documents 1-2, pp. 3-5.

189 Grayevski (supra n. 130), pp.5-6, document 3: letter from James Finn, British consul, Jerusalem, 1 Sivan 5609, (June 8, 1849); Blumberg (supra n. 182), pp. 50-55, entries for July 27, 1849, July 28, 1849, October 29, 1849, October 30, 1849 and November 7, 1849.

190 Blumberg (supra n. 182), p. 55, entry for November 7, 1849.

1,200 *grush* (approximately £11) annually to the Talmud Torah. This modified agreement was contingent on the approval of the leaders of the Prushim community in Vilna.[191] On December 13, 1850, Rabbi David Berliner and Rabbi Arieh Ne'eman, representatives of the Prushim in Jerusalem, came to Consul Finn to give notice of the affirmative answer that had been received from their leaders in Vilna.[192]

An additional agreement was concluded on January 5, 1851 between the Amzalaks and the Prushim, stating that if the annual payment were not remitted the contract would revert to the conditions agreed upon in 1839.[193]

During the following years the Prushim community paid the Amzalaks 180 *adumim* (approximately £84) and the Amzalaks contributed 1,200 *grush* (approximately £11) to the Talmud Torah of the Prushim. In 1864, with the completion of the Beit Ya'akov Synagogue in the Hurva Compound, the principle of 3,000 *adumim* (approximately £1,400) was returned to the Amzalak family. Consequently, the lease of the compound was returned to the Prushim community, and thus the connection of the Amzalak family with the Hurva Compound drew to an end.[194]

---

191 Grayevski (supra n. 130), pp. 6-12, document 4: agreement between the leaders of the Prushim community in Jerusalem on the one hand and Rachel Amzalak, Haim Amzalak, Solomon Amzalak and Raphael Amzalak on the other hand, Jerusalem, 8 Heshvan 5610 (November 4, 1849), (Hebrew); Blumberg (supra n. 182), p. 56, entry for December 5, 1849; Morgenstern (supra n. 110), pp. 410-412.

192 Grayevski (supra n. 130), pp. 13-14, document 5: letter from Rachel Amzalak, Haim Amzalak, Solomon Amzalak and Raphael Amzalak, Jerusalem, 14 Heshvan 5610 (November 10, 1849), (Hebrew); Blumberg (supra n. 182), p. 78, entry for December 13, 1850.

193 Grayevski (supra n. 130), pp. 15-17, document 6: letter from Rachel Amzalak, Haim Amzalak, Solomon Amzalak and Raphael Amzalak, Jerusalem, January 5, 1851; document 7: letter from Rachel Amzalak, Haim Amzalak, Solomon Amzalak and Raphael Amzalak, Jerusalem, 1 Shvat 5611 (January 2, 1851), (Hebrew); document 8: letter from Benjamin Mordechai Navon, Jerusalem, 3 Shvat 5611 (January 4, 1851), (Hebrew); Blumberg (supra n. 173), p. 85, entry for January 6, 1851.

194 Grayevski (supra n. 130), pp. 18-23, document 9: receipts of payments for the years 5611 (1850-1851), 5622 (1861-1862), 5623 (1862-1863), and 5624 (1863-1864) from Rachel Amzalak, Haim Amzalak, Solomon Amzalak and Raphael Amzalak, Jerusalem, to the Prushim community (Hebrew); document 10: letter from Rachel Amzalak, Haim Amzalak, Solomon Amzalak and Raphael Amzalak, Jerusalem, October 25, 1864; document 11: letter from Meir Moshe Elimelech, Jerusalem, 1 Av 5624 (August 3, 1864) (Hebrew); Blumberg (supra n. 182), p. 113, entry for November 26, 1852; *HaMagid*, vol. 8, no. 42, 3 Heshvan 5625 (November 2, 1864), p. 331; Morgenstern (supra n. 110), p. 418.

The Amzalak House

Another part of the inheritance left to Rachel Amzalak and her sons was the large house of Joseph Amzalak. The house was rented out on different occasions, providing an income for the family. Two accounts, those of Titus Tobler and G. Williams, inform us that in the late 1840s and early 1850s the house was occupied by the Protestant bishop of Jerusalem, Samuel Gobat. Tobler wrote that the house of the Protestant bishop was not near the church, but instead on David Street near Hezekiah's Pool, and that two *kavasses* (armed constables) would escort him to the church.[195] Williams noted that the bishop's house had been built for a wealthy Jew, Amzalak. He continued by saying that it was a comfortable house, but that the surroundings were noisy. The house was across from the former Crusader wheat market, which during the nineteenth century had been transformed into a vegetable market filled with the screaming and haggling of women and vegetable vendors.[196]

In October 1853, Haim Amzalak, representing the interests of his mother and brothers, came before Consul Finn with the lessee, Simeon Rosenthal — a converted Jew who served in the British consulate — to discuss the conditions of the rental agreement. In May of the following year the agreement was worked out and the house was rented for 3,550 piaster (approximately £32) for one year.[197]

In 1857 the house was rented to Samuel Gobat. The Amzalaks gave the bishop notice in June of that year that they would be requiring their house in about two months, when the lease should expire.[198]

During the 1870s and 1880s, the Amzalak house continued to be rented out; the street level was used for shops, while the upper floors were converted into the Mediterranean Hotel in around 1870. J.A. Bost, in his book *Souvenirs d'Orient*, wrote that the hotel was owned by the Hornsteins and located near Jaffa Gate and the Church of the Holy Sepulchre. In fact, the Hornsteins only rented it from the Amzalaks. The Baedeker and Murray travel guides to Syria and Palestine both mention the hotel; the latter informed travelers that the hotel, belonging to the Hornsteins, had good rooms on the upper floor, but that the lower ones were moldy and poorly aired. The manager of the hotel, Moses Hornstein, a Jew from Odessa who had converted to Christianity, was an

195 Titus Tobler, *Topographie von Jerusalem*, 1, Berlin 1853-1854, p. 380.
196 G. Williams, *The Holy City...*, 1, London 1849, appendix, p. 20.
197 Blumberg (supra n. 182), pp. 139, 142, 164, 170, entries for October 5, 1853, October 27, 1853, May 15, 1854, and August 24, 1854.
198 Blumberg (supra n. 182), p. 259, entry for June 17, 1857.

influential figure in Jerusalem. He served as translator for the German consulate and later as a representative of the Thomas Cook Travel Company until his death in 1885.[199]

The rental income from the hotel was paid to Rachel, Haim and the widows of Raphael and Solomon. The family also received a rental income from the shop below the hotel. In 1885 the shop was rented to Joseph Hayat. The widow of Raphael sold her share of the shop to her nephew, Joseph Navon, for two hundred and ten napoleons (approximately £168), in order to pay off debts incurred, provide for her large family and deal with whatever needs might arise.[200]

In 1895 a dispute with regard to the rental of the house was brought before the British consul. Haim Amzalak brought to his attention an injustice committed against his brothers' widows. Their only remaining income then came from the rent of the hotel, an annual sum of 40 to 45 napoleons (approximately £32 to £36) each. Solomon's son David had let a room in the building for 11 napoleons (approximately £10) without permission. Haim requested that the consul put this matter right and return the amount to the widows.[201]

Today the impressive three-storey building stands inside Jaffa Gate at the beginning of David Street, and has been renamed the Petra Hotel. As in the past, the street level of the building is used for stores and the two upper floors as a hotel. [see Plate 24]

Business Activities

The second generation of the Amzalaks entered the second phase of entrepreneurial activity — the reinvestment of amassed capital, in their case in land. After the Crimean War of 1853-1856, the Ottoman government introduced the *Khatt-i Humayun* (The Imperial Rescript), introducing reforms

199 Ben-Arieh (supra n. 30), pp. 385-388; J.A. Bost, *Souvenirs d'Orient*, Paris 1875, p. 327; Karl Baedeker, *Palestine and Syria; Handbook for Travellers*, Leipzig-London 1876, p. 114; John Murray, *Handbook for Travellers in Syria and Palestine*, London 1875, p. 117.

200 ISA, 123-1 J22/9 787, letter from Haim Aaron Valero, Jerusalem, to Count Bernhard Graf Caboga-Cerva, Austrian consul, Jerusalem, February 2, 1880 (French); letter from Bolissa Amzalak, Jerusalem, to Noel Temple Moore, British consul, Jerusalem, February 29, 1880 (French); letter from Angeline Amzalak, J. Amzalak, Reine Amzalak and Bachéva Amzalak, Nablus, to Noel Temple Moore, British counsul, Jerusalem, November 7, 1885 (French).

201 ISA, 123-1 J22/9 787, letter from Haim Amzalak, British vice-consul, Jaffa, to John Dickson, British consul, Jerusalem, June 18, 1895.

Plate 24: The Amzalak House, inside Jaffa Gate, 1990
(Source: Courtesy of Rehav Rubin, 1990)

designed to gain the sympathy of its allies. It granted equal rights to non-Muslims, the protection of their persons and property, freedom of worship, and the right to an education for children of all religions. This legislation also granted, at least theoretically, permission for foreigners to acquire land, which until then had been forbidden without a special firman, issued only rarely by the Sultan. Only in 1867 was an additional law passed permitting foreign citizens of countries that signed a protocol with the Porte to acquire urban and rural lands. The agreement with Great Britain was signed in 1869.[202]

Under these conditions the Amzalaks, individually and together, purchased tracts of land in Palestine. Before the passing of the Ottoman land laws they had circumvented the restrictions on land purchase by foreigners by registering lands under the name of an Ottoman subject. A separate contract between the actual owner and the person whose name appeared on the registration protected the rights of the owner. In 1873 Solomon and Haim Amzalak wrote to their consul that because of the former laws prohibiting foreign citizens from purchasing land, they had been involved in a deal for the purchase of land outside of Jerusalem which was registered in the name of Yitzhak Zion, an Ottoman subject. At the time of the transaction they had concluded a contract with Yitzhak Zion which stated that the land belonged to the Amzalaks and that

202 Kark (supra n. 26), pp. 357-359.

Plate 25: Certificate of Registration for Solomon Amzalak, April 14, 1875
(Source: Central Zionist Archives, A152/9/1 Joseph Navon Bey Archives)

he had only served as their representative. They requested of the consul that he ask the *mutasarrif* of Jerusalem to permit them to transfer the registration of the land purchase from Yitzhak Zion's name to their respective names upon presentation of the contract.[203]

In 1869 Solomon and his brothers Haim and Raphael, of English citizenship, wished to purchase a store located underneath Solomon's residence in Jerusalem from Haj Yusef Effendi Al Khaldi and Badar Effendi Al Khaldi. They requested that the British consul write a letter urging the *mutasarrif* to take the appropriate steps following an announcement of the parties' willingness to sell.[204] [see Plate 25]

In 1872 Solomon Amzalak, representing Haim and Raphael, wrote to the British consul that they had concluded a deal with Sa'id Abu Al Harak and

203 ISA, 123-1 J22/9 787, letter from Solomon Amzalak and Haim Amzalak, Jerusalem, to Noel Temple Moore, British consul, Jerusalem, 1873 (Arabic).
204 ISA, 123-1 J22/9 787, letter from Solomon Amzalak, Jerusalem, to Noel Temple Moore, British consul, Jerusalem, 1869 (Arabic).

Kwagar Hanah Kadour for the purchase of a warehouse and adjacent land beneath the Amzalak's Jerusalem house. They requested that the consul take the proper steps for the transaction to proceed via the *mutasarrif*, according to law.[205]

Their purchases were not confined to urban tracts, but also extended to agricultural lands. Solomon wanted to buy a tract with vines and olive trees in the village of 'Ajul, in the Beni Zuber subdistrict west of Jerusalem. He applied to the British consul in 1869 to forward this request to the *mutasarrif*.[206]

Another land purchase is recounted in the British consulate documents of 1873. Rabbi 'Azaria Boton had received from Haim Amzalak, then residing in Jaffa, power of attorney allowing him to deal with a particular tract land outside Damascus Gate, bordering the lands and residence of Bugoff Effendi Zakar and those of the consul of Austria. It had been sold to the orphans of Suleiman Taji for 458 napoleons (approximately £366) in the form of three promissory notes to be paid over a period of seven years. The agreed payments were not made, so at the request of Haim Amzalak steps were initiated to sell it.[207]

The Amzalaks were also involved in the renting of land, some of which belonged to the *wakf* (religious endowment), and the granting of loans. The British consular diary of 1854 mentions that Sheik Hassan en Nezek, acting for Sheik Ebda'ir, appeared before the consul to open a case against the Amzalaks about a house. He produced a lease of the house issued by the former *mutawalli* (administrator, usually of the *wakf*), the term of which had by then expired. One of the Amzalaks produced a later lease given by the *mutawalli* then in office and valid for another year, in which the rent was raised from 500 to 600 piasters (approximately £45 to £55). The consul ruled that the former paper was no longer valid, and that only the second deed could be considered.[208]

The experience that Haim Amzalak had amassed in these land transactions would prove beneficial during his later years in Jaffa. He would serve as an agent for the new Jewish agricultural settlements in the environs of Jaffa as well as continuing his own land investments in the area.

205 ISA, 123-1 J22/9 787, letter from Solomon Amzalak representing Raphael Amzalak and Haim Amzalak, Jerusalem, to Noel Temple Moore, British consul, Jerusalem, 1872 (Arabic).
206 ISA, 123-1 J22/9 787, letter from Solomon Amzalak, Jerusalem, to Noel Temple Moore, British consul, Jerusalem, April 6, 1869 (Arabic).
207 ISA, 123-1 J22/9 787, letter from 'Azaria Boton, Jerusalem, to Noel Temple Moore, British consul, Jerusalem, January 6, 1874 (Arabic).
208 Blumberg (supra n. 182), p. 172, entry for October 27, 1853.

Activities in the Community

The Amzalak family continued to play a significant role in the Jewish community of Jerusalem and the city as a whole. One member of the family, either Solomon or Raphael, was a representative on the municipal council, the *Mejlis-i Belediya*. The Jerusalem municipality was one of the first local governments to be established in the Ottoman Empire. While there is confusion as to the year of its official establishment, it is certain that the Jerusalem municipality began to function in the 1860s. Before the promulgation of the 1875 law governing elections to the municipal councils, council members were apparently appointed by the governor together with the heads or leading members of the communities. The appointment of one of the Amzalaks to the Jerusalem council was announced in the newspapers *Hamagid* and the *Jewish Chronicle*, and was a source of joy and pride for the Jewish community in Jerusalem and abroad. The following is an excerpt from a *Jewish Chronicle* article dated September 4, 1868:

> ...a board of magistrates has lately been composed without regard to creed or nationality, and that in consequence of these liberal proceedings, two Jewish gentlemen by the names of [Haim Aaron] Valero and Amselig [sic], have been elected to represent their coreligionists....[209]

Amzalak served as a representative for both the Jewish population and citizens of foreign nations residing in the city. Preceding Amzalak's appointment, the foreign consuls had feared that the proposed municipal council would infringe on their authority. The British consul had requested that foreign residents be represented on it to protect their interests. Amzalak — Solomon or Raphael — may have received his position on the council as a result of British pressure. His role as representative entailed involvement in the administration of the city, cleanliness, urban planning and the improvement of living conditions.[210]

Solomon Amzalak was among the leaders and supporters of the Jewish community of Palestine. Like his father Joseph, he was a patron of a synagogue. A list of Sephardi institutions for the year 5622 (1862–1863) includes a synagogue in the house of Solomon Amzalak.[211] In 1869 he was chosen as a

209 *HaMagid*, vol. 12, no. 29, July 22, 1868, p. 228; *The Jewish Chronicle and the Hebrew Observer*, 10, September 4, 1868 (17 Elul 5628) p. 8.

210 For further detail on the Jerusalem Municipality see: Ruth Kark, "The Jerusalem Municipality at the end of Ottoman Rule," *Asian and African Studies*, vol.14, no.2 (July 1980), pp. 117-141.

211 Gaon (supra n. 39), I, p. 131.

member of the Sephardi Community Council. During the early 1870s his signature appeared with those of other leaders of the Sephardi community on requests for financial support and donations from Diaspora communities, which were published in newspapers such as *Hamagid* and *Habazeleth*. His activities as a representative of the Jewish community also took him on fundraising missions to Constantinople in 1870 and Marseilles in 1872.[212]

In 1871, a branch of the Alliance Israélite Universelle aimed the promotion of Jewish settlement in Palestine was established in Jerusalem, with Solomon Amzalak serving as board member. Earlier that year, Rabbi Yehuda Alkalai had arrived in Palestine in order to solicit the support of the leaders of the Sephardi, Ashkenazi and Maghrabi (Moroccan) communities in Jerusalem for the establishment of this local branch. Chief Rabbi Avraham Ashkenazi (1869-1880) assembled the council of the Sephardi community, which expressed its willingness to support such a society if reciprocal support could be attained from the Ashkenazi community. However, Rabbi Meir Aurbach, the leader of the Ashkenazi community, feared that the founding of this society would reduce his community's share of the *halukkah*. He therefore remained noncommittal, stating that the power to make any decision lay solely in the hands of the chief rabbi. In the end, prominent members of the different Jewish communities went ahead and decided to establish such a society. Rabbi Meir Panagel served as its president, with Rabbi David ben Shimon, the head of the Maghrabi community, as his deputy. The committee consisted of five members: Rabbi Nissim Baruch, Rabbi Shalom Moshe Hai Ganim, Rabbi Moshe Peretz, Solomon Amzalak and Rahamim Yosef Franco. Later Rabbi Fischel Lapin,

---

212 *HaMagid*, vol. 14, no. 7, 15 Adar I 5630 (February 15, 1870), p. 5 (Hebrew); *Habazeleth*, vol. 2, no. 31, 23 Iyar 5632, (May 31, 1872) p. 244 (Hebrew); CZA, Joseph Navon Bey Archives, A152/9/1 laissez passer issued to Solomon Amzalak by Noel Temple Moore, British Consul, Jerusalem, August 1, 1870; For an example of a request to Diaspora communities for the support of Sephardim in Palestine which includes Solomon's signature see: Gaon (supra n. 39), 1, pp. 252-255; An additonal reference to Solomon Amzalak has been found in Mordechai Eliav, "Journey to Jerusalem in the Year 5645 (1884-1885)," *Sinai*, 67 (Spring 1970), p. 164 (Hebrew), which reproduces the journal of the visit of Abraham Greenbaum, with footnotes. On January 1, 1885 Greenbaum went with Ya'akov Shaul Eliachar, Eliyahu Navon, Joseph Navon and Zamalik (זאמאליק) to see the pasha of Jerusalem. Eliav assumed that this was Solomon Amzalak, but this is impossible since he had died nine years earlier, in 1876. The possible identities of this member of the Amzalak family are numerous, he could have been one of Solomon's or Raphael's sons or even Haim Amzalak or his son Joseph, who had been in Jerusalem two months earlier and may have stayed on longer as mentioned in *Habazeleth*, vol. 15, no. 4, 19 Heshvan 5645 (November 7, 1884), p. 28 (Hebrew).

from the Ashkenazi community, joined the committee.[213] The following was the society's official creed:

> The Holy land during all times has been a fertile land. It is a land of milk and honey. And its springs filled with bounty, have not been depleted nor destroyed, and the exalted hills and the plateaus will not forever be covered in thorns and thistles. And today what is wanted is only to open these springs and to clear the stones that hurt it and to be worked by the industrious, this land that since the past was well-blessed. The Alliance Israélite Universelle society has placed before itself the task and has completed it, to found a school for the learning of agricultural labour in the holy city of Jaffa, near the holy city of Jerusalem.[214]

The Widow Rachel Amzalak

After her husband's death, Rachel was provided for through the incomes derived from different properties left to her. She took an active part in the various negotiations over the debts owed to her and her family by the Prushim community. James Finn, in his personal diary, mentions visiting the *Hacham Bashi* (chief rabbi) in his *Bet Din* (rabbinic court of law) on July 28, 1846, so as to solicit his assistance in favor of a rabbi from Safed who was negotiating with the Amzalak family. Joseph Amzalak, before his death, had contracted the rabbi to study the Talmud on his behalf, but this agreement was not legally binding due to want of certain formalities. Finn hoped that the Amzalaks would take pity on the rabbi and honor the contract notwithstanding the fact that it

---

213 Yosef Shapiro, *A Century of Mikveh-Israel (1870-1970)*, Tel Aviv 1970, pp. 89-94 (Hebrew); *HaMagid*, vol. 15, no. 41, 10 Heshvan 5632 (October 25, 1871), p. 32 (Hebrew); *HaMagid*, vol. 15, no. 32, 29 Av 5631 (August 16, 1871), p. 312 (Hebrew). Rabbi Meir Panagel, who was a member of the *Bet Din HaGadol* (Supreme Religious Court) in Jerusalem. He became the chief rabbi in 1880, serving until his death in 1893. Rabbi David ben Shimon immigrated from Jerusalem from Morocco in 1855. He became the leader of the Mughrabi [North African] Jewish community in Jerusalem until his death in 1881. Rabbi Nissim Baruch was the president of Sephardi *Bet Din* (Religious Court). Rabbi Shalom Moshe Hai Ganim was a rabbi at the Beit-El Yeshiva in Jerusalem. Rabbi Rahamim Yosef Franco served as an emissary of the Jerusalem Jewish community during the 1870s. From 1879 until his death in 1900, he was a rabbi in Hebron. Rabbi Fischel Lappin was a wealthy Jew who immigrated to Jerusalem in 1863. He was involved in various philanthropic projects in Palestine.

214 Part of the proclamation of the Alliance Israélite Universelle in Palestine from 1869 as quoted in Gaon (supra n. 39), 1, pp. 101-102.

was not incumbent on them. However, Finn doubted that this request would have any effect:

> After varied conversations the family were sent for, and as I had been taught to expect, the widow's [Rachel] tongue and haughty manners bespoke a self will which defied the Chief Rabbi, [Abraham Haim Gagin] and at the end of her defence she cursed the Rabbi who held the document and had applied for its fulfilment.[215]

Despite her harsh behavior in this incident, Rachel usually maintained an amicable and respectful relationship with foreign visitors. During the summer of 1855, the Montefiores visited Jerusalem for their fourth time. On that occasion they were accompanied by Mr. and Mrs. Haim Guedalla, and the wife kept a diary of their tour. Mrs. Guedalla mentioned a number of meetings with the Amzalaks. Upon the party's entry to Jerusalem, "Mrs. [Rachel] Amzalag [sic] came out on horseback to meet Sir M[ontefiore] and Lady." A few days later, on July 25, 1855, Mrs. Guedalla was called on by "Madame Amzalag and her family." Again on August 5, 1855, "the Mesdames Amzalag came to see" her and Lady Montefiore.[216] Unfortunately the diary does not detail the conversations that ensued.

Another facet of the widow's personality can be understood from the best-documented incident involving Rachel Amzalak. In 1858 she had borrowed a pair of matching gold chain bracelets and mislaid one of them. Rachel Amzalak was quick to wrongly accuse a servant woman of stealing it. Charges were pressed against this woman, although no definitive proof existed. The editor of the James and Elizabeth Finn consular diaries, Arnold Blumberg, made note that "a disproportionately great amount of space in the diary for 1858 is devoted to a discussion of the value of the missing bracelet. Fortunately, the entire tempest in a teacup ended peacefully when the lost bracelet was found."[217] One interesting aspect of the episode is the very fact that Rachel had borrowed the bracelets, which may point to the deteriorating financial state of the family.

---

215 YIBZA, James Finn Archives, Diary 7, entry for July 28, 1846. This behavior towards Chief Rabbi Abraham Haim Gagin on the part of Rachel Amzalak does not appear abnormal since there existed a longstanding dispute between Gagin and the followers of his predecessor, Rabbi Yehuda Raphael Navon, related by marriage to the Amzalaks; see: Elmaleh (supra n. 166), pp. 182-203.

216 Mrs. H. Guedalla, *Diary of a Tour to Jerusalem and Alexandria in 1855 with Sir Moses and Lady Montefiore*, London 1890, pp. 44, 46, 52.

217 Blumberg (supra n. 182), pp. 282-283, 290, 305, entries for February 9, 1858, February 11, 1858, February 12, 1858, and June 7, 1858.

After renting out the large Amzalak house in the 1850s, the matriarch of the Amzalak family evidently resided in one of her children's homes. Documented in the census of 1875 is that Rachel lived with her daughter-in-law Angeline in the Valero courtyard, as she had probably done before when her son Raphael was alive. But that same year, with the aid of Sir Moses Montefiore, Angeline moved to Mishkenot Sha'ananim, the first Jewish neighborhood built outside the old city walls in 1855-1860. No information has been found as to whether Rachel moved with her daughter-in-law, remained in the Valero courtyard, or moved to some other place.[218]

In Rachel's later years, other Amzalak family members decided to take direct responsibility for her needs. In 1878 an agreement was made to provide for her livelihood. According to the terms of the agreement, she was obliged to transfer the titles of the Amzalak house and other buildings registered in her name to her son Haim, and to the estates of Solomon and Raphael Amzalak's inheritors, in three equal shares. In return, Haim and the respective trustees of the two estates, Haim Aaron Valero and Eliyahu Navon, undertook to give Rachel 100 piasters (approximately £0.9) a week out of the income of the buildings, plus the rent for her lodging and what she needed for coal, oil and wheat. Rachel agreed to this arrangement on the condition that the widows and the female orphans were to have enough for food until the latter married.[219]

It is known that Rachel Amzalak suffered a serious injury in the autumn of 1875. A cedar tree fell upon her and a doctor was immediately summoned. To the chagrin of the family no Jewish doctor was willing to administer treatment; though missionary doctors readily offered their assistance, it was refused. In spite of the lack of medical attention she survived this blow, living for at least three more years.[220] The latest document with any reference to Rachel Amzalak alive is from August 13, 1878, but no record of the date of her death has been found.

Esther Amzalak-Navon

Esther, the only daughter of Joseph, was betrothed to Eliyahu Navon at a young age. This was a union of two prominent Sephardi families in Jerusalem. The Navons, a family of rabbis, scholars and businessmen originating in Turkey, had strong roots in the city.

---

218 JMA, Montefiore Census of 1875 (photocopy) p. 25.
219 ISA, 123-1 J22/9 787, letter of agreement between Haim Amzalak, Eliyahu Navon and Haim Aaron Valero, Jerusalem, 1 Ab 5638 (August 13, 1878) (Hebrew).
220 *Habazeleth*, vol. 7, nos. 2-3, 2 Heshvan 5636 (October 20, 1875) p. 24 (Hebrew).

Eliyahu's father, Rabbi Yehuda Navon, was an administrator and supervisor of the affairs of the Sephardi Kolel. He was the author of *Degel Menachem Ephraim*, which was never published. In the beginning of 1841 he was appointed to the position of Chief Rabbi of the Sephardi Jewish community in Jerusalem. Yehuda was unhappy in this position, having to contend with opposition to his appointment and with the numerous controversies connected to it. He served in this capacity for less than a year, when he was replaced by Rabbi Abraham Haim Gagin, his rival . He died in Jerusalem on December 4, 1845 (23 Kislev 5605).[221]

Eliyahu Navon Effendi, born in 1821, was a businessman whose transactions and dealings took him from Jerusalem to various centers in the Levant, including Constantinople, Saloniki and Adrianople. He served as one of the Jewish representatives of the *Majlis al Idara*, the administrative council of the Jerusalem district. This council had its origins in the period of Egyptian rule (1831-1841). It originally functioned as an advisory body for the local population on taxes and commerce, and it also attempted to improve the judicial position of non-Muslims. The Ottoman Council in Jerusalem, which underwent a general reorganization in 1849, had fourteen members, including four to five non-Muslims. The members of this council used their appointments as a means of enhancing their position and influence. Eliyahu, in this manner, established social and business connections with the leaders of the Muslim community. The wedding of his daughter Joya to Haim Kalmi was attended by numerous guests from the Muslim community: the *Kadi* and many government officials, including Ra'uf Pasha, the governor of Jerusalem.[222] [see Plate 26]

Eliyahu was involved in various activities on behalf of the Jewish community. Like his father, he served as the administrator of the Sephardi Kolel which he represented, and together with the Ashkenazi community he purchased the tomb of Simeon the Righteous and its surroundings, to the north of the city walls of Jerusalem. Eliyahu represented the Magen David Yeshiva, at which he had studied, and managed the contributions from the Portuguese community in Amsterdam. He was also involved in the distribution of *halukkah* funds to Yeshivat Hessed LeAvraham VeBinyan Shlomo in Jerusalem. Eliyahu and his son Joseph were among the founding members of 'Ezrat Nidahim, a society for

221 Glass (supra n. 24), pp. 23-24; Elmaleh (supra n. 166), pp. 179-181.
222 Glass (supra n. 24), pp. 24-25; *HaMagid LeYisrael*, 19, 2 Sivan 5656 (May 14, 1896), pp. 155-156 (Hebrew); *HaMagid LeYisrael*, nos. 20-21, 15 Sivan 5656 (May 27, 1896), pp. 169-170 (Hebrew); *Habazeleth*, 17, 21 Shvat 5645 (February 6, 1885), pp. 130-131 (Hebrew); Elie Eliachar, *Living with Jews*, Jerusalem 1980, pp. 655-657 (Hebrew); Maoz (supra n. 52), pp. 87-101.

Plate 26: Eliyahu Navon, Esther
Amzalak's husband
(Source: Elie Eliachar, *Living with
Jews*, Jerusalem 1983, between
pp. 608–609)

the aid of the poor Yemenite immigrants to Jerusalem, established in 1883. He
served on the managing committee of this society as one of its seven Sephardi
members.[223]

As an important figure in the Jewish community and a member of the *Majlis
al Idara*, Eliyahu received distinguished visitors to Jerusalem. He greeted Baron
Ferdinand de Rothschild of London and the Crown Prince Rudolph of the
Austro-Hungarian Empire on their respective visits in 1880 and 1881.[224]

Although much is known about Eliyahu's life, Esther's life is poorly
documented, as was the case with most women in traditional Jewish society in
nineteenth-century Jerusalem. Esther's primary role in life was as wife and
mother. She was supported by her husband, but also received a modest pension
of 210 piasters (approximately £19) per annum from her father's estate. In 1878,

223 Glass (supra n. 24), p. 25; *Habazeleth*, 16, 14 Shvat 5645 (January 30, 1885), pp. 122-123
(Hebrew); *Habazeleth*, 2-3, 7 Heshvan 5647 (November 6, 1886), p. 9 (Hebrew);
HaMagid, 3, 19 Tevet 5644 (January 17, 1883), pp. 20-21 (Hebrew).
224 Glass (supra n. 24), pp. 25-26; *Habazeleth*, 23, 29 Adar 5640 (March 12, 1880), p. 165
(Hebrew); *Habazeleth*, 22, 29 Adar II 5641 (March 30, 1881), pp. 161-162 (Hebrew).

an arrangement was formalized between her and the rest of the Amzalak family. Haim Amzalak and the two trustees of the estates of the late Raphael and Solomon Amzalak — Eliyahu Navon and Haim Aaron Valero — agreed to pay her 12,000 piastres (approximately £109) so as to free themselves from their commitment towards her.[225]

Only one incident involving Esther is known. James and Elizabeth Anne Finn mention in the British consular diary entry of October 28, 1853 that the sister of the Amzalaks, Esther, complained of being robbed in the street by a *bashi bazouk* (mercenary of the Turkish irregulars), and that the man was soon arrested. But in the street a fellow mercenary fell upon the *kavass* named Hussain who was escorting the arrested mercenary and beat Hussain. Another *kavass* was sent to the *aga* (commanding officer) to complain, and the two *bashi bazouks* were brought before the *aga*, who took down his *nabbut* (quarterstaff) and broke it across the back of one of them. The other ran away but was pursued to the village of Silwan on the outskirts of Jerusalem, brought back and then very severely beaten. The Amzalaks begged for mercy on the delinquents, but were sent away as the case was then between the delinquents and the consul. The original malefactor was again beaten and imprisoned. Consul Finn, on learning this, sent a representative, his *dragoman* (interpreter) to have the troops drawn out in line and harangued by the *aga*.[226]

Esther and Eliyahu had six children: two sons, Yehuda and Joseph, and four daughters, Rebecca, Zimbul, Sarah and Joya, with Zimbul dying in childhood. Their eldest son Yehuda died in the winter of 1886 at the age of thirty-six, after succumbing to pneumonia, one of the many illnesses which plagued the population of Jerusalem that winter. Yehuda's passing was deeply felt; his bereaved father entered a long period of depression which continued until his own death.[227]

The couple raised their family in the Navon family courtyard located on the eastern side of the Jewish Quarter. This courtyard was named after Rabbi Mushan (Moses) Navon, Eliyahu's nephew. [see Plate 27] Ya'akov Eli'ezer, in his work *Courtyards of Jerusalem*, described the place as follows:

> To the courtyard one entered from the north. The gateway of the house was exceptionally built with an ornamented lintel with various openings.

225 ISA, 123-1 J22/9 787, letter from Haim Amzalak, Jaffa, to John Dickson, British consul, Jerusalem, June 18, 1895 (French).
226 Blumberg (supra n. 182), p. 142, entry for October 28, 1853.
227 JMA, Montefiore Census of 1855 (photocopy) p. 1; Eliachar (supra n. 222), p. 690; *Habazeleth*, 17, 6 Kislev 5647, (November 11, 1886) p. 37 (Hebrew).

Plate 27: A view of the Jewish Quarter form the east, Jerusalem, circa 1910
(Source: Jerusalem Municipal Archives, Jerusalem, 15363)

Beside its two door posts were built-in benches, the height of a chair, and above them were arches, the width of the benches. These were built with concave and protruding stones which gave the entrance a special eastern beauty. A small corridor continued from the doorway to the large courtyard paved with large coloured flagstones surrounded by a number of rooms. To the right of the corridor stairs led to the second floor and further to the balcony. Part of the courtyard was three-storeyed. It is possible to say that the courtyard was pretty and well-kept. It was among the more beautiful courtyards of the city.[228]

During the later years of Esther's life she lived with her son Joseph. As recounted by Elie Eliachar, Esther's great-grandson, Esther frequently squabbled with her daughters-in-law, Bolissa (Gisa) née Frumkin, the wife of Joseph. The house, which remains until today on Jaffa Road, was one of the

228 Ya'akov Eli'ezer, *Courtyards in Jerusalem*, n.p., n.d., pp. 84-85 (Hebrew).

most impressive homes in late nineteenth-century Jerusalem. It was described in the following manner:

> The atmosphere of the house and garden was enveloped in glamour. It was a two-storey house with a basement, an area for the storage of possessions. On the first floor lived Navon's mother, Esther Amzalak, and in the second wing, on the second floor, lived Navon, his wife and daughters. The house was built in a Middle Eastern architectural style in accordance with the tastes of the artist-engineer Conrad Schick. Its walls were more than a meter thick, the floors from red marble....[229]

The relationship between Esther and Bolissa was strained by the fact that Esther owned the remaining one-fifth of her son's home, where Bolissa was forced to reside after her husband's bankruptcy and self-imposed exile in Paris and London.

Eliyahu died on April 28, 1896 (15 Iyar 5656) after many years of depression over his eldest son's untimely passing. Eliyahu's death was mourned by the Jewish community of Jerusalem with the chief rabbi and notables of all communities in attendance. The funeral procession to Eliyahu's grave on the Mount of Olives was headed by children of Jerusalem's *Talmud Torahs* and students from the *Dorshei Zion Yeshiva*. However, no information has been found as to when Esther died.[230]

The Widows of Raphael and Solomon Amzalak

Angeline, Raphael's Widow

On June 1, 1874 (27 Shvat 5634) Raphael Amzalak died, leaving behind his wife Angeline (Yael) and five children. The young widowed Angeline lived off an income that had been provided for her in her husband's estate. Her brother-in-law Eliyahu Navon served as a trustee of the estate, part of which consisted of Raphael's portion of the family house. The income, as previously mentioned, was 40 to 45 napoleons (approximately £32 to £36) per annum in 1895. As this was insufficient for the maintenance of the widow and her daughters, G[?], Reine, and Bachéva, they sold part of their one third of the shop below the

---

229 Eliachar (supra n. 222), pp. 686-687, 689-690.
230 *HaMagid LeYisrael*, 5, 2 Sivan 5656 (May 24, 1895) pp. 155-156 (Hebrew).

Mediterranean Hotel in 1885 to Joseph Navon. The purpose was to pay off debts, care for the large family and prepare for any eventualities.[231]

According to the Montefiore census of 1875, the widow of Raphael Amzalak resided in the Valero courtyard. Her household was listed as numbering eight persons, but only seven were enumerated: the widow, two orphaned sons, two orphaned daughters, the widow's mother-in-law and a servant.[232]

Angeline Amzalak's predicament became so grave that in 1875 Moses Montefiore, while on his seventh visit to Jerusalem, gave her a house on his estate in Mishkenot Sha'ananim. It was house number 8, the one nearest the windmill. The houses of this philanthropic neighborhood were constructed with the money bequeathed by Judah Touro of New Orleans for the betterment of the poor of Jerusalem, the land having been bought with Touro's money by Sir Moses Montefiore in 1855. The original neighborhood had twenty-six apartments in one row, including two synagogues. In 1869 four apartments were added to the neighborhood, and it was in one of these that Angeline resided. This arrangement was made through the British consul of Jerusalem, and Montefiore wrote: "I shall feel obliged if Consul Moore would put Mrs. Amzalak in possession of the premises of which she is to remain in occupation during my pleasure and subject to her conforming to all the rules and regulations by which the houses are governed." No information has been found as to the duration of Angeline's residence in this neighborhood although evidence exists that she was still residing there in 1879.[233] [see Plate 28]

In 1887, Angeline Amzalak purchased a house in the new commercial neighborhood of Mahane Yehuda off of Jaffa Road. This neighborhood, which was to provide for the housing needs of medium-sized families with monetary means, was founded by her nephew, Joseph Navon, along with Shalom Konstrom and the Swiss-German banker Johannes Frutiger. Her house consisted of two two-room units situated side by side. The terms of payment

231 ISA, 123-1 J22/9 787, letter from Angeline Amzalak, J. Amzalak, Reine Amzalak and Bachéva Amzalak, Nablus, to Noel Temple Moore, British consul, Jerusalem, November 7, 1885 (French); letter from Haim Amzalak, Jaffa, to John Dickson, British consul, Jerusalem, June 18, 1895.

232 JMA, Montefiore Census of 1875 (photocopy) p. 25.

233 ISA, 123-1 J22/9 787, letter from Sir Moses Montefiore, Jerusalem, to Noel Temple Moore, British consul, Jerusalem, 16.8.1875; see Ben-Arieh (supra n. 30), pp. 74-79, which includes the rules and regulations of Mishkenot Sha'ananim; and Ruth Kark, "Notes on 'Batei-Tura'," *Cathedra*, 18 (January 1981), pp. 157-187 (Hebrew); Private Collection of Mishkenot Sha'ananim, Jerusalem, letter of confirmation signed by the residents of Mishkenot Shaananim, Jerusalem, to Sir Moses Montefiote, n.p., November 5, 1879 (Hebrew).

Plate 28: The neighbourhood of Mishkenot Sha'ananim, from the east, 1910
(Source: Central Zionist Archives, Jerusalem, 10168)

called for a down payment, which Angeline paid — 2,000 piasters (approximately £18) for the first plot and 1,689 piasters (approximately £15) for the second on September 30, 1887. Annual mortgage payments would be made over a period of thirteen years until the cost of 163 napoleons (approximately £130) for each unit was paid off. The houses were completed by the summer of 1888. Among Angeline's neighbors were important members of Jerusalem society: her brother-in-law Eliyahu Navon; the editor of the newspaper *Habazeleth*, Israel Dov Frumkin; the Chief Rabbi of Jerusalem, Rabbi Meir Panagel; and the well-known educator, Ephraim Cohen-Reiss.[234]

234 Glass (supra n. 24), pp. 72-79; CZA, A152/7/2, list of payments for Mahane Yehuda, 1887 (French).

After Angeline's death the ownership of the house in Mahane Yehuda was evidently transferred to her son Samuel. In 1902 a request was made to use the two-storey house for collateral on a mortgage of 150 napoleons (approximately £120) over a three-year period. This also points to the addition of a second storey, probably during Angeline's lifetime, to the original one-storey structure.[235]

Bolissa, Solomon's Widow

As we have seen, little information is available on the women in the Amzalak family. With regard to Bolissa Amzalak, one existing document points to her capability in managing her husband's business affairs while he was abroad, although she was illiterate.[236]

Solomon Amzalak's health was poor in 1876. In May of that year, he traveled with his wife Bolissa and one of their children to Vienna for medical treatment. Shortly after his return to Jaffa on September 18, 1876 (the eve of Rosh Hashannah of 5637), he died. He left a wife and five children — two of whom were Ben-Zion and David.[237] The executor of Solomon's estate was the Jewish banker Haim Aaron Valero, who was in a compromising position since he also held some of Solomon's debts. In December 1879 Valero twice wrote to the British consul that he had presented the widow and orphans of Solomon Amzalak with an account of Solomon's outstanding debts. He mentioned that he had requested to relinquish his power of attorney over Solomon's estate, but that the request was turned down. He petitioned the consul to intercede on his behalf so that he would be relieved of his position as the executor of Solomon's will.[238] [see Plate 29]

Bolissa responded to Valero's petition, which had been forwarded to her by the British consul. Her letter mentioned certain discrepancies between Valero's accounting records and her own recollections of the debts owed by her deceased husband. She stated that she would be willing to take an oath to the effect that

---

235 ISA, 123-1 J22/9 787, letter from Marcus Yochanan Ben Salant, Jerusalem, to John Dickson, British consul, Jerusalem, September 2, 1902 (Arabic).

236 ISA, 123-1 J22/9 787, letter from Bolissa Amzalak, Jerusalem, to Noel Temple Moore, British consul, Jerusalem, January 15, 1874 (Arabic).

237 CZA, A152/9/1 laissez passer issued to Solomon Amzalak by Noel Temple Moore, British consul, Jerusalem, August 1, 1870; *Habazeleth*, vol. 7, no.4, 9 Heshvan 5637 (October 27, 1876), p. 22 (Hebrew).

238 ISA, 123-1 J22/9 787, letter from Haim Aaron Valero, Jerusalem, to Noel Temple Moore, British consul, Jerusalem, December 9, 1879 (Arabic); letter from Haim Aaron Valero, Jerusalem, to Noel Temple Moore, British consul, Jerusalem, December 26, 1879 (Arabic).

Plate 29: Bolissa Amzalak, Solomon's wife and her son David [?]
(Source: Amzalak Family Archives, National Library Archives, Jerusalem, 4°1613/3)

her husband had told her before his death that he owed a sum less than that specified by Valero.[239]

Consul Moore summoned the parties to the dispute to appear in person or through their attorneys before the consular court. The summons to Valero was forwarded through the Austrian consul, Bernhard Graf Caboga-Cerva.[240] The verdict reached by the consular court was that the heirs of Solomon owed 209 napoleons (approximately £168) to Haim Aaron Valero. Solomon's heirs explored diverse ways of repaying the debt, and in the end sold some of their property to their relative Joseph Amzalak, Haim's son.[241]

The inheritance that Solomon had left for his wife and children was insufficient for their needs. Haim Amzalak wrote that his nephew, Ben-Zion, had been orphaned and left without financial support. Haim stated that he had paid for his nephew's education at a college in Beirut. This claim notwithstanding, part of Ben-Zion's tuition was in fact paid from his father's estate. Haim did, however, attempt to further his nephew's education and approached the Alliance Israélite Universelle, requesting that they send Ben-Zion to university in France or elsewhere in Europe.[242]

By 1895, Bolissa's income had been reduced to whatever rent was received from the Amzalak house, amounting to only 40 to 45 napoleons (approximately £32 to £36) per annum. It was insufficient to support Bolissa and her unmarried daughter, who had been seriously ill for many years. Compounding their plight, her son David syphoned off some of this money, pocketing the rent from one of the rooms himself. This, however, was contrary to the 1878 agreement that stipulated the income from this property be used first and foremost for the support of the widow and her unmarried daughters. The male orphans could only enjoy the surplus. Upon learning of David's infraction, Bolissa's eldest son, Ben-Zion who up until then had supplemented the widow and her daughter's income from his own pocket, brought David's actions to the attention of the acting British Consul Jago. The enraged Ben-Zion and his uncle Haim Amzalak

239 ISA, 123-1 J22/9 787, letter from Bolissa Amzalak, Jerusalem, to Noel Temple Moore, British consul, Jerusalem, February 29, 1880 (French).

240 ISA, 123-1 J22/9 787, letter from Bolissa Amzalak, Jerusalem, to Noel Temple Moore, British consul, Jerusalem, February 29, 1880 (French).

241 ISA, 123-1 J22/9 787, letter from Bolissa Amzalak, Jerusalem, to Noel Temple Moore, British consul, Jerusalem, December 6, 1880 (Arabic); letter from Bolissa Amzalak, Jerusalem, to Noel Temple Moore, British consul, Jerusalem, August 7, 1880 (Arabic).

242 CZA, Mikveh Yisrael Archives, J41/201, letter from Haim Amzalak, Jaffa, to Charles Netter, Mikveh Yisrael, April 29, 1881 (French); ISA, 123-1 J22/9 787, letter from Bolissa Amzalak, Jerusalem, to Noel Temple Moore, British consul, Jerusalem, February 29, 1880 (French).

demanded that the acting consul intervene immediately and force the return of the income syphoned off by David Amzalak.[243]

Incidents

The consular diaries of James and Elizabeth Anne Finn between the years 1850 and 1858 provide a different perspective on the Amzalak family: not as the law-abiding family that worked for the betterment of the Jewish community but as a group that had run-ins with the law. Under the Capitulation agreements between the Sublime Porte and foreign powers, foreign citizens under the protection of their respective consulates were subject to consular jurisdiction. The consuls had the power to judge their subjects, pass sentences, including the imprisonment of offenders in consular jails, and carry out their rulings. The diaries tell of various incidents in which the Amzalaks were involved as subjects of British protection.

In July 1850, notice from the French consulate was given to Consul Finn that a man by the name of Ibrahim Simon had absconded with a large sum of money and was thought to have concealed it in the Amzalak house. A *kavass* from the British consulate was sent to search the house, but nothing was found.[244]

On July 9, 1851, Haim Amzalak was imprisoned overnight in the British consulate as means of preserving public peace. Charges of committing a violent act against an unmentioned party were brought. He was detained, although the charges were not formally pressed. The following day, he was released upon depositing two bonds, each for 1,000 piasters (approximately £90) as securities against his keeping the public peace. In addition to this episode, mention was made of a case in which Haim's wife was accused of gross cruelty.[245]

Another affair involving Haim Amzalak occurred on March 11, 1852. This case involved an altercation between Haim, a British subject, and an Ottoman subject. In such cases it was the role of the consul to bring the situation to the attention of the pasha of Jerusalem in order to reach a settlement. Consul Finn went to visit the pasha on behalf of Haim, who had been insulted in the street by a fellah (peasant), and justice was satisfied.[246]

On June 24, 1853 Raphael was accused of gambling and of breaking open a charity box. He was imprisoned in the consulate for three days. On the twenty-

---

243 ISA, 123-1 J22/9 787, letter from Haim Amzalak, Jaffa, to John Dickson, British consul, Jerusalem, June 18, 1895.
244 Blumberg (supra n. 182), p. 74, entry for July 13, 1850.
245 Blumberg (supra n. 182), pp. 88-89, entries for July 9, 1851 and July 11, 1851.
246 Blumberg (supra n. 182), p. 102, entry for March 11, 1852.

sixth of that month, in the presence of his brother and Rabbi Jacob Dabbahl, Raphael was released upon promising not to play cards again.[247]

The diary entry of August 12, 1853 describes the relationship between Haim and his brother-in-law from Hebron. After three years of quarreling the two came before the consul in order to make peace. The entry does not give the details of the disagreement between them.[248]

Summary

The second generation of Amzalaks in Jerusalem was elevated to prominence by Joseph Amzalak. He had seen to it that they were financially provided for, leaving them as the holders of the mortgage of the Hurva Compound, and the heirs to his house and his remaining assets. He had provided for their future by arranging their marriages into prominent families in Palestine. Joseph Amzalak attempted to grant his children the best possible conditions in which to live out their lives. However, it would appear that two of his sons were not suited for community leadership, and that the economic climate of Jerusalem was adverse to advancement. Raphael and Solomon both died in the prime of life without leaving their respective widows and orphans with sufficient means of support. Their sons living in Jerusalem faded from public view during the end of the nineteenth century, an exception being Solomon's son, Ben-Zion who was raised in Jaffa by his uncle, Haim. On the other hand, Esther had married into an affluent family, the Navons, as Joseph Amzalak had provided for her needs early on. Esther's son Joseph Navon Bey became a well-known figure in Jerusalem and in Diaspora Jewish communities. Haim Amzalak apparently inherited his father's business abilities. He uprooted himself to Jaffa, a city of opportunities, and established himself there financially and socially. The next chapter will expand upon Haim's life in Jaffa.

---

247 Blumberg (supra n. 182), p. 131, entries for June 24, 1853 and June 26, 1853.
248 Blumberg (supra n. 182), p. 135, entry for August 12, 1853.

CHAPTER FOUR

HAIM AMZALAK IN JAFFA (1828-1916)

During the late 1850s Haim Amzalak established himself in Jaffa. His move was connected to his business affairs in the realm of international trade. Already in 1852, Haim traveled through the eastern Mediterranean after having been in Lombardy, the Venetian States and the Austrian territories. At Trieste he had received a laissez-passer from the British consul general allowing him to pass freely "without let or hindrance," and requesting that he be afforded all assistance on his journey to Smyrna by way of Corfu. From Smyrna he continued to Jaffa via Beirut.[249] It would appear that his travels then were connected to his business affairs, although no definite proof of this can be found.

Jaffa was the natural place to settle in Palestine for someone involved in international commerce. At the time it was in the midst of development as a port serving Jerusalem and a growing center for the agricultural hinterland. Jaffa at the beginning of the nineteenth century was ruled by Muhammad Aga Abu Nabbut (1804-1818), who developed its fortifications, buildings and commercial facilities. Later, during the period of Egyptian rule (1831-1841), the city's development was accelerated through the increased numbers of pilgrims passing through it, improved security and greater tolerance on the part of the regime. Egyptian peasants settled in Jaffa and its environs, engaging in farming and the growing of fruit trees. Jews, first North Africans and later Ashkenazim, also settled there. During the following decade, Jaffa experienced rapid economic and physical development, which gained momentum with the end of the Crimean War in 1856. The Jewish community during the late 1850s consisted of approximately sixty-five families, of which only three were Ashkenazi. Its members were merchants and shopkeepers; many lived by manual labor, as porters, sailors, messengers or mechanics. Cultivation of agricultural lands and citrus orchards was intensified, thus enlarging Jaffa's

---

249 NLA, 4°1613/5, laissez-passer issued to Haim Amzalak by the British consul general at
    Trieste, August 5, 1852.

economic hinterland. The city was the site of stepped-up European involvement, expressed through the establishment of consular agencies, churches, schools, welfare services and commercial facilities. Towards the 1880s its population had increased to such an extent that settlement expanded beyond the city walls.[250]

Haim Amzalak's Family

Haim Amzalak was twice married; his first wife was Esther, the daughter of Joseph Levi of Hebron. Esther entered the marriage with certain assets which she invested in 1875 in the purchase of an orange grove near Jaffa on the road to Jerusalem. The couple decided to strike roots in Jaffa and raise a family there. They had six children: Joseph, Abraham, Luna-Bolissa, Rosa, Kaleb and Sultana. Little is known about the children during their early years. Moses Montefiore described them as "the most amiable young family" on his visit in 1875. Bolissa, of all the children, developed a special relationship with Montefiore. Joseph enjoyed the privileges of the eldest son; he was often mentioned together with his father since he accompanied him on many occasions. Haim, in his later years, fathered four daughters — Rachel, Rozina, Gamila and Fortuni — probably by his second wife.[251]

After his brother Solomon's death, Haim raised his nephew, Ben-Zion, in his house. Haim sent Ben-Zion to college, and when the young man reached marrying age he wed Haim's daughter, Luna-Bolissa.[252]

Haim Amzalak's House

Haim Amzalak resided within the walls of Jaffa, near the port of the city and not far from the customs house. His impressive three-storey house, with a British flag flying above it, was protected by Afghani guards. Eventually Haim gave up this house because of the great amount of traffic noise in that bustling vicinity. He moved to the Manshiya neighborhood, where his nephew and son-

250 Kark (supra n. 117), pp. 16–20, 23-26, 32–38.
251 Tidhar (supra n. 183), 2, p. 816; AFP, record of circumcisions; mention is made of the circumcision of Joseph Ben-Zion Amzalak as well as the birth of four daughters by a second wife; Loewe (supra n. 152), 2, p. 274; see the section on Montefiore and his relationship with the Amzalaks.
252 Interview with James Amzalak conducted by Ruth Kark, Jerusalem, June 12, 1985.

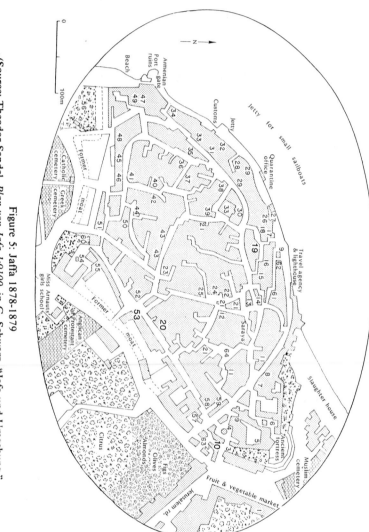

Figure 5: Jaffa 1878-1879
(Source: Theodor Sandel, *Plan von Jafa 1:9100*, in G. Schwarz, "Jafa und Umgebung,"
Zeitschrift des Deutschen Palästina Vereins, 3 (1880), op. p. 44)

10. Old Gate to the City
19. Synagogue
20. Synagogue and the home of Kayyat
53. New Gate

in-law, Ben-Zion, had established himself, and resided in one of Ben-Zion's houses.[253] [see Figure 5]

In addition, Esther Amzalak owned a house and a *bayara* (watered orchard) outside Jaffa, on the road to Jerusalem near Sabil (public fountain) Abu Nabut. Montefiore, during his visit to Palestine in 1875, was a guest there, and in his diary described the hospitality afforded him by the Amzalaks:

> It must have been about seven o'clock in the evening when we arrived. The lady of the house, surrounded by the most amiable young family and some friends of the house, gave us a friendly welcome. A refreshing beverage, consisting of almond and rose water, was handed round and ten minutes afterwards a dinner was served in the best European style. An almost endless variety of dishes, partly Syrian, partly French, were handed round by waiters dressed in the French style, who spoke French, Italian, Spanish, German and Arabic. All this might have made us forget that we were in the Holy Land had we not been reminded of it every now and then, either by the overpowering heat or the bite of an intruding mosquito.[254]

Business Activities

Haim Amzalak's business activities resembled those of his family in Jerusalem; he engaged in banking and land transactions. After moving to Jaffa, he also became involved in commerce.

Amzalak's banking operations were in collaboration with Ya'akov Valero and partners in Jerusalem. In 1859 the *Jewish Chronicle* wrote: "A Jewish banker (Hyam Amzalek [sic]) sent £400 from Jaffa to Jerusalem yesterday to Mr. Valeno [sic]."[255]

In the British Consulate archives in Jerusalem, an example has been found of his banking activities. Amzalak complained in 1866 that a bill of exchange for 31,000 piasters (approximately £282) from Haim Amzalak and Co., Jaffa to Kasem il Odeh of Nablus had become due but remained unpaid. In a request to the vice consul at Jaffa, Habib Kayat,[256] which was to be forwarded to the

253 Interview with James Amzalak (supra n. 252); Yosef Braslavi, *On Unpaved Roads to Knowing the Land*, Tel Aviv 1972, p. 133 (Hebrew); see Chapter Four for further detail about the Amzalak house in the Manshiya district in Jaffa.
254 Loewe (supra n. 152), 2, p. 274.
255 Tidhar (supra n. 183), 2, p. 816; *The Jewish Chronicle and the Hebrew Observer*, vol. 16, no. 253, October 21, 1859 (23 Tishri 5620) p. 5.
256 Kayat is the spelling that will be used in this work. The name has also been rendered variously as Khayat, Kayyat, or Khayyat.

consul in Jerusalem, Amzalak asked that the pasha of Jerusalem order the governor of Nablus to bring Kasem il Odeh to Nablus and enforce payment with interest and expenses.[257]

Haim Amzalak dealt in real estate for personal speculation and as an agent for others. He retained land in Jerusalem, which was managed by his representatives there, and expanded his holdings in the area of Jaffa.

In Jerusalem, he sold some of his properties and received rental income from others. For example, in 1873 he sold a plot outside Damascus Gate to the orphans of Suleiman Taji at a price of 458 napoleons (approximately £362). They were unable to make good on their payments and his representative, Rabbi 'Azaria Boton, petitioned the British consul to take action. On the other hand, he retained part of the Mediterranean Hotel, which still provided a rental income during the 1880s.[258]

He purchased agricultural land in the vicinity of Jaffa during the 1850s and afterwards, becoming one of the first Jews to do so. It appears that he had advised his wife to invest similarly, since he understood the potential in the developing orange market. Esther acquired a vineyard located east of Jaffa along the road to Jerusalem. Over the years prior to the purchase, this tract, which contained a well and water collection pool, was ameliorated through the planting of fruit bearing trees, mainly oranges. This *bayara* served as the family summer residence. [see Plate 30]

From the 1880s, Jews purchased tracts of land in the vicinity of Jaffa in anticipation of their development for residential use. Jewish neighborhoods were being built at that time: Neve Tzedek (1887), Neve Shalom (1890), Mahane Yehuda (1896), Yeffe Nof (1897), Achuza (1900) and others. Three of the prominent figures in these transactions were Aaron Chelouche, Haim Amzalak and Joseph Moyal.[259]

Joseph Eliyahu Chelouche, Aaron's son, described in his memoirs how the process of land purchases gained momentum. He wrote that an Arab inhabitant of Jaffa offered to sell a vineyard and well to Aaron Chelouche, with the latter's clerk serving as intermediary. Chelouche purchased this first tract, upon which part of the Neve Shalom neighborhood was later built. This development

257 ISA, 123-1 J22/9 787, letter from Habib A. Kayat, British vice consul, Jaffa, to Noel Temple Moore, British consul, Jerusalem, September 28, 1866.
258 ISA, 123-1 J22/9 787, letter from 'Ezaria Buttan, Jerusalem, to Noel Temple Moore, British consul, Jerusalem, January 6, 1874 (Arabic); letter from Haim Aaron Valero, Jerusalem, to Count Bernhard Graf Caboga-Cerva, Austrian consul, Jerusalem, February 2, 1880 (French).
259 Kark (supra n. 117), pp. 100–111.

Plate 30: Esther Amzalak's *bayara* Jaffa 1983
(Source: Kark, photographed in 1983)

inspired him to continue to partake in the redemption of the Land of Israel. Aaron Chelouche began to buy one vineyard after another, either as an individual or together with Haim Amzalak and Joseph Moyal. These areas were known by the Arab inhabitants of Jaffa as "the disputed lands." A Christian inhabitant of Jaffa, Tanuss Nassar, disputed the rights of the three to the land. Amzalak and Chelouche renounced their claims, but Moyal entered into a legal battle with Nassar which lasted over thirty years. The remaining lands in their possession were sold. Chelouche, Amzalak and Moyal sold individual plots of varying size to Jews between 1906 and the outbreak of World War I at the price of 5,600 to 8,000 francs (approximately £224 to £320) per dunam.[260] [see Plate 31]

Haim Amzalak also represented other investors in real estate. With his experience in this market, including his activities as British vice consul, he was considered an expert. He received various requests from individuals and groups, such as one from Sir Moses Montefiore in 1876:

> I shall be pleased to hear of some offer of land near Jerusalem, as I intend making a purchase of a nice plot of ground for suitable purposes. Shall

---

260 Kark (supra n. 117), pp. 126, 248–249; Joseph Eliyahu Chelouche, *The Story of My Life*, Tel Aviv 1931, pp. 19-21 (Hebrew); CFA, by the gracious permission of Mr. 'A. Cohen. These archives consist of contracts and sales receipts connected to these lands. As mentioned, they date from 1906 to 1914.

Plate 31: Aerial Photograph of the environs of Jaffa, 1918
(Source: German aerial photograph, Aerial Photograph Collection, Department of
Geography, Hebrew University of Jerusalem, F72171)
1. [Esther] Amzalak's *bayara*   3. French Vice Consul Philibert's residence
2. Sabil Abu Nabut   4. American Vice Consul Hardegg's Jerusalem Hotel
5. German Vice Consul Murad's Garden

you happen to hear of any, have the goodness to let me know it, and send
me an exact plan of the land with correct measurements of its superficies
of number of trees, cisterns or buildings that may happen to be in it —
and state the lowest price of the property.[261]

In 1874, Mr. W. Bailey, a British subject, asked the British consul in Jerusalem
to permit Haim Amzalak to purchase on his (Bailey's) behalf a portion of the
Jaffa fortress on sale at the time. He had instructed Jerusalem banker Johannes
Frutiger to supply Amzalak with the purchase money, about £200, upon the
latter's application.[262] Haim Amzalak and his nephew Joseph Navon served as

261 Pinhas Grayevski, *From the Archives of Jerusalem*, no. 8, Jerusalem 1930, pp. 6-7
(Hebrew).
262 ISA, 123-1 J22/9 787, letter from W. Bailey, Jerusalem, to Noel Temple Moore, British
consul, Jerusalem, September 3, 1874.

intermediaries in the purchase of land for the first modern Jewish agricultural settlements in Palestine (see Jewish Agricultural Settlements below).

Furthermore, Amzalak was involved in international commerce. He exported grains, oranges and other agricultural produce from Jaffa and imported English goods. Joseph Navon served as the representative for his commercial activities in Jerusalem. In 1875, Haim Amzalak was appointed the representative of British Lloyd's in Jaffa. The agency prospered over the following years as a result of the growth of Jaffa as a center of trade and industry. In 1899, Lloyd's considered opening another agency in Jerusalem but accepted Haim's recommendation not to do so.[263] That same year Lloyd's acknowledged his performance on their behalf.

> I am instructed to take this opportunity of expressing to you the best thanks of the Committee of Lloyd's for the many valuable services rendered by you to this Corporation during the time that you have held Lloyd's Agency at Jaffa, and to express the hope that you may long continue to occupy that position.[264] [see Plate 32]

In 1911, Haim retired from his position as the Lloyd's agent. He recommended that Lloyd's continue their agency under his eldest son's firm of J.B. Amzalak, to which they agreed.[265]

Vice Consular Service

The position of vice consul for a foreign government in the Ottoman Empire afforded its recipient exceptional status and power. These local inhabitants enjoyed extraterritorial rights far greater than those inherent in the protection afforded to citizens of a foreign government residing in the empire. This protection entailed exemptions from personal and other taxes levied by the Ottoman government. Vice consuls were eligible for the same judicial, financial, economic and other privileges granted to Europeans elsewhere in the Ottoman Empire. Many local merchants offered their services as vice consuls, consular agents and dragomans to foreign governments, in many cases free of charge, in order to attain the attendant advantages. Those in consular service could further their business interests as representatives of a foreign flag. They were

263 Tidhar (supra n. 183), 2, p. 816; Glass (supra n. 24), p. 31; AFP, letter from Edw. Puttock, London, to Haim Amzalak, Jaffa, July 20, 1899.
264 AFP, letter from Edw. Puttock, London, to Haim Amzalak, Jaffa, July 27, 1899.
265 AFP, letter from Edw. Puttock, London, to Haim Amzalak, Jaffa, November 23, 1911; letter from Haim Amzalak, Jaffa, to Edward Inglefield, London, September 19, 1911.

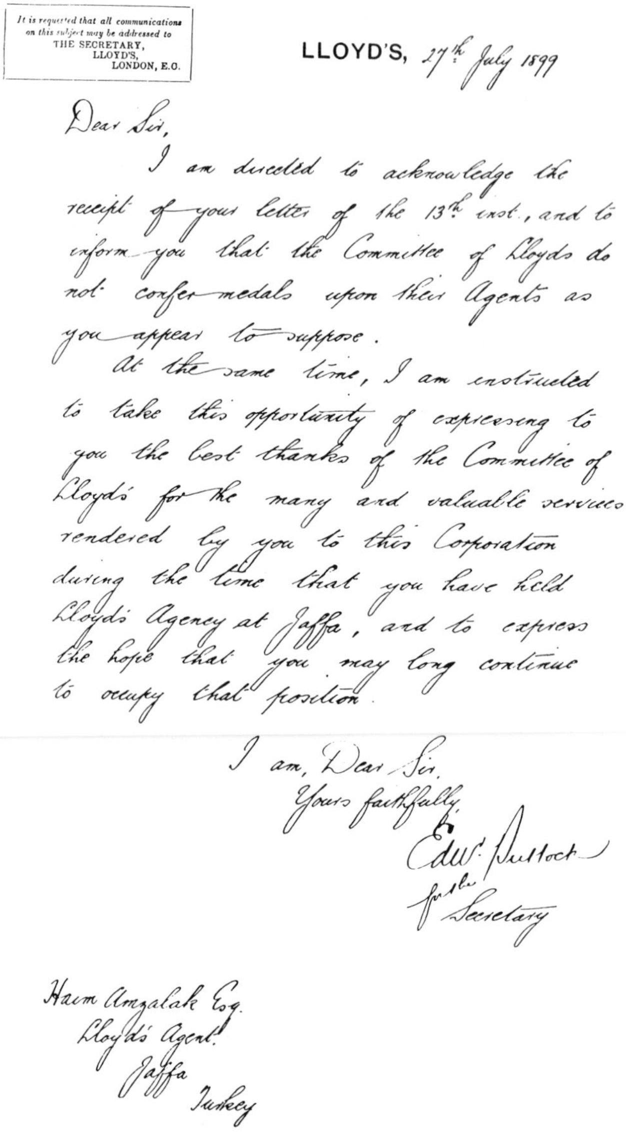

It is requested that all communications
on this subject may be addressed to
THE SECRETARY,
LLOYD'S,
LONDON, E.C.

LLOYD'S, 27th July 1899

Dear Sir,

I am directed to acknowledge the receipt of your letter of the 13th inst., and to inform you that the Committee of Lloyds do not confer medals upon their Agents as you appear to suppose.

At the same time, I am instructed to take this opportunity of expressing to you the best thanks of the Committee of Lloyd's for the many and valuable services rendered by you to this Corporation during the time that you have held Lloyd's Agency at Jaffa, and to express the hope that you may long continue to occupy that position.

I am, Dear Sir,
Yours faithfully,
Edw. Bullock
for the Secretary

Haim Amzalak Esq.
Lloyd's Agent.
Jaffa
Turkey

Plate 32: Letter to Haim Amzalak from Lloyd's, July 27, 1899
(Source: Simon Amzalak Family Papers, Jerusalem)

outside Ottoman jurisdiction and answerable only to their superiors. They enjoyed an intimate relationship with Ottoman officials. This unpaid service that they provided was usually considered indispensable by the consuls under whom they served. In short, they were at the center of affairs in their vice consular districts.[266]

Haim Amzalak received consular appointments from two nations, the first from Portugal in 1871 and the second from Great Britain in 1872. His Portuguese appointment was as consul of Jerusalem, although he did not reside in the city at the time. His activities on behalf of the Portuguese appear to have been limited, as seen from those of his correspondences that survive in the Portuguese Ministry of Foreign Affairs Archives. In fact, only seven dispatches from the years 1884 to 1886 remain, and they contain little information pertaining to the history of Palestine.[267]

An item that appeared in *Habazeleth* in 1884, and later that year in the *Jewish Chronicle*, stated that Haim Amzalak had declined an offer to become Portuguese consul in Jerusalem, suggesting that his nephew Joseph Navon serve in his place. The article reported that Amzalak's suggestion was sanctioned by the Portuguese government. No information exists in the Portuguese Ministry of Foreign Affairs Archives to confirm this information. Navon carried out various duties on his uncle's behalf in the capacity of Portuguese consul in Jerusalem, but without official sanction.[268]

In 1886, Haim Amzalak received a different appointment from the Portuguese government — that of honorary consul in Jaffa. He remained in this position until 1892, when he was replaced by Alfredo Paradi, the new Portuguese vice consul for Jaffa.[269]

On the other hand, his activities as British vice consul in Jaffa were of greater importance and much more varied. The British government had established a

266 Fawaz (supra n. 21), pp. 85-90.
267 ANTT, Mercês de Don Luiz, book 22, pp. 212-213; PMFAA, file 247, Cartas Patentes dos Consules 1855-1878, p. 110 (Portuguese); box 783, Jerusalem correspondence 1884-1886 (French).
268 Gaon (supra n. 39), 1, p. 55; Tidhar (supra n. 183), 2, p. 816; *Habazeleth*, vol. 15, no. 3, 12 Heshvan 5645 (October 31, 1884), p. 28 (Hebrew); *The Jewish Chronicle*, 817 (new series) November 21, 1884 (3 Kislev 5645), p. 12.
269 PMFAA, file 248, Cartas Patentes dos Consules 1878-1914, p. 85 (Portuguese); Ministério dos Negócios Estrangerios, *Annuario Diplomatico e Consular Portuguez Relativo aos Anno de 1889 e 1890*, Lisbon 1891, p. 121; Ministério dos Negócios Estrangerios, *Annuario Diplomatico e Consular Portuguez Relativo ao Anno de 1891*, Lisbon 1892, p. 145; Ministério dos Negócios Estrangerios, *Annuario Diplomatico e Consular Portuguez Relativo ao Anno de 1892*, Lisbon 1893, p. 105.

consulate in Jaffa in 1848 or 1849. It was subordinate to the consulate general in Beirut. From its opening until 1865, Dr. As'ad Ya'aqub Kayat served as consul. After his death, the British consul in Jerusalem, Noel Temple Moore, was anxious to annex the consulate in Jaffa, arguing that Jaffa served as Jerusalem's port and that according to the Ottoman administrative boundaries it was subsumed under Jerusalem's authority. Consequently the status of the British representation in Jaffa was lowered to vice consulate. In 1865, Habib A. Kayat, the son of the deceased consul of Jaffa, was appointed vice consul with an annual salary of £100. Habib resigned in 1869, since the Ottoman authorities, regarding him technically as an Ottoman citizen, refused to recognize his appointment. Moore notified the Foreign Office of Habib Kayat's resignation and forwarded his recommendation that Haim Amzalak be awarded the position. Moore wrote that Amzalak was the only eligible British subject in Jaffa and that the latter claimed some knowledge of Italian and English. The Foreign Office rejected this recommendation, based on information from another source that Amzalak was ignorant of English. In September 1872, Haim Amzalak was recommended again by Consul Moore for the post, and the appointment was approved on December 16, 1872. He accepted the position, but without taking a salary, believing it to be a dishonor to do so. Haim Amzalak sent letters to the vice consuls of other nations in Jaffa, informing them of his appointment. He promised to try to uphold the best relations with them and looked forward to their cooperation.[270] [see Plate 33]

The Jewish community celebrated his appointment as vice consul. *Habazeleth* wrote: "Today was a happy day for Israel, today a royal decree was read appointing Haim Amzalak the position of vice consul of Great Britain." He was given the consular seal and all the appurtenances necessary for the performance of his duties. At that time he raised the Union Jack over his home in Jaffa. The Jewish community went to visit him there, and he welcomed them. They blessed him in the name of God.[271]

In 1875 Sir Moses Montefiore visited Jaffa and expressed his sentiments about Haim Amzalak's role as vice consul:

> At four o'clock p.m. Her Majesty's Vice Consul at Jaffa (Signor Amzalak)

270 A.L. Tibawi, *British Interests in Palestine 1800-1901*, Oxford 1961, pp. 142-146; Gaon (supra n. 39), 1, p. 105; ISA, RG 67, file 451, German Consulate in Jerusalem Archives, Serapion S. Murad, Jaffa to Baron Carl Victor von Alten, German consul, Jerusalem, December 31, 1872 (German); USNA, RG 84 Box 5958, Miscellaneous Record Book 1866–1910, Haim Amzalak, British vice consul, Jaffa, to Ernest Hardegg, United States vice consul, Jaffa, November 8, 1872 (French).

271 *Habazeleth*, vol. 3, no. 5, 21 Heshvan 5633 (November 22, 1872), p. 37 (Hebrew).

Plate 33: Haim Amzalak in his vice consular uniform.

With regard to the uniform the late Dr. Vivian D. Lipman made the following comments in January 1989: "The photograph of Amzalak show him in the levee dress of a vice-consul (which consular agents were entitled to wear) but the cuffs- which should have two inches of silver embroidery on a black velvet background appear to be the white cuffs of the tropical white uniform (these cuffs, like the embroidery on the collar of the tropical uniform had to be detachable, so that the white tropical uniform could be laundered). But, most remarkable, he is wearing epaulettes with a bullion fringe which was never been part of any British diplomatic or consular uniform, but appear to have been taken from a naval uniform — probably not a British one, since the straps which held the epaulettes in position are not British. His cocked hat is probably correct but it appears lower and broader than the British style, more like a French diplomatic hat. The sword knot is also too long for British custom." We are much indebted to Dr. Lipman for his expert appraisal of the uniform.

(Source: Amzalak Family Archives, National Library Archives, Jerusalem, 4°1613/3)

accompanied by his son, two *kawasses*, with their official batons and several attendants, approached our ship. It was a source of high gratification to me to see one of my brethren, a native of the Holy Land, filling so high and honourable an office. I knew his father well. He was one of the most worthy and charitable of our brethren in Jerusalem, and I was now much pleased to have the opportunity of evincing my regard for his son, whose abilities and high character had been so honourably acknowledged by the consular functions entrusted him.[272]

Haim Amzalak's position as vice consul entailed a variety of duties. He represented the interests of the British government and British subjects either visiting or residing in the Jaffa area. Since Jaffa was a commercial port, he had the added task of reporting on the trade activities there. His information was quoted at length in nearly all the published annual reports about this district. Amzalak's reports provided detailed statistics on the annual volume of imports and exports, recounting type, quantity, and the flags of the ships engaged in this trade. His reports described trends and incidents affecting the trade and commerce in his area of jurisdiction: the annual harvest, changes in agricultural production, public works projects, plagues and, with a disproportionately large amount of information, developments in Jewish and German agricultural settlements. For example, in his report for 1881 Amzalak wrote that orange gardens constituted the best form of capital investment, yielding annual net returns of ten percent. He also described labor and industry in the area under his jurisdiction, noting that 5,000 people were employed on a daily basis for the orange picking and packing season of 1879. In his report for 1895 he communicated the increase in orange plantations not only in Jaffa, but also the nearby village of Soumeil.[273]

Haim Amzalak utilized these annual reports as a platform for voicing opinions on the state of affairs in Palestine. In his report for 1897, he opened with the following plea for the construction of a harbor in Jaffa:

272 Loewe (supra n. 152), 2, p. 274.
273 British Parliamentary Papers 1882/LXXI (Jaffa, May 1882) and 1880/LXXIV (Jaffa, February 1880) as quoted by Schölch (supra n. 21), pp. 17-18, 38; see: "Report by Consular Agent Amzalak on the Trade and Commerce of Jaffa for the Year 1881," F.O. *Consular Reports*, Commercial no. 36 (1882), p. 1159, and "Report by Consular Agent Amzalak on the Trade and Commerce of Jaffa for the Year 1882," F.O. *Consular Reports*, Commercial no. 20, (1883), p.629 cited in Gad G. Gilbar, "The Growing Economic Involvement of Palestine with the West, 1865-1914," David Kushner (ed.), *Palestine in the Late Ottoman Period: Political, Social and Economic Transformation*, Jerusalem 1986, pp. 188-210.

I feel I ought to commence my report by referring to the bad anchorage and insecure landing at Jaffa, which has caused the loss of so many lives of visitors to the sacred sites of Palestine. It would take too long to enumerate all the casualties that have taken place....just recently, a native boat carrying passengers from the Austrian mail steamer was dashed to pieces by waves upon the reef of rocks near the landing place, and left ten European and Ottoman pilgrims to the mercy of the breakers. Four out of the ten passengers perished, and the others were saved almost by a miracle....it is only by the construction of a harbour that these disasters can be avoided in the future.[274]

Consular representatives in the region played an important role in the introduction and diffusion of new technologies. With their hand on the pulse of the region they could advise foreign merchants and manufacturers as to which advances would be welcomed by the local population and whether these would be integrated into everyday use. Afterwards they would report on the degree of success or failure of recent attempts to introduce innovations, and provide explanations. Haim Amzalak, in his capacity as vice consul, advised the British Foreign Office on the marketability of various British products in the region. One example is his comments on the demand for tin plates:

... I beg to state that several consignments of tin plates have already been imported to this place from the United Kingdom, but there is not a fair demand of this article in this place as the greater part of the natives use tin of the cheap empty cans of petroleum. With regard to the quantity required by the Jewish Colonies [sic] of 'Ekron', as far as I could gather it is a trifling quantity owing to the continual decrease of the export of fruit.[275]

As vice consul, he dealt with various financial matters concerning British subjects, serving as their agent for the transfer of funds and the payment of debts, as well as witnessing and officiating at the signing of last wills and testaments. In addition, he handled the effects of deceased British subjects, transferring their property to the designated parties. However, if matter or dispute were between a British subject and a subject of another foreign nation, then Vice Consul Amzalak would enter into correspondene with that person's

274 *Report for the Year 1897 on the Trade and Commerce of Jerusalem and District*, London 1898, pp. 8-9.
275 PRO, F.O. 78/5208 (no. 42), Haim Amzalak, British vice consul, Jaffa to John Dickson, British consul, Jerusalem, July 2, 1902, as quoted by Hyamson (supra n. 176), 2, p. 565.

vice consul in the city. These two vice consuls would then attempt to reach an amicable solution without involving the Ottoman authorities. Haim Amzalak also served as an intermediary in the transfer of deeds to the name of British subjects, which entailed soliciting the *kaymakam* of Jaffa to forward a report to the *mutassarif* of Jerusalem, who was to approve the transfer.[276]

Amzalak's position also involved the entertaining of important British visitors during their stay in Jaffa. He was at Prince George and Prince Albert Victor's disposal during their visit to Jaffa in 1882. He sent his son, Joseph to escort them as far as Beit Degan while they journeyed through Palestine and Syria. Haim accompanied William Henry Hechler during his visit in 1898. Hechler was a Christian Zionist, who served as the chaplain of the British embassy in Vienna from 1885 until 1910. Hechler attempted to establish a relationship between Theodore Herzl and the Grand Duke of Baden and later between Herzl and Kaiser Wilhelm II of Germany. He joined Herzl on his 1898 visit to Palestine. While in Jaffa, Hechler was introduced by Amzalak to Dr. Hillel Yaffe, the most distinguished medical practitioner in Palestine at that time.[277]

Another aspect of his role as vice consul was the protection of the rights of British subjects. Amzalak was empowered to issue certificates of registration for

276 ISA, 123-1 J22/9 787, receipt to Haim Amzalak, British vice consul, Jaffa, from Thomas Cook, Jaffa, March 22, 1875; copy of John Larard's Last Will and Testament certified by Haim Amzalak, British vice consul, Jaffa, July 3, 1882; letter from Haim Amzalak, British vice consul, to John Dickson, British consul, Jerusalem, February 28, 1892; letter from John Dickson, British consul, Jerusalem, to Haim Amzalak, British vice consul, Jaffa, August 19, 1897; letter from Haim Amzalak, British vice consul, Jaffa, to John Dickson, British consul, Jerusalem, May 3, 1900; letter from John Dickson, British consul, Jerusalem, to Haim Amzalak, British vice consul, Jaffa, June 9, 1900; letter from John Dickson, British consul, Jerusalem, to Haim Amzalak, British vice consul, Jaffa, June 12, 1900; letter from Haim Amzalak, British vice consul, Jaffa, to John Dickson, British consul, Jerusalem, May 26, 1901; USNA, RG 84 Box 5958, Miscellaneous Record Book 1866–1910, Haim Amzalak, British vice consul, Jaffa, to Ernest Hardegg, United States vice consul, Jaffa, November 18, 1873 (French); Haim Amzalak, British vice consul, Jaffa, to Ernest Hardegg, United States vice consul, Jaffa, January 2, 1874; USNA, RG 84 Box 5959, Miscellaneous Letters 1874–1879, Haim Amzalak, British vice consul, Jaffa, to Ernest Hardegg, United States vice consul, Jaffa, January 25, 1878 (French); Haim Amzalak, British vice consul, Jaffa, to Ernest Hardegg, United States vice consul, Jaffa, February 5, 1878 (French).
277 Copy of an article from the newspaper, *The Truth*, dated June 30, 1911 in Pinhas Ben-Zion Grayevski, *From the Archives of Jerusalem*, no. 15, Jerusalem 1931, n.p.; letter from Dr. Hillel Yaffe, Jaffa, to Asher Ginzberg (Ahad HaAm), November 16, 1898, in Hillel Yaffe, *The Generation of Pioneers; Memoirs, Letters and Diary*, Jerusalem 1971, pp. 194-199 (Hebrew).

British protection, although in 1886 the British ambassador in Constantinople, Sir Edward Thorton, suggested to Consul Moore that this right be withdrawn.[278] Amzalak's duty was to represent the interests of the protected subjects before the Ottoman authorities. So ingrained was this protection in the lives of the Jewish population of Jaffa, that the concept became integrated into their speech. Yosef Braslavi, in his memoirs, wrote that it was characteristic of Jewish youths to use the phrase "in the name of the consul" as a warning when threatened by Arab youths. The latter's response to the phrase was "Come down to the sea, (where there are no witnesses) and we'll show you."[279]

The year 1882 saw the beginning of large-scale Jewish immigration to Palestine. During the following years there were three major waves of immigration: 1882-1884, 1890-1891 and 1901-1903. Between the years 1882 and 1904, the period known as the First *Aliyah*, an estimated 45,000 to 55,000 Jews reached the shores of Palestine, of whom approximately 25,000 permanently settled in the area.[280] The Ottoman government's position on immigration into the empire, and Palestine in particular, was that "it would allow any individual regardless of religion or nationality to immigrate into Turkey, but it would restrict mass settlement — that is, it would not permit an ethnic or religious group to establish a numerical majority in one specific area."[281] Thus the Ottoman government issued decrees to restrict the mass influx of Jews into Palestine in 1882, 1884, 1891 and 1901. The Western powers attempted to intervene through their representatives in Constantinople and in Palestine, but with only limited success.[282]

In 1882 the Ottoman authorities attempted to prevent the landing of Jews at Jaffa. When Amzalak confronted the *kaymakam* of Jaffa he was assured that the restrictions were meant for Russian Jews and not British Jews. Amzalak,

278 NLA, 4°1513, letter from Sir Edward Thornton, Constantinople, to Noel Temple Moore, British consul, Jerusalem, February 23, 1886.

279 Braslavi (supra n. 253), p. 139.

280 Kemal H. Karpat, "Ottoman Immigration Policies and Settlement in Palestine," I. Abu-Lughod and Abu Laban (eds.), *Settlers' Regimes in Africa and the Arab World*, Wilmett 1974, pp. 66-72; Ran Aaronsohn, "Cultural Landscape of Pre-Zionist Settlements", Kark (supra n. 24), p. 96.

281 Karpat (supra n. 280), p. 68.

282 Karpat (supra n. 280), p. 66-72; Avner Levy, "Jewish Immigration into Eretz-Israel According to the Documents of 'Ali Akram, Mutasarif of Jerusalem (1906-1908)," *Cathedra*, 12 (July 1979), pp. 164-174 (Hebrew); Mordechai Eliav, "Diplomatic Intervention Concerning Restrictions on Jewish Immigration and Purchase of Land at the End of the Nineteenth Century," *Cathedra*, 26 (December 1982), pp. 117-132 (Hebrew).

in a letter to Consul Moore, stated that this step was designed to appease the nationalistic leanings of the local Muslim population in the wake of the British occupation of Egypt.[283]

In 1898, he reported to the consul in Jerusalem, John Dickson, about Turkish soldiers having prevented four British subjects from landing at Jaffa, claiming that Jewish immigration was forbidden. Local officials sought to extend these restrictions to tourists, particularly if they were not first class travelers. Prior to this, Amzalak had carried out negotiations with the *kaymakam* of Jaffa and the local police in order to delay the deportation of these British Jews until he could inform the consul in Jerusalem, who would decide whether or not to intervene on their behalf. The disembarkation of these Jewish tourists was secured. Afterwards the general issue was taken up by the British ambassador in Constantinople who invoked the support of the Marquess of Salisbury.[284]

Another incident, the grounding of the Russian ship *Chihchov* off the coast of Jaffa during the winter of 1891, attests to Haim Amzalak's use of his vice consular powers beyond his jurisdiction, for the benefit of those not directly under his protection. This ship, carrying many Russian Jews, had broken up on the rocks two hundred meters away from the coast. Its passengers, panic stricken, crowded onto the ship's deck, awaiting assistance. The *kaymakam* had placed soldiers on the shore to guard the ship and its contents and prevent anyone from approaching it, until the Russian vice consul could join him at the scene. Members of Jaffa's Jewish community who were forced to wait helplessly on the beach called upon Haim Amzalak to intervene. Upon hearing of the incident, Amzalak immediately pressured the Russian vice consul into acting at once, fearing that continued procrastination would lead to heavy losses of human life. In turn, the combined efforts of the two vice consuls forced the *kaymakam* to lend assistance. Many members of the Jewish community aided in the successful rescue operation of all the ship's passengers.[285]

As vice consul he protected British and Zionist business interests in Jaffa. In 1903 the *kaymakam* of Jaffa demanded an official permit from the Sublime Porte for the operation of the Anglo-Palestine Bank. This subsidiary company of the chief financial instrument of Zionist policy, the Jewish Colonial Trust,

283 ISA, 123-1 J22/9 787, letter from Haim Amzalak, British vice consul, Jaffa, to John Dickson, British consul, Jerusalem, September 4, 1882.
284 Alex Carmel, "The Yishuv, the Ottoman Government, and the Foreign Consulates," Mordechai Eliav (ed.), *The First Aliyah*, Jerusalem 1981, 1, pp. 111-112 (Hebrew); Norman Bentwich, "Anglo-Jewish Travellers to Palestine in the Nineteenth Century" *The Jewish Historical Society of England --Miscellanies*, 4, London 1942, pp. 18-19.
285 Chelouche (supra n. 260), pp. 97-102.

was founded in 1902. The *kaymakam* ordered a policeman to be placed at the doors of the bank to prevent any person from entering. Haim Amzalak sent his dragoman to instruct the *kaymakam* to correspond with the vice consul rather than dealing directly with the bank, since it was a British outfit. Amzalak sent a report to the consul in Jerusalem and Consul Dickson asked Amzalak to obtain a written explanation from the *kaymakam* as to why he had interfered with the business of the company. The *kaymakam* rescinded the order, the policeman was removed, and the Anglo-Palestine Bank continued its operations without further hindrance from the local authorities.[286]

In 1882 a renowned orientalist, Professor Edward H. Palmer, was sent by the British Admiralty to persuade the Bedouin of Sinai to remain neutral during the British occupation of Egypt. He was familiar with the region since he had been among the leaders of the Palestine Exploration Fund survey expedition to Sinai, Edom and Moab during the years 1868-1869. Haim Amzalak sent his son Joseph to Gaza in order to alert Palmer's contact there to the potential dangers of such a mission. Haim later claimed a reward from the Admiralty, which was refused because his actions were viewed as merely part of his duty. He then requested a medal for his son, or at least reimbursement for his expenses. In the end Consul Moore managed to secure a present for Haim's son.[287]

With regard to the manner in which he carried out his duties, evaluations range from "efficient" and "beyond the line of duty" to "incompetent." In 1889, Consul Noel Temple Moore wrote the following to Haim Amzalak:

> I have great satisfaction in forwarding to you herewith a Gold medal which Her Majesty's Government has been pleased to confer upon you, in recognition of special services rendered by you. I would at the same time express to you my sincere congratulations on receiving this honourable distinction which you have well merited by zeal and devotion you have displayed of your duties.[288] [see Plates 34a and 34b]

Consul Moore's replacement, John Dickson, felt that Haim Amzalak was unfit for the post of vice consul. He complained that it was necessary for him

286 CZA, Herzl Archives HVIII/496, in Eliav (supra n. 284), 2, document 202, pp. 389-391; CZA, Anglo-Palestine Bank Archives, L51/78, Joseph Ben-Zion Amzalak, Jaffa, to Anglo-Palestine Bank, Jaffa, October 19, 1913.

287 Tibawi (supra n. 270), pp. 146-147; Ben-Arieh (supra n. 102), pp. 206-207; *The Jewish Chronicle*, 817 (new series), November 21, 1884 (3 Kislev 5645), p. 12.

288 NLA, 4°1613/13, letter from Noel Temple Moore, British consul, Jerusalem, to Haim Amzalak, British vice consul, Jaffa, November 13, 1889.

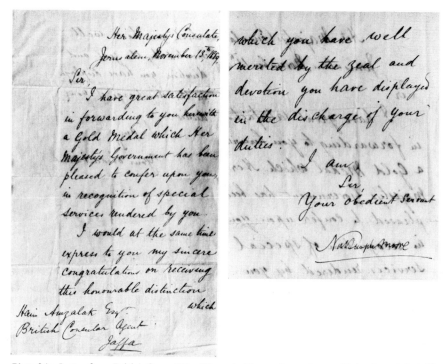

Plate 34a: Letter form British Consul Noel Temple Moore, Jerusalem, to Haim Amzalak, Jaffa, 13.11.1889;
(Source: Amzalak Family Archives, National Library Archives, Jerusalem, 4°1613/3)

Plate 34b: Gold Medal presented to Haim Amzalak. Front: For Gallantry and Humanity, From the British Government, Back: Victoria D:G: Britanniarum Regina F: D:, Side: Haim Amzalak 10th December 1874
(Source: Yael Amzalak Private Collection, Jerusalem)

to either correct or rewrite Amzalak's letters and to personally handle all British business in Jaffa. In 1891 John Dickson wrote the following to the Marquess of Salisbury:

> ...Urging his claims to allowance on account of duties connected with the Jaffa Consulate agency, where "Mr. Haim Amzalak, a Jew of Gibraltar origin, who was unacquainted with English" or French was Acting Vice Consul....[289]

Haim Amzalak ended his service as British vice consul in Jaffa in May 1903. He had always considered himself a loyal subject of the British Crown. The previous year he had sent a telegram of congratulations on the occasion of King Edward VII's coronation. During over thirty years of service he had never accepted any salary, maintaining that no financial remuneration was needed since his position was one of honor.[290]

During the following years he continued to take pride in England. He celebrated the coronation of King George V on June 22, 1911, together with members of the Anglo-Palestine Jews' Club and other British subjects, at the home of his son, Joseph Amzalak.[291]

With the outbreak of World War I in 1914, Haim Amzalak refused to renounce his British citizenship and was exiled to Egypt (see Chapter Six for further detail).[292]

Contribution to the Jewish Community

Haim Amzalak became a prominent figure in the Jewish community of Jaffa. His name was well known and respected by all and some of his acts of charity were publicized in newspapers. For example, on May 16, 1873, *Habazeleth* reported that Amzalak had arranged and financed passage aboard a European-bound British steamboat for a destitute Jew who had been stranded in Jaffa.[293]

The Jewish community of Jaffa began to organize itself in 1863, as Rabbi Yehuda HaLevi initiated the first public committee, called "*Va'ad Ha'Ir Yafo.*" Its first activity was to establish a branch of the Alliance Israélite Universelle,

---

289 PRO, F.O. 78/4367, letter from John Dickson, British consul, Jerusalem, to the Marquess of Salisbury, London, August 27, 1891 in Hyamson (supra n. 176), 1, p. 471.
290 CZA, Kא14/96/1; NLA, 4°1613/15, letter from the British Foreign Office, London, to Haim Amzalak, British vice consul, Jaffa, August 30, 1902.
291 Pinhas Grayevski, *From the Archives of Jerusalem*, 15, Jerusalem 1931, n.p. (Hebrew).
292 Tidhar (supra n. 183), 2, p. 816.
293 *Habazeleth*, vol. 3, no. 28, 19 Iyar 5633 (May 16, 1873), p. 107 (Hebrew).

with Haim Amzalak as its president. The committee later approached the Alliance Israélite Universelle, in Paris with the request that they open a school in Jaffa. On March 12, 1868, a boy's school was founded there.[294]

In 1868 the newspaper *HaMagid* reported that Sir Abraham Montefiore, while touring Jaffa, discovered that the Talmud Torah was housed in four different rented buildings spread all over the city. Calling the leaders of the Jewish community of Jaffa together, among them Haim Amzalak, he inquired as to why they hadn't constructed a structure to incorporate the scattered branches. Their reply was that they had tried but lacked the funds. Montefiore suggested that they attempt to request funds from abroad, and also donated £100 towards the £1,500 needed.[295]

With the increase of the Jewish population in Jaffa, particularly the Ashkenazi sector, as a result of the First *Aliyah* during the last two decades of the nineteenth century, the local leadership began to reorganize. Various societies were established by the Ashkenazi community, and in June 1890 the Ashkenazi Town Committee was elected. The Sephardi and North African communities were not included in this committee for various reasons. In March of the following year it was agreed to expand this committee so as to encompass all sectors of the Jewish community in Jaffa: Ashkenazim, Sephardim and North Africans. Fifty-three members of the Sephardi community, among them Haim Amzalak, his son Joseph and his nephew, Ben-Zion Amzalak, signed an agreement to join the committee. However, the unification of the communities existed only on paper; Sephardi leaders in Jerusalem opposed the appointment of the chief rabbi of Jaffa, and prevented the transfer of Sephardi community properties to the Jaffa committee. Disagreements broke out in the areas of ritual slaughter and burial. The Sephardi community generally felt disrespected and scorned by the Ashkenazim. As an expression of their sense of humiliation, Joseph Moyal, Haim Amzalak and Rabbi Joseph Ben-Nun refused to join the united Jewish committee of Jaffa. Only Aaron Chelouche served as a member, acting as the others' representative.[296]

---

294 Hannah Ram, *The Jewish Community in Jaffa from the Mid-Eighteenth Century until the First Years of the British Mandatory Rule*, Ph.D. thesis, Bar Ilan University, Ramat Gan 1982, p. 86 (Hebrew).

295 *HaMagid*, vol. 12, no. 27, 18 Tammuz 5628 (July 8, 1868), p. 211 (Hebrew).

296 Ram (supra n. 294), pp. 162-170; Ruth Kark, "Jaffa — The Social and Cultural Center of the New Jewish Settlement in Palestine," Lee I. Levine (ed.), *The Jerusalem Cathedra*, 3, Jerusalem 1983, pp. 213-218; HATAJM, (photostat in YIBZA, 4/2/5), Minutes of the Jewish Community Committee of Jaffa, 25, April 11, 1891. (The Historical Archives contain 102 minutes from the years 1890-1897).

Haim Amzalak's opposition to the committee caused much concern among its members, who hoped to win his support and to include him in their ranks. They appealed to him to reconsider, but he refused. Amzalak's opposition was sharpest with regard to transferring control of ritual slaughter to the united committee.[297]

In 1900, Rabbi Ya'akov Shaul Eliachar, the chief rabbi of Jerusalem, visited Jaffa. In the forefront of those welcoming him was Haim Amzalak, who accompanied the chief rabbi in his procession through the city until they reached the home of Ben-Zion Amzalak, where Rabbi Eliachar was to stay.[298]

Jewish Agricultural Settlement

Haim Amzalak played an active role in the development of the first Jewish agricultural settlements in Palestine, and had strong views on how this endeavor should be brought about. He was critical of the manner in which the Alliance Israélite Universelle operated the agricultural school at Mikveh Israel. The school building had been dedicated in 1870 on the outskirts of Jaffa. The purpose of the institution was to educate young Jews toward agricultural productivity in the field of agriculture. Although the rabbis of Jerusalem initially threatened the prospective students with excommunication, the director of the school, Charles Netter, managed to convince a number of families to register their children and brought a number of Jewish orphans from abroad to study there. Nevertheless, the school closed down shortly thereafter and in 1872 the Central Committee of the Alliance Israélite Universelle requested Haim Amzalak's aid in reopening it. In a letter to Charles Netter, Amzalak stated that he would be happy to help in the matter and would speak directly to Netter about it. The school reopened the following year.[299] [see Figure 6]

Yechiel Michael Pines, agent of the executive committee of the Sir Moses Montefiore Testimonial Fund, arrived in Jaffa on September 16, 1878. He visited Amzalak, who did not speak highly of the activities of the agricultural school attended at that time by about thirty pupils. Amzalak, having monitored

---

297 Minutes of the Jewish Community Committee of Jaffa (supra n. 296), 30, June 28, 1891; 31, July 5, 1891; 67, October 11, 1892, and 100, April 30, 1896; NLA, Ya'akov Shaul Eliachar Archives, 4°1271/248, letter from Haim Amzalak, Jaffa, to Nissim Hanoch and Yosef Moshe, Jaffa, 13 Iyar 5659, (April 17, 1899).

298 *Habazeleth*, vol. 30, no. 28, 5 Iyar 5660 (May 9, 1900), p. 210 (Hebrew).

299 CZA, Mikveh Israel Archives, J41/4, letter from Haim Amzalak, Jaffa, to Charles Netter, Mikveh Israel, February 28, 1872 (French).

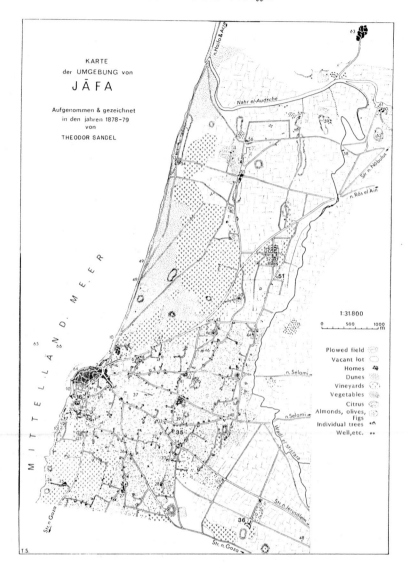

Figure 6: Jaffa and environs, 1878-1879
(Source: Theodor Sandel, *Karte der Umgebung von Jafa, 1878/9, 1:31,800*,
in G. Schwarz, "Jafa und Umgebung," *Zeitschrift des Deutschen Palästina
Vereins*, 3 (1880), op. p. 44)

16. Jewish cemetary   36. Mikveh Israel Agricultural School
35. [Esther] Amzalak's *bayara*   51. Sir Moses Montefiore's *bayara*

the situation for a number of years, declared that the project was unlikely to meet the founders' expectations. Pines agreed with Amzalak that the benefits derived from the school were limited relative to the sums which had been invested.[300]

On the other hand, Amzalak supported the activities of colonists in Petah Tikvah and later at Rishon LeZion. Petah Tikvah, known as the Mother of the Colonies, was first settled in 1878, four years before the First *Aliyah*. A group of Jews settled in Melabes, near the 'Auja [Yarkon] River, two months after the purchase of the land on July 21, 1878. The original settlers were seven in number, but after the purchase of a second plot of land twice as large as the first, they were joined by thirty-five families from Jerusalem. Several settlers died of malaria, and disputes broke out between the original seven and the later settlers. By winter of 1881, most of the settlers had left Petah Tikvah, and the rest were gone by the end of the following summer. This settlement underwent a revival in 1882, when several Jerusalemites returned, to be joined in the following year by immigrants from Hovevei Zion groups from the Bialystok area. The colony continued to grow during the following years.[301]

The extent of Haim Amzalak's involvement in the purchase of the land of Petah Tikvah is unclear, as two different sources present conflicting versions. His nephew Joseph Navon wrote that in 1876 he [Navon] had been approached by the future founders of Petah Tikvah, who asked for his aid in their search for land. After the unsuccessful attempts by these people to buy land in the vicinities of Hebron and Jericho, Navon met with his uncle and brought him up to date. Amzalak mentioned that land could be purchased near Jaffa. He later telegraphed an inquiry to the landowner, Antuan Bishara Tayan, a Christian Arab landowner from Jaffa, who replied affirmatively. Haim and Joseph proceeded to visit the land, but Tayan demanded too much for it.[302]

The settlers described the proceedings differently. In the summer of 1878, David Gutmann, Yoel Moshe Salomon, Yehoshua Stampfer, Zerach Barnett and other members of the Ashkenazi community in Jerusalem left the city to investigate the lands at Melabes in the vicinity of Jaffa. Upon their arrival there, they requested of Haim Amzalak to approach the owner, Tayan, in order to arrange for them to meet with him to see the lands. Amzalak readily complied. In the meanwhile, however, on July 30, 1878, an adjacent tract of land, 3,375

---

300 *HaMagid*, vol. 22, no. 15, May 17, 1879, p. 117 (Hebrew); *Jewish Chronicle*, 515 (new series), February 7, 1879 (14 Shevat 5639), p. 10.

301 Ran Aaronson, "Building the Land: Stages in the First Aliya Colonization (1882-1904)," Lee I. Levine (ed.), *The Jerusalem Cathedra*, 3, Jerusalem 1983, pp. 240-241.

302 Joseph Navon, "Quelques Precisions," *Le Renouveau*, 7, May 6, 1927, p. 2 (French).

Turkish dunams[303] (approximately 3,044 metric dunams) was purchased from
another Christian effendi from Jaffa, Selim Qassar. The following year the
settlers reached an agreement with Tayan, and around 10,000 Turkish dunams
(approximately 9,193 metric dunams) of his land were purchased in
installments. Some of these lands were registered under Amzalak's name.[304]

Haim Amzalak's involvement in the Jewish colonization of Palestine
increased with the efforts leading up to the founding of Rishon LeZion, another
of the first four settlements of the First *Aliyah* period. These were all established
by immigrants from Eastern Europe, some of them under the auspices of the
Hovevei Zion societies, along with individuals who came on their own
initiative. On March 19, 1882 a society called the *Va'ad Halutzei Yesod
HaMa'ala* (the avant-garde committee for the colonization of Palestine) under
the leadership of Zalman David Levontin, with Haim Amzalak as its honorary
president, was founded with the purpose of advising the new settlers. Amzalak
contributed to the society financially, and exerted his influence to advance it.[305]
[see Plate 35]

Haim Amzalak thought that the new Jewish settlements would benefit if they
were under the protection of the British government. He recommended to
Zalman David Levontin that letters be sent to certain places in London to
further this idea.[306]

When Zalman David Levontin arrived in Jaffa in 1882, a letter from
Hamburg was waiting for him, sent by Laurence Oliphant while he was en route
to Constantinople. Oliphant wrote that he was hopeful of soliciting Ottoman
support for Jewish settlement in Palestine, but that he had insufficient
information at his disposal regarding the activities of the *Va'ad Halutzei Yesod*

---

303 One Turkish dunam equals 0.9193 metric dunams or 919.3 square meters.

304 *Jubilee Book, Fifty Years to the Founding of Petah Tikvah 5638-5688*, Tel Aviv 1929,
   pp .15-18 (Hebrew); Avraham Yaari, *The Goodly Heritage*, Jerusalem 1958, pp. 79-88;
   Rami Yizre'el, "On the Historiographical Investigation of the First Years of Petah
   Tiqva," *Cathedra*, 9 (October 1978), p. 194, footnote 70 (Hebrew); Dan Gileadi, "Rishon
   LeZion under the Tutelage of the Baron Rothschild (1882-1900)," *Cathedra*, 9 (October
   1978), pp. 128, 133 (Hebrew).

305 Zalman David Levontin, *To the Land of Our Fathers*, Tel Aviv 1934, pp. 47-48 (Hebrew);
   Aaronson (supra n. 301), pp. 238-239; *Habazeleth*, vol. 22, no. 29, May 21, 1882, p. 229
   (Hebrew); *Jewish Chronicle*, 682, April 21, 1882 (2 Iyar 5642), p. 10; Shulamit Laskov
   (ed.) of Alter Druyanov's, *Documents on the History of Hibbat-Zion and the Settlement
   of Eretz Yisrael*, Tel Aviv 1982, 1, document 58: Regulations of *the Va'ad Halutzei Yesod
   HaMa'ala* in Jaffa, May 4, 1882, pp. 238-243 (Hebrew).

306 Laskov (supra n. 305), 1, document 41, letter from Zalman David Levontin, Jaffa, to
   Peretz Smolanskin, editor of *HaShachar*, March 19, 1882, p. 190.

Plate 35: Front page of the *Halebanon*
announcing the founding of *Va'ad Halutzei Yesod HaMa'ala*, May 18, 1882

HaMa'ala. He asked of Levontin that a member of this society meet him in Constantinople in order to brief him. Entertaining great expectations from Oliphant, the committee sent their most distinguished member, Haim Amzalak. On May 18, 1882, Amzalak set sail for Constantinople, where he met with Oliphant to advise him of lands possibly available for settlement. However, the political struggle between Britain and Turkey over Egypt later curtailed Oliphant's mission, making Amzalak's journey fruitless.[307]

Amzalak was involved in the purchase of the land of Rishon LeZion. Avraham Yaari wrote that " Levontin and his friends secured the help of Yosef Navon, a Sephardi Jew in Jerusalem and Chaim [sic] Amzalak to deal with the prospective Arab vendors on their behalf since they were unfamiliar with the intricacies of buying land in Palestine."[308]

Haim Amzalak purchased some of the tracts himself, while serving as an intermediary for other buyers. These transactions were nearly completed when the Ottoman authorities imposed a ban on settlement by foreign Jews. This edict was circumvented through the aid of Haim Amzalak, who purchased the lands of 'Ein Kara [later Rishon LeZion] from Mustafa Musa 'Abdellah 'Ali Dagan, and gave the settlers unofficial deeds in Hebrew. After the completion of the transaction, the Ottoman authorities made it difficult for the settlers to attain construction permits, but nevertheless, they looked the other way until the building was completed for fear of any unpleasantness with the British vice consul. Although the lands of Rishon LeZion were registered in Haim Amzalak's name, he signed a declaration that all the structures and houses on the land had never belonged to him. The settlers were indebted to Amzalak and thanked him and his nephew in an open letter published in *Habazeleth* in 1883.[309] [see Figure 7]

Sir Moses Montefiore

Haim, like his father Joseph before him, developed a special relationship with Sir Moses Montefiore. When Montefiore visited Palestine in 1875 he was

---

307 Levontin (supra n. 305), pp. 47-48; *Habazeleth*, vol. 22, no. 39, August 14, 1882, p. 302; *Habazeleth*, vol. 22, no. 40, August 25, 1882, p. 310 (Hebrew); *Jewish Chronicle*, 687, May 26, 1882 (8 Sivan 5642), pp. 5-6: *Halebanon*, vol. 19, no. 18, 29 Iyar 5642 (May 18, 1882), p. 137 (Hebrew); CZA, Zalman David Levontin Archives, A34/2/29, letter from Zalman David Levontin, Jaffa, to Yehiel Joseph Levontin, Moscow, May 7, 1882, in Laskov (supra n. 305), 1, document 61, pp. 248-249.

308 Yaari (supra n. 304), p. 113.

309 CZA, David Yodelovitz Archives, A/192/217/2ℵ, in Eliav (supra n. 284), 2, pp. 31-32, document 13; Yaari (supra n. 304), pp. 113-114; *Habazeleth*, 12, 3 Sivan 5643 (June 8, 1883), p. 162 (Hebrew); Eliachar (supra n. 222), pp. 668-669, footnote 7; *Halebanon*, vol. 19, no. 31, 2 Elul 5642 (August 17, 1882), p. 247 (Hebrew); CZA, Jewish Colonization Association, J15/7118, written declaration by Haim Amzalak, July 30, 1883 (Hebrew and French).

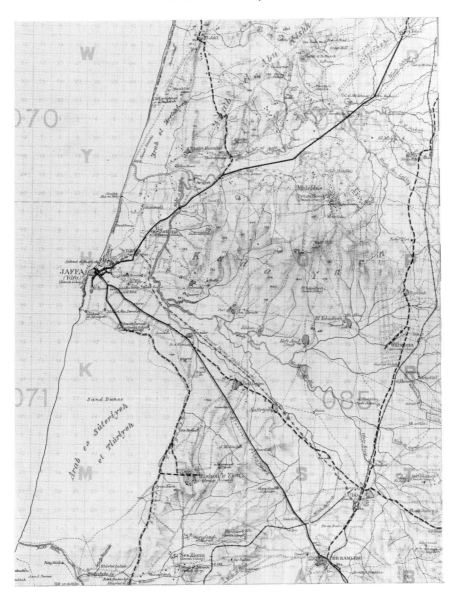

Figure 7: Jaffa and the surrounding Jewish Colonies, 1918
(Source: Survey of Egypt, *Palestine*, 1:63,360, Sheet XVI, 1918)

Plate 36: Sir Moses
Montefiore
(Source: Yad Yitzhak
Ben Zvi Archives,
Jerusalem)

greeted at the port of Jaffa by Haim Amzalak. Montefiore stayed at the Amzalak home while in the Jaffa region, and was accompanied by Haim on various journeys in the environs. [see Plate 36]

On July 13, 1875 it was arranged that Sir Moses, accompanied by his entourage and English vice consul Haim Amzalak, would conduct a complete inspection of his *bayara*, known as Pardes Montefiore. Montefiore had purchased this orchard near Jaffa in 1855, during his fourth visit to Palestine, in order to help the Jewish community of the city. On each of his following visits he inspected the *bayara*. In 1866 he had found it in ruins, and during the following years he increased his investment in this agricultural land. In the summer of 1868, five families were settled in the *bayara* to protect and maintain it, and it remained inhabited until after Montefiore's death. One informant, Jacob Rimon, wrote that in 1875 Montefiore left a budget for the cultivation and upkeep of the *bayara* in the hands of Haim Amzalak, until such time as the land would show a profit.[310]

After Montefiore left the country, and even after his death in 1885, Haim Amzalak and his son Joseph continued to take an interest in this property. The *bayara* was leased to the Alliance Israélite Universelle by Montefiore's heirs, and in 1895, as part of his consular duties, Haim Amzalak helped Nissim Bechar, Haim Aaron Valero, Serapion J. Murad and Joseph Niego, representatives of the Holy Land Relief Fund, to purchase it. These dignitaries praised Amzalak "for not sparing any effort in executing this most complex task."[311]

But before leaving Palestine in 1875, Moses Montefiore wrote to Haim Amzalak, thanking him and his family for their hospitality:

> I cannot, before leaving your hospitable roof, refrain from expressing my sincere thanks for the kind reception you and Mrs. Amzalag [sic] have given me and my party on the arrival in this town. Be assured that I fully appreciate the great attention you and your amiable family paid us to make our stay here as comfortable as we possibly could wish to be, and I shall always be glad to see yourself and Mrs. Amzalag, or any other of your family whenever you come to England. With kind regards to Mrs. Amzalag of whom I beg to do me the favour of procuring for the enclosed a little souvenir.[312]

After Montefiore's return to England, he and the Amzalaks corresponded. In a letter dated December 18, 1875 Montefiore once again thanked the Amzalaks. He also sent them a copy of his *Narrative of a Forty Days' Sojourn in the Holy Land*, and a music box for their daughter.[313]

In the following years Haim Amzalak served as a representative of Montefiore's interests in Palestine. In a letter dated February 22, 1876

---

310 Loewe (supra n. 152), 2, p. 275; Shoshana Halevi, "The Montefiore Orange Grove," *Cathedra*, 2 (November 1976), pp. 153-167 (Hebrew); Jacob Rimon, "Montefiore Neighbourhood," Pinhas Ben-Zion Grayevski (ed.), *From the Archives of Jerusalem*, 24, Jerusalem 1932, n.p., (Hebrew); Chelouche (supra n. 260), pp. 29-30.

311 AFP, letter from Joseph Sebag Montefiore, Ramsgate, to Joseph Amzalak, Jaffa, March 23, 1894; ISA, 123-1 J22/9 787, letter from Nessim Bechar, Haim Aaron Valero, Serapion J. Murad and Joseph Niego, Jaffa, to Haim Amzalak, Jaffa, April 25, 1895 (French).

312 NLA, 4°1613/6, letter from Sir Moses Montefiore, Jaffa, to Haim Amzalak, Jaffa, July 21, 1875.

313 NLA, 4°1613/7, letter from Sir Moses Montefiore, Ramsgate, England, to Haim Amzalak, Jaffa, December 18, 1875; NLA, 4°1613/8 letter from Sir Moses Montefiore, London, to Haim Amzalak, Jaffa, January 27, 1876.

Montefiore thanked Haim Amzalak for conveying to him information on the safe arrival of pumps in Jerusalem, which were among the first ones imported to Palestine. Montefiore noted that Amzalak had omitted an account of expenses the latter had incurred for the transport of the pumps.[314]

As part of their continuing relationship, Haim Amzalak occasionally sent Montefiore oranges. This gesture pleased Montefiore, who wrote the following response:

> I have to thank you for your kind letter and the oranges you were pleased to send me. They much reminded me of the happy days I spent in the Holy Land, and induced many of my friends among whom I distributed a portion of the goodly fruit, to express a desire of going to the Land in which you have the privilege of being permitted to dwell in peace and comfort.[315]

Their relationship developed to the point where the Amzalaks felt at ease in enlisting Montefiore's aid in obtaining a piano. It would appear that in the end Montefiore gave their daughter Bolissa the piano as an outright gift.[316] Bolissa thanked Montefiore for the present in a later letter, in which she used the term of endearment "grandpapa" for Montefiore. This demonstration of familiarity touched off a sensitive nerve in Montefiore's secretary, N. Johnson, and possibly in Montefiore himself. Moses and Judith Montefiore had had no children, and rumors abounded that Montefiore had fathered an illegitimate child. Such rumors were of course denied. This being the case, Montefiore's secretary wrote the following to Bolissa Amzalak:

> I am instructed by Sir Moses Montefiore, who I regret to say is somewhat indisposed, to thank you for your letter informing him of the safe arrival of the "piano" which he had the pleasure of presenting to you. Sir Moses

---

314 Letter from Sir Moses Montefiore, London, to Haim Amzalak, Jaffa, February 22, 1877, in Pinhas Ben-Zion Grayevski, *From the Archives of Jerusalem*, 8, Jerusalem 1930, p. 7 (Hebrew).

315 Letter from Sir Moses Montefiore, Ramsgate, England to Haim Amzalak, Jaffa, April 24, 1876 in Grayevski (supra n. 314), pp. 6-7.

316 NLA, 4°1613/9, letter from Sir Moses Montefiore, Ramsgate, England, to Bolissa Amzalak, Jaffa, September 9, 1878, "I have much pleasure in handing you enclosed a Bill of Lading relative to the Piano which you requested me to procure for you ['in compliance with your request' is crossed out]. I beg you will accept the same as a token of regard for your dear parents and yourself. I shall be glad to hear of its safe arrival in Jaffa and that you were pleased with the choice of the instrument which has been made by a very able Pianist. Hoping your dear parents, yourself and the rest of the family are in enjoyment of health."

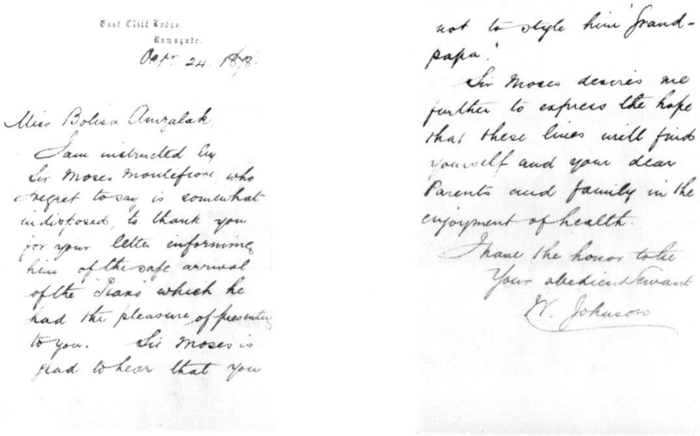

Plate 37: Section of a letter from Sir Moses Montefiore's Secretary, N. Johnson,
Ramsgate, to Bolissa Amzalak, Jaffa, October 24, 1878
(Source: Amzalak Family Archives, National Library Archives, Jerusalem, 4°1613/3)

Plate 38: Envelope to Haim Amzalak, Jaffa from Sir Moses Montefiore, Ramsgate
(Source: Amzalak Family Archives, National Library Archives, Jerusalem, 4°1613/3)

is glad to hear that you like it, and approve of the instrument chosen for
your acceptance, — but he begs me to call your attention to the
appellation of "grand-papa" by which you addressed him. Sir Moses not
having any children can naturally not be the grandfather of you or any
other person in the world. You will therefore have the goodness in future
not to style him grand-papa. Sir Moses desires me further to express the
hope that these lines will find yourself and your dear Parents and family
in the enjoyment of health.[317] [see Plates 37 and 38]

317 NLA, 4°1613/11, letter from N. Johnson, Ramsgate, England, to Bolissa Amzalak, Jaffa,
     October 24, 1878.

Summary

After taking up residence in Jaffa, Haim Amzalak rose in both rank and prominence. He expanded his entrepreneurial activities from the prior small-scale land investment in Jerusalem, to banking, international import–export trade, and land investment and development, particularly orange grove cultivation. Foremost among many achievements was his appointment as British vice consul for the port city. This position required an astute understanding of the financial and commercial activities of the city and its hinterland, which Amzalak had proven to have. The appointment entailed regular contact with members of the local government and with other foreign consular representatives. Furthermore, this position enhanced his status in the local community, creating and strengthening connections with Muslim, Christian and Jewish notables as well as foreigners either residing or visiting in Jaffa.

Within the Jewish community he was well respected and admired as one of their principal leaders. His opinion was carefully considered in any of their decisions.

Haim Amzalak not only possessed an awareness of the contemporary economic and political climate but also had a vision of a Jewish return to and settlement of Zion. On different occasions he met with distinguished promoters of this cause, such as Sir Moses Montefiore, Laurence Oliphant and William Hechler, with whom he shared certain views. Using his influence in the Jaffa region, he attempted to realise this vision. He facilitated the purchase of land for new neighborhoods outside the walls of Jaffa and for Jewish agricultural colonies in its environs. Amzalak also extended his patronage to some of these infant colonies, using his vice consular status to circumvent the hindrances placed before them by the local authorities. As vice consul, he exercised every possible means at his disposal to lift or relax Ottoman restrictions on Jewish immigration to Palestine.

Despite his insight and foresight, in his later years Haim Amzalak was relegated to the sidelines of the business world. With the increased expansion of foreign companies into the local market at the turn of the century, the scope of Amzalak's activities decreased.

Within the Jewish community, the rapid growth of the new Ashkenazi population broke the hegemony of the Sephardi leadership in the 1890s. Amzalak's position of prominence at that point began to decline rapidly. Similarly, his role in the Zionist movement declined with growing influence and domination of its European membership after the first Zionist Congress at Basel in 1897.

Amzalak's contribution to the infant Jewish agricultural settlements likewise diminished, having been eclipsed by the extensive philanthropic patronage of the Baron Edmond de Rothschild. Different Jewish settlement organizations established their own representation in Palestine and were no longer in need of Amzalak's services. Amzalak's significant role on the local scene was overshadowed by the aspirations of political Zionists who sought the large-scale resettlement of Eretz Israel.

The changes and advances of the twentieth century appeared to have passed Amzalak by. He was steeped in traditional values that were quickly disappearing before his very eyes. Nonetheless, he understood the potential of the next generation and prepared for the future by investing in the advancement of his son Joseph and his nephews Joseph Navon and Ben-Zion Amzalak — his future heirs.

Haim Amzalak's last days were spent in a bittersweet exile. On the one hand, he was away from him home in Jaffa — a city in whose development he had been instrumental. On the other hand, he was in the company of his family in Alexandria — living out his last days with them under British rule.

CHAPTER FIVE

THE AMZALAKS — THIRD GENERATION

The third generation of the Amzalak family was divided between two principal centers of Jewish settlement in Palestine during the late Ottoman period — Jerusalem, the bastion of the Old *Yishuv* and Jaffa, the rising administrative, cultural and social center of the New *Yishuv*. Of the many members of the family three were prominent in their business activities and their contributions to society: Joseph Ben-Zion Amzalak, Ben-Zion Amzalak and Joseph Navon Bey. These three fostered the interaction between the Old and New *Yishuv* in the respective cities. Each of these individuals left his respective imprint on the Jewish community in Palestine and the development of the economy and landscape of the region. This chapter will focus on these three personages and their activities in Palestine.

Joseph Ben-Zion Amzalak (1860-1944)

Joseph Ben-Zion Amzalak was born to Haim Amzalak and Esther Levi in Jaffa, in 1860. Little information has been found about his childhood or youth. He received both a traditional and a general education. As a young man he worked as an apprentice at his father's side in the field of international trade, and later rose to be one of the most respectable merchants in Jaffa. As a loyal British subject, on certain occasions he helped his father, the vice consul, in his duties. Joseph was also a prominent figure in the Jewish community and promoted Zionist aspirations, while simultaneously enjoying amicable relations with Arab residents of the region. [see Plate 39]

He married Oro, the daughter of Yehuda Asseo, and they had six children: Amanda, who died in her youth, Meir Haim (Henry), Sarina, Leon, Gentil (Naomi), Simon Mark and Eliyahu. After the death of his wife in 1926, he was remarried to a woman from Turkey. He and his family at first resided in Jaffa, but with the founding of the new neighborhood of Neve Tzedek outside the Old City walls, they moved to one of his two houses there. A wall surrounded the gardens and fountain of his residence. The entrance to the compound was

148

Plate 39: Joseph B. Amzalak
(Source: Simon Amzalak
Family Papers, Jerusalem)

Plate 40 : Amzalak House in Neve Tzedek, Jaffa, view from the rear, 1990
(Source: Courtesy of Sarit Danziger, 1990)

adorned with a monumental ironwork gate. In addition to the luxurious one-storey house, there were two additional structures: the servants' quarters and a synagogue.[318] [see Plate 40 and Figure 8]

318 Tidhar (supra n. 183), 4, p. 1467; AFP, passport issued to Joseph Amzalak, Jerusalem, October 2, 1882; Interview with Golda Amzalak conducted by Joseph Glass, Jerusalem, November 4, 1989; PRO, F.O. 617/3, Births within the District of the British Consulate at Jerusalem entry no. 80, Meyer Haim Amzalak, born June 30, 1886 in Jerusalem [and Simon Mark Amzalak, born March 10, 1898 in Jaffa] to Joseph Ben-Zion Amzalak and Oro Asseo.

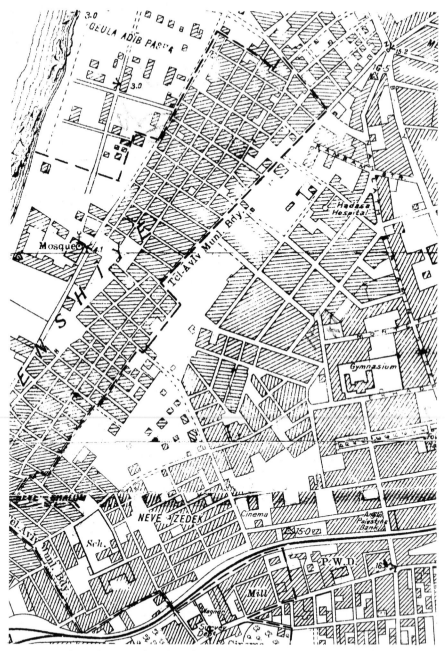

Figure 8: The residential neighborhoods to the north of Jaffa, 1925
(Source: Survey of Palestine, *Jaffa, Tel-Aviv and Environs*, 1:7,500, Jaffa, June 1925)

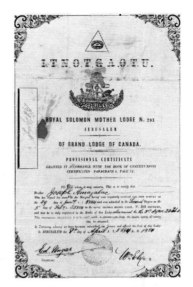

Plate 41: Royal Solomon Mother
Lodge, Jerusalem provisional certif-
icate given to Joseph Amzalak, April
8, 1884
(Source: Simon Amzalak Family
Papers, Jerusalem)

Joseph Amzalak was a member of the Freemasons. This secret society from
the seventeenth century had developed into a social organization which
cultivated a tradition of doctrines, passwords, symbols and ritual supposedly
derived from the building of the First Temple of Jerusalem. Organized masonic
activities in Palestine were begun in 1868. For the first time in centuries
Freemasons — visitors and residents in Jerusalem — congregated in the long-
abandoned Solomon's Quarries (Zedekiah's Cave), masonic utterances
breaking the silence that usually prevailed there. Notable among their members
in Palestine at the time were Heinrich Julius Petermann, Prussian consul at
Jerusalem, Charles Warren, noted archaeologist, Richard Beardsley, United
States consul in Jerusalem, Rolla Floyd, American-born travel agent and
Noureddin Effendi, *kaymakam* of Jaffa, all of which points to prominence of
Freemasons in local society. The first regular lodge in Palestine, the Royal
Solomon Mother Lodge, was founded in Jerusalem in May 1873, under the
jurisdiction of the Grand Lodge of Canada. Amzalak was admitted into its ranks
in 1884. In 1891, another lodge was established in Jaffa under the National
Grand Lodge of Egypt, and Joseph Amzalak became a member of this one too
in 1892.[319] [see Plate 41]

319 AFP, membership certificate dated April 8, 1884; membership certificate dated June 5,
    1884; membership certificate dated April 12, 1892; Abraham Fellman, "Freemasons in
    Israel," *Encylopaedia Judaica*, 7, Jerusalem 1973, pp. 124-125; Robert Morris,
    Freemasonry in the Holy Land or, Handmarks of Hiram's Builders, New York 1872,
    pp. 461-481.

Plate 42: Transportation of goods from the port of Jaffa to ships anchored off shore
(Source: D. Hermann Guthe, *Land und Lente Palästina*, Bielfeld und Leipzig 1908,
p. 127)

As a merchant, he, like his father, established trade relations in other provinces of the Ottoman Empire and many foreign countries. In 1878, Amzalak founded a commercial company for the exportation of wheat, barley, durra, sesame, olive oil, wool and other produce. That same year, he initiated the export of oranges to the United Kingdom, and his memoirs describe his involvement in this line. Years earlier, at the age of seven or eight, he would stroll with his father in the orchards around Jaffa, observing the inefficient manner in which the oranges were marketed. In 1876 he watched an attempt by Italian merchants to modernize the exporting process by the removing the fruit from the trees with scissors and wrapping it in tissue paper. Unfortunately, the Italian initiative failed because the produce remained in the ship's hold for too long and rotted. Amzalak learned from their experience and improved the management of consignments that he later exported.[320] [see Plate 42]

In 1902 he proposed a new and innovative idea for the marketing of oranges from the Jewish moshavot directly to merchants abroad. At that time the total export of oranges reached approximately half a million crates, or one third the value of all exports from the port of Jaffa. The contribution of Jewish agriculturalists was around one quarter of the volume of this trade.[321] He also

320 AFP, Memoirs of Joseph Amzalak, 1935, pp. 27-28 (Ladino).
321 Gross (supra n. 1), pp. 124-125; Owen (supra n. 13), p. 265.

hoped to interest the Hovevei Zion Association in London in this project, but they ruled that it was outside their scope.[322] The proposal, however, was quickly accepted by others, and brought much benefit and profit to the orange growers. Until then the orange trade had been entirely in the hands of Arab merchants. The produce had been sold to these merchants at very low prices and the terms of payment were greatly disadvantageous to the Jewish citrus growers.[323]

During the following years he expanded his areas of activity. In 1909 he informed the Achuzat Bayit Company, an organization for the construction of a modern Jewish garden suburb in Jaffa (which in fact became the core of the first Hebrew city in Palestine: Tel Aviv) that he had opened a store for building supplies and would be able to furnish lumber, roof tiles, bricks, lime, cement, pipes and metal of all types, iron in every dimension and tempered steel girders. The following year the Achuzat Bayit Company used his services.[324]

For twenty-five years Joseph Amzalak served as the surveyor of Lloyd's agency under his father. Haim Amzalak wrote that his son "has always fulfilled his duties in doing his upmost to secure the interests of the underwriters."[325] Once Haim Amzalak retired from his position as the agent for the British Lloyd's in 1911, his son Joseph took over for him. Similarly, after Joseph retired in 1937 the Lloyd's Agency was taken over by his son Simon Mark until the latter's death in 1956.[326]

Between the years 1899 to 1902, Joseph attempted to become the agent for the Jewish Colonial Trust in Jaffa. It appears that he had made a good impression on William Henry Hechler, whom he had met in 1898. He had hoped that Hechler, who was on intimate terms with Theodore Herzl, could help him in this pursuit. In 1899, Hechler wrote the following to Amzalak:

322 CZA, Chovevei Zion of England Archives, K11/39, letter from N. Bloomfield, Secretary of the Junior Zionist Association, Cadet Tent of the Chobebi [sic] Zion Association, London, to Joseph Amzalak, Jaffa, February 24, 1902.

323 AFP, letter from Haim Amzalak, Jaffa, to Edward Inglefield, London, September 19, 1911.

324 AFP, letter from J.B. Amzalak, Jaffa, to Mourad Yayon, Beirut, November 1, 1878; TAJMA, RG 1 file 40, letter from J.B. Amzalak, Jaffa, to Achuzat Bayit Company, Jaffa, 24 Adar 5669 (March 17, 1909); RG 1 file 89א, invoice from J.B. Amzalak, Jaffa, to Achuzat Bayit, Jaffa, May 17, 1910, for the supply of girders and pipes to Achuzat Bayit between November 22, 1909 and January 28, 1910; RG 1 file 89א, letter from J.B. Amzalak, Jaffa, to Meir Dizengoff, Jaffa, December 20, 1910.

325 Tidhar (supra n. 183), 4, p. 1467; Gaon (supra n. 39), 2, p. 107.

326 Tidhar (supra n. 183), 4, p. 1467; Gaon (supra n. 39), 2, p. 107; Interview with Yael Amzalak conducted by Joseph Glass, Jerusalem, September 26, 1989; Interview with James Amzalak (supra n. 252).

I have been to see Dr. H[erzl] on your behalf and read him your letter. He fully agrees with me....Dr. H[erzl] has nothing to do with the appointment for the bank; but as soon as you hear that it is started and that agents are wanted in Palestine; then write to the bank authorities, and refer them to Dr. H[erzl] and to me; but write to me stating you have done so that we know what to say and do.[327]

Once a decision was made to establish a subsidiary company of the Jewish Colonial Trust, it was only natural for Joseph Amzalak to apply to be their agent in Jaffa. On January 2, 1902 he wrote to this company, telling of his experience in the financial world and of the high esteem in which he was held by the British government. He forwarded letters of reference from the former British consul, Noel Temple Moore, and the British consul then in office, John Dickson. He also gave references from William Henry Hechler and Garcia Jacobs and Company, London. Joseph Amzalak was not appointed their agent. On July 21, 1903, the Anglo-Palestine Bank, the Jewish Colonial Trust's subsidary company, was opened in Jaffa with Zalman David Levontin as its manager.[328]

Joseph, like his father Haim, supported the early attempts at Jewish agricultural colonization of Palestine. He was a member of *Va'ad Halutzei Yesod HaMa'ala*, serving as its treasurer.[329]

Joseph Amzalak assisted his father in the latter's consular duties. For a period of about twenty-six years, Joseph was a clerk in the consular agency and on several occasions served as acting consular agent in his father's place. In 1901, with the approval of the consul in Jerusalem, Joseph was appointed a British assessor for the newly constituted Commercial Tribunal at Jaffa. The tribunal dealt with cases arising throughout the whole of Palestine. His responsibilities were "to attend to every sitting of the tribunal whenever required, either for hearing, rehearing, trial and decision of cases when concerning any British subject, British naturalized and protected person."[330] [see Plate 43]

Among the earlier incidents in his life was the mission in 1882 on behalf of his father to relay a message to Professor Edward H. Palmer, whom he was to

327 CZA, Joseph Ben-Zion Amzalak Archives, K11/39, letter from William H. Hechler, Vienna to Joseph Ben-Zion Amzalak, Jaffa, January 10, 1899.
328 CZA, Zalman David Levontin Archives, A34/21/6, letter from Joseph Ben-Zion Amzalak, Jaffa to the Jewish Colonial Trust, London, January 2, 1902.
329 *Habazeleth*, vol. 22, no. 29, May 21, 1882, p. 229; *Habazeleth*, vol. 22, no. 40, August 25, 1882, p. 310 (Hebrew).
330 AFP, letter of certification from Haim Amzalak, British vice consul, Jaffa, January 2, 1902; letter from Haim Amzalak, British vice consul, Jaffa, to Joseph Amzalak, Jaffa, December 1, 1901.

Plate 43: Laissez Passer to Joseph
Amzalak, October 2, 1882
(Source: Simon Amzalak Family
Papers, Jerusalem)

meet in Gaza, the gateway from Palestine to the Sinai Peninsula. Joseph's actions would place him in danger, since he was supporting British political and military aspirations in a region under Ottoman rule. As previously mentioned, Palmer was in Sinai at the same time in the service of the British Admiralty, attempting to persuade the Bedouin to remain neutral during the British occupation of Egypt. Upon hearing of the British bombardment of Alexandria, Haim Amzalak sent his son to warn Professor Palmer of the danger of anti-British backlash among local Arabs. Joseph, who was privy to Palmer's plans, was to assist the professor in any possible manner. Joseph and a *kavass* named Achmed, both disguised as Bedouin, rode to Gaza, arriving there before Palmer. Joseph enlisted the aid of an English clergyman named Shapira who was living in Gaza. Shapira provided Amzalak with information on the political climate

Plate 44: Professor Edward H. Palmer
(Source: Yehoshua Ben-Arieh, *The Rediscovery of the Holy Land*,
Jerusalem 1983, p. 207)

there. The local population was outraged by the British attack on Egypt and feared a similar action against Gaza. While awaiting Palmer's arrival, Amzalak engaged ten camels and contacted friendly Bedouin to accompany Palmer. Once Palmer arrived he was warned of the hostility toward the British harbored by the local populace. Amzalak suggested that Palmer slip out of the city in the darkness of night so as to avoid any additional risks. Palmer did so and succeeded in crossing the Sinai into Egypt, but on a later expedition into the Sinai, Palmer and his companions were killed.[331] [see Plate 44]

331 AFP, Memoirs of Joseph Amzalak, 1935, pp. 1-10 (Ladino); Tibawi (supra n. 270), pp. 146-147; Ben-Arieh (supra n. 102), pp. 206-207.

Joseph Amzalak fled from Gaza immediately after completing his mission. Fortunately for Joseph the *kaymakam* of Gaza was not in the city at the time. As soon as the *kaymakam* was informed of Joseph's presence he dispatched soldiers to arrest him. By quickly riding off to Jaffa along the seashore, thus avoiding the main road, Joseph and his companion alluded their pursuers.[332]

The English government wanted to reward Joseph Amzalak with £500. Amzalak flatly refused this reward, claiming that he had acted for his country and not for monetary gain. He was eventually rewarded by the Earl of Granville, on behalf of the British government, with a gold medal on which was inscribed, "presented to Mr. J. Amzalak by the H.M. Government, 1884."[333]

In 1882, Joseph met with Prince George and Prince Albert Victor of England. Their father, then the Prince of Wales (afterwards Edward VII), had decided that naval training would best prepare his sons for their future responsibilities, although their grandmother, Queen Victoria, agreed only with reluctance. When George was twelve, he and his elder brother Albert joined the training ship *Britannia* as naval cadets. The two brothers served on the *H.M.S. Bacchante* from 1879 to 1882, their service including a cruise around the world. On March 28, 1882, they reached the port of Jaffa and then made their way on horseback through the Holy Land. Over a period of six weeks they covered more than 960 kilometers.[334] Joseph Amzalak made their acquaintance, which he recalled at the 1911 celebration in Jaffa of the coronation of King George V:

> Mr. Amzalak then narrated one of the pleasantest recollections of his life, viz. that in April 1882, he went on board H.M.S. Bacchante to meet King George (then Prince George) and his brother the late Prince Albert on their visit to Palestine. As representative of his father who was then the British Consular Agent, he accompanied the young Princes on horseback as far as Beth-Dajan, a historical village at a short distance from Mikveh Israel.[335]

In 1892 Joseph was again rewarded by the British government for services rendered. During the winter of that year, an English steamship, the *Drewton of*

---

332 AFP, Memoirs of Joseph Amzalak, 1935, pp. 1-10 (Ladino).
333 AFP, Memoirs of Joseph Amzalak, 1935, p. 11 (Ladino); *Jewish Chronicle*, 817 (new series), November 21, 1884 (3 Kislev 5645) p. 12; *Habazeleth*, vol. 15, no. 4, 19 Heshvan 5645 (November 7, 1884) p. 28 (Hebrew).
334 Owen Morshead, "George V," L.G. Wickham (ed.), *The Dictionary of National Biography, 1931-1940*, (supplement 5), London 1949, pp. 314-315.
335 *The Truth* (supra n. 277).

Hull, was wrecked off the coast of Jaffa and ran aground on the rocks. In a concerted effort, Joseph successfully helped rescue many of its sailors, who later sent him a letter of gratitude.

> I John Bammant, Master of the s/s Drewton of Hull which stranded at Jaffa during a storm on November 25th hereby on behalf of myself and the under-signed members of my crew do heartly [sic] thanks to Mr. Joseph B. Amzalak for his untiring efforts to render assistance on that date he being constantly on the beach encouraging the native boatmen for several hours amid heavy rain and spray untill [sic] the last twelve of the crew were ultimately rescued by a native boat engaged by the said Mr. Joseph Amzalak; There is no doubt that without his assistance we should have had great danger in reaching the shore and possibly some lives might have been lost.[336]

Joseph Amzalak and Jacob Hayat, the interpreter of the British consular agency at Jaffa, were each given a plate in recognition of their services to the shipwrecked crew. The inscription on Amzalak's ran as follows: "To Joseph Amzalak, in recognition of his humanitarianism and good heart."[337]

In May 1907 a number of Jews from Jaffa and from English-speaking countries founded the Anglo-Palestine Jews' Club, with Joseph Amzalak as its president. Among its founding members were, Joel Reznek, Mr. Eleorson and Samuel Frumkin from South Africa, the latter a vigorous and educated youth; Moses Menachem Levene, the secretary of the club and an immigrant from England; and Solomon Wainer from Leeds. Besides being a social club, it also sought to facilitate the absorption of immigrants from English-speaking countries. One step in this direction was the founding of a moshavah (settlement) in the Negev for former Englishmen and subjects of the Dominions. The initiators of this project assumed that as British subjects the future settlers would be exempt from Turkish edicts against the purchase of land by Jews, and that since the new settlement was near the Gazan border it would benefit from British protection.[338]

336 AFP, letter from John Bammant, Master of the Drewton of Hull, Jaffa to Joseph Amzalak, n.p., November 27, 1892.

337 AFP, letter from John Dickson, British consul, Jerusalem, to Haim Amzalak, British vice consul, Jaffa, June 27, 1893; *HaMagid LeYisrael*, vol. 2, no. 9, 11 Tishrai 5654 (September 21, 1893); see also Tidhar (supra n. 183), 4, p. 1467 and Goan (supra n. 39), 2, p. 107.

338 Mordechai Eliav, "The Rafah Approaches (Pithat-Rafiah) in the History of Jewish Settlement," *Cathedra*, 3 (February 1977), p. 128 (Hebrew); letter to the Editor of the *Jewish Chronicle*, from Moses Levene, May 12, 1911 in response to an article from April 7, 1911, in Eliav (supra), pp. 182-184.

The club members were described in the newspaper *HaTzfirah* as pleasant and honest gentlemen who appeared to exaggerate the importance of their British nationality. The author of the article asserted that British nationality had little importance in Palestine. He felt that the club members were too busy discussing matters at length and making excuses for their inaction rather than doing anything of a concrete nature. He also mentioned that they were involved in various negotiations in the Gaza region with the aid of the British consular agent there, but that their efforts bore no fruit.[339]

After preliminary investigations by the Anglo-Palestine Jews' Club into real estate opportunities in the environs of Gaza, a company for land purchase and settlement, the Palestine Development Company, was founded on July 7, 1907. Joseph Amzalak was among its founding members. Later that year a thirty-dunam tract in the vicinity of Jaffa was purchased by the company with the aid of Alexander Anton Knesevich, the British consular agent at Gaza. This small-scale purchase was made on a trial basis, and the company tried not to attract attention to themselves and their plans.[340]

After many difficulties owing to the restrictions imposed by Ali Ekram Bey, the *mutasarrif* of Jerusalem in the years 1906-1908, on the purchase of lands by Jews, it was decided, based on a suggestion by Knesevich, to focus the attention of the company on lands in the Rapha region. This area, near the Egyptian border, four hours travel south of Gaza, was private property with no tax debt outstanding. An area of 50,000 dunams fit for grain cultivation and pasture was available for purchase. However, in 1909 another group, Agudath Israel from Bialystok, outmaneuvered the Palestine Development Company and purchased the tract.[341]

As mentioned, the coronation of King George V and Queen Mary was celebrated by the Anglo Jewish Club at the home of Joseph Amzalak on June 22, 1911. The event was described in *The Truth*:

> All the British subjects of Jaffa, as well as the doctor and staff of the English Hospital and the consular secretary, Mr. Nasri Fiani, attended. Mr. Amzalak opened with a speech in which he declared how every

339 *HaTzfirah*, 137-138, 4-5 Tammuz 5671 (June 29-30, 1911) in Eliav (supra n. 338), p. 187.
340 Eliav (supra n. 338), pp. 128-129; CZA, Central Zionist Office, Cologne, Z 2/232, letter from Prof. Otto Warburg, Chairman of the Committee for the Study of Eretz Yisrael, n.p., to David Wolfson, President of the Zionist Organization, Berlin, December 10, 1907, (Hebrew translation from original German) with enclosure of letter from A. Knesevich, British Consular Agent, Gaza, to Moses Levene, Secretary of the Palestine Development Company, Jaffa, in Eliav (supra n. 338), p. 165.
341 Eliav (supra n. 338), pp. 129-135.

member of those present felt the same patriotism, devotion and loyalty, and how their hearts went out to their sovereigns with the same sincerity as that of their friends in England.[342]

During this meeting, Rabbi Joseph Arrvas read a prayer and wished Their Majesties and the Royal Family a long, peaceful and prosperous life. Mr. Moses Levene, the secretary of the club, and Dr. Keith of the English Hospital also delivered speeches. Afterwards champagne and sweetmeats were handed round, and in conclusion Mrs. Haim Amzalak [the second wife] played "God save the King" on the piano, which was heartily sung by the whole assembly.[343]

With the outbreak of World War I, Joseph Amzalak, as a British citizen, was expelled from Jaffa and settled in Alexandria for the duration of the war. He returned to Jaffa after the war and continued to reside in his home in Neve Tzedek while his son occupied the adjacent house, until his death on February 11, 1944 (17 Shvat 5704); he was buried in Jerusalem.[344]

Ben-Zion Amzalak (1865-1935)

Ben-Zion Amzalak, born in Jerusalem in 1865, was the son of Solomon and Bolissa Amzalak. Orphaned at the age of eleven, he was left with no means of support. He was later taken in by his uncle, Haim Amzalak, who thought very highly of him. In a letter to Charles Netter, the director of Mikveh Israel, Haim Amzalak wrote that nature had endowed Ben-Zion with "vivacious intelligence, most ardent and extraordinary." Hence the elder Amzalak decided to continue the young man's education, and Ben-Zion was sent to Zaki Cohen's school in Beirut. He made suprisingly rapid progress there, completing the curriculum within three years. He mastered Hebrew, French and Arabic to such an extent that the director of the school wished to retain him as a teacher on his staff.[345] [see Plate 45]

Ben-Zion wanted to continue his education in a European university, particularly in France, but the only resources at his disposal were serious application and high hopes. Haim wrote that he was unable to support Ben-

342 *The Truth* (supra n. 277).
343 *The Truth* (supra n. 277).
344 Tidhar (supra n. 183), 4, p. 1467; Interview with Yael Amzalak (supra n. 326); Interview with Golda Amzalak (supra n. 318).
345 CZA, Mikveh Israel Archives, J41/201, letter from Haim Amzalak, Jaffa, to Charles Netter, Mikveh Israel, April 29, 1881 (French).

Plate 45: Ben-Zion Amzalak
(Source: Amzalak Family
Archives, National Library
Archives, Jerusalem, 4°1613/3)

Plate 46: Luna-Bolissa Amzalak
(Source: Amzalak Family
Archives, National Library
Archives, Jerusalem, 4°1613/3)

Zion's continued education and turned to Charles Netter and the Alliance Israélite Universelle with the request that they take up his nephew's cause.[346]

Ben-Zion married his first cousin Bolissa Amzalak, Haim's daughter. Together they had ten children: four daughters — Rebecca (Claire), Esther, Rose and Pauline — and six sons — Edward, Maurice, Daniel, James, Simon and Henry.[347] [see Plates 46 and 47]

They resided in the Muslim Manshiya neighborhood, located to the north of the walled city of Jaffa. They owned an area of 3,602 square meters, on which were built seven structures with a total floor space of 2,105 square meters. The buildings were all destroyed on May 1, 1948 during the Israeli War of Independence. Detailed information on the buildings prior to their destruction was collected by M. Stern, a civil engineer, in order to evaluate the damage caused to the owners. The compound had been surrounded by stone walls of varying height, with some ornamental wrought iron railing. Areas not built

346 CZA, Mikveh Israel Archives, J41/201, letter from Haim Amzalak, Jaffa, to Charles Netter, Mikveh Israel, April 29, 1881 (French).
347 Interview with James Amzalak (supra n. 252).

Plate 47: Ben-Zion and Luna-Bolissa Amzalak and their children
Front row: (left to right) James, Luna-Bolissa, Henry, Ben-Zion, Daniel,
Second row: (left to right) Pauline, Rose, Clair, Esther, Simon,
Background: (left to right) Edward, Maurice
(Source: Amzalak Family Archives, National Library Archives, Jerusalem, 4°1613/3)

upon were either paved with stone, concrete flags and tile, or were planted with gardens and orchards. The one- and two-storey buildings were constructed with the finest materials and were considered grand and beautiful. The walls of the buildings within the compound were of course masonry, dressed on the face, and coated with lime cement plaster. The stone was imported Lidani sandstone; the roof was of timber covered with Marseilles tiles; and the joinery was of *katrani* (Turkish pine) timber. All windows had louver shutters and all the joinery and external woodwork was painted.[348] [see Plate 48]

The houses had all the modern conveniences available: excellent sanitation, water supply and electric lighting. James Amzalak, Ben-Zion's son, related that they were among the first to have electric lighting, at a time when most houses

---

348 PPJA, Report on Amzalak Property, Manshieh-Jaffa, prepared by M. Stern, Tel Aviv, May 1949. This report was recieved from James Amzalak in January 1987.

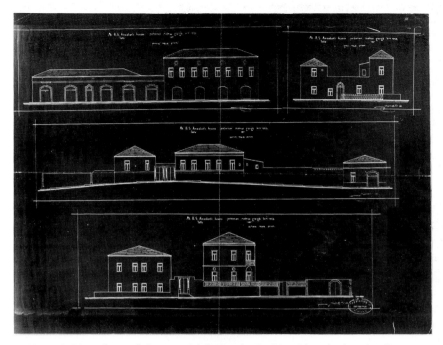

Plate 48: Plan of one of the Amzalak houses in the Manshiya district of Jaffa, 1948
(Source: James Amzalak Papers)

were lit by gas. Ben-Zion had hired a German engineer to set up a dynamo generator to supply their needs.[349]

The buildings had both residential and commercial functions. One was the house of Ben-Zion and his family, another that of Haim Amzalak, and the rest were rented to Jews and Muslims. Among the tenants mentioned by Ben-Zion's son, James Amzalak, were the Shertok [later Sharet], Feldman, Rokach, Levontin, and Haladi families. Facing the street along the eastern side of the compound were ten stores.[350]

The Amzalak compound in Manshiya was an important center in Jaffa. Its residents and tenants were prominent figures in the Jewish and Muslim communities. When the chief rabbi of Jerusalem, Rabbi Ya'akov Shaul

349 Interview with James Amzalak (supra n. 252); Report on Amzalak Property (supra n. 348).
350 Interview with James Amzalak (supra n. 252); Report on Amzalak Property (supra n. 348).

Eliachar, visited Jaffa in the spring of 1900, he toured the city and was later escorted to Ben-Zion's home, where he resided during his stay.[351]

Ben-Zion Amzalak, a leading businessman in Jaffa, purchased tracts of land in different areas of Palestine. According to his son James, he had entered into partnership with Abu Ramadan Abu Khadra from Gaza. They owned agricultural land in the vicinity of Gaza, on which they grew corn, barley and other field crops. Ben-Zion Amzalak also purchased lands around the village of Abu Gosh in the Judean mountains.[352]

His expertise in business and familiarity with the local market were well recognized by the inhabitants of Jaffa. Joseph Eliyahu Chelouche, in his memoirs, told of having met with Ben-Zion Amzalak and of receiving his advice. Chelouche was attempting to start out in business at the time and had traveled to Port Said on an unsuccessful search for merchandise. On returning to Jaffa he met with Ben-Zion, who told him of a business opportunity. A merchant who traded in iron, painted-tin, pottery, plates, glasses and other utensils was liquidating his business due to old age. Amzalak and Chelouche inspected his merchandise and together purchased it. They arranged to store it in a warehouse, but before this could be implemented they sold all their wares to a merchant from Jerusalem, making a 200 napoleon (approximately £160) profit.[353]

Ben-Zion Amzalak supported the infant Zionist movement. In 1901 he was one of 125 individuals in Jaffa who contributed a gold shekel each to the Zionist organization in Vienna. Four settlements, Jerusalem, Rehovot, Rishon LeZion and Jaffa, established Zionist organizations in accordance with the second of the four points of the Basel Congress program of 1897. The program called for: 1) the settlement of Eretz Israel by agriculturalists, craftsmen and industrial workers; 2) the organization and the union of all Jewries through local and general projects in accordance with the laws of their respective countries; 3) the strengthening of the feelings of Jewish independence and the recognition of Jewish nationalism; 4) efforts to prevail upon the governments concerned to acquiesce in Zionist aspirations.[354]

---

351 *Habazeleth*, vol. 30, no.28, 5 Iyar 5660 (May 9, 1900), p. 210 (Hebrew).
352 Interview with James Amzalak (supra n. 248). The authors were unable to locate these tracts.
353 Chelouche (supra n. 260), pp. 122-123.
354 CZA, The Zionist Office, Vienna, Z1/331, letter from the founding committee of Barkai, Jaffa, to the Zionist committee, Vienna, February 9, 1902, in Eliav (supra n. 338), pp. 370-371; see also footnote 1 to the document.

Plate 49: Portrait of Joseph
Navon Bey
(Source: Elie Eliachar, *Living
with Jews*, Jerusalem 1983,
between pp. 608–609)

The Jews of Jaffa, both Ashkenazim and Sephardim, met on January 26, 1902 to form the Barkai organization, and Ben-Zion was one of its seven members. The group's purpose was the promotion of Zionism in Jaffa, the propagation of Zionist ideas among the city's Jewish inhabitants, a growth in the number of shekel contributors and support for the Zionist organization in Vienna.[355]

With the outbreak of World War I, Ben-Zion Amzalak, as an enemy citizen, was forced to leave Jaffa for Alexandria with many of his relatives. After the war, he returned to Jaffa, where he resided until his death in 1935.

Joseph Navon Bey (1852-1934)

Joseph Navon was born in Jerusalem in 1852 to Eliyahu Navon and Esther Amzalak. He was circumsized by his uncle, Haim Amzalak. Navon studied at a yeshiva in Jerusalem, and at age thirteen was sent to France, where he received a fine secular education. He had a knowledge of Hebrew, French, Ladino and Arabic.[356] [see Plate 49]

355 CZA, The Zionist Office, Vienna, Z1/331, letter from the founding committee of Barkai, Jaffa, to the Zionist Committee, Vienna, February 9, 1902, in Eliav (supra n. 284), 2, pp. 370-371; for additional information on the Zionist movement in Palestine see: Chaya Har-El, "The Zionist movement and the Yishuv at the End of the First Aliya," Mordechai Eliav (ed.), *The First Aliyah*, Jerusalem 1981, 1, pp. 383-406 (Hebrew).

356 AFP, Record of circumcisions; it is important to note that sources like Gaon (supra n. 39), p. 455, Tidhar (supra n. 183), 1, p. 70, Eliachar (supra n. 222), p. 660 and Glass (supra n. 24) all mention that Joseph Navon was born in 1858, but the correct year is 1852. He was circumcised on 2 Adar 5612 (February 22, 1852) by his uncle Haim Amzalak. In addition, Joseph Navon at the age of four was enumerated in the census of 1855, which was conducted over a two year period; CZA, J41/62 and A152/8/2; *Le Renouveau*, 7, May 6, 1927 p. 2; 8, May 13, 1927, p. 1 (French).

Plate 50: Portrait of Gisha (Bolissa) Frumkin Navon (Source: Elie Eliachar, *Living with Jews*, Jerusalem 1983, between pp. 608–609)

Plate 51: Joseph Navon Bey's House on Jaffa Road
(Source: Elie Eliachar, *Living with Jews*, Jerusalem 1983)

Joseph Navon married the daughter of Rabbi Sandak Frumkin and sister of Dov Frumkin, the owner of the newspaper *Habazeleth*. His marriage to Gisha — or Bolissa, as she was known in Navon's Sephardi home — was one of the first "intermarriages" between Sephardim and Ashkenazim. The couple had three daughters, Leah, Rosa and Rachel-Batsheva.[357] [see Plates 50 and 51]

Upon his return to Palestine, Navon began working as a clerk in the Frutiger Bank. Within a short period of time, before reaching the age of twenty, Navon became a partner. He engaged in commercial activities, representing the interests of his uncle, Haim Amzalak, in Jerusalem. A few years later, in 1886, Navon purchased the largest trading house in Jerusalem, the German Duisberg Company, which dealt with companies located in London, Paris, Vienna, Zurich, Trieste, Milan and other commercial centers. Navon served as an agent for a number of European insurance companies which provided life and property policies as well as insurance for ships and their cargoes.[358]

Navon also assisted Haim Amzalak in a different capacity, as the latter's unofficial representative for Portuguese consular affairs. The impression given to Jewish community was that Joseph Navon was, in fact, the Portuguese consul. In 1884 *Habazeleth* reported that Navon had been appointed consul of Portugal in Jerusalem upon the recommendation of Haim Amzalak, who had declined the position. As mentioned above, the Portuguese Foreign Ministry Archives have no record of any such appointment. Nevertheless, this illusory assignment enhanced Navon's status in the community.[359]

Navon dealt in land transactions for his personal betterment and as a representative of individuals or groups, among them the Ottoman government, the Frutiger Company, and the agricultural colonies of Petah Tikvah and Rishon LeZion. The land market proved highly profitable for Navon at first, but the 1891 and 1892 restrictions on Jewish immigration and land purchase brought him great losses.[360]

357 Gaon (supra n. 39), p. 455; Tidhar (supra n. 183), 1, p. 70; Eliachar (supra n. 222), p. 660.

358 Grunwald (supra n. 30), pp. 261-262; Ben-Arieh (supra n. 30), pp. 382–384; Eliachar (supra n. 222), pp. 655-656; CZA, A152/8, bills of sale for December 31, 1885 to November 26, 1886; *HaMagid*, vol. 5, no. 29, 29 Shvat 5646 (February 4, 1886), p. 42 (Hebrew).

359 CZA, A152/6/7, blank forms of the Portuguese government; *Habazeleth*, 3, 12 Heshvan 5645 (October 31, 1884), p. 24 (Hebrew); Eliachar (supra n. 222), p. 669; Gaon (supra n. 39), p. 455.

360 *Habazeleth*, 39, 24 Av 5741 (August 20, 1881), pp. 295-296 (Hebrew); *HaTzfirah*, 39, 3 Tishrei 5742 (September 26, 1881), p. 4 (Hebrew); CZA, A152/9/14, contract of sale of lands to Frutiger, April 18, 1887 (French); CZA, A152/1, translation of kushans.

His activities did not stop with the purchase of these land holdings; he was also involved in their development. In partnership with Johannes Frutiger and Shalom Konstrum, Navon constructed the first commercial neighborhoods in Jerusalem: Mahane Yehuda along Jaffa Road (1887) and Beit Yosef in Abu Tor (1887). Navon also proposed other land development schemes, including the founding of a hotel on his holdings near the Jerusalem railway station.[361]

In 1885, Navon began his involvement in the development of public works by attempting to obtain the concession for a railway system in Palestine. The development of this project was described by Navon's first cousin, Joseph Amzalak, in his memoirs. Joseph Amzalak and Joseph Navon met with the engineer Georges Frangiya in Jerusalem. The latter suggested that a railroad could be constructed for no more than £400,000 and would provide a profit for the investors. Navon concluded with Frutiger that the concession should be attained from the Ottoman government and be resold so as to make a large profit. A statistical study of the revenues of the Jerusalem-Jaffa road was conducted, and Frangiya prepared the necessary plan for a £200 fee. Joseph Amzalak successfully solicited the support of the British consul in Jerusalem, Noel Temple Moore, and the support of the other consuls was soon to follow. In addition, Navon hoped to receive the support of Kamal Pasha, an Ottoman minister in the capital. Navon was friendly with Musa Pasha Al Hussaini, whose son was married to Kamal Pasha's niece. Before leaving for Constantinople, Navon offered his cousin a partnership on condition that the latter share in both past and future outlays. Joseph Amzalak declined the proposal.[362]

After three years of negotiations, in 1888, Navon received a concession from the Sublime Porte in Constantinople for the construction and operation of a railway line from Jaffa to Jerusalem, with an option for the construction of extensions to Gaza and Nablus. Unable to attract Jewish backers in Palestine and Europe, Navon sold his concession in 1890 to a French company. However, he retained shares in the railroad, which was completed and inaugurated in 1892. Navon was granted the title bey by Sultan Abdul Hamid II and the French

---

361 JMA, Beit Yosef File; CZA, A152/7/1, A152/7/2, A152/8/2; *Habazeleth*, 34, 23 Tammuz 5647 (July 15, 1887), pp. 256, 264; *Habazeleth*, 26, 21 Iyar 5648 (May 2, 1888), p. 193 (Hebrew).

362 CZA, A152/6/1; D.C. Loutfy Bey, *Projet d'une Ligne de Chemin de Fer Reliant L'Egypte à la Syrie, Note sur la Socièté Khédivate de Géographie du Caire 20 Mars 1891*, Cairo 1891; Selah Merrill, "The Jaffa and Jerusalem Railway," *Scribner's Magazine*, vol. 13, no. 3, (March 1893), pp. 295-297; Jaques Thobie, *Les Intérêts Economiques, Financiers et Politiques Français dans la Partie Asiatique de L'Empire Ottoman de 1895 a 1914*, 1, Ph.D. thesis, L'Université de Paris, Paris 1973, pp. 203-207.

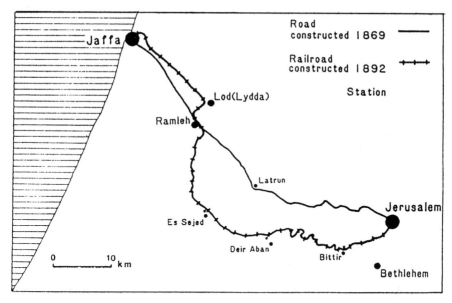

Figure 9: The Jerusalem-Jaffa Railroad, 1892
(Source: Joseph Glass, "The Biography in Historical-Geographical Research: Joseph Navon
Bey — A Case Study," Ruth Kark (ed.), *The Land That Became Israel*, New Haven and
Jerusalem 1990, p. 86)

Legion of Honor for his role in the founding of the Jaffa-Jerusalem railroad.[363]
[see Figure 9]

Navon's activities in the sphere of public works included a number of
attempts toward the development of the Jaffa area. He proposed two projects,
in 1893 and 1894 — one for the construction of a modern deepwater port in
Jaffa, which would be a logical continuation of the railway, and the second for
the development and irrigation of lands in the environs of Jaffa through
exploitation of water from the Yarkon River. Navon received an Ottoman
concession for the construction of the port, but never realized either of the
proposed projects.[364]

363 Kurt Grunwald, "The Beginnings of the Railroad from Jaffa to Jerusalem," Y. Porat, B.Z.
     Yehoshua, and A. Kedar (eds.), *Chapters in the History of the Jewish Community in
     Jerusalem*, Jerusalem 1974, 2, pp. 262-263 (Hebrew); *Habazeleth*, 36, 9 Tammuz 5653
     (June 23, 1893), p. 285 (Hebrew).
364 Shmuel Avitzur, "The First Project for the Intensive Exploitation of the Yarkon Waters
     (the Frangiya-Navon Scheme of 1893)," *Museum Ha'aretz Bulletin*, 6 (1964), pp. 80-89;
     Shmuel Avitzur, "Earlier Projects for Improved Harbour Facilities" *Museum Ha'aretz
     Bulletin*, 7 (1965), pp. 30-39; CZA, A152/6/3.

Navon's activities were not confined to commercial ventures or the economic development of Palestine; he also undertook various projects to improve the plight of his fellow Jews. In 1883, he was among the founding members of 'Ezrat Nidahim, a society which provided aid for Yemenite immigrants. The organization collected funds for the construction of houses near the village of Silwan. One of these structures, dedicated during Hannuka of 1885, bore an inscription denoting that it had been donated by Joseph and Gisha Navon. In 1886 Navon was chosen as one of the seven Sephardi representatives of the managing committee of the society. Two years later, while in Constantinople, he interceded on the society's behalf by attaining building permits, some of them retroactive, for thirty houses in the vicinity of Silwan.[365]

Navon was involved in a second project for the housing of the poor in Jerusalem, on land that he had purchased together with Shmuel Bek in 1886 near the Tomb of Simon the Righteous. Six houses known as Batei Navon, were constructed there for the benefit of the Sephardi poor.[366]

Navon was concerned with the fate of the land upon which the neighborhood Yemin Moshe was to be built. It had originally been purchased by Sir Moses Montefiore in 1855, and five years later Batei Tura (Mishkenot Sha'ananim) and the windmill were erected on the southern third of the area. The remaining two-thirds remained barren for almost twenty-five years. After Montefiore's death, his heir, Joseph Sebag Montefiore, wished to rent the northern section to the Alliance Israélite Universelle for the establishment of a school. However, since this tract had not been mentioned in Montefiore's will, it was assumed by the poor of Jerusalem he had never regarded it as his own, and that it was earmarked for their benefit. In 1886 they began the establishment of a shanty neighborhood there. In the ongoing dispute over the ownership of the land, Navon represented the interests of the poor of Jerusalem. On May 27, 1892, the land was transferred to the Sir Moses Montefiore Testimonial Fund for the establishment of a new neighborhood and the squatters were evicted.[367] A few

365 Nitza Druyan, "The First Yemenite Quarters in Jerusalem, 1882-1914," *Cathedra*, 13 (October 1979), pp. 97-100 (Hebrew); *HaMagid*, 3, 19 Tevet 5644 (January 17, 1884), pp. 20-21 (Hebrew); *Habazeleth*, 10, 1 Tevet 5645 (December 19, 1884), p. 75 (Hebrew); *Habazeleth*, 4, 2-3 Heshvan 5647 (October 31, 1886), p. 9 (Hebrew); *Habazeleth*, 24, 13 Iyar 5648 (April 24, 1888), p. 185 (Hebrew).

366 Ben-Arieh (supra n. 30), p. 221; CZA, A152/9/14, letter of agreement between Shmuel Bek and Joseph Navon, 1886 (Hebrew); *Habazeleth*, 23, 14 Adar 5647 (March 14, 1887), p. 133 (Hebrew); Gaon (supra n. 39), p. 454.

367 Kark (supra n. 233), pp. 157–187; Y. Meisl, *This is the History of the Sir Moses Montefiore Testimonial Fund*, Jerusalem 1939, pp. 70-73 (Hebrew); CZA, A152/9/12, letter from Joseph Sebag, London to Rabbis Pansiel and Salant, Jerusalem, January 12, 1887.

months later, upon Navon's return to Jerusalem for the inauguration of the railroad, he wrote in *Habazeleth*:

> ...thus as the representative of the group, I have through the government delayed the excavation and building and hereby demand from Mr. Sebag to fulfill his duty and donate the land, to tell the community to build houses for the poor and not the rich.[368]

Navon was outspoken regarding the rivalry between the Ashkenazi and Sephardi communities in Palestine, which reached a peak with the dispute over the division of *halukkah* funds from the United States in the early 1890s. In a plea published in *Habazeleth* in 1892, he called for greater understanding between the two communities, and cited his marriage to an Ashkenazi as an example of this.[369]

Besides supporting Jewish agricultural settlement in Petah Tikvah and Rishon LeZion, Navon also negotiated on behalf of the director of Mikveh Israel, Samuel Hirsh, for the purchase of lands near the villages of Yalo, Jindas and Latroun in the Judean piedmont, midway between Jaffa and Jerusalem. His involvement was not confined to the purchase of lands, but extended to aiding the colonists of Rishon LeZion and 'Ekron in attaining building permits. He also helped the colonists of Rishon LeZion in securing a loan from the Frutiger Bank.[370]

Navon at the same time realized the difficulties inherent in the attempts to settle Jews in Palestine in large numbers. He strove to use his influence to lift the 1891 Ottoman restrictions on the immigration of Russian Jews to Palestine. The year that these limitations were imposed he stood behind a project involving the Baron Maurice de Hirsch, the Alliance Israélite Universelle and Hovevei Zion for the purchase of a large tract of land east of the Jordan River designed for Jewish settlement. In the end, however, the project was not realized and he searched for alternative solutions for the "Jewish Question."[371] One such

368 *Habazeleth*, 3, 7 Heshvan 5653 (October 28, 1892), pp. 19-20 (Hebrew).
369 *Habazeleth*, 3, 7 Heshvan 5653 (October 28, 1892), pp. 17-19 (Hebrew).
370 Yaari (supra n. 304), pp. 80-82; Eliachar (supra n. 222) pp. 668-669; CZA, A152/8/2, letter from Yehiel Michael Pines and Yoel Moshe Salomon, to Joseph Navon, 1883 (Hebrew); CZA, J41/62, letter from Joseph Navon, Jerusalem, to Shmuel Hirch, Mikveh Yisrael, August 20, 1883 (French); J41/62, letter from Joseph Navon, Jerusalem, to Shmuel Hirch, Mikveh Yisrael, October 31, 1883 (French); *Le Renouveau*, 9, May 20, 1927, p. 1 (French); see also agricultural settlements in Chapter Four.
371 Zvi Ilan, "The Baron Hirsch and the Attempt to Organize an International Jewish Project for the Purchase of Lands and Settlement in Trans-Jordan in 1891" *Kivunim*, 17, pp. 111-116 (Hebrew); *Habazeleth*, 41, 8 Av 5651, pp. 326-327 (Hebrew).

alternative was Baron de Hirsch's project for Jewish settlement in Argentina, to which Navon lent his qualified support, as described by Hirsch in a memorandum:

> ...although he [Navon] is ostensibly very enthusiastic about the immigration into Asiatic Turkey, that at the bottom he would not hesitate to give preference to the Argentine republic, had he not beforehand embarked upon the other project....M. Navon believes and, it appears to me [Hirsch] rightly so, that provided Palestine be waived, the Turkish government will accept a limited number of Jewish immigrants and furnish them gratuitously, or nearly so, the necessary lands.[372]

In 1894, Joseph Navon left Palestine due to bankruptcy, never to return. During this period two prominent local bankers of European origin also went bankrupt: Peter Melville Bergheim in 1892 and Johannes Frutiger in 1896. These bankruptcies resulted mainly from the restrictions by the Ottoman government on the sale of land to Jews. With regard to Navon and Frutiger, financial losses from their investment in the Jaffa-Jerusalem railroad was also an important factor.[373]

After leaving Palestine, Navon resided in London and Paris. In Europe, Navon pursued his financial activities, some of which were still connected to Palestine. Of note was his scheme between the years 1927 and 1930 for the development and construction of a garden city to be called Beit Yosef on Mount Cana'an near Safed. This scheme never advanced beyond the planning stages. However, Navon never succeeded in reestablishing himself financially. He remained in Paris in a self-imposed exile and constantly longed for Jerusalem until his death in 1934.[374]

Summary

These three individuals — Joseph Ben-Zion Amzalak, Ben-Zion Amzalak and Joseph Navon — are conspicuous in the developments of Palestine from the 1880s until the outbreak of World War I. They began their activities about the

---

372 Baron de Hirsch's Memorandum on Palestinean Colonization, 1891 in Kurt Grunwald, *Turkenhirsch — A Study of Baron Maurice de Hirsch, Entrepreneur and Philanthropist,* Jerusalem 1966, pp. 123-125.

373 ISA, RG 67 files 456, 429, German Consulate in Jerusalem Archives; CZA, A152/12/4, A152/12/5.

374 CZA, A152/6/6, plans for Garden City on Mt. Cana'an; *Le Renouveau,* 15, July 17, 1927, pp. 4-5 (French).

same time as the First *Aliyah*, facilitating the ingression of Jewish immigrants into the region and its society. They continued the process of modernization that had begun earlier in the nineteenth century. These entrepreneurs were engaged primarily in trade, but their business undertakings expanded to banking and land, for both speculation and development. Their imprints were left on the agricultural hinterland of Jaffa, particularly the citrus orchards, and the new neighborhoods outside the walls of Jerusalem. Joseph Navon went further; he expanded into the realm of public works, the area in which the risks were the greatest but the profits highest. His first cousin too, Joseph Amzalak, had the opportunity to invest in the Jerusalem-Jaffa railroad; however, his more conservative approach to business kept him outside this project.

Nevertheless, the question arises of why these three Amzalak family members stood out among the rest of their generation. There appears to be a great contrast between the magnitude of the dealings of the three individuals discussed above and those of their relatives. The explanation lies in the social standing, education, personality and capabilities of each individual. All three possessed the necessary tools for future success. Furthermore, another common denominator should be pointed out: they enjoyed the support and trust of Haim Amzalak. The patronage of Haim Amzalak, which included a period of apprenticeship for all three, helped mold them. Joseph Amzalak enjoyed the status of being Haim's eldest son, a special position in the family framework. Ben-Zion Amzalak, orphaned at a young age was seen by his uncle as a promising and honest youth. Ben-Zion's union with Haim's daughter Bolissa further consolidated the bond between the two men. Lastly, Joseph Navon was also favored by his mother's brother Haim, although the basis for their special relationship cannot be clearly pinpointed. One possible explanation may lie in Haim's need for a trustworthy and capable family member in Jerusalem, who would represent his interests there. It is possible that the intimate relationship between them simply evolved over the years. Whatever the reason, the bond did exist.

This being the case, the third generation should be seen in the light of its relationship with Haim Amzalak. He had chosen these three men and groomed them for success in their future dealings. Joseph Amzalak, Ben-Zion Amzalak and Joseph Navon were Haim's selected heirs; following his lead they took up positions of leadership in the Jewish community and attained distinction in the business world of Palestine at the time.

CHAPTER SIX

THE AMZALAK FAMILY IN EXILE

The Expulsion from Jaffa, 1914-1915

The outbreak of World War I on August 1, 1914 brought about catastrophic results for the majority of the Jewish community in Palestine, and a provisional pause in the hundred-year presence of the Amzalak family in the land. The war gave rise to

> expulsions, banishment, summary executions, unjust accusations, exorbitant taxation, forced military service and labor, and suppression of all outward Zionist activity....The passage of armies, requisitioning of property and severance from the outside world almost completely disrupted its [Palestine's] economy. Added to all these were a disastrous locust plague in 1915 and other ravages of nature. Finally, when the end was in sight, Palestine became the scene of fighting, and for a time the front line ran across the country.[375]

On September 8, 1914, the Ottomans annulled the Capitulation agreements which had been made with foreign governments. Jews who were nominal subjects of Britain, France and Russia were considered enemies of the Ottoman Empire and many of them came under threat of internment or expulsion from Palestine. An option was given to them to become naturalized Ottoman subjects. Many prominent figures in Palestine supported a campaign for the Ottomanization of the Jewish population, believing this to be in the Jewish interest. However, this was not a viable solution for the Amzalak family. They

---

375 Yaari (supra n. 304), p. 347; an extensive literature exists on the effects of World War I on the Jewish Community in Palestine; for example, see: Zvi Shilony, "Changes in the Jewish Leadership of Jerusalem during World War One" *Cathedra*, 35 (April 1985), pp. 58-90 (Hebrew); Ron Bartour, "American Consular Aid to Jews in Eretz Yisrael in the Twilight of the Ottoman Rule, until the outbreak of the first World War," Ph.D. Thesis, Hebrew University of Jerusalem, Jerusalem 1985, pp. 197–219 (Hebrew); Nathan Efrati, "The Jewish Community in Eretz Yisrael during World War I, 1914–1918," Ph.D. Thesis, Hebrew University of Jerusalem, Jerusalem 1985 (Hebrew).

had been loyal to the English crown for decades; Haim Amzalak had been British vice consul in Jaffa for over thirty years, and Joseph Amzalak had aided the Palmer Expedition in Sinai in 1882 and was the Anglo-Palestine Jews' Club president. It would have been unthinkable for any of them to relinquish their British citizenship.

Once the war broke out the nationals of enemy states — England, France and Russia — were left virtually unprotected, except for the help that was provided by the United States. The American diplomats in the area had become the sole representatives of a neutral nation. The plight of the Jewish population of Palestine became an important concern for the United States government, under pressure by American Jewry to intervene on behalf of their imperiled brethren. The American ambassador in Constantinople, Henry Morgenthau Sr., a Jewish philanthropist with prominent status in the American Jewish community, was in a tenuous position, having to answer to both the State Department and his coreligionists. But after being informed of the Ottomans' intention to intern subjects of belligerent nations who remained in Palestine, he approved the suggestion forwarded by the American consul in Jerusalem, Otis Glazebrook, that "since Turkish facilities for transporting Jews were inadequate, the *U.S.S. Tennessee*, then in the waters of the eastern Mediterranean, should be used to carry refugees to Port Said."[376]

On December 17, 1914 the first expulsion of Jews from Jaffa took place. Beha ed-din Effendi, an Ottoman Ministry of Interior expert on Jewish affairs in Palestine who had been appointed *kaymakam* of Jaffa three months earlier, issued orders that non-Ottomanized belligerents be deported that same afternoon at four o'clock. Captain Decker of the *U.S.S. Tennessee* provided details of the deportation in a report to his superiors, based on his conversations with the refugees. He noted that the police had indiscriminately rounded up the Jewish inhabitants of Jaffa from the streets and their houses. These people were dragged to the port without being allowed to collect their belongings. As Jaffa's port offered only offshore anchorage for large vessels, rowboats were needed to transport people and goods to awaiting ships. Many Arab boatmen took advantage of this situation by beating and robbing the refugees. The space available for the transportation of these people was limited, and many families were separated. By January 1915, over 6,000 Jewish refugees had been carried from Jaffa to Egypt on various ships, among them members of the Amzalak

376 Frank E. Manuel, *The Realities of American-Palestine Relations*, Washington 1949, pp. 122-123; Mordechai Ben-Hillel Hacohen, *War of the Nations: An Eretz Israel Diary 1914-1918*, I, Jerusalem 1981, pp. 31-65 (Hebrew); see also Yaari (supra n. 304), pp. 348-354.

Plate 52: Ships landing refugees at Alexandria
(Source: Central Zionist Archives, Jerusalem)

family who were taken to Alexandria on the *U.S.S. Tennessee.* In all, 11,277 Palestinian Jews were expelled to Egypt during the years 1914 and 1915.[377] [see Plate 52]

As most of the refugees had been forced to leave their possessions behind, they were destitute upon their arrival in Egypt. Initially, many of them were housed in camps set up by the British. Later a Jewish council called the Assistance Committee for Palestine and Syria, composed of the exiled Palestinean leadership and representatives from the native Jewish community in Alexandria was established in Alexandria to shelter, feed and clothe the refugees during the initial stage. It subsequently tried to provide the refugees with employment and their children with an education.[378]

Upon fleeing Jaffa, the Amzalaks abandoned most of their possessions and property to plunder and destruction, but managed to smuggle out some jewels

377 Manuel (supra n. 376), pp. 127-128; Ben-Hillel HaCohen (supra n. 376); Shimon Rubinstein, *To Leave or Not to Leave?: "Yeridah" to Egypt at the Outset of World War I,* Jerusalem 1988, p. 30 (Hebrew).

378 Nurit Guvrin, "The Encounter of Exiles from Palestine with the Jewish Community of Egypt During World War I, As Reflected in Their Writings" Shimon Shamir (ed.), *The Jews of Egypt: A Mediterranean Society in Modern Times,* London 1987, pp. 177-191; Jacob M. Landau, *Jews in Nineteenth Century Egypt,* New York 1969, pp. 68-70.

and gold. They believed the war would last only three or four months, but as it dragged on they rented a villa in Hadeni Bey Souk, Tabakhine, Alexandria. Abraham Amzalak, Haim's son, had already been residing in Egypt, and his presence probably facilitated matters for the rest of the family. According to the account of family members, Abraham enjoyed a position of authority and importance in the Egyptian administration. His children later emigrated to Australia.[379]

Haim Amzalak died in exile on December 12, 1916 (7 Kislev 5676). His grandson James vividly recalls that on that day Haim Amzalak was scheduled to visit Sultan Fuad of Egypt. He had finished dressing and preparing for the visit, and then asked for a glass of water. Within moments Haim Amzalak died at the age of eighty-eight, with all his family around him. He was buried in the Shatbi Sephardi Jewish cemetery in Alexandria.[380]

Sources on the history of the Jews of Alexandria and the Jewish Palestinian refugees there during World War I make no reference to the Amzalak family. Several explanations are possible. For example, the Amzalaks may have brought with them sufficient financial resources to maintain themselves, or may have been supported by local family members; in either case, they were not dependent upon the services provided by the assistance committee, and were not listed among its beneficiaries.[381]

Military Service during World War I

The Amzalak family supported the British war effort during the First World War. Many members of the family volunteered for active service in the British army, either in regular units or the Jewish Legion.

The Zion Mule Corps was formed in March 1915. Its volunteers were Palestinian Jewish refugees who had refused to be Ottomanized and were expelled to Egypt, and also young Egyptian Jews. The idea of forming the corps had originated with Ze'ev (Vladimir) Jabotinsky, a renowned Russian Jewish journalist who promoted the "Hebraization" of the Diaspora and Jewish self-

---

379 Interview with James Amzalak (supra n. 252); interview with Golda Amzalak (supra n. 302); BHMA, photocopy of British War Office Records — list of Zionist Transport Corps, n.d.

380 Interview with James Amzalak (supra n. 252).

381 Guvrin (supra n. 378); Landau (supra n. 378) pp. 31-34, 68-70; Ya'akov Yisrael Malkov, *From Egypt to Here*, Jaffa 1922 (Hebrew); David Yudelovitz, "Palestinian Exiles in Egypt", serialized in *MiYamim Rishonim* (monthly supplement to *Bustenai*), 1 (December 1934-May 1935), (Hebrew).

Plate 53: Zion Mule Corps in Alexandria
(Source: Central Zionist Archives, Jerusalem)

defense. An ardent supporter of Zionism, he had served in 1908 in the Zionist information service in Constantinople. With the outbreak of World War I, his hopes for the attainment of Zionist aspirations were pinned on the British. Among the Jewish Palestinian refugees in Egypt was Joseph Trumpeldor, an ex-officer in the Russian army who had lost an arm in the siege of Port Arthur during the Russo-Japanese War (1904). He had immigrated to Palestine where he joined the *kvutza* (commune) at Migdal in 1912 and later the one at Degania. Jabotinsky traveled to Egypt and met with Trumpeldor, and they agreed to propose the idea of a Jewish combat unit to the British military authorities. The British assented to the formation of such a unit, but gave no assurance that it would serve on the Palestine front. Under the Army Act these soldiers could not enroll as fighting troops, but could be employed as mule-drivers. Jabotinsky, in disappointment, abandoned the project but Trumpeldor undertook the organization of the corps. The commander of the Zion Mule Corps was Lieutenant-Colonel J. H. Patterson, and Captain Trumpeldor served as his deputy.[382] [see Plate53]

On April 17, 1915 the Zion Mule Corps sailed to Gallipoli. The 650-man unit lost eight men in battle, and fifty-five were wounded. Its ranks were further decreased by disease and desertion, and the detachment of two companies.

382 Shulamit Laskov, "Joseph Trumpeldor — Diary of the Zion Mule Corps (Alexandria, 24.1.1916-7.10.1916)" *Cathedra*, 7 (April 1978), pp. 204-206 (Hebrew); Vladimir Jabotinsky, "The Jewish Units in the War," Michael Adler (ed.), *British Jewry Book of Honour*, London 1922, pp. 59-64.

Upon the corps' return to Alexandria at the end of 1915, it numbered only ninety, and it appeared likely that the unit would be disbanded. The events taking place in the camp in Alexandria are recorded in the diary entries of Joseph Trumpeldor between the dates January 24, 1916 and October 7, 1916. Mention is made of a non-commissioned officer named Amzalak, who has been identified as Int. Sergeant Maurice [Moses] Amzalak, Ben-Zion's son:[383]

> 1.2. 9:30 a.m. Yesterday I was in the camp until nine in the evening (starting from twelve noon). I observed the routine there. At six in the evening [2nd Lieutenant Geronim] Mer carried out inspection. It appeared to me that 37 men were present, that is to say that about one hundred men were absent without permission. But these things are unimportant. The main thing is that there is no order in the camp.... Screaming like a hoodlum and swearing, Amzalak metes out punishments...[384]
>
> 28.3. This morning (at eleven), while I was still in the city, a lieutenant-general arrived at the camp. He carried out an inspection. He asked Amzalak certain questions..., which he [the latter] answered.... Afterwards the General said that he had heard a very good opinion of our work in Gallipoli. Amzalak confirmed [this opinion] (which was inappropriate on his part): "Yes, we worked very well." It is said that Amzalak was very frightened (and he partially confirmed this) when he spoke to the General. His legs shook.[385]
>
> 14.5. The mood of the junior officers, especially [2nd Lieutenant Jacob] Gouldin, is not particularly good. Only Amzalak is satisfied. He walks around like a puffed up goose. And is it unimportant he is to receive a commission? And I don't want to believe that the Zion Mule Corps will finally die.[386]

Three other sons of Ben-Zion and Bolissa Amzalak — James, Edward and Daniel — also enlisted into the British Army during their exile in Egypt. Daniel

---

383 Laskov (supra n. 382), pp. 206-207; Additional entries exist with references to Amzalak from the dates April 18, 1916, 7 p.m., April 30, 1916, 10 a.m. and May 16, 1916, 7 p.m.; List of Zionist Transport Corps (supra n. 379).

384 Laskov (supra n. 382), p. 212.

385 Laskov (supra n. 382), p. 220.

386 Laskov (supra n. 382), p. 224; Joseph Trumpeldor and six of his comrades were killed defending Tel Hai on March 1, 1920. Trumpeldor became a heroic figure in the history of Eretz Israel and has been remembered for his last words, "It is good to die for our country." See: Yaari (n. 304), pp. 445-475.

Plate 54: James (Jimmy)
Amzalak
(Source: Amzalak Family
Archives, National Library
Archives, Jerusalem, 4°1613/3)

Amzalak was a sergeant-major in charge of all rationing at the Suez Canal town of Kantara. Edward Amzalak, a doctor, reached the rank of captain in the medical corps and was stationed in Cairo. After the war he settled in New York, where he was assigned to a hospital as a specialist in the field of breast cancer.[387] James (Jimmy) Amzalak was also assigned to the medical corps. For over two years he was stationed at the Bombay Presidential Hospital in San Stefano, Alexandria. Twice during this period he served on a hospital ship that sailed from Alexandria to the Dardenelles to collect the wounded and take them back for treatment in Alexandria. James, in an interview, related that he had donated his salary from the British government to the Overseas Club of London. After the end of the war, James remained in Alexandria. In 1920 he returned to Jaffa, only to proceed to the United States via France. He eventually settled in California, his present place of residence. Capitalizing on the experience he had accumulated at his father's side during his youth, he entered various business ventures there. Noteworthy among these was his participation in the founding of the Hollywood State Bank. During the Great Depression he successfully prevented a run on the bank, thus averting its failure.[388] [see Plates 54 and 55]

387 Interview with James Amzalak (supra n. 252).
388 Interview with James Amzalak (supra n. 252); NLA 4°1613, letter from Over-Seas Club, London to James Amzalak, n.p., November 1917; receipt from Over-Seas Club, London, in the name of James S. Amzalak, January 18, 1918; letter from Over-Seas Club, London, to J.S. Amzalak, Alexandria, February 15, 1918; letter from Over-Seas Club & Patriotic League, London, to James Amzalak, Alexandria, April 24, 1919; laissez passer from Egyptian Expeditionary Force, Jaffa to James Amzalak, Jaffa, 1920. These documents were kept by James Amzalak for many years and only recently were donated to the Jewish and University Library in Jerusalem.

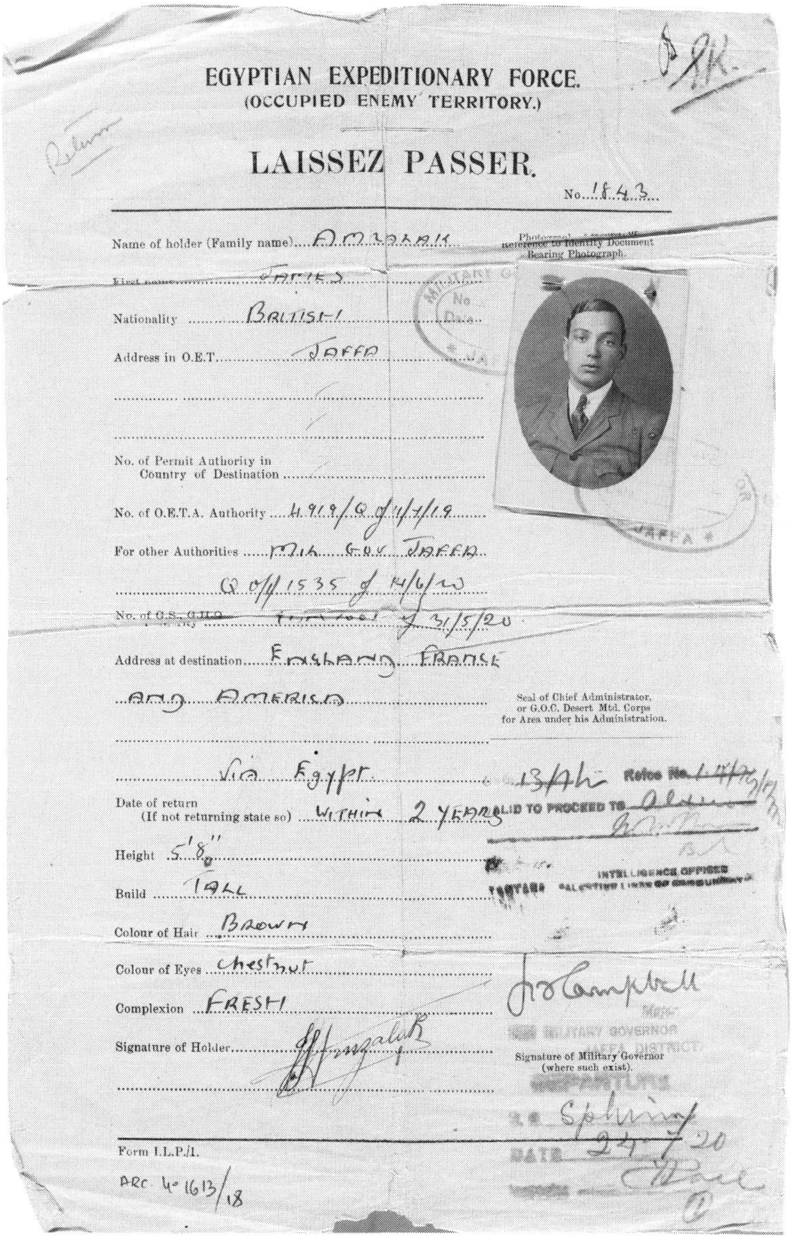

EGYPTIAN EXPEDITIONARY FORCE.
(OCCUPIED ENEMY TERRITORY.)

LAISSEZ PASSER.

No. 1843

Name of holder (Family name) AMZALAK

First name JAMES

Nationality BRITISH

Address in O.E.T. JAFFA

No. of Permit Authority in Country of Destination

No. of O.E.T.A. Authority 4919/Q of 1/7/19

For other Authorities MIL GOV JAFFA

Q 0/1/1535 of 14/6/20

No. of G.S. G.H.Q. ... of 31/5/20

Address at destination ENGLAND FRANCE AND AMERICA

Via Egypt

Date of return (If not returning state so) WITHIN 2 YEARS

Height 5'8"

Build TALL

Colour of Hair BROWN

Colour of Eyes chestnut

Complexion FRESH

Signature of Holder J. Amzalak

Photograph, or Reference to Identity Document Bearing Photograph.

Seal of Chief Administrator, or G.O.C. Desert Mtd. Corps for Area under his Administration.

VALID TO PROCEED TO ...

INTELLIGENCE OFFICER

J. Campbell
Major
MILITARY GOVERNOR
JAFFA DISTRICT.

Signature of Military Governor (where such exist).

DEPARTURE
24.7.20

Form I.L.P./1.

ARC. 4° 1613/18

Plate 55: Laissez-Passer issued to James Amzalak
(Source: Amzalak Family Archives, National Library Archives, Jerusalem, 4°1613/3)

After the war, many members of the Amzalak family returned to Palestine, among them Ben-Zion and Joseph Amzalak, along with some of their kin. Others, like Joseph's son Eliyahu, settled in England. Eliyahu worked as a medical practitioner in London.

CONCLUSION

Among the central issues in contemporary research on the Middle East is periodization, i.e., the definition of the beginning of the modern era in the region. In dealing with this question historians and social scientists have presented various conceptual frameworks, each of which has been subject to varying degrees of criticism. One scheme traces the pattern of linear progression from tradition to modernity, which was propelled in one way or another by Western influences. Another focuses on the dichotomy between internal and external forces, while emphasizing the role of the former type in the process of change.

In the absence of a universally accepted scale of measurement for dating the beginning of the modern era, a more practical approach has been suggested: the use of a list of developments characteristic of modern society, with no causal or sequential relationship between them, as a guideline. In metropolitan centers, these were expressed through institutional changes — the restructuring of the central government, the introduction of legal reforms, the seeking of new technologies and capabilities by the military, and the intervention of the central treasury in the economy and the fiscal system. The social structure of society, particularly its ruling elite and intellectual leadership, played a major role in guiding the processes of transformation, and in the conceptualization and absorption of new ideas. In peripheral areas like Palestine, the list of characteristic developments differs from that of the core due to the absence of central institutions. In the outlying provinces, these developments find their expression in the decline of long-established social organizations as well as the enhanced status of minority religious groups, the emergence of a new entrepreneurial elite and changes in the infrastructure, economy, organizational framework and local administration.[389]

Until recently, research on nineteenth-century Palestine had adopted the model of linear progress from tradition to modernity, with singular emphasis on the influence of external forces from the West — churches, missions, consuls and settlers — on the processes of change. The greatest weight was placed on

---

389 Charles Issawi, *The Economic History of the Middle East, 1800-1914*, Chicago 1966; Shamir (supra n. 57), pp. 214-231.

the New *Yishuv* — those who had immigrated to Palestine from the 1880s onwards and who were considered the harbingers of modernization. On the other hand, research on the Old *Yishuv*, the Jewish community predating this modern settlement and synonymous with tradition, has focused upon the community's organization, social structure, institutions and spiritual and religious life, while neglecting economic and settlement aspects.

The tradition-versus-modernity approach inevitably dated the beginning of the process of change towards the end of the nineteenth century. However, current research points to the first half of the previous century as the beginning of the modern era in Palestine. By then developments characteristic of the modern era can be seen in the spheres of settlement and economy.[390]

Among the internal influences were several local entrepreneurial families — Muslims, Christians and Jews — that served as intermediaries between the local community on the one hand and the Ottoman Empire, its political apparatus, and international economic bodies on the other hand.[391] The Jews in this category came mainly from the ranks of the native Sephardi elite or those who had emigrated from Mediterranean (Morocco and Turkey) and Middle Eastern (Syria and Iraq) countries in the early or mid-nineteenth century.[392] Among this group were the Valero, Navon, Amzalak, and Yehuda families in Jerusalem and the Chelouche and Moyal families in Jaffa.

This book has spanned more than a century of the Amzalak family history, starting with the establishment of the family patriarch in Palestine at the beginning of the nineteenth century. It portrays one portion of the larger mosaic composed of many such family histories. Familiarity with this mosaic has enhanced our understanding of how local and internal factors contributed to changing Palestinian society and economy. Other related subjects that are ordinarily relatively neglected have been elaborated upon, such as day-to-day family life, housing, furniture, dress, the role of women and children, religious frameworks, and relations between neighbors.

The activities of the Amzalaks transcend the supposed periodization of the modern era as beginning with the establishment of Jewish agricultural settlements in the 1880s. The Amzalaks' pursuits, in fact, illuminate processes originating at the beginning of the nineteenth century and continuing through the end of Ottoman rule in Palestine.

Certain aspects of the Amzalaks' lives reflect developments in the Jewish and general communities. On the other hand, some of their attributes and pursuits

390 Schölch (supra n. 21); Kark (supra n. 117).
391 Fawaz (supra n. 21).
392 Parfitt (supra n. 108).

are clearly unique. The arrival of Joseph Amzalak and his family in Palestine in the early nineteenth century fits the trend of Jewish immigration predating the First *Aliyah* (1882-1904). His settling in the port city of Acre and integration into its commercial activity were steps that deviated from the common pattern. His later move to Jerusalem was in chime with the religiously-motivated tendency of most Jews to settle in one of the four holy cities — Jerusalem, Safed, Tiberias and Hebron.

Joseph's vast wealth facilitated his rapid integration into the Sephardi elite of Jerusalem, which dominated the Jewish community of the city until the 1880s. He enhanced his family's status by establishing bonds of marriage with two different branches of the eminent Navon family. The rapidly-growing Ashkenazi population in Jerusalem came to partially eclipse the Sephardi elite. Only select families with a strong economic or political basis in the city — such as the Navons, Valeros and Eliachars — continued to exert an influence after the 1880s. The second- and third-generation Amzalaks in Jerusalem, whose status and livelihood were based only on their inheritance from Joseph Amzalak, were devoid of influence and stature.

Certain members of the Amzalak family relocated in the port city of Jaffa in order to further their activities. Opportunity abounded there due to the city's growing agricultural hinterland, while Jerusalem remained economically stagnant. The contrast between these two cities is highlighted by a comparison of Haim Amzalak to his brothers, Solomon and Raphael. Haim Amzalak, a very successful merchant in Jaffa, received the prestigious and pivotal post of British vice-consul, thus further enhancing his status. Throughout his residence in Jaffa was considered one of the foremost leaders of the city and of the Jewish community in Palestine. Likewise, his son Joseph and his nephew Ben-Zion attained similar rank around the turn of the century. On the other hand, Raphael and Solomon, who remained in Jerusalem, participated only to a limited extent in the leadership of the Jewish community, while declining financially and fading into unimportance on a communal level.

The Amzalaks promoted the aspirations of pioneering Jewish settlement in Palestine from its outset in the late 1870s for both ideological reasons and the possible financial benefits connected. Haim Amzalak and his nephew Joseph Navon assisted the settlers of Petah Tikvah and Rishon LeZion in the procuration of land and interceded on their behalf before Ottoman officials. Many members of the family belonged to various societies supportive of Jewish settlement endeavors, and later supported the Zionist movement.

The Amzalak family stood out in maintaining good working relations with Jews, Christians and Muslims alike, both localites and foreigners. They developed a complex network of connections in Palestine with consuls of the Great Powers, Christian missionaries, rabbis from the Sephardi and Askenazi communities, Jewish settlers from Eastern Europe, merchants and bankers. Their relationships transcended the borders of Palestine, reaching Constantinople and other European capitals, and important commercial centers along the Mediterranean basin. This was facilitated by their British citizenship and unswerving loyalty to the Crown. In addition, their knowledge of foreign and local languages greatly eased these interactions. The Amzalaks were cosmopolitan in their nature, lifestyle and activities while maintaining a high level of Jewish identity and involvement.

In the wake of the disintegration of the Palestine they had known, and their exile in Egypt during World War I, the Amzalak family eventually found itself dispersed throughout the world. Possessing language skills, well-rounded educations and experience in economic fields, they integrated into society and business undertakings in London, Paris, Lisbon, Alexandria, New York and later California. A few members returned to Palestine after the war, but found a society that was rapidly changing in a direction not suited to their life styles, and again left. Others reestablished themselves in Eretz Israel after the exile, choosing to continue their long-standing emotional and economic ties with the land.

APPENDIX I

AMZALAK FAMILY TREE

ERETZ ISRAEL BRANCH

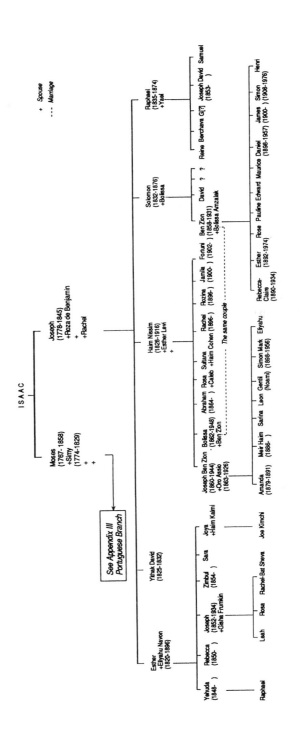

APPENDIX II

THE LISBON BRANCH OF THE AMZALAK FAMILY

Portugal during the late eighteenth century saw the beginning of liberalization of the attitude towards Jews. A central figure in this process was the Marquis de Pombal, Sebastião Jose de Carvalho e Mello. Pombal felt the Inquisition had been detrimental to the reputation of Portugal abroad and the economic prosperity of the kingdom. He observed that the Christãos Novos (New Christians) who had fled Portugal had contributed greatly to the economic prosperity of the markets in Bordeaux, London, Amsterdam and other towns. In 1768 Dom José I ordered the suppression of the list of New Christians so that they could no longer be distinguished from the general population. During the following years laws were enacted that abolished all discriminatory treatment between the king's subjects, whatever their origin, and that limited the activities of the Inquisition.[1]

In this environment of tolerance, New Christians were no longer outwardly persecuted, and Jews from outside Portugal began to move to Portugal. Jews from Gibraltar, who held British citizenship, were among the first Jews to return. They had the advantage of being protected by various treaties between Portugal and England permitting the English, including Jews, to practise their religion freely but in privacy. Others came from Tangiers, Tetuan and Mogador in Morocco. A small community was formed in Lisbon in the 1800s. In 1801, a section of the English cemetery da Estrella at Lisbon was acquired by the Jews of Lisbon. In 1813, Rabbi Abraham Dabella founded *Sha'ar Shamayim* (Gate of Heaven) Synagogue at Lisbon. A Jewish community has existed in the Azores since 1818. In 1820 João VI officially allowed Jews to

---

1   Cardozo de Bethencourt, "The Jews in Portugal from 1773 to 1902," *The Jewish Quarterly Review* (old series), no. 15, (1903), pp. 251-260; E.H. Lindo, *The History of the Jews of Spain and Portugal*, London 1848, p. 375; for additional bibliographical references to Portuguese Jewry during the nineteenth and twentieth centuries, see: Robert Singerman, *The Jews in Spain and Portugal: A Bibliography*, New York 1975, pp. 301-319.

settle in Lisbon. The following year the Inquisition at last ceased to exist. Yet another Jewish community was founded in Faro by 1830.[2]

The Amzalak family arrived in Lisbon during this period. Moses Amzalak and his first wife Simy (1784-1829) had seven children. After his wife's death Moses settled in Jerusalem. He remarried two more times according to information provided by the Portuguese branch of the family. After his immigration to Jerusalem all contact between him and the Portuguese Amzalaks was discontinued.[3]

The oldest grave in the aforementioned da Estrella cemetery, dating from 1804, belongs to a member of the Amzalak family. Its epitaph bears the following inscription: "AQUI . IAS . IOZE. AMZALAGA QUE MORREU EM XXVI D FEUEREIRO D 1804" (Here lies Joseph Amzalaga who died on the twenty-sixth of February, 1804).[4]

The part of Moses Amzalak's family that remained in Lisbon was prominent in the Jewish community and Portuguese society, as an 1889 *Jewish Chronicle* article referring to his grandson, Moses Abudarham Amzalak, attests:

> The Jewish Community of Lisbon enjoys the protection of Royal Family and Government and expects the formal sanction to the building of a synagogue worthy of the capital. Mr. Moses Amzalak (who is now in London on business connected with the founding of a new bank at Lisbon, 'the Africa and Brazil,' of which he is a founder) is one of the foremost members of the community and is a persona grata with the Portuguese Royal Family. On August 15 last, he was graciously received by Her majesty the Queen [Victoria] to whom he presented a letter praying for the recovery of the King.[5]

The Amzalaks played an important role in the establishing of a new synagogue, *Sha'are Tikva* (Gates of Hope) in Lisbon. Before its construction, the synagogues in the city were all in poor condition and located in small rented structures. Leão (Judah) and Isaac Amzalak, the sons of the elder Moses Amzalak, were among the organizing committee of the synagogue during the mid-nineteenth century, contributing time and money and bequeathing a legacy

2   Bethencourt (supra n. 1), pp. 264-265; Jose Maria Abecassis, *Hebrew Genealogy: Portugal XIX and XX Centuries — An Epigraphic Study and Listing of Existing Graves in the Jewish Cemetery of Faro*, Faro 1986, pp. 1-2; Lindo (supra n. 1), p. 377.
3   Jose Maria Abecassis, *Genealogy of Some Jewish Families in Portugal*, Lisbon 1976 (unpublished manuscript).
4   Bethencourt (supra n. 1), p. 265.
5   *Jewish Chronicle*, October 11, 1889, p. 6a.

ק״ק שַׁעֲרֵי תִקְוָה

COLONIA ISRAELITA DE LISBOA
ESTA PEDRA FUNDAMENTAL DA SYNAGOGA PORTUGUEZA

SHAARE TIKVA

FOI COLLOCADA EM 18 DE YIAR DE 5662
25 DE MAIO DE 1902

POR ABRAHAM E.LEVY

SENDO PRESIDENTE DO COMITÉ, LEÃO AMZALAK
PRESIDENTE DA SECÇÃO DA EDIFIGAÇÃO, A. ANAHORY
E THESOUREIRO DA COLONIA, SALOMON DE M.SEQUERRA

ARCHITECTO, VENTURA TERRA.

Plate 56: Plaque from interior of Sha'are Tikva Synagogue, Lisbon 1989.
(Source: Glass, photographed in 1989)

to this cause. The project was not realized during their lifetimes. On May 25, 1902 the cornerstone of the synagogue was laid, with Leão (Judah) Benoliel Amzalak, the grandson of Moses, presiding over the ceremony.[6] [see Plate 56]

The following description provides insight into the role of the Amzalak family in Portuguese society at the turn of the century, and the social goings-on at the time:

> One of the drawing rooms which appealed to the non-Jews and attracted them was that of the Amzalak family who then lived in the building which now houses the warehouses of Chiado and which in those days was known as the "Barcelinhos Palace" (the name of its owners, the Viscount

6   Moses Bensabat Amzalak, *A Sinagoga Portuguesa "Sha'are Tikva" (As Portas da Esperanca)*, Lisbon 1954; Abecassis (supra n. 3); Bethencourt (supra n. 1), pp. 269-271.

Barcelinhos). Thanks to the charm and the goodness of its members, this family had a distinguished position among both the Jews and the non-Jews. To the Jews they were always ready to extend a helping hand, a good word to alleviate the pain, the moral and the material support which they bestowed on the needy. For the non-Jews they showed personal charm, elegance and good manners. Through their generously open drawing room passed many distinguished figures of their time, whom the ladies of the house as well as the head of the household, who was a merchant and very estimated in the business world, director of the Lisbon Commercial Association, greeted with sympathy. These drawing rooms were visited by poets such as Tomaz Ribero and Gomes Leal, the "beaux" of the day such as the three Lima Mayer brothers: Adolfo, Augusto and Carlos (who later belonged to the famous "winners of life" group), Carlos Cirilio Machado (later Viscount de Santo Tirso); known families such as the Ulrichs, the family of Jose Luciano de Castro (who later succeeded Anselmo Braacamp as head of the progressive party and future president of the council of ministers). The traditions of that family still shine with fervour in one of the ladies of this house, Dona Anette Amzalak who is highly esteemed in the Portuguese society and equally, our dear cousin, Professor Dr. Moses Bensabat Amzalak who inherited the virtues of his ancestors.[7]

The most prominent member of the Amzalak family in Lisbon was Moses Bensabat Amzalak, born on October 4, 1892. His activities in the fields of academics, economics, history and politics received international acclaim. Rising through the ranks of the academic world, he attained full professorship in 1927 at the Higher Institute of Commerce in Lisbon, vice rectorship in 1931 and rectorship in 1956 at the Technical University in Lisbon. He wrote an extensive number of economic histories of Portugal and ancient Greece and Rome, as well as studies on the history of Portuguese Jewry. Bensabat Amzalak served as an economic advisor for the Portuguese government. He was offered the post of Minister of Commerce, which he declined in order to remain in the academic world.[8] [see Plate 57]

The Amzalak family resided not only in Lisbon but also in the southern Portuguese coastal town of Faro. An individual by the name of Dinar Amzalak was interned in the Jewish cemetery of Faro in 1894.[9]

7 Aldolfo Benarús, *O Antisemitismo*, Lisbon 1937, pp. 19-20.

8 Abraham Elmaleh, *Le Professeur Moses Bensabat Amzalak, sa Vie et son Oeuvre Litéraire, Economique, Historique et Scientifique*, Jerusalem 1962; Abecassis (supra n. 3).

9 Abecassis (supra n. 2), p. 10.

Plate 57: Professor Moses
Bensabat Amzalak
(Source: Amzalak Family Archives,
National Library Archives,
Jerusalem, 4°1613/3)

The Amzalak family also had a prominent branch in Brazil. Isaac, the son of Moses the elder, immigrated to Bahia, Brazil in the early nineteenth century. He had sought a tropical climate as a cure for his rheumatism. It seems that he opened a subsidiary of a Lisbon- or London-based commercial company which traded with the West Indies. In Bahia, he developed the best of relationships and was held in high esteem by the Marquez de Paranagua and the Baron de Cotegipe. His descendants were prominent members of Brazilian society, serving in the military and the civil service.[10]

Another branch of the Amzalak family settled in the Portuguese colony of Angola. Jacob Abudarham Amzalak, son of Leão (Judah), was employed by the Angola Sugar Company. Family sources indicate that although Jacob did not marry, he had some seventy children. All his children were given a gold chain with his photograph, which served his grandchildren as identification when they visited the family in Lisbon.[11]

10   Abecassis (supra n. 3).
11   Abecassis (supra n. 3).

APPENDIX III

AMZALAK FAMILY TREE

PORTUGUESE BRANCH

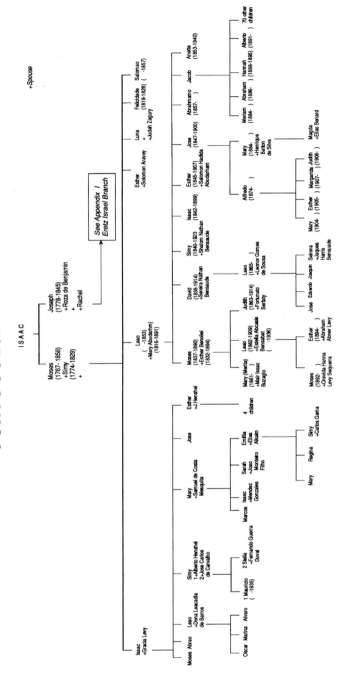

INDEX

01/09 ②

3
3/10
9/18 ④

CASA DE AMANTES

C A S A
D E
AMANTES

LOURDES VENTURA

PLAZA & JANÉS EDITORES, S.A.

Primera edición: septiembre, 2000

© 2000, Lourdes Fernández Ventura
© 2000, Plaza & Janés Editores, S. A.
  Travessera de Gràcia, 47-49. 08021 Barcelona

Printed in Spain – Impreso en España

ISBN: 84-01-32831-4
Depósito legal: B. 28.154 – 2000

Fotocomposición: Comptex & Ass., S. L.

Impreso en Limpergraf
Mogoda, 29. Barberà del Vallès (Barcelona)

L 3 2 8 3 1 4

A Charo Martínez,
desde los días de Portobello

Gracias a Ignacio Aranaz, Silvia Bastos, Manuel Bear, Maritxu Catalán, Asunción Fernández, Manuel Hidalgo, Ana Parrilla, Arantxa Sola y Fernando Verdugo, que han seguido esta historia desde sus inicios.

Nosotros olvidamos al cuerpo, pero el cuerpo no nos olvida a nosotros. ¡Maldita memoria de los órganos!

E. M. CIORÁN

1

Mi hermana me obligó a detenerme en medio del camino para ver las bocanadas de fuego que salían de aquellos labios de ángel caído. Me arrastró hasta un corrillo de curiosos apiñados en torno a una rueda de hachones encendidos en cuyo centro exacto un hombre rubio y extranjero lanzaba llamaradas por la boca. Tenía esa palidez mortecina o seráfica, según se mire, de algunos emigrantes del Este y un cuerpo apetitoso de huesos perfectos. Mi hermana lo llamó comefuegos y yo pensé más bien que era un lanzallamas. Faquir o tragasables. Hubiera dado lo mismo. Marta lo miró con sus ojos de samaritana y yo adiviné que, una vez más, había visto en él el resplandor de las fogatas bajo los puentes, y la soledad de las fronteras cruzadas a pie con un atado de ropa por todo equipaje, y los atardeceres fríos de los parques europeos cuando un puñado de chiquillos, como en aquel domingo luminoso del Retiro, se empujaban unos a otros para ver al lanzallamas en primera fila. Está mal que yo lo diga, pero a mi hermana, la verdad, se le hizo la boca agua.

Un día, hace un par de años, en casa de nuestra madre, Marta me llevó a la cocina y me dijo: «He desnudado a un vagabundo con la barba rojiza de un escocés y los ojos azul Paul Newman; lo he lavado, he restregado la mugre que se había pegado a su piel y he rasurado sus mejillas hasta sacar a la luz unos rasgos asustados y nuevos.»

Cuando me cruzo con un mendigo joven por la calle, pienso algunas veces en esa imagen. Mi hermana Marta en su cuarto de baño resplandeciente, la luz del pequeño jardín tamizada por la persiana, el hombre sentado en el borde de la bañera ya limpio, desconcertado y envuelto en una toalla de color crema.

¿Cuántas veces hay que cambiar el agua de un baño para que la mugre de un pordiosero vaya desapareciendo? Conociendo a mi hermana imagino que tuvo que quitar en varias ocasiones el tapón de la bañera para ver cómo el agua sucia se perdía entre los torbellinos del sumidero. Imagino que mientras el mendigo estaba recostado contra la porcelana blanca, ella vaciaría el baño y volvería a dejar correr el grifo del agua caliente y a verter gel para que saliese espuma, hasta que el nivel del agua volvía a cubrir al hombre y la espuma humeante alcanzaba su pecho velludo, no tan caliente protestaría él, y mi hermana, de rodillas sobre una alfombrilla de felpa, con la melena rubia sobre los hombros, como en una de esas estampas de místicas atravesadas por el rayo de la santidad o del placer, vaya usted a saber, frotaría con un guante de crin, con infinita paciencia, empezando por la espalda y el cuello, por detrás de las orejas, seguro, tal como nuestra madre nos lavaba de niñas, un poco más tarde no, un poco más tarde éramos nosotras quienes teníamos que obligar a nuestra madre a lavarse, cuando todo lo olvidaba, cuando los dedos de su novio Hipólito le trepaban por las piernas.

14

A lo mejor a Marta se le ocurrió poner música de fondo, un coro conventual, o algo parecido, pero no me lo dijo, o al menos no lo recuerdo. Secó al náufrago con una toalla de color crema rosada, eso lo sé, del mismo color que los jabones de La Toja, le prestó el albornoz blanco que tiene dispuesto para los que arriban a su isla sin equipaje y lo sentó frente al espejo con un cepillo de dientes sin estrenar. No hay más que ver las manos expertas de Marta en asuntos masculinos para saber que lo afeitaría con sumo cuidado y con el albornoz puesto, y luego le daría un masaje de barbería de lujo con el aftershave olvidado de alguno de sus amantes de paso.

Supe que el vagabundo, agradecido, abrazó con torpeza a mi hermana convencido de que era una santa. Con ojos de Lázaro resucitado aquel hombre se miró en el espejo sin reconocerse.

Marta me dijo en casa de nuestra madre que después lo dejó dormir muchas horas sobre las sábanas limpias de su propia cama. Unos días más tarde, en una cafetería de la calle Princesa, me contó la verdad.

2

Podrían pensar que hay una desmesura en todo este asunto de Marta y el vagabundo, y lo cierto es que he tratado de empezar a contar mi propia historia de otro modo, pero no se me ocurría nada más estrafalario para despertar su interés que las inclinaciones afectivas de mi hermana, por inverosímil que resulte la fascinación de una mujer de aspecto normal por los sin techo.

No pretendo decir con esto que lo que a mí me ha pasado y he decidido registrar para acallar mi conciencia o para tratar de descifrar algunos detalles confusos, sea carente de interés, o demasiado corriente o irrelevante. Aunque en realidad es ambas cosas, porque, como he podido comprobar, los edificios de apartamentos de cualquier ciudad están llenos de mujeres y hombres que hacen el amor a deshora en cuartos alquilados o prestados y abren las puertas con sus propias llaves y cierran el ascensor con el mayor sigilo para desaparecer más tarde del lugar del crimen. Siempre piensas que eres la única mujer infiel del planeta y al final te enteras de que hay multitudes en tu caso. Multitudes.

Como probablemente ya habrán adivinado, lo que van a

leer en estas páginas es una historia más de adulterio (sí, ya sé que están cansados de madame Bovary y de toda su descendencia, qué le vamos a hacer), y, cuando les diga que todavía guardo, camufladas entre los dedos deshabitados de un guante de lana, oculto en las profundidades de un armario que nadie abre, las llaves de un apartamento de una ciudad del norte, comprenderán que yo soy la adúltera.

A veces nos ocurren las cosas sin entenderlas bien, y luego tenemos necesidad de escucharlas en voz alta, de encontrar palabras para ordenar los acontecimientos, igual que hacen los detectives o los policías, desplegando las secuencias y atando cabos para ver si esto casa con aquello, para saber si la hora en que salió del bar el malhechor coincide con el momento exacto del paso del autobús por aquella calle —sólo de ese modo pudo llegar el sospechoso al lugar donde cometió su tropelía, puesto que no tiene coche ni cómplices y ningún taxista recuerda a un pasajero de esas características—. A veces intentamos averiguar cómo llegaron a ocurrir las cosas o por qué tuvo lugar determinado suceso en vez de otro, y nos empeñamos en rastrear nuevos indicios que se presentan justo cuando estamos a punto de dormir y entre sueños creemos descubrir el retazo que ilumina los hechos y nos hace ver claro, pero es sólo un segundo, un chispazo pasajero de luz, porque al despertar, y durante los siguientes días, no podemos recordar en qué consistía aquel detalle insignificante que nos asaltó en la noche y lo esclarecía todo.

Mi pretexto para seguir adelante no es calmar los nervios, ni saber en qué va a acabar todo esto que todavía colea, porque la vida sigue su curso y de pronto te encuentras con un atajo con el que no contabas; ni pretendo azuzar el deseo morboso de revolcarme de nuevo en las imágenes de esa guarida en que me he refugiado lejos de casa durante algunas horas; sino explicarles a ustedes por qué la existencia de un apartamento en una ciudad del norte embarulló los destinos de unos desconocidos entre sí, cuyo único vínculo, en principio, era la cama que compartían con otros hombres o mujeres que no eran sus maridos o compañeras.

Sé que es una locura contarlo todo así, de golpe y embarullado, pero las explicaciones llegarán a su tiempo. Antes de ir más lejos, tengo que reconocer la evidencia: durante los últimos meses he estado traicionando a Miguel. Aunque a decir verdad ya había empezado a serle infiel antes, por lo menos en mi cabeza. O, mejor, mucho mejor, yo no habría sido capaz de engañarle ni siquiera en mi imaginación siendo la que yo era hasta entonces, pero el caso es que me convertí en otra, y esa otra acabó cansándose del gesto torcido de Miguel y de la enorme televisión encendida que presidía, y todavía preside, nuestras vidas. No quiero decir que la mujer en la que me había convertido fuera peor, más quisquillosa y con menos escrúpulos que la que se casó con Miguel; simplemente era distinta. Y tampoco deben pensar que no le daba lo mejor de mí al hombre con el que dormía todas las noches cuando ocurrió lo que ocurrió, pero a fin de cuentas conocí a Álvaro Arriaga, con quien jamás he dormido, y me dejé llevar por la corriente.

Algo tan tonto como una carta vino a complicarlo todo. Yo no había previsto que Álvaro Arriaga me escribiese una carta de amor. Y es que, señoras y señores, nada hay tan peligroso como las misivas acusadoras. Si me preguntan a mí, les diré que destruyan en el acto cualquier papel comprometedor, palabras ardientes, diarios idiotas, barquitos de papel con mensajes cifrados que navegan a la deriva hasta que un experto en huellas encuentra las claves y se convierte en fiscal husmeador, o peor, en una jauría de policías que ronda las pesadillas implacables de nuestras noches. Pero nadie podía saberlo entonces. Me acostaba con Álvaro a muchos kilómetros de Madrid, eso es cierto, y él se empeñó en inventar el deseo con letra de miniaturista, la tinta negra cada vez más condensada, volviéndose líneas y puntos, me costaba entender cada palabra, patitas de araña retorcidas sobre una pradera nevada, sin encabezamiento ni firma. Tuve que achicar los ojos hasta entenderlo todo; leí muchas veces aquel papel unos minutos después de haberme entregado el sobre, me gustaba leerlo a solas acurrucada en el sofá del apartamento.

Sí, supongo que ustedes pensarán que yo cometí un error imperdonable al extraviar la carta de mi amante. Una noche al despedirnos después de uno de nuestros encuentros, Álvaro dijo: te he escrito una carta. Yo le pregunté: ¿una carta? Él me dijo: hay cosas que prefiero decirte por escrito. Y entonces me dio un sobre sin membrete y un beso de película. Al día siguiente olvidé el sobre encima del sofá. De todos modos, yo no imaginé que un desconocido podría tener algún interés en sustraer una carta ajena.

Fue entonces, hace unos meses, cuando tuve la sensación, conforme pasaban los días, de que a lo largo de toda la relación con mi amante y, en concreto, mientras nos veíamos en lo que creíamos la protectora soledad del apartamento 4A que yo alquilaba, y todavía alquilo (porque no he cancelado mi contrato con la agencia), en esa ciudad del norte, se desplegaban muy cerca de nosotros otras historias que han acabado por enredarse con la nuestra. No digo que no sea frecuente que las vidas de los seres humanos se desplieguen y se anuden como los ovillos deshilachados de una caja de costura, sino que a mí me desconcierta.

Las cosas se pierden y tú te mareas de tanto buscarlas. De pronto te has metido en un remolino y todo se vuelve del revés. Buscas una cosa, y tropiezas con otra con la que no contabas. Siempre ocurre así. Yo buscaba un sobre perdido y me di de bruces con Yolanda, la secretaria, y con Julio Oroz. Los dos se acostaban en el apartamento 4A, pero no juntos sino con otras personas, y otros días de la semana. El hecho de que estemos implicados varios amantes a la vez —aunque no entre nosotros y no simultáneamente, como creo que habrán ido comprendiendo— empantana la historia en mi cabeza y la vuelve más enrevesada.

El caso es que acabé enterándome de que tres mujeres casadas, y yo era una de ellas, nos dábamos cita en secreto con nuestros amantes en el mismo apartamento (aunque parezca raro, cada una tenemos asignados dos días a la semana, según acuerdo con la agencia), y lo más desorientador, y quizá éste es el hecho que está en el origen de mi desasosiego y de estas páginas, es que existen indicios para pensar que el amante de la mujer de los viernes, en realidad mi propio amante, hoy mi ex amante, para ser exactos, pudo haber sido, de confirmarse las sospechas, el responsable de la locura de la esposa de Julio Oroz, el amante que acudía a encontrarse con la mujer de los miércoles, y que en estos momentos está esperándome en Hendaya. Sí, ya sé que a estas alturas se han hecho un lío y barruntan que esto es una lombriz retorcida que nunca acaba de salir del barro, pero les suplico un poco más de paciencia.

Empezaré, pues, por buscar un comienzo, si es que como dice Oroz alguien puede ver con nitidez el principio y el fin de un suceso. Él desconfía de la cronología. ¿Es que no te das cuenta de que es por completo indiferente saber *dónde y en qué momento vivimos*? Es el tipo de interrogantes que suele lanzar aunque yo no acabe de entenderle. Y sin embargo, no puedo evitar agotarme para revisar una y otra vez los pasos andados hasta dar marcha atrás e imaginar cómo pudo iniciarse este episodio determinado de mi vida, porque sin ese inicio yo no hubiera conocido a Álvaro Arriaga, mi amante durante unos meses y hasta hace muy poco, ni tampoco hubiera tropezado con Julio Oroz, ni me hubiera enterado de las cosas que he tenido que enterarme.

Es cierto que de no haber perdido la carta de Álvaro, yo no habría conocido al resto de los inquilinos del 4A. Por culpa de una negligencia tuve que meterme a hurgar en vidas ajenas. Supe que Yolanda la secretaria y su jefe acudían al apartamento los lunes o los martes, o los dos días, y que Julio Oroz se veía con su amante los miércoles, aunque también podrían haberlo hecho los jueves puesto que la agencia exigía un alquiler mínimo de dos días. Tampoco habría leído un libro de Oroz y otro de Ciorán, ni visto las instalaciones artísticas de Mara Barbieri; no hubiera sabido, de haber destruido la carta de Álvaro o de, simplemente, haberla guardado en el aparador, junto a nuestra botella de Chivas, que la mujer de Julio Oroz quedó medio trastornada desde que un coche arrolló a su hija frente a un parque.

Ya sé que todo esto resulta un galimatías, tengan calma. El mundo es una bobina de lana, por así decirlo. Lo único que tengo que hacer es encontrar el cabo del hilo. Eso es. Empezar por el principio de la historia. Aunque he de advertir, para que se comprendan algunos pormenores, que tengo la impresión de que hay situaciones que se incuban mucho antes. Por eso estoy convencida de que todo ocurrió a causa de mi voz.

Hace pocos años mi vida emprendió un camino imprevisto. Ahora acabo de cumplir los treinta, pero cuando me convertí en *la voz* yo tenía veinticinco años, mis horas se extendían ante mí como un desierto y mi hermana ya llevaba mucho tiempo girando alrededor de los hombres como un torbellino sexual. Quiero decir que antes de ser *la voz*, yo no era nada. Trabajaba en una entidad bancaria, me había casado con un compañero de trabajo, y además de hacer números todos los días en el banco, hacía números en casa para llegar a fin de mes.

Seguramente ustedes me han escuchado cientos de veces. No han visto mi rostro, que es anodino y sin ningún interés, pero han oído mi voz en montones de anuncios televisivos. Es mi voz la que susurra detrás de automóviles rutilantes que alguien quiere comprar, y también soy la voz con que habla esa mujer de piel transparente que embadurna sus mejillas con una crema que promete juventud eterna. Parece que la claridad de mi pico de ángel acompaña la belleza de esas Barbies hidratadas que sonríen al mundo invitando a probar el producto salvador y que, casi seguro, en la vida real, hablan en otro idioma, o tienen unas voces roncas, o vulgares, o demasiado chillonas. Yo me encargo de que los mensajes lleguen con suavidad hasta el cerebro de los espectadores. Soy locutora de publicidad, ése es mi trabajo, y también doblo documentales y grabo cuñas radiofónicas y vídeos para campañas políticas. Así fue como me liberé del banco para siempre y así fue, también, como conocí a Álvaro Arriaga.

Miguel, mi marido, sigue en el banco haciendo números y contando billetes, pero yo soy libre, ahora soy *la voz* y una de las mejores en mi profesión, tengo unas tarifas considerables y vigilo con sumo cuidado el estado de mi garganta. No siempre tengo sesiones de grabación, de modo que, como el horario es variado, algunas mañanas me quedo en la cama haciendo gorgoritos para desentumecer las cuerdas vocales y leyendo en voz alta: hocico de oro, murmullo estremecido de hada madrina antes de entregar la carroza a Cenicienta, un chorro de dulzura por la boca caliente, la punta de mi lengua recorriendo el paladar de miel. Voz-de-or-gas-mo, como dice Julio Oroz. Más vale que se hagan una idea.

Es una vida bastante buena para una chica criada en un piso oscuro de un barrio dormitorio de las afueras de Madrid, con una madre desquiciada y un padre viajante que se fugó hace años con una manicura teñida de walkiria, llevándose consigo los discos de *soul*.

Quizá alguien quiera saber, y con toda razón, cómo entré en contacto con Álvaro Arriaga. La cosa empezó a través de un teléfono. Fue la primera vez que oí hablar de Arriaga y Asociados. La agencia de comunicación que dirige Álvaro quería contratarme para un trabajo, pero teníamos que grabar en su ciudad. Soy parca al teléfono, procuro no gastar saliva, puse mis condiciones y Álvaro aceptó. Todo lo demás vino después.

Anoche, por enésima vez, después de que Miguel anunciase benévolamente que esperaba una decisión definitiva por mi parte, evoqué lo que sentí cuando conocí a Julio Oroz y también imaginé estatuas incandescentes que arden por dentro y están heladas por fuera, o al revés. Cuando vi en el Retiro las bocanadas de fuego del lanzallamas angélico y cuando escuché el discurso incendiado de Julio Oroz, pensé lo mismo: habrá problemas.

3

Yo no buscaba un amante, se instaló hace unos meses en mi vida, tontamente, como se instaura en lo cotidiano una costumbre nueva; un queso, por ejemplo, un queso que se ha comprado por primera vez en el supermercado sólo para probar, porque alguien lo mencionó en una ocasión o lo leímos en una revista, un queso que se compra de nuevas porque tropezamos con esa variedad por casualidad en el estante de los lácteos y entonces recordamos que hemos oído hablar de él, y al probarlo en casa nos gusta, nos gusta tanto que decidimos volver a buscarlo la siguiente semana, y también la otra, así hasta que la adquisición de ese determinado queso se convierte en un acto imprescindible que pasa a formar parte de nuestros pequeños rituales y de nuestros hábitos de cada día.

Lo crean o no, así entró Álvaro Arriaga en mi vida, a lo tonto, como una nueva variedad de queso, como un sujetador de blonda recién estrenado, tan blanco al principio, mucho más favorecedor que los otros que vamos arrinconando en el cajón, como un sabor nuevo al que me empecé a acostumbrar sin darme cuenta.

Entretanto, Miguel y yo caminábamos igual que sonámbulos con las manos extendidas, buscándonos el uno al otro por la casa, pero tropezábamos con los muebles y abríamos los ojos para descubrir que estábamos solos, que habíamos abrazado una silla vacía. Hacía ya tiempo que no nos encontrábamos, aunque nos queríamos, aunque dormíamos en la misma cama y se fundían nuestros cuerpos algunas noches. O pudo ser entonces, hace menos de un año, cuando caí en la cuenta, cuando el regusto de los besos de Álvaro me convenció de que la boca de Miguel sabía a rutina, debió de ser por entonces cuando supe que nos lanzábamos miradas inexpresivas, sin vernos bien, con los ojos borrosos de los catatónicos.

Es cierto que hay hechos contundentes que se dejan pasar, sospechas que se ocultan debajo de la almohada, pruebas irrefutables que nadie quiere ver. Yo seguía con mi trabajo y con la organización doméstica sin que Miguel notara que había empezado a acostumbrarme a un sabor nuevo. O eso creía yo. El tiempo que Miguel y yo pasábamos juntos transcurría, como ahora, entre el sofá y la televisión, las sesiones de cine de algunos sábados, cuando no hay partido, y las salidas esporádicas de los viernes con amigos que cada vez me interesan menos, o que ya han dejado de interesarme por completo. Los domingos nunca han sido míos, los domingos son de la madre de Miguel y de los clubes de fútbol.

Recuerdo ahora una de aquellas cenas de viernes por la noche. Yo acababa de conocer a Álvaro. Entre copas y señales de humo a alguien se le ocurrió la idea de ir a bailar. Todos habíamos bebido más de la cuenta. Nos metimos en un local pequeño, sin gorila a la entrada, oculto entre callejas. La música era atronadora y a Miguel le entró complejo de peonza bajo la luz lunar de la discoteca. Yo empecé a encogerme en el asiento, me encogía cada vez más y callaba. De todos modos, por mi trabajo no me conviene forzar la voz y había que hablar a gritos en aquella bombonera de plata para entenderse. Miguel hacía esfuerzos por pasárselo bien, eso se veía. Sacó a bailar a las chicas de nuestro grupo, después solicitó a las llaneras solitarias que pescaba en la barra y en otras mesas, pedía más bebidas, hacía piruetas en la pista, bastante borracho y bastante harto, pensé yo, harto de su vida, harto de mis silencios y mis encogimientos, harto de no poder estallar, por eso giraba como un loco, como un derviche, como una peonza sin rumbo. Hay veces que bailamos a favor, y otras en contra. Miguel, esa noche, bailaba en contra del mundo, bailaba contra mí, bailaba contra sí mismo. Si hubiera tenido arrestos habría dado vueltas en la pista hasta acabar con todo, hasta caer derrengado bajo las luces galácticas, pero era consciente de su cobardía, mantenía un punto de control, se sabía demasiado cuerdo para danzar como un maldito hasta la extenuación. Yo, en mi asiento, sumergida en el hondo vaho del whisky (la misma marca que había bebido la primera noche con Álvaro, pero no la que hemos estado bebiendo durante meses y de la que todavía queda una botella en el aparador del apartamento), me trasladé con facilidad a otro escenario. Lo hago muchas veces. A decir verdad, lo he hecho desde niña. Todo empieza con un pálpito en las sienes. Tengo que elegir, o dolor de cabeza o el tobogán. Elegí también ese día el tobogán y me deslicé por una pendiente que ya conozco y que me deposita en un rectángulo luminoso de arena. Aquel viernes, en la discoteca, detrás del pálpito de mis sienes no habitaba Miguel girando como un derviche loco. Detrás de mis sienes a punto de crisparse en una migraña feroz se abría la cuesta abajo por la que me dejé rodar hasta aterrizar en la cama de un hotel de lujo. Yo daba zarpazos de placer contra la nada y allí estaba Álvaro Arriaga con la cabeza hundida entre mis piernas.

Cuando regresamos a casa, Miguel me hizo sentar en la cama. De golpe se le había pasado la borrachera. Pensé que en su danza de guerra había expulsado los malos espíritus. Me preguntó que dónde estaba yo desde hacía tiempo, me acusó de vivir en otro lugar. Me dijo que me veía detrás de un cristal. Hace mucho que no puedo llegar a ti, creo que dijo, estamos separados por una mampara de cristal. Me quedé rígida frente a él. Si alguien hubiera doblado con fuerza mi cuello en ese momento lo habría tronchado como una rama. Sólo le pude decir eso. Le expliqué lo de mi cuello agarrotado porque no le podía hablar del tobogán, ni de Arriaga entre sábanas reptando por mis piernas. Ladeé la cabeza y señalé mis omoplatos con gesto de niña malcriada y dolorida porque quería que Miguel me diese uno de sus masajes. Así de sencillo, sus dedos explorando mis cervicales, despejando mi nuca, los dedos de Miguel. Y otra vez sentí sobre mi piel la presión y el calor de aquellas manos, las únicas capaces, hasta hacía poco, de disolver mi cuerpo en el vacío.

Momentos como ése nos hacían olvidar el tedio y Miguel y yo volvíamos a acercarnos y a buscarnos como en los primeros días, cuando empezábamos a vivir juntos. No es normal que el compañero de trabajo sea un experto masajista, pero Miguel lo era, magnífico, manos de santo, decían sus compinches del equipo de fútbol cuando Miguel les enderezaba los huesos.

La primera vez que nos vimos fuera del horario del banco me temblaban un poco las piernas. Quedamos un sábado por la noche en un bar de la calle Huertas. Llegué tarde y sin paraguas. Llovía. Me dijo que parecía una ardilla con el pelo mojado. Lo peiné hacia atrás con los dedos, para aplacarlo. Se quedó todo pegado, mi pelo corto. Miguel me besó en ese mismo instante. En la boca, mordiéndome los labios, buscando mi lengua, a lo bestia, como yo imaginaba desde hacía cuatro meses de tropezarme con sus manos en el angosto espacio de nuestra oficina. Luego jugueteó con mis cigarrillos sobre el mármol helado de la mesa. Le miré a los ojos de frente, muy cerca, por primera vez; comprendí por qué yo pensaba que se daba un aire a un león joven: melena desordenada de león, barba de león, ojos de selva.

—Blanca —me dijo—, lo que yo quiero es encerrarme contigo en tu casa y no salir en una semana.

—Soy claustrofóbica, me angustian los espacios cerrados —mentí.

—Mientes —dijo seguro.

Le expliqué que siempre tenía ganas de escapar cuando me presionaban. No son los espacios, sino las personas, le dije. Si me rodean me reducen a la condición de prisionera. Me pesa la rutina compartida. Es lo que más me agobia del trabajo en el banco, dije, los días por delante, todos idénticos.

—Dame una semana, sólo una semana —rogó.

Me volvió a besar a conciencia. Miguel esperaba rendirme en el primer asalto. Yo estaba ya rendida, para qué iba a luchar.

—Hoy es sábado, el lunes es fiesta, tenemos tres noches —respondí.

—¿No está tu hermana? —preguntó, los ojos fijos.

—Marta está en Marruecos.

Un chico larguirucho depositó en la mesa un plato de almendras. Miguel miraba las almendras y luego a mí como si buscase una relación. Se comió una almendra y acarició mi boca con un dedo. Noté el sabor de la sal en los labios.

—¿No has imaginado alguna vez —preguntó—, una habitación inmensa, vacía, sólo con un colchón y sábanas frescas, y al fondo una terraza sobre el mar?

—El mar me da miedo, no sé nadar, me aterra el mar.

—¿No sabes nadar?

—No sé flotar, me hundo en el agua.

—Flotar es como hacer el amor. Lo mejor es dejarse ir, no juzgar, no observar. Puede que te trague el amor, o puede que te trague el agua, lo mismo da, pero no se debe pensar en ello cuando tratamos de ser un corcho en la superficie. Es la única manera de flotar. Si te paras a analizar el proceso, pierdes pie, cobras peso, te hundes. Dicen que cuando tienes miedo al agua, tienes miedo al sexo. Miguel hablaba como el monitor de gimnasia que un día quiso ser.

—Yo no tengo miedo al sexo —protesté, y noté un suelo resbaladizo bajo mis pies—. A mí me gusta hacer el amor, Miguel, me gusta perder la memoria. Cuando hago el amor me vuelvo amnésica. Cuando amo me olvido de quién soy, me dejo ir, como tú dices. Pero en el agua, no, en el agua me hundo como un ancla.

Miguel enmarcó mi cara con sus manos. Yo todavía no era *la voz*, pero él quiso saltarse un capítulo.

—¿Sabes qué dice Alarcón?

Me encogí de hombros.

—Dice que tienes la voz más convincente del banco, que te tenías que meter a sindicalista.

Me eché a reír. No llegué a terminar el ron con coca-cola,

me sacó del local en volandas. Tres noches en volandas. Me acariciaba con sus dedos de masajista y al minuto la sangre hervía. Horas y horas a la horizontal, de la cama al sofá, haciendo el amor y contándonos en los intervalos las sórdidas historias de su madre viuda y de mi madre loca. Parecíamos un concurso de vidas tristes, y eso nos daba risa. A salvo por fin, a salvo en nuestra torpeza, en nuestro encierro. El martes por la mañana llegamos juntos a trabajar. Él llevaba la misma ropa del sábado. Nadie tenía por qué saberlo.

4

Cuando Miguel se fue de casa los cuadros quedaron enderezados en las paredes, las macetas regadas, las revistas apiladas en una mesita, los vasos en su sitio en la cocina, los ceniceros limpios. Muy poco tardé en darme cuenta de que Miguel era el orden personificado. Lo único alborotado de Miguel era la melena de león, melena indomable que le gustaba llevar en aparente tumulto. Creo que para compensar. Dos días más tarde, cuando se empeñó en quedarse a dormir en casa, aprovechando que Marta no había vuelto de su viaje, supe ya de sobra que yo formaba parte de sus planes y que pediríamos un préstamo para comprar un piso soleado y vivir juntos.

Fuimos al juzgado con su madre de negro y unos cuantos amigos. Marta, mi hermana, también vino. Mi padre estaba de viaje y mi madre en las nubes, como siempre. Fuimos al juzgado con nuestros vestidos de todos los días y ropa interior recién estrenada, no sé por qué. Estaba nublado y yo me sentía confinada en una nave como uno de esos astronautas cabeza abajo. Miguel, en cambio, me contemplaba con el mismo aire satisfecho que se exhibe al distribuir la ropa en armarios y cajones después de plancharla, o después de cuadrar satisfactoriamente un balance o pegar las fotos de las vacaciones en un álbum. Para Miguel era una cuestión práctica. Nos casamos, tras varios meses de vivir juntos, para poner las cosas en orden. Como si antes de firmar los papeles nuestra vida fuera un barullo, y al casarnos, al poner, como dice Miguel, las cosas en orden, nuestra existencia hubiera entrado en un cauce tranquilo y sosegado. Miguel nunca se olvida de los plazos del piso, ni de las revisiones del coche, cambios de aceite, declaraciones de la renta, citas con el dentista, horarios de sus entrenamientos, ni tampoco de las visitas a su madre todos los domingos.

Raras veces asisto a los encuentros dominicales entre madre e hijo. Durante esas comidas la madre de Miguel suspira más que habla. Al menos cuando yo estoy delante. Puede que esté equivocada, pero en esos suspiros de la madre enlutada detecto siempre un reproche lanzado contra mí. Contra mí que me he llevado a su hijo, pobrecillo, a saber qué comerá en mi casa, cómo le zurciré los calcetines, si es que se los zurzo, si es que no va con un gran boquete que las uñas hicieron y nadie se encargó de remendar, a saber qué desaguisados estoy haciendo con la vida de su hijo que seguiría divinamente atendido bajo la tutela de su madre de no haberse casado conmigo, tan bajita, tan suficiente, y ahora para colmo ganando más que su hijo con ese oficio raro de ponerle voz a los anuncios, seguro que le miro por encima del hombro, pedir la excedencia en el banco por un trabajo tan poco serio, coches para hombres entre susurros, mujeres que jadean para promocionar un perfume, esto no puede ser trigo limpio. La madre de Miguel dice todo esto sin decirlo, lo dice en la triste mirada y en los *ay señor* que lanza al aire sin darse cuenta y deja flotando durante un tiempo hasta que se condensan en una nube amarga. No voy a las comidas de los domingos en la casa familiar de Miguel porque me desazona el luto perpetuo y me cansan las palabras lastimeras de su madre; no voy, porque no me gustan las víctimas que disparan suspiros con un fondo de latigazo.

Me he ido por las ramas. Miro con cierto asombro —hace tanto que no escribía— el despliegue de páginas que ya se amontonan sobre la mesa; pero me es imposible tirar del hilo sin perderme. Ahora debo centrarme en Álvaro y dejar de lado la negrura de Herminia, mi suegra, que reaviva cada día su dolor, del mismo modo que otros echan leña al fuego o le sacan brillo al panteón familiar. Aunque a decir verdad, tengo que reconocer que la segunda vez que me acosté con Álvaro, una semana después de nuestro primer encuentro, mencioné de pasada a la madre de Miguel. Supongo que es una cosa rara comentar con el amante asuntos referentes a la madre o a otros miembros de la familia del marido, aunque sólo sea de pasada. O a lo mejor no es tan raro, a lo mejor los amantes aprovechan la traición para desfogarse, para poner de vuelta y media a la parentela de sus consortes. Al menos ésa es la impresión que saqué después de hablar con Yolanda la secretaria, la inquilina de los lunes y martes del apartamento, la que se acuesta con su jefe el abogado, ese jefe que sabe desenfocar los ojos al mirarla en el despacho ante el resto de los empleados, y que aprovecha sus encuentros con ella para despotricar de su suegro el magistrado y de su mujer, acaso anoréxica y terriblemente ambiciosa, según me contó la secretaria. Pero eso viene mucho más tarde.

Puede que Álvaro lo tuviera todo pensado cuando nos acostamos por segunda vez. Puede que la idea surgiera sobre la marcha y sobre la marcha se acordara de esa agencia de alquiler de fama dudosa, eso no me lo dijo pero lo deduje por la sonrisa nauseabunda al decir que era un negocio discreto, poco común, que disponía de apartamentos por días, o por semanas, en la parte nueva de la ciudad, cerca de su despacho. Yo podía alquilar un apartamento sólo para los viernes. En realidad es una especie de aparthotel, dijo Álvaro. Mucho más barato y más disimulado que un hotel. La gente sube y baja constantemente en los ascensores de esos edificios de apartamentos en los que también hay oficinas. Nadie pregunta, nadie mira con insistencia a nadie. Él era demasiado conocido en los pocos hoteles de lujo de la ciudad, yo lo tenía que imaginar.

Lo imaginé al instante: vi salones con tapices y reuniones de ejecutivos con manos cuidadas y relinchos alegres, y vi tipos calvos encargando puros y lo más caro de la carta en largos almuerzos de negocios, y salas de conferencias cuajadas de damas respetables con cabellos de color celeste y rigidez de laca, vi a un par de periodistas arrogantes haciendo una entrevista a un individuo bruñido sentado en un diván, vi camareros con botellas de champán y hombres que hacen sonar propinas como campanillas para comprar genuflexiones. Admito que las moquetas, los maîtres asfixiados con su propia pajarita y los chicos que se comen el mundo pueden con mis nervios, y estoy convencida de que en otro momento yo hubiera vomitado, pero confieso que ahora me cautivaba recrearme en los movimientos confiados y atléticos de un Álvaro protagonista de todas esas imágenes que desfilaron durante un segundo por mi cabeza. Comprendí que sus pasos estaban adiestrados para andar con firmeza por extensiones de mármol y alfombras espesas. Deseé entonces arrancarle de ese escenario iluminado, desgarrar con mis dientes los botones de su camisa impecable, encerrarle en la oscuridad de cuatro paredes desnudas, obligarle a perder el control y hacerle gritar como a un oso babeante. Sabía que tarde o temprano nos alcanzaría la marea y quise probar el sabor del desastre inminente ahogándome con él en una guarida despoblada.

Álvaro esperaba una respuesta, sería preferible que él no diese la cara, tuvo la cortesía de no hablar de gastos, daba por sentado que soy una mujer solvente, quería que yo alquilase el apartamento para varios meses. Eso me permitiría viajar cualquier viernes desde Madrid. Él podía escaquearse algunos viernes, estoy segura de que utilizó esa palabra, «escaquearse», con el pretexto de cenas con amigos o de trabajo. Su mujer prefería acostarse pronto los viernes, a menos que tuvieran un compromiso inaplazable, Begoña no salía, pero no impedía que él lo hiciese.

Los sábados Begoña juega al golf, el golf requiere la máxima concentración, por eso no le gusta salir los viernes. Álvaro no tiene paciencia para el golf. Algunos viernes cena con sus amigos, hombres solos, sin las mujeres, él piensa que eso lo encontramos raro los de Madrid, un puñado de tíos dispuestos a comer como dioses y a emborracharse durante horas hasta meterse en broncas o perder el sentido. Si lo miras bien, es como lo de los ingleses, me dijo, se reúnen en el club precisamente porque quieren librarse de las mujeres, deshacerse de ellas durante unas horas. No recuerdo en qué momento exacto hizo Álvaro ese comentario. Puede que fuera en algún encuentro posterior. Lo que sí me dijo aquella segunda noche es que Begoña jugaba al golf todos los sábados. Él necesitaba seguir mordiendo mis pezones y lamiendo mi piel. Quería seguir viéndome, se volvería loco si no me veía, si no me escuchaba, si no hacía el amor conmigo. Pero eso sí, tenía que ser en viernes.

Tuve que dudar, acurrucada entre sus brazos como estaba, tuve que pensar en Miguel cansado, Miguel traicionado definitivamente, manos de masajista sosteniendo el diario deportivo, ajenas a mi engaño. Tuve que haber musitado negativas, dudas, dificultades. Pero sólo recuerdo mi determinación al marcar, al día siguiente, el teléfono que Álvaro había anotado en un papel.

Acordé con un tipo de voz pastosa que alquilaría el apartamento los viernes y los sábados, aunque nunca me he quedado a dormir un sábado, siempre me voy por la mañana, antes del mediodía. El precio era módico e incluía limpieza y ropa de cama. No había teléfono. No respondían de los objetos o accesorios guardados en los armarios de una semana a otra. Una empleada se encargaría de cambiar las sábanas y adecentar el apartamento los viernes a primera hora; se ocuparía también de todo después de mi marcha, me dijeron. Tenía que saber que otras personas ocupaban el apartamento el resto de los días de la semana. La confidencialidad estaba garantizada. Cuando estuviese dispuesta, dijo el hombre, se encontraría conmigo para entregarme las llaves y firmar los papeles.

Ese segundo viaje, como el primero, lo hice en avión, por cuenta de Arriaga y Asociados. Todavía quedaban pendientes unas cuñas para la campaña de radio que tuve que grabar antes de cenar con Álvaro aquella noche. Al día siguiente no me acompañó al aeropuerto. Nos habíamos despedido a las tres de la mañana en el hotel. Loco si no volvía a lamer mi piel, había dicho, y yo, sin creerle, pero marcada todavía por las huellas de su lengua, alquilé el apartamento.

Miguel en Madrid me miraba sin interés. Le conté que habían surgido nuevos trabajos en la ciudad del norte, inventé vagos documentales para la televisión local que iban a requerir mi voz, hablé con opacidad, nos viene bien separarnos un poco de vez en cuando, echarnos de menos, dije, a lo mejor necesitamos aire. ¿Me oyes, Miguel, me estás oyendo?

5

A veces me han dicho que si se cierran los ojos al escucharme unas motitas de luz empiezan a hacer cosquillas en el interior de los párpados. Me lo decía Miguel al principio, cuando me descalzaba a la vuelta del banco y me daba masajes en las plantas de los pies.

—Pobrecilla, tienes los pies de china, vaya par de muñones informes, y qué dedos más cortos. Voy a dejarte como nueva. Aunque sólo fuera por eso, deberías contarme la historia de la tía abuela monja de tu madre, que me gusta mucho.

—La tía abuela Elvirita —empezaba yo por enésima vez— había cumplido quince años cuando se tropezó con Augusto da Silva, un vendedor ambulante que se quedó en el pueblo varios días porque tuvo el pálpito de que en aquel erial de La Mancha iba a encontrar a la mujer de su vida. Venía de Lisboa y traía toallas de rizo americano y mantelerías bordadas como nadie vio jamás en la comarca.

La tía abuela Elvirita no había hecho otra cosa en la vida que ir de las eras trigueñas a su casa encalada y de su casa encalada a las eras trigueñas. Cuando naufragó en los ojos azul marítimo de Augusto da Silva le dio por pensar en el océano que nunca vería y se puso a llorar a cántaros… Pero Miguel, si te sabes el cuento de memoria.

—Que no, que se me ha olvidado cómo escaparon al amanecer y cómo devolvieron a Elvirita al pueblo los guardias civiles con su hatillo de ropa y el mantel de hilo que le obligó a aceptar el portugués como regalo de despedida.

Miguel se acordaba perfectamente, lo que pasa es que le gustaba escucharme y luego me engatusaba con lo de que mi voz le hacía cosquillas en los párpados. Lengüita de dulce de mango, sonsonete musical de mis relatos, yo venga a hablar como una descosida, él batiendo palmas ante las monerías de la muñeca parlante, agilidad de la lengua humedísima, cambio de ritmo del rechupar de labios al ombligo del hombre que escucha y ahora quiere manosear a la narradora, trajinando la lengüecilla musical hacia la maleza de Miguel, escalando la boca parlanchina por el tótem erguido de Miguel, aquí se habla y se come al mismo tiempo, la boca llena, Miguel pedía más y más historias y lengüetazos hasta que se aburría y me dejaba con la palabra en las fauces, arrinconada y desconectada porque le llamaban las piernas peludas de los futbolistas de la tele.

Me han dicho que podría ganar unas elecciones sólo con mi voz, pero no lo he creído. Eso fue lo que insinuó Álvaro Arriaga poco antes de empezar el trabajo para el que su agencia de comunicación me contrató. Álvaro se había fijado en mi voz en televisión, en un anuncio de colonia para hombres. Me dijo que le repugnaba el olor de aquella fragancia, pero que cada vez que veía el anuncio le entraban ganas de acudir a una perfumería y repetir muchas veces la marca en el oído de la dependienta. Según Álvaro, mi voz daba credibilidad al producto, despertaba el deseo, conectaba con el consumidor. Por eso se puso en contacto conmigo a través de los estudios de grabación de Madrid. Arriaga y Asociados realizaban la campaña televisiva de un partido político para las elecciones municipales de una ciudad del norte y Álvaro necesitaba que mis palabras calasen en las mentes de los votantes. Aceptó mis tarifas. Fijamos los detalles. Anunció que estaría esperándome en el aeropuerto.

—Vivimos en la era de la información —sentenció mientras en el coche me observaba de reojo—. Para el ejercicio del poder ya no sirve de nada la fuerza, el control político se ha desplazado a la persuasión. Si lo miras bien, lo único que tiene que hacer un líder es colapsar los medios de comunicación con una presencia convincente y conquistar sin más contemplaciones a los electores. Seducción mediática, eso es lo que necesitamos, erotismo político.

Álvaro conducía con la misma suavidad con que un cisne se desliza de una orilla a otra de un lago. Mientras hablaba, parecía saborear los pequeños detalles de su coche deportivo: acariciaba el diseño aerodinámico del volante, miraba con lujuria el salpicadero de caoba, rozaba sensualmente los asientos tapizados en cuero. Este tío tiene un orgasmo cada vez que piensa en la perfección de su máquina, me dije. Hay coches que no huelen a nada y otros que huelen a dinero. El coche de Álvaro olía a ascensión hacia la cumbre y eso le ponía cachondo.

—El poder consiste en conseguir de los demás el comportamiento que nos interesa, supongo que eso lo ves claro —prosiguió—. Y para movilizar las energías en la dirección adecuada, estamos nosotros. Que cuando los electores vean a los políticos en televisión, quieran abrazarlos y se sientan seguros y protegidos. Convencer por la vía racional es el primer paso, de acuerdo, pero tenemos que arrancar la adhesión emotiva y para ello no hay más remedio que persuadir.

Me preguntó si yo entendía lo que me quería decir. Respondí que sí y supuse que Álvaro estaba entrenado para hablar con ideas condensadas, palabras de neón en la oscuridad, un mapa de imágenes que se fija con nitidez en la imaginación. Está orgulloso de su ronquera de macho, pensé, ha amaestrado la voz para que le salga de lo hondo del sexo, acabará con pólipos en la garganta, si es que no los tiene. Imaginé también su cuerpo desnudo bajo el traje de chaqueta: brazos fuertes sobre el volante, muslos firmes, culo de hierro, sin duda iría al gimnasio, ni una gota de grasa. Me reí para mí misma pensando que era uno de esos hombres que se pueden definir con mensajes publicitarios: puro músculo, un triunfador, sin escrúpulos. Seguramente un hijo de puta, decidí, acaso porque me irritaba que me gustase a mi pesar. Y encima está convencido de ser imbatible en la cama. Ladeó un poco la cabeza al intuir mi sonrisa, pero no dijo nada.

Me di cuenta de que era de los que saben permanecer con la vista fija, les haces una pregunta y parece que no te escuchan, vuelves a preguntar, te miran de repente, extrañados, como si llegasen de otro planeta y, cuando menos te lo esperas, te han vendido algo con las palabras justas, sin el menor esfuerzo, sin gastar saliva. Sus clientes querían ganar las elecciones municipales. Y él aseguró que las ganarían.

Los spots de la campaña televisiva fueron un éxito. Mi voz sobrevolaba los parques de esa ciudad del norte en la que hasta no hace mucho he sido la inquilina de los viernes y sábados del apartamento 4A (aunque en realidad sólo he pernoctado en el apartamento un viernes de cada mes, así durante los últimos meses).

No sé si se han fijado, pero casi todos esos documentales que venden paraísos urbanos para que un partido político se lleve el gato al agua, son iguales. Siempre adivinas en ellos algún monstruo escondido en las alcantarillas, pero en la superficie todo es perfecto y encantador como en las películas de Doris Day.

En el nuestro había niños que correteaban por la hierba con sus cometas de colores, y madres jóvenes paseando y empujando cochecitos, igual que un día, Elena, la mujer de Oroz, tuvo que haber paseado y empujado el cochecito de su niña, hasta que se produjo el accidente, hasta que se acabó todo, y también se veían grupos de chicos y chicas en vaqueros, de camino al colegio o a la universidad, y matrimonios de jubilados de aspecto saludable y muy acicalados.

Las tomas se habían realizado en un día radiante, aunque en esa ciudad llueve a menudo, y sobre el verde césped y las viejas piedras de edificios históricos se fundían imágenes de fábricas, unas fábricas de otra galaxia, edificios futuristas de cristal y aluminio de los que salían cuadrillas de metalúrgicos con cascos y unos monos impolutos, hombres jóvenes y fuertes, tan guapos que parecían bomberos, por lo atléticos, supermanes obreros de un planeta pluscuamperfecto saludando con sonrisas dentífricas a los espectadores.

Sonaba una música dulzona, y en segundo término, la melodía del partido, con notas que se elevaban cada vez más, encaminadas a inocular optimismo en todas las rendijas de la ciudad. Después se escuchaba mi voz en *off*. Yo fui capaz de decir, estas manos limpias son nuestras manos, y estar pensando en otra cosa, y también pude pronunciar sin temblor y con toda convicción las palabras «progreso», «libertad», «paz», y recordar al mismo tiempo las promesas siempre incumplidas de los partidos y ver ante mis ojos los titulares de los periódicos contando perrerías un día tras otro.

Verán, no siempre creo en las propiedades milagrosas de una crema nutritiva, pero es mi trabajo, alguien tiene que hacerlo. Oroz dice que más vale tener una conciencia muy delimitada, no confundir al emisor con el contenido, para no sentirse inquieto después de lanzar ciertos mensajes. No le falta razón; trato de ver la cuestión de un modo objetivo. Procuro no torturarme pensando que mis comentarios van a adquirir un alcance funesto. Yo sólo tenía que vender un sueño con el mismo tono que utilizo para vender un aroma o un coche velocísimo.

En cuanto a los electores, creyeron en mi voz y dieron su confianza a los políticos. Ahora, retrospectivamente, reconozco que mientras grabábamos mi locución yo ya había empezado a pensar en Álvaro, a preguntarme cómo acariciarían las manos de un chico listo con quijada a lo Kennedy, un chico duro que con sólo pulsar un botón despertaba deseos en los ricos y ansiedades en los pobres. El peligro consistía en que aquel chico que hablaba de los publicitarios de la avenida Madison, el peligro para mí, voz susurrante de esos señuelos apetecibles, imprescindibles, envidiables, besos húmedos deslizados a traición, lo turbador, digo, era que Álvaro Arriaga, estudioso del comportamiento de un rockero frente a una nueva crema de afeitar y pregonero de detergentes tocando la fibra íntima de las amas de casa, había envalentonado mi cuerpo, la sangre empezaba a bombear, un tren a toda velocidad entre mis muslos, ganas de oxígeno. Que venga el príncipe y se coma de una vez a Blancanieves.

Mientras grababa los mensajes políticos, Álvaro no me quitaba la vista de encima. Me entraron ganas de ponerle nervioso, no sé si me explico. Hablé con el mimo y la calidez que se utiliza para cuidar a los niños con fiebre y alentar a los convalecientes de una larga enfermedad, y también con la sensualidad que vibra en la garganta un minuto antes de hacer el amor con alguien por primera vez. Hablé desde la contemplación de un crepúsculo y sumergida en una pompa tornasolada porque el cuerpo de Álvaro me estaba narcotizando desde algún lugar del estudio. El tam-tam del sexo, la llamada salvaje del Caribe, la química desatada: todo. Por eso pude vender a los votantes un espejismo con la sorda dulzura con que una mariposa muerta cae sobre la tierra.

Pero Álvaro no parecía darse cuenta del tam-tam y seguía a lo suyo: los electores anhelan una ciudad luminosa, decía, sin sobresaltos, una ciudad imaginaria. Mi voz, la tonalidad de las palabras que yo iba a pronunciar desde dentro de una campana de cristal resonando en un valle, tenía que encarnar los deseos de los habitantes de esa ciudad utópica.

—Blanca, estamos vendiendo una fantasía. La audiencia tiene que engancharse a tu voz como un bebé se aferra a los pechos de su madre. ¿Te das cuenta? A nadie le gusta su realidad. Nosotros somos ilusionistas; les vamos a seducir con un discurso cargado de promesas. Para eso estás tú aquí, tú eres la hipnotizadora, Blanca. Tienen que engancharse a tu voz como a una teta.

Dos directores creativos rapados a cepillo al estilo Bruce Willis asintieron con sonrisas de discípulos aplicados. Tuvimos suerte. El partido que había contratado su campaña con Arriaga y Asociados ganó las elecciones. Álvaro, en adelante, haría el amor con su mujer pensando en mi voz.

Las sesiones de trabajo se prolongaron durante cuatro días. La cordialidad, la eficacia de los chicos Bruce Willis me agobiaba tanto como la lentitud del director de campaña, que provocaba interminables esperas porque se empeñaba en supervisar cada uno de los spots y en reunirse con los candidatos para ver los vídeos ya sonorizados y dar el visto bueno definitivo. El estudio de grabación era demasiado pequeño para el continuo deambular de tanta gente. Cada dos por tres uno de los miembros del equipo de Álvaro me ofrecía café. Álvaro hablaba sin parar por el teléfono móvil y entraba y salía con el director de campaña. Recuerdo las idas y venidas de la asesora de prensa del partido, Ana Iribar, cuya hiperactividad me agotaba y me sigue agotando.

Por lo que sucedió después, la entrada en escena de Ana Iribar tiene su interés, o lo tuvo el hecho de que fuera ella, sin calibrar la posibilidad de que contribuía a enmarañar una madeja, quien me puso en la pista de Julio Oroz. Almorzó conmigo y con uno de los chicos Bruce Willis, el primer día. Quería que supiera que se ponía a mi completa disposición; de ninguna manera tenía que sentirme sola en la ciudad, para eso estaba ella.

Se me ocurrió que Ana Iribar era una mujer con un secreto. Yo no tenía ningún dato objetivo para suponerlo, pero bajo su aspecto de bajar con naturalidad por las escalerillas de los aviones y despachar con soltura abrazos y palabras francas, bajo esa característica suya de acercarse confidencialmente a políticos y periodistas, bajo su aire de estar disponible para los jefes a horas intempestivas y de llevar siempre en el bolso tiritas, *tampax* y medias nuevas para solventar cualquier emergencia, detecté una sombra que convenía ocultar, un recuerdo no del todo dormido de su vida pasada; imaginé una doble vida, unos pasos cautelosos, una amenaza que podía salir a la luz y que ella trataba de enmascarar con una avalancha de gestos y palabras. Ahora sé que, de un modo u otro, todas las mujeres tenemos un secreto.

Yo temía su intromisión en mis únicas horas de soledad; ella se extrañaba de mis ganas de encerrarme por las noches en una habitación de hotel. Una tarde accedí a acompañarla a un bar. Chicos barbudos, bien rasurados o de gesto pensativo revoloteaban en torno a ella como moscas. Yo no aspiraba a divertirme ni me interesaban las breves declaraciones de Ana Iribar condensando la biografía de unos y otros. De haber podido dibujar un objetivo en una diana, habría optado por unos solitarios ojos grises que, esquinados en una mesa a salvo de mi amiga y de sus conocidos, se abismaban ante una copa de vino que adiviné triste.

Me alojaba en un hotel pagado por la agencia y la libertad de las últimas horas de la tarde me protegía. Ser una desconocida, eso me gusta, que nadie detenga en mí su mirada. Las miradas de los demás son como bofetadas o achuchones que me agobian o hacen daño. Lejos de la gente de Arriaga y Asociados, lejos de ceños interrogativos y de pestañeos desconfiados o benévolos, daba un paseo por la parte vieja de la ciudad antes de cenar sola en mi habitación, y me acostaba pronto para estar fresca por la mañana.

El último día de trabajo descubrí en Álvaro un asomo de complicidad, un buen humor secreto que le ataba a mí y volvía sus ojos burlones. Me pregunté qué iría a ocurrir. Creí comprender cuando me invitó a cenar aquella noche.

Ya he dicho que Álvaro Arriaga es un hombre atractivo, si te gustan los hombres que gastan aires de comerse el mundo; uno de esos ejecutivos publicitarios con los que en Madrid ya me había acostumbrado a tratar; todos sonríen mucho, enseñando mucho los dientes, todos cultivan una voz un poco hinchada y bastante afable. Gente con ases en la manga, chicos y chicas cinco estrellas transportados al mundo real desde el universo perfecto de los anuncios. Álvaro es parecido a todos los demás, la misma ropa impecable, moderna pero no modernísima, con estilo pero no demasiado clásica, muy cara pero que no se note, o sí, que se note, bueno que se note pero que no se note; no llevan corbata, o la llevan un poco floja, corbatas de Kevin Klani, Keliani, Tartalani, Armani, Zutani, de alguien. Chicos que no sudan, no se irritan, no escupen, no se manchan de sopa las corbatas de Kevin Klani, Keliani, Tartalani, Armani, Zutani, de alguien. Chicos a quienes no les estallan los números rojos a fin de mes. Chicos supercómodos, a todo confort. Confort, ésa sería la palabra.

Álvaro parece salir de un anuncio donde todo, la casa, los niños, los sillones y la mujer, es confortable. Vi en una ocasión, durante esos días, a su mujer. Una rubia de mechas, muy bronceada, con abalorios de oro en las manos y en la garganta. Creo que tenía silicona en los labios porque le salía un morrito extraño, disparado, como de pato. Sonreía sin parar, igual que los chicos Bruce Willis, y saludaba a todos con amabilidad y una voz gangosa con una esquirla estridente en los agudos.

Así que Álvaro tenía una vida de anuncio, una mujer de anuncio, una casa de anuncio y unos niños de anuncio, pero cuando hacía el amor, dentro de su cabeza resonaba mi voz. Yo era la voz que animaba a Álvaro a crecerse en la noche y a abrirse camino entre las piernas de su mujer. Naturalmente, yo eso no podía saberlo en nuestra primera cita, no suelo salir a cenar con los publicitarios, aunque sean los directores de las agencias, mi trabajo termina a la puerta de los estudios de grabación, ni tampoco nunca antes había tenido un amante, de modo que era difícil saber entonces que la enredadera de manos, piernas y lenguas de los amantes se traslada sin el más mínimo respeto a las sábanas de los esposos. Un barullo de cuerpos propios y ajenos, en las camas legales. Aunque, misteriosamente, en las camas furtivas no ocurre lo contrario, y si ocurre, mal asunto. Por lo menos eso es lo que me explicó algo más tarde, con otras palabras, Julio Oroz. En la red circense de los amantes, no hay sitio para nadie más, porque en el centro de una aventura uno deja de ser uno mismo y allí no hay salvavidas con cabeza de cisne ni retratos de infancia ni enormes bolsas de pañales ni visitas al supermercado ni frascos de medicinas en las mesillas de noche. En las camas prohibidas se apagan los focos y el resplandor proviene de otras regiones, a las que los trapecistas ensartados, entreviendo sólo con la piel y las bocas, se asoman a ciegas.

Ignorante de todo esto yo sólo me pregunté qué hacer para combatir mi pereza ante una velada de atenciones, un probable asedio por cortesía y una cena para dos en un restaurante elegante. Pensé que por mi culpa Álvaro no vestiría la deslumbrante armadura de los héroes. Un Casanova de diseño no iba a gastar su artillería con una mujer insignificante. Yo no estaba a la altura, mi única munición era mi voz, si guardaba silencio, sería Eva expulsada con malos modos del paraíso. Álvaro Arriaga busca mujeres que atrapan y desprenden luz y yo soy la pura opacidad, me torturé.

Pensé en piernas de seda, en maniquíes de porcelana con bocas entreabiertas, en ojos orientales lanzando anzuelos. Luego, con fría determinación, me dije que las manos de Álvaro podrían obedecer a otras consignas: cuerpos desnudos enardecidos por el mero deseo, sin trampas, sin disfraces, empujados a la búsqueda del placer en lo alto de un trapecio con red. ¿Por qué no podía Álvaro Arriaga prender una hoguera en un cuerpo agazapado tras la mediocridad pero deseando arder en llamas como el mío?

Creo que entonces no lo vi con tanta claridad, pero algo en mi interior me llevó a perfumar a fondo el escote y la nuca. En un alarde, me puse un traje de chaqueta gris sin camisa debajo. Imperdible oculto para que las solapas no se abriesen demasiado. Aun así yo respiraba y el pecho caliente se agitaba bajo la lana fría. Soy pequeña, tengo conciencia de mis piernas cortas y musculosas cuando me pongo faldas. Medias negras. Mi pelo es de muchacho e ingobernable, pero ese día lo peiné hacia atrás con un pellizco de brillantina. Aires de tango. Súbitamente transformada. Un poco de rojo en los labios, el resto de la cara sin pintar, mis rasgos son pálidos y sosos, inútil intentar mejorarlos con pinturas de guerra. Hacía sólo unos días que Álvaro me había visto por primera vez en el aeropuerto. No podía saber, por tanto, que jamás antes me había tomado la molestia de estirarme el pelo con gomina.

Puede que el peinado tuviera algo que ver con la metamorfosis. En la cena me sentí tan diferente que sonreí como si fuera otra, me hundí en el vino como si fuera otra, sucumbí a sus encantos, escuché sus palabras, imaginé el vello de su pecho y le deseé con los mismos ojos de duermevela con que las protagonistas de los anuncios devoran a esos machos atléticos que se acaban de rociar el torso con colonia.

Dijo que yo era un gato montés, refrenando mi naturaleza salvaje con el controlado parapeto de mi voz. Pensé que era un donjuán de los que lanzan teorías sobre las mujeres por ver si se cumplen; me quise defender, pero cada vez que la punta de los dedos de Álvaro Arriaga rozaba por descuido mi piel, yo me veía como un felino saltando sobre una presa apetitosa.

Nos acercábamos sigilosos. Yo ya sabía que iba a traicionar a Miguel. En el coche jugueteó con mi mano. Tropecé con las marchas, con su pierna, con su entrepierna. Me besó en un semáforo, o yo quería que me besara, no recuerdo. Me besó, de eso estoy segura, en el aparcamiento del hotel, mis manos en su cuello, yo había bebido, eso ayudaba, ahora quería beberme aquella saliva con sabor a *pipermint* (en el trayecto me había ofrecido un chicle de menta, pero comprenderán que queda mucho más fino decir *pipermint*). A partir de aquel momento no hizo falta disimular. Él quería tomar la última copa en mi habitación y yo estaba de acuerdo.

Hice el amor con él como si me hubiera convertido en una mujer distinta y creo que por eso pronuncié las palabras que él imaginaba que una pantera debe pronunciar en estos casos. Entonces él me dijo: dime que me deseas y dime que te gusta que te haga el amor una y otra vez. Estoy tan acostumbrada a musitar mensajes publicitarios que supe enseguida que él quería ser el Adán de mis sábanas blancas y suaves, el Apolo que todo lo puede, el del pene más duro, el macho más vigoroso que hubiera pasado jamás por cama alguna. Estaba a horcajadas sobre mí, en pleno zafarrancho, cuando se puso un preservativo.

Nunca supe de dónde los sacaba, ese primer día, desnudo como estaba, y he seguido sin saberlo en los encuentros posteriores. Aquel prestidigitador de gomas sin envoltorio cerrado, sin bolsitas plateadas y firmemente selladas que hubiera tenido que abrir por el borde, aquel malabarista que no alargaba el brazo para recurrir a un cajón de la mesilla, o a un bolsillo, puesto que estaba ya desnudo, acaso había colocado los preservativos sin funda debajo de la almohada y los sacaba sin que yo me diera cuenta; ese malabarista, al que parecían crecerle condones en los dedos, estaba a horcajadas sobre mí después de un sudoroso cuerpo a cuerpo preliminar; colocó entonces con mucha atención el preservativo caído del cielo, desenrolló con cuidado el elástico rosado hasta la base de sus genitales, y lo dejó impecable y bien tensado como el que encasqueta una capucha a un niño pequeño. Creo que lo hizo todo tan despacio (despacio en términos relativos, dada la agitación del momento, ya me entienden) para que yo no perdiera detalle de la dimensión de su sexo excitado. En el calor de la jungla Álvaro tenía una verga de Tarzán, qué duda cabe, y estaba dispuesto a que un coro de violines acompañara su erección. Ahora sé que él estaba pidiendo a gritos un aplauso, una ovación. Tal vez, empujada por ese ruego inconsciente de mi amante, en medio del fragor, descubrí que *la voz*, que mi voz, había cobrado autonomía y se había puesto en marcha como la grabación de un magnetófono.

No sé qué impulso me llevó a hablarle entre jadeos ni por qué me atreví a decirle todo aquello en aquel hotel de la ciudad del norte en la que luego he seguido viéndole un viernes al mes, en un apartamento alquilado. El caso es que se lo dije, y he seguido repitiéndoselo una y otra vez en nuestras citas posteriores. Le dije entonces que deseaba ser atravesada por su lanza enhiesta y recorrida por su lengua, que nadie me había ensartado y lamido como él, que todos mis sueños tendrían en adelante el color de su mirada efervescente y la calentura de su piel contra la mía. Le dije que mi cuerpo no podría sobrevivir en adelante sin el suyo y que nunca nadie me había mordido con tantos dientes. Le hablé de los huesos de sus rodillas largos y fuertes como los de un Cristo crucificado, de la tonicidad de sus tensorios y suspensorios (él se reía), de sus orejas pequeñas y de la perfección de su mentón de Kennedy. Yo iba a reconocer el peso exacto de sus testículos con mi boca, a horadar su ombligo a lengüetazos, a explorar la raíz central de sus nervios entre sus piernas fuertes. Mi voz le excitaba, decía, que siguiera hablando, que todo empezaba de nuevo, que iba a darme placer hasta hacerme arañar las paredes (esto me sonó a mí a bolero), quería follarme en nombre de todos los hombres que se habían acostado conmigo, aprendería a volverme loca, montaría un incendio en la cima de mi clítoris, haría lo que yo quisiera, pero necesitaba seguir escuchándome, no dejes de hablar, Blanca, decía, sigue, dale a la lengua, chupa o habla, pero no te detengas.

Cuando se puso la corbata y me dio un beso para regresar a la cama de su mujer con mechas y un poco estridente en los agudos, noté que aquel hombre había crecido unos centímetros. De él parecía salir luz y yo estaba a punto de convertirme en un montoncito de cenizas con las últimas brasas apagándose entre mis muslos. Supe que yo misma me acababa de condenar a ser el sostén esporádico de su ego.

6

Es difícil saber cómo se organiza la rutina de un adulterio. De pronto te encuentras en la cueva del amor con toda una serie de ritos milimetrados, ritos sin ningún tipo de fisura, rituales más rígidos que los hábitos de tu propia casa, tal vez porque a las neuronas les viene bien una planificación maniática, una planificación doméstica muy sólida para que no te engulla el desconcierto, para no tener que pensar en el mundo que se queda fuera girando sin ti, o tú girando sin él, vete a saber.

Nosotros teníamos, y allí seguirá, si es que no ha acabado con ella otro inquilino, una botella de Chivas en el aparador. Álvaro la reponía puntualmente. Bebíamos todo el tiempo. Bebíamos como cosacos encerrados en una taberna en plena ola de frío. No hay más remedio que beber para crearse la ilusión de que todo está sucediendo de verdad y no es un culebrón televisivo. El alcohol funciona como un anestésico: al cuarto whisky confundes a tu amante con un desconocido que te gustó en una gasolinera, y tú misma no sabes si eres tú misma o una muñeca hinchable.

La gente se equivoca muchas veces. Hay quien cree que

los amantes cuando vuelven a encontrarse después de un mes sin verse se devoran en el acto arrancándose la ropa con los dientes por los pasillos, como muestran en las películas. Pero no es cierto. Las cosas suceden de otro modo. Después de varias semanas sin vernos, Álvaro y yo nos comportábamos con absoluta normalidad, con una normalidad patológica, diría yo, como si fuese tan normal encontrarnos en el apartamento 4A de esa ciudad del norte en la que yo no tenía que poner mi voz a ningún anuncio, ni ninguna otra cosa que hacer más que abrirme de piernas a montones de kilómetros de mi casa.

Imaginen la escena: el galán llama al timbre (los furtivos han llegado a la conclusión de que sería más discreto que él no tuviera llave) y da un beso a Rosamunda que espera tejiendo y destejiendo su nerviosismo. El galán entonces es invitado a sentarse como si fuera una visita. Se bajan las persianas o se aplacan las luces, según la hora, y se preparan las bebidas. Ella le pregunta por las cosas más tontas, por las campañas de publicidad o por la varicela de los niños. El galán y Rosamunda se enzarzan en las discusiones más insospechadas. Van y vienen de su pasado a su presente, parlotean de todo y de nada, ríen sin motivo, atacan cualquier tema por el gusto de quitarse la palabra de la boca. Los amantes actuarán durante los primeros minutos como dos cotorras compulsivas. Se bebe, se fuma y se habla muchísimo en los preliminares. Después la conversación y los vapores etílicos los van enlazando, las piernas y los labios se traban. Sólo entonces, si no les da pereza (a veces se remata la faena en el diván), los amantes pasarán al dormitorio para los fuegos artificiales.

Era en el dormitorio donde Álvaro Arriaga quería oír mi voz. Durante meses hemos repetido esa colisión de peroratas, alcohol y sexo que a ambos nos dejaba extenuados y nos cargaba las pilas al mismo tiempo. A las dos o tres de la mañana Álvaro desaparecía. Nunca se ha quedado a dormir conmigo. Nunca he sabido de qué costado duerme ni si pone una mano debajo de la almohada ni si se acurruca como un cachorro en un extremo de la cama. Tampoco he llegado a saber qué lado prefiere para dormir o de qué humor se levanta por las mañanas. Crees que has penetrado en la intimidad de tu amante, y a la hora de la verdad no sabes casi nada de él. Si de pronto se quedaba adormilado después de hacer el amor, se sacudía la pereza y se levantaba con toda diligencia al cuarto de baño. Una vez que había decidido marcharse, nunca se quedaba remoloneando en la cama, ni me daba ese último abrazo pegajoso con que se eternizan las parejas que duermen juntas.

Cinco minutos más, le decía yo a Miguel cuando nos levantábamos a la misma hora para acudir a trabajar al banco por las mañanas. Pero Álvaro no tenía pereza, me dejaba desnuda en la cama para vestirse él con toda atención, como si fuese a empezar la jornada laboral. Álvaro se peinaba el pelo hacia atrás, se daba un sobresaliente en el espejo y recogía su cartera, el mechero, las llaves, el pañuelo, el tabaco, esos restos del naufragio que los hombres desparraman en las mesillas.

Alguna vez me levantaba de la cama para despedirle. Me ponía la camisa más sexy de mi vestuario (jamás me llegó a ver en bata ni en pijama, mejor así) y le besaba a la puerta, con la misma expresión indefinible con que una esposa Minie Mouse despide a su marido Mickey para ir al trabajo. Pero él no tenía que ir al trabajo a esas horas, eran las dos o las tres de la mañana, él volvía a su casa a meterse en la cama con su mujer después de una supuesta cena de trabajo y algunas copas.

Nunca he sabido qué excusas pondría Álvaro. En qué restaurantes decía haber cenado con amigos o clientes, ni a qué bar o discoteca aseguraba haber tenido que acompañar a los tenorios con ganas de juerga hasta altas horas de la noche. Nunca le pregunté por sus pretextos. ¿Para qué? Yo sólo pensaba en que no le vería hasta dentro de varias semanas, en que al día siguiente yo tendría que conducir cuatro horas escuchando la radio, y en que tendría tiempo de tomar un café al llenar el depósito de gasolina.

¿Creen que alguna vez me propuso salir a cenar? Pues se equivocan. Si me entraba un ataque de hambre, antes de que llegase Álvaro, tomaba un sándwich en la cafetería de la esquina donde ya me conocían. Yo era una reclusa de amor encerrada entre cuatro paredes. La calle constituía un peligro. Nuestro universo estaba comprimido en los tabiques de un apartamento. Yo tenía un Tarzán en mi cama. ¿Para qué quería más?

A los seis meses de este plan Álvaro Arriaga tuvo un calentón y me escribió una carta de amor. Me dijo que no la leyese hasta que él se hubiera ido. Una carta sin membrete y sin firma que él nunca debería haber escrito, o yo nunca debería haber perdido. Sí, ya lo sé, una amante debe ser cuidadosa con esas cosas, pero yo abandoné la carta en el apartamento como quien se olvida la gabardina en el guardarropa del restaurante en un día de sol.

No mucho después de que Álvaro me entregara la carta, mi hermana tuvo gripe y quise pasar unos días a su lado. Me instalé en su casa con una cesta de zanahorias y puerros y pechugas de ave para caldos y pepitorias. Llegaba dispuesta a hacer de madre Teresa, a tapar mis problemas con su tos cavernosa y a refrescar sus sienes en las horas de fiebre.

Desde que era pequeña los estados febriles de Marta van acompañados de pesadillas, sudores y accesos de pánico. A veces, cuando ya éramos adolescentes y mi madre pasaba temporadas en el sanatorio, en medio de la noche Marta empezaba a dar brazadas en sueños. Soñaba con un mar embravecido, con olas gigantescas que se tragaban todo y derribaban muros y ventanas hasta arrasar la casa en que ella se encontraba. Batallaba con todas sus fuerzas, golpeándose con bultos flotantes, se aferraba con las uñas a las paredes, a los picaportes de las puertas, pero, pese a la lucha, su cuerpo era arrastrado por las aguas. Por más que intentaba nadar y salir a flote, me contaba Marta, siempre un golpe de mar volvía a hundirla hasta el fondo.

Ese sueño y otros parecidos se repetían con frecuencia. Marta decía que no podía soportar la angustia. Prefería ahogarse a seguir debatiéndose contra la avalancha de agua, por eso al final del sueño desistía, se dejaba caer como una piedra, sin pelear, y, en ese momento, despertaba.

Ya para entonces, ambas habíamos aprendido a vivir solas, o con una madre ida, que a fin de cuentas era lo mismo, con el dinero escaso que puntualmente nos entregaba mi padre, o Estrella, la manicura, que resultó ser, y todavía es puesto que sigue viviendo con mi padre, una mujer generosa y preocupada por nuestra situación, y empezábamos a hablar hasta el amanecer de nuestro futuro. Puede que otras niñas con más suerte especulen con el olor de la madera de veleros ingleses y con la caricia de abrigos de pieles de bellos animales en extinción. Puede que vayan a la universidad mientras imaginan mansiones de fábula con maridos que se ocupan de todo y niñeras para sus hijitos de algodón y perros y piscinas a la luz de la luna. Con razón a las niñas afortunadas les gusta soñar con imágenes triunfales, construir castillos en el aire. ¿De dónde íbamos a sacar nosotras fantasías de villas en la costa y tíos rubios como el *gran Gatsby* vestidos de blanco almidonado, pasando sus dedos de oro por nuestras espaldas? ¿Sabíamos algo sobre muebles de diseño, sobre áticos iluminados con velas perfumadas, sobre coches deportivos, zapatos italianos o vestidos de seda tornasol, más allá de lo que veíamos en algunas revistas o en el cine? No, nosotras estábamos condenadas a tener los pies en el lodo. Sólo podíamos aspirar a una formación rápida en academias baratas con buenas perspectivas para colocarnos cuanto antes. Yo no era mala con las cuentas, trabajaría en un banco y haría teatro en grupos de aficionados (no me decidía a matar mis esperanzas antes de tiempo, pero mi sueño, el teatro, quedaba reducido a un escenario polvoriento en un hangar abandonado).

Marta tenía facilidad para el inglés, decía que era por haber escuchado tantas veces desde pequeña los discos de *soul* de mi padre. Se sabía de memoria *Never let you go, If you need me, Sky's the Limit, I'll come running back to you*, y le encantaba decir que ella hablaba inglés con acento de negra porque había aprendido de tipos como Marvin Gaye, Wilson Pickett, Sam Cooke y Los Temptations.

Viajar; eso es lo que Marta quería, perderse por el mundo con una mochila, cerrar los ojos en las calles de Calcuta y escuchar el estrépito de la humanidad, ir a California, liar canutos y patinar con los viejos hippies de largas melenas rubias en Venice Beach, empezar a correr y tragar kilómetros y llegar a lugares que no vienen señalados en los mapas. Yo le decía que todos los hippies se habían muerto y que sus hijos eran los tiburones elegantes de Wall Street. No jodas, decía Marta, algún hippie quedará.

La agencia de viajes donde se colocó al cabo de los años, y donde aún trabaja, no es un universo muy grande pero desde allí se emiten billetes de avión a destinos remotos. Refrenar el espíritu errante hasta que llegan los días de vacaciones, algo es algo, dice Marta. Si yo no hubiera conocido tan pronto a Miguel habría acompañado a mi hermana en alguno de sus viajes. Pero Miguel agitó las guedejas de león y extendió su mano para que mi mesa del banco no pareciera tan lúgubre. Yo, atrapada, yo varada en Madrid, yo exploradora en la laberíntica selva de unos ojos.

Me costaba concentrarme en la lectura, sentada una de aquellas tardes a los pies de la cama de Marta, tal vez por la escasa luz que se filtraba a través de los visillos o tal vez por ese sopor que nos invade cuando estamos velando a una persona enferma que duerme profundamente y todo está en silencio a nuestro alrededor. A veces la sentía agitarse un poco o esconder un brazo debajo de la almohada. Me preguntaba qué soñaría en aquel momento. Recordé que Marta me había contado hacía tiempo que un psicólogo había acabado de un manotazo con sus pesadillas del temporal. Arrancados de golpe sus fantasmas por obra y gracia del señor Freud. Había hablado tanto de esas imágenes y de sus posibles significados, me dijo, que se habían desgastado en su cabeza hasta desaparecer por completo.

Cerré los ojos yo también, como quien convalece, y pensé en Álvaro y acto seguido en Miguel. Después de nuestra boda entendí que me había casado con Miguel y con un batallón de forofos del fútbol que se presentaban en casa cada dos por tres. Mientras yo me escabullía al cine con Marta, él abría cervezas con sus amigos frente al televisor, lo pasaban en grande, cada partido lo veían juntos en una salita de estar casi idéntica. Cuando tocaba en la nuestra yo dejaba la nevera llena y no volvía hasta media noche, hasta saber que reinaba el silencio. Empezaron sus broncas y mis mutismos y hoy me gustaría saber si fue en ese momento de gestos desabridos y espaldas mudas, cuando empezó la astilla de hielo a clavarse en nuestros ojos.

Yo trabajaba junto a Miguel cada día y en el banco volvíamos a ser compañeros más que marido y mujer. Reíamos de otra manera, comentábamos los periódicos, gastábamos bromas, tomábamos cañas a la salida con los demás. Hay hostilidades matrimoniales que desaparecen en el trabajo. Son olvidos que sobrevienen sin darnos cuenta, hostilidades que se diluyen con la actividad y que al cabo del tiempo ya no se recuerdan o exigirían cierto esfuerzo para sacarlas de nuevo a la luz: qué ocurrió, cómo fueron los hechos, cuál era aquella palabra que nos arrojaron y causó tanto daño, dónde quedaron las marcas de los insultos como azotes y por qué al despertar los ojos aparecieron hinchados. Nos amparábamos en las risas de la quiniela imposible y colectiva, en las reivindicaciones salariales, en el deseo fugaz: Miguel se enredaba, como todos, en el cruce de piernas de Natalia, larguísimas piernas para faldas tan cortas, y yo relajaba mis sienes cada vez que Alarcón despeinaba mi pelo de chico con sus dedos de actor italiano. El trabajo compartido era para nosotros una tabla de salvación, pero cuando yo dejé el banco y me convertí en *la voz*, Miguel tuvo la impresión de que se quedaba a la deriva y solo.

Se quedaba con Basilio, con Loli, con Berta la gorda y

con Zamora, con los otros a los que tratábamos menos, y también con Natalia y con Alarcón. Alarcón que hundía los dedos en mi pelo revuelto, Alarcón sindicalista, bigote de turco y ojos incandescentes, de color cerveza o amarillos, a veces un poco irritados, para mí que fumaba demasiado o follaba demasiado, ojos de vividor, eso seguro, un cuerpo duro como una roca, Alarcón de película neorrealista italiana, yo me lo imaginaba en camiseta abrazando a Claudia Cardinale. Las chicas a solas estábamos convencidas de que se lo hacía como Dios, la gorda Berta, al poco de llegar nueva a la sucursal, lo soltó un día en el lavabo con esas mismas palabras: este tío se lo tiene que hacer como Dios. Todas nosotras, con esas u otras palabras o incluso sin palabras, lo habíamos pensado, lo habíamos sentido alguna vez. Cuando Berta hizo aquel comentario en el cuarto de baño, Natalia no dijo nada. No habló de las idas y venidas de Alarcón a su apartamento. No confirmó ni echó por tierra lo que las demás intuíamos y ella debía a esas alturas saber a ciencia cierta.

Yo tampoco he sabido que Natalia se acostaba con Alarcón hasta hace unos meses. Miguel me lo dijo a la vuelta de uno de mis últimos viajes a la ciudad del norte. Pienso ahora que acaso Miguel esté también acostándose con Natalia. Puede que ella le haya confesado lo de Alarcón en uno de esos momentos de intimidad que siguen al reposo de los amantes. Los amantes se cuentan más secretos que los matrimonios. O al menos se cuentan ciertos secretos que están vedados entre matrimonios. Acaso porque los amantes infieles saben de antemano que su pareja comparte la cama con otra persona. En eso los adúlteros tienen una ventaja sobre sus compañeros oficiales que ignoran que su mujer o su marido se acuesta con una tercera persona. Por eso seguramente los componentes de una pareja legítima no quieren saber demasiados detalles sobre los hombres o mujeres que pasaron con anterioridad por la vida de sus consortes. Quizá en algún momento, durante los primeros meses, cuando todo lo del amado nos interesa y vivimos bajo la hipnótica seguridad de la conquista, tenemos el valor de enfrentarnos a los álbumes de fotos de su pasado: indagamos nombres, nos familiarizamos con los rostros y los cuerpos que nos precedieron, escuchamos los pormenores de historias de amor que ya se cerraron o que nosotros damos por canceladas. Pero al cabo del tiempo es mejor olvidar, no mencionar ciertos nombres, no hundir las manos en el agua pasada, hacemos tabla rasa. Borrón y cuenta nueva.

Los amantes, en cambio, vivimos en total promiscuidad, sabemos que el cuerpo que tomamos prestado durante unas horas no nos pertenece, es un cuerpo al que tiene derecho otra persona, por eso entre nosotros podemos hablar con toda confianza sobre historias y aventuras anteriores, al menos al principio; después, cuando pasa el tiempo, según he sabido, hay amantes que se vuelven tan posesivos como un segundo esposo, ya no quieren saber de otros hombres ni de los escarceos del pasado, se sienten amenazados, unidos al marido en indignación y celos.

Tal vez estoy divagando demasiado. No puedo recordar con exactitud dónde estaba. Sólo puedo escribir estas páginas de noche y de noche olvido algunas cosas y otras vuelven a mí con nitidez. Todavía no les he hablado de Julio Oroz y, sin embargo, su rostro sin afeitar, en un hotelucho de San Sebastián, se presenta ante mí machacado y vengativo aunque todavía no sea el momento.

Yo hubiera podido hablarle a Álvaro de Alarcón, de haber querido, podría haber comentado cómo Alarcón me pasaba la mano por el pelo, y cómo a veces encontraba pretextos para buscar algo en la pantalla de mi ordenador y acariciar en broma mi mejilla, era un juego inocente pero me fijé que lo hacía en los momentos en que Miguel estaba ocupado con un cliente o despachando con el director al otro lado de la cristalera.

Quizá Natalia se ha acostado solamente una vez con Miguel, justo hace unos meses, cuando Miguel me lo dijo porque necesitaba hablar de Natalia, sacudirse la culpa y al mismo tiempo resucitar el recuerdo nombrándola, trayendo a Natalia a colación. Acaso Miguel deja pistas como el ladrón que quiere ser cazado. Por eso me dijo que Natalia se había acostado con Alarcón. No sé cuántas veces, quizá no una sola vez sino muchas y regularmente como yo con Álvaro, al fin y al cabo Natalia no vive con nadie, puede hacer lo que le dé la gana, no tiene que mentir a una tercera persona, en todo caso es Alarcón quien tendrá que lidiar con su conciencia y con María, su mujer y sus tres niños, como mi culpabilidad tuvo que lidiar con la presencia cotidiana de Miguel, aunque la verdad es que no tuve tiempo de pensarlo, ni siquiera fui consciente de que tenía un amante y engañaba a mi marido hasta fechas recientes, cuando me di cuenta de que había desaparecido la carta, cuando se complicaron las cosas y tuve que conocer a Yolanda la secretaria y a Julio Oroz.

No tengo buena memoria, pero una de las frases de la carta escrita por Álvaro me viene ahora a la cabeza y pensé también en ella en casa de mi hermana mientras Marta dormía la siesta con la respiración pesada de la fiebre y yo escuchaba en mi cerebro un chisporroteo de fusibles a punto de fundirse. Era una frase que quedaba hacia el centro de la cuartilla, después de unas referencias a lo mucho que le excitaban mis palabras en la cama y antes de las alusiones a mis pechos: *quiero que me beses los pies y que succiones mis dedos uno a uno como si fueran penes minúsculos que esperan tensarse y estallar dentro de tu boca.* Algo así. La referencia a los pies me chocó la primera vez que leí la carta porque nunca había yo besado ni chupado los dedos de Álvaro, sin duda la única porción anatómica de Álvaro que yo no había chupado ni besado, y también estuve pensando en ello mientras conducía aquel sábado por la mañana de regreso a casa.

A pesar de la ducha, yo olía a Álvaro. Y Álvaro olía a su colonia de siempre, ese aroma de lobo marino de alta costura que se alza vencedor después de una larga batalla contra las furias huracanadas del mar. En algún momento abrí un poco más la ventanilla y traté de recordar las palabras que me había escrito y que yo había leído varias veces por la noche al quedarme a solas. Pensé que la carta estaba en mi bolso, pero en ese mismo instante me asaltó la duda y noté un encogimiento de estómago al tiempo que estiraba la mano y revolvía el interior del bolso que viajaba negro y silencioso en el asiento del pasajero. La carta, naturalmente, no estaba. Ahora lo veía claro. Yo no había llegado a guardarla, la había doblado después de leerla quién sabe cuántas veces y la había metido en el sobre, pero se quedó encima del sofá cuando me acosté esa noche después de marcharse Álvaro. Seguirá allí cuando el lunes a las 8 de la mañana llegue la mujer de la limpieza, me dije aterrada. Yo estaba a menos de cien kilómetros de Madrid y había llamado a Miguel para avisarle de la hora aproximada de mi llegada. Ahora no podía dar la vuelta. En realidad no tenía por qué preocuparme, me tranquilicé, la gente no va por ahí leyendo cartas ajenas. La asistenta vaciaría los ceniceros y volvería a dejar la carta en una esquina discreta. Yo la encontraría allí dentro de tres o cuatro semanas. Álvaro había tenido la precaución de no firmar con su nombre —sólo un garabato de iniciales ilegibles y entrelazadas—, no aparecía ningún membrete de Arriaga y Asociados ni dirección ni ningún otro dato comprometedor. Seguro que no iba a pasar nada.

Durante los días siguientes me aferré a la posibilidad de que nadie más, salvo la asistenta, iría al apartamento hasta mi próxima visita. Me dije que la agencia tendría muchos otros pisos para alquilar en el mismo edificio y en otros bloques del ensanche nuevo de la ciudad. A lo mejor, pensé, soy la única inquilina del 4A y las botellas que había visto en los armarios de la cocina, un día que se me ocurrió fisgar, no eran más que los restos de la fiesta de alguien que alquiló la casa antes que yo. Dediqué toda la semana a darle vueltas.

Así, mientras mi vida seguía y me comportaba con naturalidad en el estudio donde tuve que grabar las cuñas de un centro de estética para la radio, yo no dejaba de rumiar malos presagios. Estaba incubando un miedo indefinido, un miedo que parecía acarrear un futuro desastre que me obsesionaba y amenazaba con romper algún tipo de orden. No había cambiado nada en mi rutina con Miguel, pero la aprensión me atenazaba el vientre o la garganta, según el día, y siguió flotando sobre mí mientras yo hacía caldo y pepitorias para mi hermana enferma, o trataba de concentrarme en la lectura a los pies de su cama.

—¿En qué piensas? —Era Marta que se había despertado.

Mi hermana estaba al tanto de mis encuentros con Álvaro Arriaga.

—En algo estúpido que me ha ocurrido —le dije—. El

último viernes, antes de marcharse, Álvaro me entregó un sobre. Una especie de carta de amor, medio erótica, como prefieras. Me pidió que no la leyese hasta que él se hubiera marchado, así que la leí esa misma noche antes de dormir. A la mañana siguiente, cuando ya estaba llegando a Madrid, me di cuenta de que había olvidado la carta en el apartamento y empecé a ponerme nerviosa.

Marta se incorporó en la cama. Tenía mejor aspecto y esbozó una sonrisa tranquilizadora.

—Nada, Blanca, no va a pasar nada. A lo mejor te cae una bronca, como mucho, pero más vale que no se lo digas. Además, a nadie se le va a ocurrir curiosear un sobre abandonado. De todos modos, me parece que buscabas algún tipo de riesgo cuando te metiste en esto. A ti la convivencia con Miguel te pesa una tonelada y esta aventura con Álvaro ha vuelto tu vida mucho más ligera. ¿O no?

—Las cosas sucedieron, Marta, ni siquiera estoy segura de cómo empezó todo.

—No conozco a Álvaro y admito que un buen polvo a tiempo es una victoria; tú por lo menos vuelves de esas excursiones como una malva, pero por lo que me has contado de él me parece que a mí no me gustaría.

A pesar de la melena un poco pegajosa sobre la frente, el rostro de Marta seguía terso y dulce sin las ojeras oscuras de los griposos. Vi que sus palabras no iban cargadas de mala intención, pero me irrité.

—No sé por qué dices eso.

—No me fío de los hombres perfectos y prepotentes —siguió Marta—. Tengo la impresión de que nos miran con un alfiler escondido en algún sitio igual que coleccionistas de mariposas. Los veo en la barra de un bar con una mano metida en el bolsillo del pantalón y me parece que van a desenfundar el *colt* de un momento a otro. A lo mejor son cosas mías, pero desconfío de los tipos que llegan al poblado con el aire matón de los vaqueros. Algunos están convencidos de llevar una pistola entre las piernas. Claro que a ésos les excita tanto su propia erección que se les dispara el arma antes de tiempo. No me fío, Blanca, al final, de un modo u otro, acaban haciendo daño. Antes no era así, ya lo sabes. Yo era más valiente que nadie. No sabía vivir sin tener un tío cerca. Me servía cualquiera. Pero ahora me siento demasiado cansada para defenderme de los seductores profesionales. Prefiero a los hombres sin esperanza, derruidos, sin ambiciones. Acostarse con uno de ellos es como hacer el amor con un condenado a muerte. Puro vértigo.

Me vi obligada a defender a Álvaro.

—Álvaro no es un cazador de mujeres.

Marta hizo un gesto para incorporarse del todo y yo me levanté para acercarle la bata.

—¿Cómo puedes estar tan segura? —preguntó mientras sentada en el borde de la cama se ponía las babuchas.

Vi a Marta con la bata de piel de ángel reflejada en el espejo del tocador que había frente a la cama y alcé los hombros pensando que efectivamente yo lo desconocía todo de Álvaro Arriaga. Marta se quedó pensativa en la puerta del cuarto de baño mirándome con una sonrisa comprensiva y algo enigmática. Por una vez ella volvía a ser la hermana mayor y yo la patosa y confundida hermana pequeña.

7

A los pocos días del restablecimiento de Marta y de mi regreso a casa con Miguel, me sentí enferma mientras grababa el anuncio de un perfume francés. A los franceses les gusta mucho que chicas andróginas con aspecto de ninfa correteen por la pantalla con guirnaldas de flores entre zumbidos de libélulas y risillas de gnomo. A mí me tocaba, hociquito de Alicia, gorjeo de Lolita juguetona, cosquilleante y cosquillosa Lolita, lamedora de muslos de los tres cerditos, chupeteadora de capullos en llamas, convertirme en la voz de la reina de las hadas.

El director de márketing de la firma estaba en el estudio escuchándome con interés. Era un hombre de mediana edad, con la cara rosada como un salmonete y los ojos acuosos; un hombre sin duda acostumbrado a firmar cheques con pulso firme y a tratar a sus subordinados con una paternidad algo fingida, sobre todo a su secretaria, a la que llamaría *niña*, que le adoraría y encontraría muy atractivo. Me pregunté si compartiría con ella apartamento furtivo y Chivas, y si le escribiría mensajes porno que ella olvidaría como una idiota entre los papeles del despacho. De repente, mientras pensaba esto, comprendí que el asunto de la carta era una bola gigante en mi cabeza que iba de una esquina a otra, encendiendo luces y haciendo saltar muelles, como en aquellas máquinas *flipper* de los bares.

—Estás en las nubes, mi amor —me regañó Héctor con su acento arrastrado y cariñoso.

Héctor Wetelman es feo, cincuentón, argentino y grande como un oso. Tiene fama de ser un buen técnico de sonido y cualquier mujer estaría satisfecha de dormir entre sus acogedoras garras de peluche. Hay algo en sus movimientos pausados, en sus ojos sabios y en su melena y barba blanca a lo Moustaki que le hace interesante. Él nunca habla de ello pero me han contado que fue profesor de universidad en Buenos Aires y que a su mujer la detuvieron una madrugada durante la dictadura militar y no volvió a saberse de ella nunca más.

—Hay que repetir esa toma —dijo Héctor desde la mesa de sonido.

—De acuerdo —dije yo, y esperé a ver el avance de los fotogramas del spot por la pantalla y a que apareciera el código que daba paso a mi locución.

Cuando terminé mis frases y me llevé la mano a la frente tuve la impresión de que tenía fiebre. Sentía los labios húmedos y un poco salados de los que tienen sangre en la boca. Son las muelas, me dije, porque recibí una descarga en las encías y pensé que se me iban a caer todos los dientes a la vez. Desde el control el director de márketing que parecía un salmonete me contemplaba satisfecho.

—Perfecto, ha quedado perfecto —dijo a través del interruptor.

—Está bien, Blanca, la última vale —confirmó Héctor.

Yo permanecí quieta con una desagradable sensación de mareo.

—¿Te encuentras mal? —preguntó la voz de Héctor desde la lejanía.

Con el subterfugio de que algo caliente me sentaría bien, el hombre rosado se empeñó en acompañarme a una cafetería. Me extrañó que aquel hombre-pez se moviera con normalidad fuera del agua, aunque detecté en él una respiración anómala, igual que si tuviera que tomar mucho aire cada vez que inspiraba. Lo imaginé metiendo la cabeza bajo el chorro del grifo, dando boqueadas de felicidad soñando con la inmensidad del mar abierto.

—En realidad —me dijo el hombre salmonete después de un trago de whisky—, la naturaleza sabe muy bien lo que se hace. Los dones están repartidos cojonudamente. Tú, por ejemplo, eres más bien poca cosa, si no te molesta que te lo diga, pero tienes esa voz increíble.

No me molesta ser poca cosa, estoy acostumbrada, la verdad, pero sí me molesta que un desconocido de rostro colorado me lleve a una cafetería para recordármelo cuando estoy a punto de desmayarme. En ese instante, todos los ruidos del local se elevaron sobre mi cabeza con un estrépito ensordecedor y las cosas y las personas empezaron a girar a mi alrededor. Quise sujetarme al asiento y miré al salmonete sin protestar, con la misma expresión desesperada con que un borracho miraría una farola un segundo antes de derrumbarse junto a ella.

—Una voz de lujo, niña. Una voz para poner cachondo a cualquiera.

El hombre soltó una carcajada y lo último que yo vi fue el dibujito repetido de *Las Meninas* de su corbata. Yo me desvanecía mientras *Las Meninas* daban vueltas con sus faldones de colores, tan bonitas.

Cuando recuperé la consciencia, Héctor me atendía solícito en la misma mesa de la cafetería y el director de márketing se había esfumado.

Al hacer memoria me acuerdo ahora de que aquel hombre tenía las pestañas blancas. Los ojos de pez y las pestañas blancas. No sé por qué tuve que ir a tomar nada con aquel individuo cuando lo único que yo quería era marcharme a casa. Siempre es la misma historia: llevan corbatas elegantes y me dejan pasar a mí primero poniendo con suavidad la mano en mi cintura o en mi espalda, como si animasen a seguir andando a una niña pequeña, pero en cuanto pueden, relacionan mis cuerdas vocales con las sacudidas de su bragueta.

He mencionado lo de las pestañas blancas porque al cruzarse ahora, en la distancia, mi mirada con la suya veo, con la claridad de un foco iluminando sus ojos descoloridos, que él era un hombre débil y desconcertado por una nimiedad fuera de su control. Quizá por esa misma razón todavía me asquea más la forma en que aquel tipo escabulló el bulto, nunca mejor dicho, en la cafetería. Acaso me indigna que fuera simplemente cobardía la razón por la que el hombre con el rostro demasiado encendido (me pregunto si se expone con demasiada frecuencia a rayos UVA o si padece hipertensión, lo que también podría explicar el tono subido de su epidermis) se desentendió de mí sin contemplaciones una vez que me vio desvanecida en aquel establecimiento en el que ninguno de los dos conocíamos a nadie. Estoy segura de que tuvo que darle una buena propina al camarero para que se ocupase de mí mientras él regresaba al estudio de grabación a buscar a

Héctor, para no comprometerse personalmente, para no perder su valioso tiempo, como si yo fuera un pequeño problema que se resuelve con un dinero extra, del mismo modo que esas personas acostumbradas a adquirir lo mejor a cualquier precio, consiguen excelentes localidades en el teatro deslizando una cantidad suplementaria a la taquillera que vende las entradas. Estoy segura de que le expondría la situación al camarero, él era director de márketing y no me conocía apenas, veníamos de los estudios Armonía de grabar un anuncio, yo era la voz de uno de sus productos, una empleada al fin y al cabo, esto no lo diría pero lo pensaría, el camarero fue muy amable, entendió todo perfectamente. Se ocupó de mí mientras llegaba Héctor, haciendo una almohada con un mantel doblado y acomodando mi cabeza hasta que quedé tumbada en el asiento, con las piernas colgando. Yo no molestaba a nadie, una mujer indispuesta, qué le vamos a hacer, una mujer nada aparatosa por otra parte, una joven bajita e insignificante, muy poca cosa, como había dicho el salmonete antes de abandonarme al cuidado del camarero. Al recordar lo sucedido lo que más me llama la atención es que aquel hombre me trató como si yo fuera un bulto inservible. Desvanecida, sin voz, yo no era nada, algo inútil, una bolsa de plástico con desperdicios olvidada en cualquier esquina de una estación. Una presencia molesta como lo había sido, durante mi adolescencia, para los acompañantes de Marta, cuando en verano, en el pueblo de mi padre, no tenían más remedio que cargar conmigo, la hermana pequeña.

Si no hubiera sido por lo guapa que era Marta y porque a los catorce años fumaba porros y no le importaba dejarse besar junto al río o en la oscuridad, jamás hubiéramos salido con los hijos mayores de los veraneantes. La gente de Sotoespino hablaba de los veraneantes con una pizca de desconfianza y, acaso, de desprecio. Para mi padre aquellos jóvenes que vivían en chalets con piscina a las afueras del pueblo y conducían sus propios coches o los coches de sus padres, no eran más que un hatajo de gilipollas. Durante los dos veranos en que nos vimos con los veraneantes, y también con Fredy, el chico de los autos de choque, mi padre estuvo de mal humor. Ahora creo que él intuía que más allá de la plaza del pueblo nuestra infancia se acababa y que la amistad con aquellos muchachos mayores que nosotras nos cambiaría para siempre. Aunque teníamos total libertad para ir y para venir, incluso hasta altas horas de la noche, mi padre insistía en que yo, un año más pequeña, no me separase nunca de mi hermana.

Después no hubo más veranos en Sotoespino porque el abuelo murió y se vendió la casa, mi padre se fue a vivir definitivamente con Estrella y mi madre se convirtió en una enferma mental a la que teníamos que ingresar durante algunas temporadas. Fue precisamente en aquellos veranos de nuestra adolescencia cuando empezó a crecer en mí el miedo a convertirme en una carabina molesta para los amigos de Marta, que me ignoraban y me dejaban olvidada en un rincón como no hace mucho me dejó olvidada el hombre salmonete, y también para Fredy, el chico de la feria, que me gustaba casi tanto como a Marta.

Aunque Fredy acabó fijándose en mí el último verano de Sotoespino, buscando mi cuerpo cuando no tuvo a mano el de mi hermana, por rabia o por despecho, pero yo me alegré, por una vez dejé de ser un bulto sin identidad y permití que Fredy se ocupara de mí con sus propias manos y con la alambrada eléctrica que recorría todo su cuerpo.

A Marta le traía sin cuidado que nos obligaran a ir siempre juntas a todas partes, en vez de fastidiarle mi presencia decía que se sentía más segura, que no le importaba adentrarse en el monte con uno de aquellos chicos al regreso de las fiestas de los pueblos cercanos mientras yo esperaba en el coche con la radio puesta. Cuando durante varios días yo veía que el chico que bailaba con Marta y nos llevaba luego en su coche era el mismo, yo creía que la cosa iba en serio, pero enseguida el novio de turno era sustituido por otro, y desde entonces cada vez que Marta cambiaba de pareja no me daba por enterada y miraba al nuevo acompañante con la misma sonrisa inocente con que había mirado a sus antecesores. Yo le preguntaba a mi hermana si le gustaba alguno de ellos. Pero a Marta el único que de verdad le gustó por aquella época fue Fredy, el rubio parecido a James Dean de los autos de choque.

—Al primer tío que os dé una hostia a mala fe, le salto los piños.

Eso fue lo que nos dijo Fredy nada más conocernos cuando se puso de pie sobre el pescante de nuestro coche. Lo dijo mirando a Marta que iba a mi lado mientras yo esquivaba a volantazos los impactos de los demás conductores. A partir de ese día no podíamos evitar cierta satisfacción cuando Fredy viajaba con nosotras encaramado a la barra metálica mientras oteaba las intenciones de los automóviles hostiles, como un pirata vigila los movimientos de un navío enemigo en el horizonte.

Fredy era la verdadera atracción de la feria, rubio de tanto sol y con esa piel aindiada de los que pasan mucho tiempo al aire libre, un golfo guapo de diecisiete o dieciocho años con la delgadez atlética de los modelos y un culo perfecto embutido en unos levis desgastados. A veces se desplazaba por la pista sin camisa, saltando de un coche a otro con la ligereza de Dick Turpin mientras las chicas aguantábamos la respiración. Decía que había nacido en Cannes, de madre francesa, pero se ganaba la vida con el negocio de su padre por las ferias de los pueblos y había quien aseguraba que Fredy y su padre tenían sangre gitana.

Todas las tardes, a la hora de la siesta Marta y yo salíamos de casa y nos íbamos andando hacia el río, atravesando el pueblo y dejando a un lado las instalaciones de la feria. En varias ocasiones vimos de lejos a Fredy regresando a su caravana con bidones de agua que traía de una fuente cercana. Iba despreocupado silbando o canturreando y saludando a otros feriantes cargados también con garrafas en dirección a otras roulottes.

Nos gustaba quedarnos adormiladas a la orilla del río, en un recodo solitario, cerca de un bosquecillo muy tupido. Yo buscaba la sombra de los árboles y la mayoría de las veces ni me quitaba la ropa pero Marta se tendía al sol en biquini y se bañaba cuando apretaba el calor para volver a tumbarse boca arriba un buen rato hasta que, de nuevo, yo sentía el chapoteo de su cuerpo al entrar en el agua.

Una tarde me pareció ver acercarse a alguien entre los árboles, por detrás de las ramas entrecruzadas. En el acto me incorporé y me senté contra un tronco sin dejar de vigilar la espesura mientras Marta seguía tumbada un poco más lejos con los ojos cerrados, entre sol y sombra, cerca de la orilla. Quedé a la espera de que el intruso saliera a la luz. No me había equivocado, muy pronto apareció Fredy con una camiseta de Bob Marley y un pantalón de baño.

—¿Qué hacéis, chavalas? —preguntó sin más.

—¿No lo ves? Dormimos la siesta —fue lo único que atiné a decir.

Volví a sentir la opresión leve y pasajera que en los últimos días me acometía cada vez que me tropezaba con él.

—Oye, mocosa, le preguntaba a tu hermana.

Marta entornó los ojos, ladeó un poco la cabeza para poder vernos, le hizo un gesto de complicidad a Fredy y se echó a reír. En ese momento Fredy se quitó la camiseta, se acercó a ella y se quedó de pie mirándola desde arriba.

—Qué morena estás —comentó, totalmente concentrado en el rostro de Marta y en la acogedora sonrisa con que era invitado a sentarse.

—Tú también, Fredy.

La sonrisa de mi hermana siguió encendida entre los dibujos de las ramas que sombreaban su cara hasta convertirse en una bienvenida tan cordial que Fredy aprovechó para pedir un poco de espacio en la toalla. Marta le hizo un sitio y volvió a cerrar los ojos.

—¿Y ésta tiene que estar aquí todo el rato? —preguntó Fredy acercándose mucho y hablando en un susurro.

Por el rabillo del ojo vi a Marta alzando los hombros.

—¿A que no te atreves a bañarte desnuda? —dijo de pronto Fredy, incorporándose y esperando la respuesta de mi hermana, que ahora le miraba con unos ojos completamente translúcidos.

Marta se echó a reír, se quitó el sujetador y en dos zancadas se metió en el río con las minúsculas bragas del biquini.

Fredy se quedó un momento sentado, me miró de reojo y dejó su pantalón de baño sobre la toalla. Con una carrera entró en el agua desnudo y alcanzó a Marta. Me recosté en el árbol y quise pensar en otra cosa; les oía reír y chapotear y supe que se iban nadando al otro lado del recodo. Al rato sólo se escuchaban risas ahogadas, silencios y chapoteos otra vez entre risas. Cerré los ojos y en ese momento deseé con todas mis fuerzas estar en el lugar de Marta.

Así empezamos a ver a Fredy a la hora de la siesta cuando el pueblo dormía y nuestros amigos veraneantes, o más bien los amigos veraneantes de Marta, hacían la digestión en los porches de sus casas mientras los mosquitos se ahogaban en el agua viscosa de las piscinas familiares.

A Marta no le importaba quedarse desnuda del todo delante de Fredy, como no le había importado desnudarse cuando éramos mucho más pequeñas y el abuelo nos llevaba a la finca de Olga Navas (de Olga ya hablaré a su tiempo). Yo cerraba los ojos. Sabía que se abrazaban en cueros en el río. Contenía el aliento y me hacía la ciega o la dormida. Los otros desaparecían de mi vista, escuchaba el golpeteo de sus brazos contra el agua, intentaba olvidarme de ellos, me ponía a pensar en otras cosas, mentira, mentira, no podía dejar de ver sus cuerpos estrechados bajo el agua. Ahora sé que a veces hacían el amor en el río. Ella enroscaba sus piernas de trapecista alrededor de la cintura de él. A mí me entraban ganas de morir.

Yo entonces no lo sabía o no lo supe hasta el verano siguiente, en plenas fiestas del pueblo, cuando Marta se largó acabado el concierto con el batería del grupo que no había dejado de fulminarla durante toda la actuación. Me quedé sentada en un banco de la plaza contando las estrellas y mirando a las chicas y chicos desperdigados que no acababan de irse a rematar la noche a otro sitio. Yo tenía que esperar hasta que regresara Marta. Se había levantado aire y hacía frío, pero no me atrevía a volver a casa sin ella. Fredy apareció por la plaza después de cerrar los coches de choque, traía la cara desencajada y se sentó a mi lado en el banco. Me quedé paralizada como una tonta y le di una calada al porro que me ofreció, yo que nunca me había atrevido a fumar un porro.

—He visto a un hijo de puta metiéndole mano a tu hermana en la discoteca —dijo con rabia—. Más vale que no la esperes. Te vas a quedar como un témpano, vete a casa.

Entonces me puso su cazadora por los hombros y me atrajo hacia él con aire protector. Le miré a los ojos para darle las gracias y vi que estaba a punto de llorar, aunque puede que fuera por el hachís, y que sus pestañas eran muy largas y espesas.

—Todas las tías sois unas zorras —dijo alargándome el pitillo.

Di unas cuantas caladas y empecé a sentir un mareo que me empujaba hacia Fredy. Era una cosa rara, tenía ganas de tragar y de que me tragaran. Me apreté contra él, me miró interrogante, me ovillé entre sus brazos y noté que empezaba a darme lametones en el cuello. Yo le dejé hacer, quería que siguiese, sigue, sigue, decía yo por dentro, viendo girar sobre mi cabeza las bombillas de colores de la plaza. Cuando quise darme cuenta yo chupaba también su cuello convertida de golpe en la novia de Drácula. Era extraño, te quedabas pegada a aquel James Dean como a un cable de alta tensión. En un santiamén descubrí un torbellino de lenguas dentro de mi boca y un cuerpo que se restregaba contra el mío, me pareció que a Fredy le habían crecido dedos por todas partes, unos se deslizaban por debajo de mi camiseta acariciando mis pechos, otros medían mis caderas, se metían dentro de mi pantalón, sobaban mis bragas, acercándose hasta una humedad que me avergonzaba y al mismo tiempo me envalentonaba para explorar con mis manos aquel bulto que latía por debajo de los levis de Fredy y cada vez crecía más entre sus piernas.

—Ten cuidado, tía, estás loca, vamos a largarnos de aquí si no quieres que me corra en plena plaza.

No me creía lo que me estaba pasando. No dejó de abrazarme en todo el camino hasta el río. Se había levantado un ventarrón y a veces mis dientes castañeteaban entre beso y beso.

—Te voy a calentar yo a ti, verás cómo te voy a calentar —me dijo cuando dejamos de ver las luces del pueblo.

La noche era una boca de lobo cuando me tumbó bajo los pinsapos y siguió besándome y apretando mis tetas como un demente. Creo que me llamó Marta y puta, y que me dijo cosas en francés, pero yo estaba mareada y prefería no escuchar nada, sólo quería que Fredy siguiera tocándome sin parar. Nunca había pensado que fuera a ser tan rápido. No sé ni cómo me arrancó los pantalones y las bragas y me atravesó de un embate a la primera estocada. Casi no me dolió y me pareció que acababa en un santiamén.

—Tú también tenías ganas, ¿eh? —dijo Fredy después de salir de mí, de lanzar algo viscoso a la oscuridad y de subirse los calzoncillos y los pantalones que no se había llegado a quitar del todo—. Tu hermana está más buena y es más guapa, pero tus tetas son más grandes.

Nadie se enteró de que Marta y yo no volvimos a casa juntas aquella noche. Todavía nos reímos cuando nos acordamos de los veranos de Sotoespino. Marta siempre dice lo mismo.

—¿Qué habrá sido de Fredy?

A veces yo también lo pienso. No sé si seguirá yendo de feria en feria por los pueblos, ahora ya propietario del negocio, sustituyendo a su padre que se habrá retirado para llevar una vida más sedentaria, seguro que ya no se desliza entre los coches sin camisa como Dick Turpin, permanecerá en la cabina cobrando a los adolescentes o cambiando la música, con cien ojos o de mala gana, igual que hacía su padre, o acaso habrá regresado a Cannes, la ciudad de su madre, para llevar el pequeño café familiar. Recuerdo que él soñaba con ser un famoso jugador de baloncesto, se lo dijo muchas veces a Marta, y ahora me doy cuenta de que era uno de esos sueños absurdos porque había dejado la escuela muy joven y que nosotras supiésemos no jugaba, ni había jugado nunca, ni pertenecía a ningún equipo local o aficionado, cómo iba a entrenar si no vivían mucho tiempo en el mismo sitio, siempre de un lado para otro, además no era lo suficientemente alto, pero él insistía, hablaba de su fantasía con una seguridad pasmosa, la abrillantaba como el que cuida un tesoro, cada día le agregaba un detalle nuevo, un adorno que lo hacía más fabuloso, de pronto le fichaban para la NBA, o le salía un contrato millonario con un equipo australiano. Me pregunto hasta cuándo habrá mantenido a flote su sueño. En qué momento habrá dejado Fredy de soñar para conformarse con la realidad, con el modesto café regentado por la madre en alguna pequeña ciudad francesa, o con la pista de autos de choque de siempre y la vida nómada de las caravanas y los feriantes.

Creo que Marta siguió pensando en él durante algún tiempo. Desde entonces mi hermana lo tuvo claro: le dolían las muelas si no se revolcaba con un contingente inagotable de aventureros sexuales. Decía que el sexo a lo bestia le hacía olvidar la ansiedad que le producía una taladradora que hacía boquetes en su cabeza. Empezó a abrazar a la humanidad entera, se apuntó a la carrera de bólidos de una cama rodante, sobrevoló todos los límites de velocidad, subía y bajaba de los ceguerones sexuales en plan montaña rusa. Vomitaba tras los excesos y volvía a tener hambre. Ya he dicho que se gastó mucho dinero en tumbarse en los divanes de los brujos de la tribu, esos señores con pipa y enigmáticas cejas levantadas que en sus peores sueños le meten una bala en la frente a Sigmund Freud. Un día le dijeron que tenía dentro de ella una madre muerta y que le iba a resultar muy difícil sacudírsela. Ella no lo entendió, pero yo sí.

A veces arrastro los pies como una tortuga aletargada y ciega y entonces me asusto y me veo en la piel de mi madre y me dan ganas de gritar y no me sale el grito. Y en lugar de cepillarme al primero que encuentro como hace mi hermana Marta, yo hablo. Me pongo a hablar en voz alta, despacio, con calma, una avalancha de palabras hasta que las variaciones sobre el mismo tema se convierten en una espesa salsa cerebral. Y cuando escucho mi propia voz, me tranquilizo, pienso que ya he recobrado el control y me quito de encima las escamas de pescadilla amnésica y sin ojos que me ronda.

Nunca me arrepentí de dejarle hacer a Fredy. Pensé que era como pasar un examen: cuanto antes mejor. Además, como después me explicó mi hermana, Fredy sabía lo que se traía entre manos, manejaba con pericia los dedos, la lengua, la calentura previa, resolvía con eficacia la tarea de colocar el preservativo. Según Marta era lo que yo necesitaba para tirarme al monte del todo, para no andarme con remilgos: un verdadero profesional. Y Fredy lo era.

Yo había visto a las niñas bonitas de los chalets traficando con su virginidad, que sí pero que no, más vale no llegar hasta el final del todo, a menos que vayan en serio, los padres de fulanito están forrados, mejor una mamada para abrir boca, de momento. Pero a Marta y a mí, y a las chicas guerreras de nuestro barrio, el himen nos traía sin cuidado. Estábamos condenadas a trabajar para salir adelante, excluidas de un golpe de suerte, a nadie le importaba que nuestro virgo estuviese o no intacto. Cuanto antes, mejor, pensé cuando Fredy, sin más miramientos, me atravesó del primer embate a la orilla del río.

Lo que les estoy contando se me escapa de las manos, lo reconozco. Todos queremos que esto avance, pero yo estoy molida, las noches no son el mejor momento del día para perseguir un hilo recto entre mis laberintos mentales, pero qué quieren, no tengo otro momento, me pongo a escribir y aparece el hombre salmonete que me lleva hasta Fredy cuando yo intentaba seguirle la pista a una carta perdida. Tengan paciencia. ¿Ustedes creen en las casualidades? Yo no creía hasta que alguien me explicó que en las ciudades pequeñas hay infinitas probabilidades de que el azar se cruce en el camino y ponga en marcha un mecanismo trastornador que puede desviar por completo los pasos previstos.

8

Álvaro siguió llamando como si tal cosa. Un día preguntó por la carta, que qué me había parecido, se reía el condenado y yo lívida al otro lado del hilo, me gustó Álvaro, qué le iba a decir, me gustó mucho, ahora no puedo hablarte, mentía yo, hay alguien aquí conmigo, mejor lo comentamos en otro momento, en cuanto nos veamos. Álvaro tan tranquilo convencido de que su misiva estaría a buen recaudo o pulverizada y convertida en un puñado de papelillos que habrían sido lanzados por la taza del retrete con el ademán nostálgico y esperanzado de quien tira confetis en Nochevieja o los deja volar desde un barco que leva anclas. Mejor hubiera sido.

Una carta de amor hecha confetis tragada por la catarata del váter y no en manos de un extraño que se preguntaría a esas alturas cómo demonios los dedos de un pie pueden tener el mismo sabor que un puñado de penes en miniatura.

Esa imagen me perseguía. Era lo único de la carta que recordaba. El resto de las palabras se habían borrado o se confundían con otras parecidas que nos habíamos dicho algunas veces en la cama. Me entró la paranoia. Empecé a andar de puntillas. Espiaba mis espaldas por si alguien seguía mis pasos. En medio de aquel vértigo interior salían a flote culpabilidades de todo tipo y sólo me faltaba estirar los brazos como una acusada para que un carcelero colocase grilletes en mis muñecas. Es lo mismo que sucede en las parejas, un buen día alguien hace una perrería y todas las maldades anteriores se abren paso para formar una suma gigante que se lanzan a la cara él o ella en un juicio final adelantado.

Miguel me miraba con el mismo estupor con que hace dos años yo empecé a vigilar a mi hermana a su regreso de un viaje a la India. Yo escudriñaba pequeños cambios, detalles casi imperceptibles que empezaron a modificar a Marta sin que nadie más se diese cuenta, movimientos sutiles que yo trataba de interpretar cuando coincidíamos en casa de mi madre, o cuando hablábamos por teléfono, o en alguna de nuestras salidas juntas para ir al cine.

Marta siempre ha sido alta, rubia y celestial, el tipo de chica a la que en los colegios de monjas seleccionan curso tras curso para hacer de virgen María en las funciones de Navidad. De haber ido a un colegio de monjas Marta hubiera sido la virgen del Belén y yo, con toda seguridad, una humilde pastorcilla o la que arrea el burro o una lavandera o cualquier otro personaje de rango inferior. Pero nosotras no fuimos a un colegio privado ni vimos una toca en nuestro horizonte ni capillas ni flores a María ni adoración a las chicas virginales ni falta que nos hizo.

A Marta, en el fondo, le traen sin cuidado los gestos de admiración de los demás. A veces he pensado que le horroriza ser tan guapa. Arrastra su físico con resignación, como el que carga con un fardo molesto. Vive su belleza como algo prestado, algo que tiene que devolver y regalar a los demás.

Nada más verla en su papel de samaritana sexual, intuyes que sería capaz de alimentar a batallones de neuróticos, a masas de fresadores en paro, a columnas de depauperados o a un enjambre de moscas. Siempre temo que un día su belleza se apagará como una vela derretida y Marta se convertirá en una mujer sin facciones, los rasgos emborronados por tanto desgaste.

Por eso me dediqué a observarla con atención cuando al poco de regresar de la India empezó a dar pasos desorientados, y a desenfocar la mirada y a reírse con risa de trombón cuando no venía al caso. Algo pasaba.

Un día me llevó a la cocina de nuestra madre y me dijo que había bañado en su casa a un vagabundo. Pero fue unos días más tarde, al citarnos en una cafetería de la calle Princesa, cuando me preguntó qué pensaría de ella si me dijese que había hecho el amor con aquel hombre sin domicilio que dormía bajo los puentes.

—Joder, Marta, ¿has tenido cuidado? —Creo que fue lo único que se me ocurrió decir.

—Eso es lo de menos —me dijo—. Siempre estarás tú ahí para recoger mis pedazos. —Le salió una risa seca—. ¿Sabes lo que te digo? A la gente le parece normal que una mujer se case con un hijo de puta limpio y bien vestido aunque de vez en cuando la muela a golpes, pero hacérselo con un desarrapado es un escándalo. Y a ti también te espanta, no digas que no. Mira, Blanca, a veces pienso que hay una línea invisible entre los seres normales y los que andan a la deriva envueltos en harapos. En lugares como Calcuta cualquiera puede convertirse en mendigo o en loco en un instante. Basta con cerrar los ojos y rebasar esa línea hacia el lado oscuro. Los abres y ya no sabes quién eres, ni de qué color es tu piel, ni qué estás haciendo ahí entre la escoria. Hay turistas a los que les roban el bolso y las tarjetas de crédito y el pasaporte. Tu cabeza se ablanda y en mitad de la calle te da por pensar que una batidora ha mezclado tus ideas en una papilla pastosa. Empieza el viaje al infierno. En pocos días las ropas acaban siendo andrajos y tienes que buscar cualquier cosa para comer en los basureros de los grandes hoteles. En uno de esos hoteles se habría quedado tu maleta y tu identidad. Yo podría haber caído en el agujero negro. No es tan difícil cruzar el límite. ¿Lo entiendes? Supe eso en Calcuta. Hay una fuerza que me retiene en esa orilla del Ganges, entre los leprosos que se salpican unos a otros a carcajadas. Por eso necesitaba estar con ese hombre, saber qué ocurre dentro de la cabeza de uno de ellos.

Fue entonces cuando pensé que sus ojos se habían vaciado. Ella seguía frente a mí, vestida correctamente, con su tenue maquillaje de siempre, con su sonrisa inalterable que no evidenciaba tristeza o desesperación, sino una dulzura casi culminada, como si al entregarse al vagabundo hubiera coronado una etapa de un largo viaje. Yo tengo un sensor especial para los embrollos de cama de Marta, de modo que antes de saber lo del vagabundo me había temido lo peor. Lo que no sabía es que la imaginación de mi hermana se había quedado haciendo turismo sexual con las castas más bajas que pueblan las aguas espesas del Ganges.

—Supongo que lo importante es que controles la situación —le dije.

—Lo sé, pero no creas que estoy a punto de perder la cabeza.

—No, no es eso —vacilé—, o sí; quiero decir que te comprendo.

En varias ocasiones mi hermana había visto a aquel hombre con barba rojiza caminando por el parque del Oeste. No tenía el aspecto de los demás mendigos y Marta me juraba que era un hombre guapo. Puede que no tuviera cuarenta años y, según Marta, sus dientes y sus ojos habían conocido otro tipo de vida. Un día Marta acudió al parque después de salir de la agencia de viajes, ya tarde, y vio al vagabundo caminando con una botella de vino en dirección a un viejo edificio abandonado bajo cuya marquesina extendían los sin techo sus hatillos. Marta se sentó en un banco no lejos de allí y lió un cigarrillo de hachís. Perdió la noción del tiempo. Recordaba que siguió fumando hasta que fue noche cerrada y entonces sintió una fuerza que la empujaba a amontonarse con aquellos seres. No me podía explicar por qué lo hizo, pero se dirigió a la marquesina, se acurrucó junto a aquel hombre y le pidió de beber.

—Cada vez está más oscuro —dijo mi hermana por decir algo.

El mendigo se acercó más a ella, encendió un pitillo arrugado y acercó la llama al rostro de Marta hasta que la cerilla se le apagó entre los dedos.

—¿No tendrás miedo, eh, señoritinga? —preguntó alargándole la botella y pasándole un brazo por el hombro.

—No tengo miedo —dijo Marta.

—No me conoces de nada, soy un vagabundo —dijo el hombre inspeccionando con su mano el cuello y las orejas de Marta.

—En cierto modo yo también soy una vagabunda.

—No jodas; no pareces una vagabunda, tu cuerpo está caliente. Las vagabundas tienen el cuerpo frío, los pies fríos, las manos heladas, la cara fría, hasta en verano; es un frío que nunca llega a quitarse del todo, un frío que penetra en los huesos y se queda allí para siempre. Tu cuerpo en cambio está caliente, caliente como las madejas de lana que apretaba mi madre entre las piernas.

El mendigo desabrochó el abrigo de mi hermana. Buscaba un hueco, desbocando el cuello, me contó Marta, para deslizar su brazo por debajo del jersey.

—La palma de tu mano está fresca. Me gusta sentirla debajo de mi ropa —le dijo Marta.

—¿No serás una de esas drogadictas piradas? —desconfió el hombre.

Marta negó con la cabeza. Tomó las manos del mendigo entre las suyas. Esperaba que fueran ásperas, pero eran resbaladizas y suaves.

—No tienes las manos ásperas.

—Tú sí que tienes una piel suave, chica, y está tibia. Me da miedo ensuciarte, mis manos tienen mugre. Por más que me lavo en las duchas de esa mierda de albergues nunca consigo quitar del todo esta capa de mugre.

Ese hombre, contaba Marta, tenía las manos pulidas como piedras y cada vez que tocaba su cuello lo hacía con sumo cuidado, como si evitase contaminarla. Las manos de ese hombre eran las manos de un asesino, me dijo Marta, lo supo mientras él le hablaba de su época de trotamundos por Europa. Él no era un mendigo corriente, le dijo a mi hermana, él hablaba idiomas y había viajado por medio mundo.

—Maté a un tipo bajo el puente de Vauxhall, en Londres —dijo el vagabundo.

—¿Mataste a un hombre?

—Él me lo pidió —siguió el vagabundo—. Estaba muy enfermo, aquel viejo se estaba muriendo. Dormía entre cajas de cartón, estaba hecho un asco de los pulmones. Apenas podía respirar; la mujer que vivía con él hacía la calle para poder comprarle medicinas. No quería ir a un hospital, el muy jodido. Una noche se le pusieron los ojos en blanco y empezó a retorcerse como una anguila. La zorra de su mujer se había largado con un negro. El tipo escupía sangre y deliraba en medio del dolor. Me pidió que le tapase la cara con unos trapos. Quería acabar cuanto antes. A mí me importaba un carajo si el viejo quería palmarla de una vez por todas. Así que le hundí los trapos en la boca con todas mis fuerzas. El viejo mamón pataleó hasta que dejó de respirar. Me largué de allí. Hubiera muerto de todos modos.

Mi hermana bebió más vino para soportarlo.

—¿Serías capaz de cortar mi respiración si yo te lo pidiera? —preguntó Marta.

—No. Claro que no. Estás pirada. ¿Por qué quieres morir?

—Era sólo una idea —dijo Marta.

El vagabundo llevaba una vieja trenca recogida en el ropero de alguna parroquia. Los pantalones estaban atados a su cintura con un cordón. Marta me dijo que sintió el deseo de saber si aquel ser estaba vivo como hombre. Acarició su pecho, que era fuerte, y dejó resbalar una mano por su cintura.

—¿Por qué hundes los dedos en mi bragueta?

—No llevas calzoncillos. Me gusta sentir el calor de tus muslos.

—Deja mis pantalones en paz, no busques nada ahí; el pájaro está muerto —dijo el hombre.

—No está muerto, está solamente dormido. Los pájaros dormidos pueden despertarse —dijo Marta.

—Saca tu mano de ahí, tía, no tengo ganas.

—¿No te gusto? —preguntó Marta.

—Estoy sucio. No follo con mujeres como tú. Huelo mal. Es muy jodido sentirse asqueroso y tropezarse con una mujer que se baña todos los días, ¿entiendes eso, chica?

—Podrías venir a mi casa y darte un baño.

—¿Y luego, qué? Dormir unas horas entre sábanas limpias, saciar esa boca hambrienta que tienes ahí abajo. Sois todas iguales, más putas que gallinas y luego nos dais la patada. Lárgate. Quiero que me dejes en paz. Estás loca.

Marta bromeó:

—Entonces yo me revolcaré en la mugre hasta que huela como tú. Me haré mendiga, te seguiré a todas partes como un perro. ¿Me follarías entonces?

Marta me dijo que el hombre se quedó pensativo, volvió a beber de la botella y luego la besó suavemente con sabor a vino barato.

—Antes de vivir en la calle —le dijo el hombre—, conocí a una mujer que se parecía a ti. No era tan guapa, pero se parecía a ti.

Fue al día siguiente. Marta lo recogió con el coche en la esquina del parque del Oeste donde estaban citados. Había decidido no ir a trabajar por la tarde y acababa de comprar dos botellas de un vino excelente. Supo que el vagabundo venía de ducharse del albergue. Llevaba las greñas peinadas hacia atrás y le temblaban un poco las manos.

Esa tarde, cuando el hombre estuvo bañado y afeitado, lo dejó dormir durante muchas horas.

Por la noche el vagabundo y Marta hicieron el amor. Marta no entró en muchos detalles pero no me dijo que hubiera *follado* con el vagabundo. Me dijo: esa noche hicimos el amor.

No quiso quedarse a dormir con ella. Mi hermana lo volvió a llevar en coche a los alrededores del parque del Oeste. No hablaron mucho durante el trayecto, pero el hombre comentó de pasada que iba a buscar una ciudad más cálida antes de que empezase a hacer frío de verdad.

El día que Marta quedó conmigo en una cafetería de Princesa supe que los ojos vacíos de mi hermana no eran el preludio de la locura ni del precipicio, sino la conciencia de la fragilidad de nuestros pasos. Y a pesar de saber que Marta estaba bien yo seguí vigilando sus reacciones durante un tiempo para estar segura de que sus actos, cualesquiera que fuesen —porque yo desconocía qué hacía Marta cada día—, no se volvían contra ella. Tal vez por eso me empezó a vigilar Miguel después de perder el sobre de Álvaro, aunque él no supiera que yo había extraviado la carta de un amante. Acaso porque sospechaba que a mí me ocurría algo que quedaba fuera de su alcance y que se podía volver contra mí, algo que hacía mi sueño más agitado y ligero que de costumbre y me llevaba a andar de puntillas y a mirar nerviosa a mis espaldas por si alguien había seguido mis pasos.

9

A Julio Oroz le conté en San Sebastián, o en Hendaya, no recuerdo, la historia de mi hermana y el vagabundo. ¿A santo de qué aparece ahora Julio Oroz?, preguntará el coro de lectoras y lectores indignados. Todavía no sabemos nada de ese Julio Oroz… Tienen toda la razón. A mí tampoco me gustan estos virajes bruscos, pero yo estoy aquí, ante ustedes, mientras Miguel duerme, descartando unas sombras y dando la bienvenida a otras, y los pensamientos me traicionan, me ofuscan, brincan y rebotan en mi cabeza. No crean que esto es fácil. Por el río revuelto de mi mente circula a la deriva el nombre de Julio Oroz, aunque no puedo imaginar qué estará haciendo en estos momentos Julio, ni si espera todavía una palabra mía, un movimiento que cambie mis circunstancias y las suyas. Pero todo llegará a su tiempo, porque cuando empecé a andar con el sigilo de un malhechor y Miguel me vigilaba como yo había vigilado a Marta, temiendo esos ojos vacíos que a veces recuerdan a los de nuestra madre, yo no sabía nada de la existencia de Oroz, o lo iba a saber un poco después. Supe de Julio Oroz cuando regresé unas semanas más tarde a la ciudad del norte y descubrí que la carta escrita por Álvaro había desaparecido del apartamento. Entonces no se me ocurrió pensar que la caída de una ficha de dominó puede desequilibrar toda una ordenada hilera de fichas blancas y negras, aparentemente estables, y derrumbarlas una tras otra, igual que cuerpos fulminados por equivocación. No se me ocurrió que la mala suerte es eso: estar justo debajo de la ventana desde la que un puñetero niño al que no conoces de nada lanza un botellón de dos litros de coca-cola que te acierta precisamente a ti.

Una vez más era viernes y yo estaba en la ciudad del norte, tres semanas después de mi último viaje. Lo primero que hice al abrir la puerta del 4A fue recorrer con la mirada el escaso espacio del salón buscando un sobre. Pero no había nada a primera vista. Busqué con gestos nerviosos y la garganta seca. Yo quería descubrir un rectángulo de papel blanco brillando sobre una mesa o repisa, arrugado entre los almohadones del sofá o bajo los sillones, guardado discretamente en el aparador o en algún cajón de las mesillas de noche. Mientras me arrastraba debajo de la cama, abría armarios y cajones, sacudía asientos e inspeccionaba los bajos de los muebles, la mirada desconfiada de Álvaro me perseguía, como la de un juez severo, esperando una explicación endeble para condenarme.

Álvaro se disgustaría si llegaba a saberlo. Tendría que engañarle, claro, no mencionar la carta en absoluto, comportarme como si nada hubiera ocurrido. Me lo notará, notará algo raro y no parará hasta enterarse. No seré capaz de soportar un interrogatorio. Estaba segura y no me podía tranquilizar confiando en mis armas para acallar su indignación con arrumacos. Tal vez la única idea consoladora era imaginar la carta arrugada como un papel cualquiera en la bolsa de basura que la empleada de la limpieza habría depositado varias semanas antes en el contenedor. Pero puesto que nunca se podría comprobar esa suposición, mi vida en adelante sería una zozobra, pensaba yo.

Me dije que las señoras de la limpieza de hoteles o aparthoteles para seres furtivos y transeúntes, suelen ser muy miradas con los documentos y pertenencias de los huéspedes. Están acostumbradas a pasar con sigilo sobre las vidas ajenas y a dejar las cosas en el mismo sitio donde han sido encontradas. Yo sabía que una empleada iba los viernes a las ocho de la mañana a limpiar el apartamento y a cambiar las sábanas por cuenta de la agencia; regresaba también el lunes a la misma hora y seguramente otros días entre semana. De ocho a diez, según me habían informado al firmar el contrato. Dos horas bastaban para que la limpiadora borrase los rastros de los inquilinos anteriores. Cambiaría las toallas y haría la cama, vaciaría los ceniceros (ya he dicho que la infidelidad va acompañada de mucho humo), y lavaría los vasos si había quedado alguno sucio en la cocina. Estuve segura de que nunca se habría tropezado con un látex usado y olvidado por descuido en un cenicero o en un rincón del dormitorio. Al menos nunca después de nuestra estancia en el apartamento. Así como jamás he sabido de dónde sacaba Álvaro los preservativos, tampoco supe qué hacía con ellos una vez habían cumplido su misión. Desaparecían como por ensalmo del mismo modo que habían entrado en escena. Lo cierto es que jamás encontré uno debajo de la cama (Álvaro nunca se quedó a dormir conmigo, pero yo dormía en el apartamento y antes de marcharme revisaba la casa para comprobar que todo estaba en orden), ni a la vista en la papelera del baño cuando yo tiraba el envoltorio de unas medias nuevas. Entonces creí recordar que Miguel los tiraba a la basura, aunque no estaba segura, nunca se me había ocurrido pensar en ello hasta ese momento, son los hombres los que se ocupan de ese asunto; es su asunto, al fin y al cabo, un asunto pegajoso encapsulando un fluido caliente y desperdiciado.

Y si la señora de la limpieza había vuelto a dejar todas las cosas en el mismo sitio, quedaba la hipótesis de que alguno de los otros huéspedes, por así llamarlos, o visitantes del apartamento hubiera sustraído la carta. No podía, sin embargo, recurrir a la agencia. La máxima discreción, me habían advertido. Además, no se responsabilizaban de objetos perdidos. No había ninguna posibilidad de telefonear y preguntar por la identidad de los inquilinos que, acaso como yo, alquilaban el apartamento el resto de los días de la semana. Por eso, mientras esperaba a Álvaro inspeccionando puertas de altillos y vitrinas vacías, andaba yo buscando una solución que no encontraba.

Pero les he escamoteado algo. En ese registro de la casa, tropecé por primera vez con el nombre y la fotografía de Julio Oroz. En un primer momento no le di importancia. Yo había abierto el último cajón de una cómoda o tocador que hay en el dormitorio. En varias ocasiones había visto allí folletos, y algún libro, pero nunca me había atrevido a curiosear. Esta vez me entretuve en revolver. Yo era una espía y buscaba indicios. Acaso la carta de Álvaro estaba entre aquellos papeles. No había muchas cosas: el catálogo de la exposición de una pintora llamada Mara Barbieri, un librito titulado *La cueva de los locos*, escrito por un tal Julio Oroz, cuyo retrato venía en la contraportada, el folleto explicativo de una compañía de seguros y un libro grueso, muy gastado, de relatos de William Faulkner.

Me senté en el suelo y observé las reproducciones de aquellas obras incomprensibles de Mara Barbieri. Leí el texto que acompañaba a las imágenes sin entender apenas nada. Desmantelación del concepto de arte. Propuestas que ponen en crisis los valores estéticos. Objetos susceptibles de ser convertidos en fetiches. Iconos cotidianos que fascinan y repelen. Frases que me inquietaban y se subían a mi cabeza como vino caliente. Al final del texto en letra grande venía el nombre del autor: de nuevo, Julio Oroz.

Volví a mirar *La cueva de los locos* y leí los datos biográficos de Oroz. Había nacido en la ciudad del norte y había estudiado Filosofía y Letras. Las chicas como yo preferimos cerrar los ojos cuando tropezamos con una mirada tan triste. Así que no me extrañó que Oroz fuera también el autor de un poemario titulado, *Día de perros.* Tenía 40 años, una chaqueta gastada de espiguilla y la expresión flotante del que acaba de bajar de una avioneta y ha tenido que vérselas con la ingravidez.

Comprendí que un escritor llamado Julio Oroz o alguien relacionado con él, era uno de los visitantes de la casa.

Nada más ver a Álvaro con sus zapatos de diplomático y sus piernas cruzadas con esa elegancia de embajada que algunos chicos ambiciosos consiguen con el tiempo, supe que iba a ser un encuentro de mucho ajetreo. Debo aclarar las cosas. Debo explicar que los resortes de mi cuerpo se ponían en acción en cuanto Álvaro entraba por la puerta. Mi cabeza les dirá a ustedes lo que quiera, pero yo me sumía en una delirante y agradable confusión cada vez que Álvaro Arriaga ponía su boca contra mi oreja. El mundo se acababa con los ojos cerrados. Abracadabra de besos suaves, luego más profundos, empezaba la combustión interna. Bebí todo el whisky que pude, dejé que mis fibras tomasen sus propias decisiones, y aclaré mi garganta mientras se encendía el piloto automático de mi megafonía sexual.

Puesto que la rutina del sexo es más o menos parecida, les ahorraré en esta ocasión la descripción de nuestro esplendoroso cuerpo a cuerpo en el dormitorio. Sólo les diré que Álvaro estaba excitadísimo y que al cabo del cuarto combate él seguía con ganas de ganar algún tipo de campeonato y yo ya había empezado a mirar al techo.

De pronto Álvaro volvió a preguntarme por la carta y yo me apresuré a besarle con una lengua que se enroscó en su campanilla para que se le quitasen las ganas de seguir hablando del tema. No sé bien a qué hora se fue, ni cómo conseguimos despegarnos el uno del otro ni qué me dijo al despedirse, pero por la mañana yo estaba sola en una cama extraña, me dolían los huesos y odiaba al hombre que no era capaz de quedarse a dormir una sola noche conmigo.

Podía haberme olvidado de la carta. Podía haber abandonado a Álvaro ese mismo día. No es fácil explicarlo: un chico ambicioso sube en un ascensor velocísimo hasta el piso más alto de un rascacielos. Entre dos plantas, ha seducido a la ascensorista para sacar brillo a su ego de escalador. Al llegar a la cima del rascacielos el chico ambicioso comprueba que los zapatos de diplomático están sin mácula y sale del ascensor sin acordarse de la ascensorista que se recupera del encontronazo, enderezándose como puede mientras recoge un jirón de encaje de bolillos, de seda o de algodón, como prefieran, que ha sido desgarrado sin miramientos por el chico ambicioso ganador de todos los premios, la ascensorista con las uñas astilladas de asirse a la pared resbaladiza, deslizante, escurridiza pared, dolorida de abrirse de piernas contra las esquinas de un cubículo, mujer araña, recoge los pedazos de su corazón roto y de sus bragas rotas, él ni siquiera ha dicho adiós, y ella abrocha los botones de su blusa como Dios manda.

Supe que Álvaro nunca iba a dormir una noche entera con la ascensorista.

Entonces se me ocurrió la idea de convertirme por unos días en detective. Debía prepararme para buscar al autor de *La cueva de los locos*. En realidad, creo que había empezado a pensarlo de madrugada, entre sueños, cuando estiré un brazo y sentí que Álvaro ya no estaba. Tenía que permanecer en la ciudad del norte, acechando el bloque de apartamentos, hora tras hora, hasta que apareciera un escritor llamado Julio Oroz. Seguro que él sabía algo de mi carta. Los escritores son gente extraña. Son capaces de sacar punta a cualquier cosa, por ridícula que parezca. Dediqué parte de la mañana a urdir mi plan. De ningún modo podía abandonar la ciudad sin dejar el asunto resuelto. Quiero que entiendan que en ese momento pensé que era la solución adecuada. En parte para librarme de la bola de culpabilidad que había convertido mi cabeza en una máquina *flipper*, y en parte porque no tenía ganas de volver a Madrid con Miguel. Por suerte esa semana no había en mi agenda ningún compromiso de trabajo urgente.

Nunca he tenido teléfono móvil y ahora me alegro, así que tuve que hacer varias llamadas desde la cafetería. A Miguel le dije que las cosas se habían complicado. Tenía que quedarme unos días más en la ciudad del norte, habían surgido problemas con uno de los capítulos del documental que estábamos grabando. Pasaría el fin de semana con Ana Iribar. Luego marqué el número de la agencia. Se puso el mismo tipo de voz pastosa con quien hablé la primera vez, pero no el mismo que se encontró conmigo en la portería del edificio, hacía varios meses, para entregarme las llaves y hacerme firmar un contrato. Hablé con mi tono más convincente de mujer de negocios. Le dije que era importante, que debía permanecer toda la semana en la ciudad y que necesitaba alquilar un apartamento idéntico al mío, en el mismo bloque, en la misma planta a ser posible. Yo era muy maniática, me acostumbraba a los lugares, a ciertas alturas, al paisaje que se contempla desde una determinada ventana; quizá alguno de aquellos apartamentos en el mismo piso estaban libres, quizá me podían alquilar el 4C o el 4D. El hombre carraspeó, primero me dijo que la mayoría de los apartamentos disponibles se alquilaban por meses, tendría que mirar; después hubo un silencio y escuché el teclear de un ordenador. Me pidió que esperase un momento. Me comí una uña. Esperé un poco más. Habló con alguien y tecleó de nuevo. Mi osadía iba a funcionar, yo cruzaba los dedos. Al cabo de un breve lapso, la voz anunció benévolamente que puesto que yo era una clienta de toda confianza, podían facilitarme el 4E. ¿El 4E…? Desde luego que me interesaba el 4E. El 4E me parecía perfecto.

Podría haberme quedado a dormir el sábado en nuestro apartamento, pero preferí instalarme enseguida en el 4E, en cuanto una chica de la agencia, con gesto de aburrimiento y unas medias de rombos de colores, se reunió conmigo a la puerta del edificio y me entregó las llaves. No quería ver las sábanas deshechas de la cama recién compartida ni notar en la tapicería del sofá el olor de Álvaro, el mismo olor de su colonia para hombres audaces de la mar océana que se quedaba debajo de mi piel muchas horas después de habernos separado a pesar de los baños de espuma y a pesar de mi propio perfume y de cascadas de agua y desmemoria.

Supervisé sin interés el nuevo apartamento. Era muy parecido al nuestro. Lo único que me interesaba era saber si iba a tener un punto de vista ventajoso sobre el descansillo. Me resulta difícil expresar con exactitud mi nerviosismo, mi estado de euforia cuando comprobé que desde la mirilla se podía ver una esquina del ascensor, y a lo lejos, como desde el ojo cóncavo de un pez, al fondo de un pasillo, se divisaba la puerta del apartamento 4A.

Así pues, el sábado por la mañana, después de hacer acopio de víveres (nunca antes había entrado en un supermercado de la ciudad del norte), pensando en el cerco de Numancia, me dirigí a una librería para comprar *La cueva de los locos*, de Julio Oroz. No debía manosear un ejemplar ajeno, o acaso evitaba dejar mis huellas en el libro guardado en la cómoda. Después supe orientarme hasta un restaurante de la ciudad vieja en el que un día había comido con los chicos Bruce Willis. Pensé que me arriesgaba a tropezarme con Álvaro, con su mujer, con sus niños, con sus suegros y con alguno de sus clientes, pero creo que no me importó nada. Y además Begoña estaría jugando al golf y Álvaro, con toda seguridad, habría llevado a los niños a la casa de campo de sus suegros. Me apetecía comer bien, me apetecía disfrutar de mi libertad, del vino estupendo, de la amabilidad familiar y acogedora propia de los buenos restaurantes que no llegan a ser pretenciosos. Me hubiera gustado, pensé de pronto, que un escritor con chaqueta de espiguilla con la expresión funámbula de Oroz estuviera sentado frente a mí.

Por la tarde, mientras leía el libro recién adquirido, una especie de diario o reflexiones o pensamientos impenetrables, se me ocurrió que Ana Iribar tenía que conocer a Julio Oroz. No sé cómo se organizan los detectives; supongo que dan rodeos y más rodeos hasta que ven una moneda brillando en el asfalto con unas huellas dactilares; Oroz era mi única pista, y ahora sé que llamar a Ana Iribar fue una buena idea.

Esgrimí una mentira complicada cuando llamé a Ana. A mi madre le estaban haciendo unas pruebas en una de las clínicas privadas de la ciudad. Nos habían recomendado al doctor X (inventé un nombre), uno de los mejores neurólogos del país. Yo tenía algún tiempo libre y me apetecía volver a verla. También a Ana le agradaría verme. Tuve suerte porque Ana Iribar no parecía saber nada de neurólogos, ni le importaba demasiado la enfermedad de mi madre de la que no llegó a preguntar nada más, ni insistió en saber esos detalles insignificantes que algunas personas se empeñan en saber cuando les cuentas cualquier historia no sé si porque desconfían de tus explicaciones o porque tienen alma de porteras. Le confesé a Ana que, de paso, quería preguntarle por una persona de la ciudad de la que tal vez ella sabía algo. En realidad, dije desenfadada, se trata de algo muy tonto, tengo que dar una información a una amiga y creo que puedes ayudarme. No pareció sorprenderse. No hizo preguntas. Ana es una de esas mujeres amables, siempre dispuesta a resolver cualquier situación, a interceder entre unos y otros. Nos podemos ver mañana, dijo, a las ocho en el café Internacional. Yo conocía el café. Todo el mundo en la ciudad conoce el café Internacional.

En la fotografía no se podía ver cómo eran las manos de un escritor llamado Julio Oroz; resultaba difícil imaginar cómo se inclinaría para convencer a un interlocutor, el único dato fiable era la caída de la chaqueta de espiguilla sobre sus omoplatos delgados, eso sí se podía ver en la foto.

Al día siguiente, mientras hablaba con Ana, el rostro de Julio Oroz, al menos la expresión y el pelo flotante de aviador que mostraba la fotografía del libro, se había pegado a mi memoria como un chicle. Traté de sacudirme el chicle mientras Ana Iribar hablaba, pero el rostro de Oroz estaba tan presente ante mí como si estuviese sentado en una de las dos sillas libres.

Al principio me quedé arrinconada en la mesa sin saber cómo empezar. Ya le había vuelto a contar a Ana, de pasada, el pretexto por el que estaba en la ciudad. Ahora sólo tenía que dejar caer el nombre de Julio Oroz.

Preferí entrar a saco:

—Verás, Ana, tengo una amiga que está enamorada de un tal Julio Oroz —dije sin más preámbulos—. Lo conoció en Madrid en la presentación del libro de un amigo. Sabe que vive aquí y quiere saber más cosas de él. ¿Lo conoces?

—Un hueso duro de roer, Julio —dijo Ana después de escrutarme. Creo que no se tragó lo de la amiga y se preguntaba si colgarme a mí el enamoramiento—. Mejor le dices a tu amiga que se olvide. Un bicho raro, Julio, aunque las tías se lo rifan. No lo entiendo. A mí es que la tipología del siniestro me ataca los nervios. Ya sabes: tono un poco depresivo, rostro impenetrable, comentarios cínicos, mala leche. Demasiado Ciorán para mi gusto.

Pensé que Ana conocía bien al personal masculino de la zona. Me hizo gracia que los tuviera clasificados en tipologías. Así que Julio era del tipo siniestro. ¿Quién diablos era Ciorán? Yo por la foto sólo hubiese dicho que Oroz era un hombre triste, como si le hubieran obligado a bajar del columpio o de la avioneta a su pesar. Por eso el viento agitando el cabello y los ojos perplejos. Me pregunté si Ana se habría acostado con él alguna vez. Creo que al ver mi concentración acabó convencida de que era yo la enamorada.

—¿Tú no lo conoces? —preguntó.

—No lo he visto nunca —dije para disipar sus dudas—, ya sabes que apenas vengo por aquí. Mi amiga me ha pedido que le compre *La cueva de los locos*. Se me ha ocurrido hojearlo pero soy bastante negada para ciertos libros.

Ana había vuelto la cabeza para saludar a un par de tipos que se sentaban en la mesa vecina.

—Oroz escribe bien —dijo Ana—, pero vive encerrado en sí mismo. Y lo malo es que bebe demasiado, bueno, como todos aquí. Yo también bebo lo mío, qué remedio —dijo clavando la mirada en su gin-tonic—. O bebemos por desesperación, o bebemos para matar el tiempo. Aunque el pobre Julio tiene razones serias para beber.

—¿Razones serias?

Ana me miró con un atisbo de desconfianza. Creo que se preguntó si merecía la pena ponerme al día en las historias de la ciudad, al fin y al cabo yo era alguien de fuera, una desconocida, por mucho que mi voz hubiera contribuido al triunfo de las elecciones de su partido. Tuve miedo de que no siguiera hablando. Me hubiera quedado convertida en una gárgola con la boca abierta y las orejas al acecho. Una gárgola a punto de pulverizarse, porque en aquel momento yo quería saberlo todo de Julio Oroz.

—Aquí anda en boca de todo el mundo, de modo que no es ninguna indiscreción ponerte al día —dijo. Yo intuía que mi interés había despertado en ella cierta cautela—. Hace un tiempo un coche atropelló a la hija de Julio. —Tragué saliva y ella siguió—. Era una niña de meses, su madre cruzaba la calle con el cochecito cuando una furgoneta se llevó a la niña por delante. Parece que Elena, Elena es la mujer de Julio —se vio obligada a aclarar—, cruzó por donde no debía; eso ya era raro, porque es una avenida amplia, de muchísimo tráfico. Julio vio el accidente desde el balcón. Tal vez eso es lo más terrible de todo. A él no se le ha quitado de la cabeza que fue una imprudencia de Elena y vive amargado. Pero el caso es que ella desde entonces está medio ida.

Me quedé petrificada. No sabía qué decir y me sentía hurgando en el dolor ajeno, como en esos programas basura de la tele.

—Tuvo que ser horrible.

—Desde su casa Julio pudo ver la expresión del rostro de su mujer. Le debió costar unos segundos comprender aquel gesto y luego se lanzó a la calle. No se pudo hacer nada. La niña se había golpeado la cabeza y estaba muerta cuando llegó Julio. No sé qué ocurrió después. Estuvieron un tiempo fuera, creo que en Madrid. Los padres de Elena viven en Madrid. Julio es documentalista en la biblioteca municipal y me parece que pidió una baja por depresión. Lo hace de vez en cuando. Cuando volvieron se comentaba que ella estaba cada vez más desquiciada. No, loca no, sino como aturdida. Eso es, con un enorme aturdimiento. Julio empezó a salir más por la noche. Empezaron los problemas entre ellos. Ella quería tener otro hijo, pero Julio no se atrevía, con su mujer en esas condiciones, cualquiera sabía. A veces te la encuentras en el parque leyendo. Se sienta en el mismo banco y mira a otros niños, hasta habla con ellos. Julio me dijo un día que tenía miedo de que Elena raptase a uno de aquellos pequeños. Igual que en las películas. Ya sabes, la mujer desesperada que ha perdido un hijo, coge a un niño en brazos y echa a correr con él hacia paradero desconocido.

—¿Hace cuánto tiempo? —pregunté.

—Han pasado dos años pero todo sigue igual. Creo que Julio se ve con alguien. No sé en Madrid, pero aquí esas cosas hay que llevarlas en el más absoluto secreto. Si estás casado y tienes un lío más vale que no lo sepa ni tu sombra, aquí nos conocemos todos, ya sabes. Oroz se ve con otros escritores, claro, va al cine, queda con amigas, pero me parece que hay alguien más, algo serio, una mujer con la que se acuesta.

—Supongo que se largará de la ciudad de vez en cuando.

—Julio lleva años diciendo que se quiere ir de aquí. Dice que se ahoga. Lo decía incluso antes de que Elena tuviera a la niña. Para Julio esta ciudad es una tumba, pero tampoco creo que se pudiera adaptar a Madrid. Lo ha intentado en varias ocasiones, frecuenta a otros escritores allí, pero cuando vuelve dice que los de Madrid son unos frívolos, que nadie habla de literatura, que lo único que les importa a todos es lo que pagan las editoriales. Dice que es inútil escapar, que a las pequeñas ciudades se acaba volviendo siempre. Yo creo que Julio está perdido. A los hombres de aquí no se les permite mostrar debilidades, ¿sabes? Por eso Julio se tiene que desahogar con el alcohol, pero me parece que además se está tirando a una tía, porque ahora lo veo más tranquilo.

Yo escuchaba a Ana hablar de Julio Oroz con la vergüenza de saberme capaz de hurgar en la bolsa de inmundicias de cualquiera.

—Le diré a mi amiga que no insista.

Ahora Ana me miró confiada.

—De todos modos, te lo puedo presentar, si todavía te vas a quedar aquí unos días. Ha escrito el catálogo para la exposición de Mara Barbieri. La exposición se inaugura el jueves. A lo mejor está Álvaro. Aunque creo que no irá. Álvaro no se lleva bien con el marido de Mara Barbieri.

Pasó a hablarme de Álvaro. Creo que ella sospechaba que nos veíamos de vez en cuando en Madrid. Cómo le iba a explicar a Ana Iribar que hacía dos noches nos habíamos visto y que yo pasaba un viernes al mes en su ciudad, encerrada como una reclusa en el mismo apartamento donde tal vez Julio Oroz se veía con una mujer, y donde, según supe un día más tarde, una secretaria llamada Yolanda, se acostaba con su jefe los lunes y los martes. Todos casados, todos seguramente conocidos en una ciudad tan pequeña.

—Álvaro es distinto, se lo ha montado bien.

Pero a mí no me interesaba hablar de Álvaro ni de su mujer con boca de pato. Yo sabía de Álvaro todo lo que necesitaba saber. Sabía cómo doblaba el brazo para peinarse antes de salir y cómo me atrapaba por la cintura en la puerta cuando se despedía hasta el mes siguiente. Aunque nunca lo decíamos. Nos despedíamos como si él se fuese a trabajar, como si tuviese un trabajo nocturno y tuviese que salir a la calle a las dos o tres de la mañana y yo me quedase esperándolo en aquella casa desangelada, sin preguntarle cuándo vas a volver, o cuándo nos veremos otra vez. Nos despedíamos a la puerta como los que van a encontrarse al cabo de las horas, aunque dos noches antes no me enteré de su partida, me quedé en la cama soñando que en el último cajón de la cómoda había un libro escrito por Julio Oroz, de la tipología de los siniestros, según Ana Iribar.

Le dije a Ana que me acercaría a la exposición de Barbieri, si no me había marchado el jueves. Me explicó dónde estaba la galería. Le rogué también que no le dijera a Álvaro

Arriaga que me había visto. No iba a poder llamarle y no quería quedar mal. Las cejas de Ana Iribar se alzaron imperceptiblemente, pero dijo que comprendía. Ahora pienso que no comprendía nada. Ana Iribar me miró, pensativa, cuando se fue a buscar el coche. Yo regresé andando por donde había venido. Había sido una buena tarde para una detective de medio pelo.

Pensé que había muchas posibilidades de que Julio Oroz se hubiera llevado la carta. A los escritores se les ocurren esas cosas. Demasiado Ciorán, había dicho Ana. El lunes por la mañana entré en la misma librería del sábado y pedí que me aconsejasen un libro de Ciorán. Algo me empujaba a acotar al máximo el territorio de Julio Oroz.

Y ha resultado que me gusta mucho Ciorán y que escribe mucho más claro que Oroz; la gente se cree que las chicas de barrio somos unas taradas. Leí a Ciorán en voz alta en el apartamento 4E para pasar el tiempo y para tratar de comprenderlo mejor. Es algo que hago a menudo para trabajar la voz. Por la mañana hay que calentar las cuerdas vocales con una especie de gargarismos y después leo en voz alta durante un buen rato. Cualquier cosa. Invento voces. Leo metafísica como si fuera la mujer golondrina, o leo los periódicos imitando la voz desmayada de Blancanieves después de despertar en brazos del príncipe.

Leí a Ciorán con la misma voz con que animo a que el pelo quede brillante y muy suave usando un determinado champú con acondicionador. Eso producía un efecto raro, pero muy estimulante; parecía que las palabras del escritor cobraban otra dimensión. Me hacía gracia el discurso malhumorado del viejito que decía no luchar contra el mundo, sino contra su fatiga del mundo. Recité un párrafo con voz alegre y resultaba que sus frases tenían mucha ironía y una punta de maldad divertida: «¿Cómo superar los ataques de furia, esa necesidad de estallar, de partirle la cara a todo el mundo, de abofetear universos? Habría que dar inmediatamente un paseo corto por un cementerio o, mejor aún, un paseo definitivo.» Abofetear universos, eso me gustó mucho. Sin conocer a Oroz supe que tenía cara de eso: cara de abofetear universos.

De todos modos Julio Oroz no me habló de Ciorán cuando nos encontramos en la exposición de Mara Barbieri, ni tampoco pude saber entonces si él había sustraído la carta del apartamento. Tampoco hablamos de Ciorán cuando vino a verme a Madrid una semana después ni hemos mencionado al escritor rumano en nuestros encuentros posteriores. Yo tampoco le he confesado que le vi un miércoles de refilón en la puerta del 4A, despidiéndose de una mujer a la que apenas pude ver, ni le he explicado que hablé con Yolanda la secretaria y que durante unos días me comporté como una rata espiando por la mirilla de la puerta y husmeando respiraciones ajenas a través de los tabiques.

10

Por fortuna la labor detectivesca me dejaba mucho tiempo libre para caminar de un lado a otro del apartamento, para bajar a tomar pinchos a la cafetería o picotear páginas de los dos únicos libros que me acompañaban, el de Ciorán y el de Julio Oroz. También pensaba. Pensaba en lo pronto que me había hecho mayor. Cierras los ojos y te han crecido las tetas. Vuelves a cerrar los ojos y ya tienes vello púbico y el corazón hecho añicos por dos o tres desgracias que te han sacudido cachiporrazos cuando menos te lo esperas. Como en las marionetas. Toma, toma, toma.

Desde los catorce años tuve que empezar a hablarle a mamá como si ella fuera mi hija y yo su madre. Se quedaba mirando las sábanas colgadas de las cuerdas que dibujaban un aspa de una ventana a otra sobre el agujero gris del patio y al rato se preguntaba qué estaba haciendo allí. Se acordaba entonces de cosas de su pueblo, de un novio que tuvo a los quince años que acabó de carnicero en Ciudad Real o en Guadalajara, no recordaba bien el lugar, repetía su nombre en voz alta como si lo tuviese delante, *Hipólito, Hipólito, Hipólito*; que le arañaban las espigas, musitaba mi madre mirando al patio oscuro sin ver nada, que sus manos eran muy velludas para ser tan joven, que no la estrujara con tanta fuerza que podía venir alguien. Le gustaba el aire fresco que le levantaba la falda y ver la loma a lo lejos y las manos de Hipólito encaramándose poco a poco por sus piernas y los milanos flotando en el aire, pide un deseo decía Hipólito, y ella sopló muy lejos el milano y se arrodilló y besó la tierra y pidió un piso a estrenar con bañera y cocina alicatada y lavadora en una ciudad grande y macetas en los balcones y un marido que no tuviera las manos ásperas como lijas. ¿Te acuerdas, Hipólito? No quise decirte lo que había soñado para que no descubrieras que iba a casarme con otro, yo qué sabía, yo no sabía que acabarías siendo carnicero en Guadalajara o en Ciudad Real, tú ibas para campesino, como tu padre y tu abuelo, como todos los de nuestro pueblo, yo quería un marido con manos de señorito, me arañaban las espigas en los muslos y los pellejitos de tus dedos avanzando como arañas, avanzando como arañas delgadas hasta mis bragas, despacio, la araña peluda, que me haces cosquillas, Hipólito, no seas golfo que puede venir alguien.

—¿Con quién hablas, madre?

—¿Quién, yo? Yo no he dicho nada. Habrá sido el viento.

—Estabas otra vez hablando con Hipólito. Decías no sé qué de unas arañas.

—Puede ser, a veces se me va la cabeza. Estaba a punto de llevar la comida a mi abuelo que está trillando en la era.

—Tu abuelo murió hace muchos años, mamá, estamos en Madrid, yo soy Blanca, tu hija.

Entonces me escrutaba sin entender del todo. Su cara pálida y los ojos de niña asustada, mirándome con pena hasta que me reconocía y preguntaba por mi padre.

—Está de viaje, mamá, ya lo sabes.

Otras veces nos trataba, a mi hermana y a mí, como si fuéramos las hijas de los vecinos que habían venido de visita. Caricias y parloteos para nosotras entonces. Decía que a sus pobres hijas se las había llevado su marido. Ya no las veía, ya no le quedaba nadie de su familia. Daba tristeza verla perder la cabeza de día en día, volviendo a su pueblo en los delirios, olvidada de nosotras y de las tareas de la casa. Quemaba los cazos porque se olvidaba de poner el agua en los hervidos, o subía de la tienda con dos docenas de tarros de mermelada. Alguien tenía que hacerse cargo, pero mi padre cuando estaba en Madrid paraba más en casa de Estrella, la manicura, que en la nuestra. Alguien tenía que tomar las riendas. Yo no lo pedí. Yo no pedí dejar los libros en la consola del vestíbulo y correr hasta la cocina para encontrar un amasijo carbonizado de coles y alcachofas y una humareda por todas partes de ruinas después de un bombardeo, y un olor chamuscado a crematorio. Mi madre lloraba en silencio sentada en un taburete junto a la cocina. La confusión se disipaba con una bronca suave. Se volvió sumisa como un ángel arrinconado en una esquina tras haber perdido las alas. Yo la reñía sin alzar la voz, Marta nos miraba aturdida y mi madre bajaba la cabeza. Yo, catorce años y el único deseo de empezar a subir por una montaña empinada a paso muy rápido y no bajar nunca. Al final le rogamos que no se ocupara de la casa, que nos dejara hacer; nosotras nos encargaríamos de todo.

Mi hermana y yo hacíamos equilibrios para mantener cierto orden en la vida doméstica. A veces Marta me miraba basculando sobre un cordel, a punto de caerse desde nuestra altura de equilibristas. Yo era más pequeña, pero me convertí en la estratega de la familia. Obligaba a mi madre a ducharse y vestirse antes de irnos a clase, la dejaba plantada frente al televisor, veía cualquier cosa, hablaba en sueños con Hipólito, se adormecía en el sofá, arrullaba a hijos imaginarios, mecía a un chico, a veces murmuraba que había tenido un hijo de Hipólito, que se lo habían robado, que en las mañanas de lluvia se le aparecía. En mis horas libres me apunté a expresión corporal y a contabilidad. Respirar hondo y vaciar todo el aire del cuerpo con bufidos de perro apaleado, eso era lo que yo necesitaba. A veces me sorprendía en plena clase de expresión corporal pensando en los garbanzos que debería poner en remojo esa misma noche. Los ojos se me llenaban de garbanzos, perdía el ritmo y terminaba de hacer los ejercicios con la energía furiosa de un descargador. Yo pensaba en garbanzos y Marta en entregar su cuerpo a los novios de guardia que la esperaban con moto o coche a la salida del instituto. Yo admiraba la facilidad de mi hermana para encontrar novios motorizados.

Estudiar para colocarme pronto en un banco. Eso hacía yo por las noches cuando mi madre dormía gracias a los tranquilizantes y Marta guardaba en el bolso una caja de Durex para lanzarse a alguno de sus maratones nocturnos. Me convertí en un búho. Todos los ojos y los oídos eran pocos, oteaba en la oscuridad, vigilaba el resuello que llegaba desde el dormitorio de mi madre, reconocía los sonidos de la escalera, los ladridos de los perros a lo lejos y las cisternas nocturnas del viejo del tercero, el golpe de la puerta del coche que llevaría a Marta de bar en bar, o a un descampado, a veces era el ruido de una moto, sentía el motor al arrancar y también los pasos de Marta al regresar tambaleante, varias horas más tarde, de madrugada. Yo era un búho y dormía con los ojos abiertos.

Algún día se pondrá bien. Eso pensábamos. Pero mi madre seguía empeorando, andaba por las habitaciones cada vez más ausente, cada vez más incapaz de reconocer las siluetas de sus hijas o la sombra de un marido que ya no se detenía en casa más que para llevarse muda limpia y darnos dinero, o para preguntarnos a Marta y a mí si estábamos bien, si necesitábamos algo. Mi madre habitaba en un mundo de silencios y mi hermana y yo tuvimos que acompasar nuestros pasos y el sonido de nuestras voces a aquellas paredes que se llenaron de murmullos. Se acabó la música a toda pastilla en nuestra habitación o en la salita cuando mi padre ponía sus viejos discos de Wilson Pickett, *if you need me, call me, don't wait too long*, y nos hacía bailar con él, mi madre no podía seguir el ritmo, quita, quita, le decía a mi padre cuando la atraía hacia él obligándola a llevar el paso, para músicas estoy yo, se acabaron también las broncas que llegaban desde la habitación de mis padres, los portazos nocturnos, los llantos apagados en medio de la noche. En cierto modo, llegó a ser cómodo vivir mudas o a media voz, aunque el silencio pesado de la mirada de mi madre sentada a la mesa, cada vez más ausente, nos aplastaba a Marta y a mí.

Mis gritos de niña quedaron sepultados entre aquellas cuatro paredes. Mi voz se convirtió en un susurro. Mudé la voz como los muchachos adolescentes. Un día el pitido de los chiquillos se transforma en el ronquido de un trombón desafinado. Los niños cantores de Viena con unos vozarrones de estibadores. A los chicos les desconciertan sus gallos y se extrañan también del cohete que despega y aterriza entre sus piernas. A mí se me puso tono de telefonista de la esperanza. Cuando una gruta en mi laringe se tragó esos maullidos chillones que gastan las chicas malcriadas pensé: maldita sea, ahora nadie me regalará un osito de peluche.

A los chicos de clase les avergonzaba la muda de la voz. A mí no. De pronto yo tenía una voz de mujer mucho más clara y pausada que la de las demás niñas. Voz de mujer y cuerpo de mujer, a los catorce años, como si ya hubiera gastado mi vida.

Yo entonces no lloraba nunca. No sé por qué, pero no lloraba. En secreto sólo pensaba en correr y en dejar en la estacada a mi madre. No se lo decía ni siquiera a Marta. No es que quisiera deshacerme de mi madre, pero en algún lugar de mis sueños había un chico delgado conduciendo un coche a toda velocidad por una carretera sin retorno a casa.

Nosotras no sabíamos qué le hacían en el hospital pero cuando regresaba de alguna de sus estancias cortas veíamos cómo volvía a su rostro la expresión de su juventud, la expresión apacible de muchacha de pueblo, la que tuvo antes de casarse con mi padre, la que acaso aún podría reconocer Hipólito, ese carnicero de Ciudad Real o de Guadalajara, que la había amado antes de ser carnicero, cuando sólo era un chico de campo con las manos ásperas.

Al cabo del tiempo, mi tía Leonor se quedó viuda y se ofreció a vivir con mi madre y a cuidarla. Nosotras empezábamos a ganarnos la vida y alquilamos un piso en el centro. Necesitábamos respirar, el resto de la familia y los médicos aprobaron la idea. Bastantes palos nos había dado ya la vida.

Me acordé en el apartamento de los mandobles de las marionetas porque muchas veces lo habíamos hablado Marta y yo. Vas andando tan tranquila con la cestita y cuando menos te lo esperas te han atizado un papirotazo. Llegas en plan ricitos de oro a casa de los encantadores ositos, y un lobo feroz que pasaba por allí te viola y te despedaza. Lo que más envidio de las personas como Álvaro no es su dinero, ni esa guapura de Ken, el novio de Barbie, ni la altura del rascacielos desde donde contemplan el mundo, lo que más me admira es que parecen gente sin rasguños, gente que se desliza por la vida sin tropezar, sin que nadie les ponga zancadillas, personas que jamás han perdido una partida y que se comen el mundo con la sonrisa de los vencedores. Pensé en eso el lunes por la mañana y volví a pensar en ello el lunes por la noche después de hablar con Yolanda la secretaria.

Ya sé. Tengo que recuperar el ritmo de los acontecimientos. Divago un poco y se me escapa la perspectiva. Eran casi las tres de la tarde del lunes cuando sentí el ruido del ascensor. Me asomé a la mirilla igual que una chismosa se asoma a un patio de vecinos. Un hombre bien trajeado de unos treinta y tantos años cerró despacio la puerta del ascensor como si no tuviese prisa en llegar, se arregló la corbata y escuché el sonido de unas llaves. Unos minutos más tarde una mujer joven entraba al 4A con su propio llavín. Los dos tienen llaves del apartamento, pensé, y desde luego, ese tipo no es Julio Oroz. Después hubo un silencio de dos horas. Me adormecí en el sofá sin dejar de escuchar cualquier ruido que pudiese llegar del rellano de la escalera. A las cinco en punto se cerró una puerta, imaginé que sería la del 4A y vi por la mirilla cómo el mismo hombre que había entrado antes, pedía el ascensor y se marchaba. Esperé unos minutos y pensé que la mujer se había demorado en el apartamento por alguna razón. Era mi oportunidad. Tenía que hablar con ella, preguntarle por mi sobre perdido, descartar otra posibilidad.

A las cinco y cuarto llamé al timbre. No iba a ser fácil explicar todo aquello. Nerviosísima, le dije a la joven que me abrió que yo había alquilado ese mismo apartamento hacía un par de semanas, que, por descuido, había olvidado allí una carta, una carta importante, quería saber si, por casualidad, ella la había visto. Era una chica guapa, no tendría más de veinticinco años. Parecía trastornada por algo, el rostro contraído, aunque muy bien maquillada, seguramente se estaba terminando de arreglar cuando yo llamé a la puerta. No abrió enseguida, me había inspeccionado por la mirilla antes de abrir.

Tengo que advertir que no me gustaba lo que estaba haciendo; pensaba lo mismo que ustedes: ¿Por qué le da tanta importancia a esa dichosa carta? ¿Por qué no se olvida de ella y se vuelve a casa con Miguel?

Puede que la carta no fuera tan importante, pero lo era para mí, era importante para mí saber que aquel papel no andaba rodando por la ciudad del norte, aunque no sé si me aterraba más que la carta cayese en manos de un desaprensivo que pudiera reconocer la escritura de Álvaro, o que Álvaro llegase a enterarse de que yo había sido capaz de perder aquellas declaraciones tan íntimas. Por eso le dije a la secretaria, luego supe que se llamaba Yolanda, que la carta era importante.

—¿Una carta? —dijo con la voz ronca de quienes han pasado mucho tiempo fumando y bebiendo—. No tengo ni idea, como no esté caída por ahí, déjame mirar.

Durante unos segundos, Yolanda me observó en medio de su agitación, me invitó a sentarme en el sofá, movió ceniceros, sacó un vaso del aparador, miró detrás del respaldo de las butacas, hasta que negó con la cabeza en un silencioso movimiento que yo interpreté como un gesto de desolación. Acto seguido empezó a caminar de un lado a otro de la salita, como se mueven los niños nerviosos, como si el ir de esquina a esquina buscando la carta perdida pudiera calmar su inquietud. Después se sentó, sirvió whisky para las dos (su vaso y la botella, de otra marca distinta a la nuestra y que yo no había visto nunca en la cocina ni en el aparador, estaban en la mesita, como si ella hubiera seguido bebiendo después de irse él) y empezó a decir frases incoherentes, o al menos incoherentes entre sí, porque me pareció que hablaba de varias cosas a un tiempo, pero las frases salían mezcladas y yo tuve que hacer un esfuerzo para diferenciar lo que decía sobre mi carta que enseguida adjudicó a un amante, y para comprender que también se quejaba del encuentro que acababa de tener con el hombre que acababa de salir del apartamento.

No me atreví a interrumpirla y esperé a que las palabras cobrasen sentido o a que se decidiese a hablar con claridad de alguno de los asuntos que parecía llevar entre manos.

—Es mi jefe —balbuceó y me di cuenta de que estaba bastante bebida—. Puedo hablarte con confianza, ¿no? Sí, ya veo que tú también andas metida en algún lío. Ya te he dicho que él es el jefe, bueno, yo soy su secretaria, trabajo codo a codo con él, para que me entiendas, te puedes imaginar lo que eso significa en un despacho de abogados, significa que ante los demás tenemos que actuar como si fuéramos de hielo, quiero decir que nuestras miradas se cruzan al día muchas veces, a todas horas en realidad, pero no nos vemos, él tiene una forma rara de mirarme sin verme delante del resto de la gente, como si se volviese ciego o se le quedasen los ojos en blanco, a mí me da hasta miedo, ha de tener mucho cuidado, claro, para que su mujer y la familia de ella que es muy influyente no puedan sospechar nada, no sé si me explico.

Dije que comprendía. Yolanda encendió un cigarrillo y bebió el último trago de whisky de su vaso haciendo el gesto de que lo encontraba fuerte. Tenía ganas de seguir hablando y sirvió más bebida en su vaso ante mi gesto de no querer más.

—La pura verdad es que no sé por qué te cuento todo esto —dijo sacudiendo la melena—. Bueno, sí, te lo cuento porque estoy harta. Yo estoy convencida de que Jorge es un cabrón. Lo único que le importa es la posición social de su mujer, ya te lo puedes imaginar, un apellido ilustre, muchas relaciones, el padre es magistrado, un pez gordo, y además están forrados, casa de verano en Biarritz, chalet en Suiza, o sea, que lo que ocurre es que Jorge ha dado un braguetazo, así de claro, en realidad no soporta a su mujer, una inútil que ha vivido siempre entre algodones, un hatajo de huesos vestido con lo mejor, yo creo que vomita por la noche como las bulímicas, a mí me parece que a ella no le interesa el sexo, como que le da asco. Jorge conmigo se lo pasa bien, para qué nos vamos a engañar, conmigo hace lo que le da la gana, yo le digo amén a todo, a mí me gusta el sexo, me gusta mucho hacer el amor con él, ésa es la verdad, también me gusta mucho hacer el amor con Roberto, mi compañero, nos queremos muchísimo, aunque te parezca raro, nos hemos criado prácticamente juntos, somos novios desde los quince años, el único hombre de mi vida hasta que apareció Jorge. Pero Jorge se lo tuvo que trabajar, no creas. Yo al principio no quería, un par de besos en el coche en el aparcamiento a la vuelta de una fiesta de Navidad. Pero él erre que erre. Un año detrás de mí. ¿Qué podía hacer yo? Era mi jefe, ¿no?, era mi jefe y me llevaba a la hora del almuerzo a unos restaurantes preciosos en pueblos de los alrededores, allí todo el mundo le conoce, por eso me hacía ir con carpetas de trabajo, para que se viera claramente que teníamos una relación laboral, él cuida mucho esas cosas, aunque los de los restaurantes se las saben todas, tú pregúntale a un camarero, no se les escapa un lío. Mejor que psicólogos, los camareros.

En ese momento Yolanda pareció acordarse de algo, sacó del bolso un espejito y se pintó los labios de rojo.

—Pero esta vez lo dejo —dijo decidida, guardando la barra de labios en el bolso—. Lo dejo de una vez por todas. A ti te lo puedo decir, si no te importa; me parece que las dos estamos hundidas en esto hasta el cuello. Siempre acabo bebiendo más de la cuenta. Estoy harta de recibir sus órdenes, harta de que me trate sin ninguna consideración. Lo malo es que luego me arrepiento. Porque me gusta y porque al fin y al cabo es mi jefe. Una no puede acostarse con su jefe y mandarle a hacer gárgaras así como así. El que paga, manda. Así de claro.

Yo asentía fascinada. Era como estar escuchando a una pariente cercana.

—Soy su secretaria desde hace tres años —prosiguió Yolanda—. Yo ya vivía con mi novio cuando empecé a trabajar con Jorge. Mi novio es uno de esos parados sin remedio; llegaba a casa y siempre lo veía desanimado, deprimido, al final una se cansa de dar ánimos, de currar, de llevar la casa. A mí me agota mi novio, ésa es la verdad, a veces tengo la impresión de que lo cargo como un saco a la espalda, se queja de todo, de los trabajos temporales que le salen, de que llego tarde. Nunca está contento. Y en éstas, te encuentras con un jefe con pinta de tratar a las chicas como a reinas: educado, detallista, siempre pendiente de ti. Y además no está mal. Una especie de Papá Noel, vamos. ¿Y tú qué haces? A ver qué haces tú cuando te lleva a comer a un restaurante bucólico y se va de viaje y te trae un bolso que te mueres.

Encendí un cigarrillo porque vi que aquello iba para largo. Era extraño estar de visita en la habitación en la que Álvaro y yo nos habíamos abrazado unos días antes. Era raro estar sentada con una desconocida en el mismo sofá en el que Álvaro y yo empezábamos nuestras caricias, y donde alguna vez, ávidos y con pereza de trasladarnos hasta el dormitorio, habíamos hecho el amor y, seguramente, donde Yolanda y su jefe también lo habrían hecho en más de una ocasión.

—Lo que tengo que hacer es cortar con él de una vez por todas —dijo Yolanda como si se tratase de una idea fija—. Pero no creas que es fácil —prosiguió, dejando caer los hombros como si su intención se desvaneciera de pronto—, lo he intentado montones de veces, no es sólo por mi novio, sino también por mí. No me respeta, este hombre se desfoga conmigo, pero no creas que me da placer. Es de los que creen que las mujeres no tenemos más que abrirnos de piernas y empezar a dar suspiros, como si fuéramos máquinas tragaperras. Ellos meten la moneda y nosotras empezamos a agitarnos y a suspirar. Cariño, eso es lo único que le pido, cariño y un poco más de tiempo; que sea tierno conmigo, pues nada, que si quieres arroz. Aquí te pillo aquí te mato; en media hora ha terminado y quiere desaparecer a toda pastilla del lugar del crimen. Que le produce claustrofobia el apartamento, dice. Más claustrofobia me da a mí que acabe en un santiamén y me deje a dos velas en una cama que no es la mía. Yo le pido que me abrace, que se quede un rato conmigo, pero él una vez que se ha desahogado, se esfuma. Qué le vamos a hacer. Tienes suerte si tu amante te escribe cartas. Supongo que estarás casada.

Me horrorizaba entrar en contubernio. Pensé en mentir, pero no me pareció justo; ella había compartido su secreto conmigo y yo no quería hacerla sentir como un bicho raro. Empezaba a darme cuenta de que éramos una multitud.

—Sí, estoy casada, pero no vivo aquí. Vengo sólo de vez en cuando, una vez al mes.

—Una vez al mes, qué suerte. Yo los lunes y martes, permanente, como la funeraria. Al principio me decía que tenía problemas con su mujer, que acabarían separándose, que yo era como una bocanada de aire fresco. Ponía de vuelta y media a su mujer, y al padre de su mujer, yo creo que me utilizaba para lavar sus trapos sucios. Que yo le relajaba. Eso me decía al principio, como una bocanada de aire fresco. Yo tenía veinticuatro años cuando empezamos, era una cría. Y además el apartamento lo alquilo yo, no creas, decía que era muy comprometido para él. Me subió el sueldo, pero me lo hubiera tenido que subir de todos modos. Lo malo es que no puedo hablar de esto con nadie. Con nadie. En la oficina no lo entenderían, ni mis compañeras ni los demás abogados, es un bufete muy serio, no lo verían bien, la secretaria que se lía con el jefe, como si no fuéramos legión. Tenemos que actuar con mucha cautela, además a Jorge se le caería el pelo, por su suegro, sobre todo. Al principio era más divertido, al principio creo que a los dos nos excitaba el riesgo, a mí me traía sin cuidado que me vieran en coche con él, y él me gastaba bromas haciéndome llevar todas aquellas carpetas. Al principio era muy fuerte. Cuando acabábamos de empezar la relación y todavía no teníamos el apartamento, en una ocasión nos lo montamos en el cuarto de las fotocopias. Hay una fotocopiadora y máquinas de coca-cola y café, el cuartito lo llamamos todos, un poco sala de fotocopias y almacén.

Pues bueno, un día a la hora de comer nos pusimos a manosearnos en el cuartito, ya sabes, yo sentada encima de él, sentada sobre sus rodillas y él me había quitado las bragas y me estaba follando con el dedo, no veas qué corte, yo no podía más, pero no me iba a poner a dar gritos de placer allí mismo, así que cuando volvimos a su despacho yo estaba que ardía y tuvimos que cerrar la puerta con llave. Fue la única vez que lo hicimos en su despacho. Tuvimos suerte. Nadie llamó a la puerta. Ninguna otra secretaria, ni sus socios ni nadie. Metió el condón usado en un sobre para que yo lo hiciera desaparecer. Es absurdo que te cuente esto, pero para mí fue un trago. No podía dejarlo en la papelera, ni me atrevía a tirarlo por el váter, por si se quedaba flotando o atascado, así que guardé el sobre en un cajón de mi mesa hasta que terminé el trabajo, y luego lo metí en mi bolso hasta que encontré una papelera en la calle. Después empezamos a venir a este apartamento.

11

Ahora me pregunto si el compañero de la secretaria le habrá dicho alguna vez que la veía a través de un cristal. Puede que sea un extraño signo, un signo que unifica a las mujeres que tienen amantes, que se acuestan con otros a espaldas de sus maridos o compañeros, una pantalla de cristal que hace que se vaya difuminando nuestra presencia, como si no estuviéramos del todo en ningún sitio, como si estuviéramos veladas. Como es natural no le pregunté nada de eso cuando me senté con Yolanda en el sofá, en el mismo sofá que yo utilizaba un viernes al mes, aunque en realidad podría haberlo utilizado cada viernes, ya que tengo derecho a utilizarlo todos los viernes y sábados que quiera, incluso ahora que ya no veo a Álvaro, aunque nunca me llegué a quedar un sábado, al menos no en el 4A, me iba siempre antes del mediodía. Pensé muchas veces que podría haberme quedado si Álvaro me lo hubiera pedido, pero Álvaro los sábados se debía a su mujer y a sus hijos; los sábados no eran míos, lo único mío, en todo caso, era un segmento de viernes, de ocho de la tarde a tres de la mañana, como mucho; después Álvaro tenía otras cosas más interesantes que hacer y yo conducía durante cuatro horas para regresar a Madrid.

Yolanda, la secretaria, no tiene que conducir tantas horas para ver a su amante, en realidad se ven todos los días puesto que trabaja con él en el despacho contiguo, en realidad se ven casi todos los minutos del día porque una secretaria ve a su jefe todo el tiempo, tiene permiso para irrumpir en el despacho siempre que quiera, o para pasarle avisos telefónicos en cualquier momento, y además se encuentran en el apartamento casi todos los lunes a la hora de comer, y también los martes, según me dijo, también a mediodía, o a veces por la tarde si a él le ha surgido una comida de trabajo. Pero salen y entran del despacho siempre por separado, y también llegan y se van del apartamento siempre por separado, dejando el espacio de unos minutos, a veces él primero y ella después, gracias a lo cual yo pude oír la puerta, espiar por la mirilla y ver que él se iba solo. Aproveché esos minutos en que ella se quedaba recogiendo, tirando las colillas de los cigarrillos, como hacía yo algunas noches, o al día siguiente por la mañana antes de irme, apilando las copas en el fregadero, abriendo las ventanas, y ventilando el dormitorio. Yolanda no cambiaría las sábanas, pero al menos cubriría la cama hasta el día siguiente, porque la señora de la limpieza no iría hasta el miércoles de ocho a diez, para dejar la casa a punto para los siguientes inquilinos.

El martes pasé por alto los ruidos de puertas que me llegaron desde el rellano al mediodía. Yolanda y su jefe habían quedado descartados de mi investigación. Era una tontería seguir encerrada en casa, así que busqué un restaurante discreto para comer y pasé la tarde en una sala de minicines que hay en el barrio.

Y así fue como el miércoles, a las cuatro de la tarde, vi por primera vez a Julio Oroz desde el ojo de pez de la puerta. Se despedía de una mujer que se metía en el ascensor y a la que sólo pude ver fugazmente y de espaldas. Me pareció alta y llevaba el pelo ensartado con un pasador. Les oí abrir la puerta y hablar, pero no les había sentido entrar en el apartamento. Pensé que Julio Oroz y su amante también aprovechaban el momento del almuerzo para verse, pero por alguna razón la mujer tenía prisa por marcharse. Con la puerta del ascensor abierta, ella ya dentro y lejos de mi campo visual, seguían hablando en voz baja. De pie en el descansillo, Oroz, mucho más alto que en mis fantasías, se pasaba la mano por la mejilla como si tuviera que tomar una decisión. Pero yo sólo escuchaba el murmullo de las voces, ninguna palabra. «De acuerdo», dijo finalmente Oroz, la puerta del ascensor se cerró y él volvió a entrar en el apartamento.

Imaginen ustedes mi estado de nervios. ¿Asaltaría a Oroz como había asaltado a Yolanda? ¿Podía permitirme dejarle marchar? ¡Tantas horas perdidas para nada! Tenía que salirle al encuentro, pero me faltaba valor. Me latían las sienes, me latía un párpado, me latía el corazón a punto de estallar. Cuando estaba decidida a abordar a Julio Oroz en el descansillo, tuve que recordar dónde estaban las llaves para no quedarme en la calle y corrí a buscar mi bolso al dormitorio. Fue una de esas dilaciones fatales. Un segundo después, oí de nuevo golpes de puertas. Oroz acababa de desaparecer en el ascensor.

Ya me había metido en una ratonera, así que tendría que esperar hasta el día siguiente para conocer al hombre que, con toda seguridad, sabía algo de mi carta perdida. Si por segunda vez se me escapaba Oroz en el apartamento, o si el jueves no aparecía con su amante, no me quedaría más remedio que acudir a la inauguración de Mara Barbieri.

El jueves me mantuve al acecho toda la mañana. Después de las doce empecé a controlar la puerta del 4A, asomándome a la mirilla al menor ruido. Se abrieron otras puertas del rellano, pero no hubo ningún movimiento en el apartamento 4A. Me sentía avergonzada de mí misma. Mis pensamientos eran como murciélagos aleteando sobre mi cabeza. Me espantan los murciélagos y yo estaba allí perdida luchando contra ellos. Me daba cuenta de que había ido demasiado lejos. Todo había resultado inútil. Pero me negaba a desperdiciar mi último cartucho. Muy bien. Aunque te escondas bajo tierra, Julio Oroz, acabaré encontrándote. Y le encontré, unas horas más tarde, en la exposición de Mara Barbieri.

Llegué a la galería de arte cuando la sala estaba ya muy concurrida. Hice tiempo a propósito para estar segura de coincidir con Ana Iribar. Pero Ana, mujer de mundo, tantas citas, tantas cosas que resolver a lo largo del día, no había aparecido. Les parecerá infantil, pero yo estaba asustada. No soy carne de cóctel, no sé qué cara poner al contemplar un lienzo blanco con una red metálica con un pájaro muerto, un pájaro de verdad, reseco o disecado, ni qué decir ante televisores rotos con muñecas Cindy dentro con el vestido desgarrado y aspecto de marujas maltratadas; tampoco sé estar con mucha gente ni domino el arte de sonreír, besar y sostener la copa al mismo tiempo, ni se me ocurre qué hacer cuando mi interlocutor me deja sola en medio de un salón para ir a saludar a otra persona; no sé rotar buscando el sol que más ilumina o el invitado más conveniente para pegar la hebra, soy de las que tienden a las esquinas mal iluminadas, de las que acaban medio escondidas junto a un cortinón de terciopelo.

Más intrusa que nunca, traté de moverme con familiaridad en un ambiente que no era el mío. Por otra parte, yo sólo tenía un objetivo, un solo astro en torno al cual girar aquella tarde. Y allí, en medio de la galería, ajeno a una loca que le buscaba, recién aterrizado de algún sitio, un halo furioso de aviador clandestino sobre la cabeza, estaba plantado Julio Oroz. La agonizante Blanca reculó hacia un extremo de la sala y agradeció el encontronazo con un señor de pajarita que llevaba una bandeja. «¿Una copa?», preguntó el camarero mientras yo le miraba con agradecimiento alargando la mano para zambullirme en una copa de vino. Mientras vigilaba la puerta para ver aparecer a Ana Iribar, me fijé en que había dos tipos de invitados, unos que se movían de esquina a esquina, saludando a todo el mundo, y otros que se quedaban quietos en el mismo sitio, dejando que los demás se acercasen a ellos. Julio Oroz pertenecía a los inmóviles, pero su parcela estaba siempre bien concurrida. Yo soy poca cosa, me quedo debajo de las mujeres altas, pero tuve la impresión de que, por un instante, los ojos de Oroz se cruzaron con los míos. Fue una mirada neutra pero insistente, esa mirada que gastan los vigilantes de los grandes almacenes y los policías.

Durante unos minutos ensayé una expresión de entendida. Yo hacía como que me interesaban mucho los cuadros, las *instalaciones*, me corrigió más tarde Ana Iribar. Descubrí a la pintora, que podía ser muy joven o no tan joven, hermética, misteriosa como sus cuadros. Llevaba una levita de terciopelo, falda larga, botines y la melena lacia dividida por una raya recta. Maquillada con palidez artificial, párpados profundos y labios de color zarzamora para contrastar, la espiritual pintora recibía besos y felicitaciones, sin apenas sonreír, con esos ojos asombrados y atentos que lucen las personas sorprendidas por su propio éxito. Divisé a su marido. Lo supe porque se buscaban mutuamente, gestos imperceptibles mandando mensajes. Él sonreía mucho. Parecía un buen relaciones públicas de su mujer, sin corbata, un traje de plena moda, zapatos de diplomático, como los de Álvaro. Pinta de diseñador o de artista también. En todo caso de artista con dinero, o con el dinero de padres generosos, o de mecenas generosos. Ana me dijo en otro momento que la madre de Mara emigró a Buenos Aires y se casó con un argentino forrado. Mara nació en Argentina, pero creció aquí. Imaginé a la pintora y a su marido en una casa enorme y luminosa, blanca, con las extrañas obras de ella en las paredes, con pocos muebles. Todo muy moderno, todo muy caro. Sin duda Julio Oroz y su mujer irían a cenar con ellos alguna vez, pensé deambulando cada vez más impaciente y extrañada de no ver a Ana Iribar.

Yo intrusa, yo observando todo desde fuera, ignorada por la colmena hacendosa que iba y venía dando besos. Sólo Oroz había reparado en mí, o eso creí.

Ana Iribar llegó por fin. Me encontró, me saludó, me presentó a los dos chicos que la acompañaban y me dejó hablando con ellos de arte conceptual. Yo decía a todo que sí cuando Ana volvió y me arrastró hasta Julio Oroz. Fue una conversación para tartamudos.

—Blanca te admira muchísimo, Julio. Ha leído *La cueva de los locos*.

—Así que Blanca ha leído *La cueva de los locos* —repitió Julio socarrón.

—Has oído su voz montones de veces —volvió a la carga Ana Iribar—. Blanca se dedica a grabar anuncios de la tele. Ha puesto voz a la campaña de un partido político en nuestras municipales, pero no te vamos a decir el partido.

Julio pareció de pronto fijarse en mí.

—Me interesa mucho más la publicidad de la tele que las campañas políticas. ¿Sabes cuáles son mis anuncios preferidos?

—No. No lo sé —dije yo.

—No te fíes de su tono de superioridad, Blanca. Va a soltar algo desagradable —dijo Ana Iribar, que se fue detrás de una bandeja con copas y me dejó a solas con Julio.

—Los de medias. Piernas de mujer, sin tronco, sin rostro, sin cerebro. Un universo de piernas maravillosas subiendo y bajando escaleras o cruzándose y descruzándose en el aire. Una cosa surrealista, algunos de esos anuncios de medias.

—No me fijo en las imágenes de los anuncios —dije—. Sólo estoy pendiente de las voces. Deformación profesional, supongo.

—Me parece asombroso creer en algo, hasta el punto de ponerle voz —dijo Julio.

—Yo no creo en todo lo que me toca anunciar —me defendí—. No me considero responsable de los mensajes que otros lanzan. Únicamente presto mi voz.

—Ya. Más vale tener una conciencia muy delimitada y no confundir al emisor con el contenido, ¿no es eso?

Nos volvieron a interrumpir. Alguien me empujó. Julio me pidió una tarjeta. Iba a menudo a Madrid. Teníamos que hablar de *La cueva de los locos* y de los anuncios. Le parecía un trabajo curioso. Curioso, dijo, lo recuerdo muy bien. Luego alguien se llevó a Julio hasta el grupo de la pintora y su marido. La colmena reía. La colmena me ignoraba y yo no había avanzado nada en mi investigación. Me despedí de Ana Iribar en cuanto pude. Al día siguiente regresé a Madrid con dos ideas: intentar olvidar a Álvaro Arriaga y volver a ver a Julio Oroz.

12

Un sábado por la mañana llamó Julio Oroz. Estaba en Madrid y quería verme. Pasó una cosa rara. La voz se me rompió como se le quiebran los pretextos a un acusado que es culpable, y me quedé paralizada en el sofá. ¿De qué era yo culpable? Julio Oroz pidiéndome una cita en un bar de Madrid se convertía en una garra que atenazaba mi garganta. Tenía que haber un error. Yo era la perseguidora y él el presunto malhechor. ¿Por qué Julio Oroz me buscaba a mí? Una cafetería de Gran Vía, pensé. Cuanto más impersonal, mejor, cuantos más mostradores de formica, camareros mareados, tortitas con nata y sirope, escaleras flotantes de hierro y mesas con cuatro sillas junto a los ventanales, mejor. En Nebraska, le dije, muy cerca de Callao. A las siete.

Miguel estaba a esas horas en casa. Sentado en la mesa del comedor, detrás de las hojas del diario deportivo, seguía la órbita de un balón imaginario hasta la red amiga o enemiga, vete a saber. Ya no trato de entender por qué se aferra a la camiseta de un árbitro o al despido de un entrenador. Traspasos millonarios y alineaciones ideales en un inacabable juego de chapas de la niñez, ésa es su vida. Hace tiempo que no digo nada. Cuántas veces, viéndolo acompañar esa órbita azarosa o calculada de un balón, he pensado que Miguel estaba buscando una salida. Él convertido en balón, él dibujando una trayectoria en el espacio, impulsado por el patadón de un jugador invisible, él despedido a una velocidad de vértigo, pero ¿hacia dónde? Supongo que cada uno se escapa como puede.

Escuchó el teléfono desde su rincón y me sintió hablar.

—¿Quién era? —preguntó.

No resultaba fácil urdir una respuesta. Qué sabía yo quién era Julio Oroz. Había leído su libro y su texto para el catálogo de una exposición, y sabía que se citaba con una mujer, de la que no pude ver el rostro, en el mismo apartamento en que yo me acostaba con Álvaro; estaba enterada de que leía a Ciorán, porque me lo había dicho Ana Iribar, y había observado, al verle, que la chaqueta de espiguilla le colgaba como si no quisiese llevarla y la chaqueta, sin embargo, se empeñase en abrazar su cuerpo, aferrándose a los huesos largos y descarnados. Pero cómo contestar a la pregunta de Miguel. ¿Quién era Julio Oroz?

—¿Quién era? —insistió Miguel.

—Un tal Oroz; llama de parte de Arriaga y Asociados —mentí—. No lo conozco. Quiere que vea unos textos que tendré que grabar las próximas semanas.

Cuando puse la mesa para comer, los ojos de Miguel estaban brillantes. La pantalla del televisor le esperaba. Iba a ser un magnífico fin de semana de fútbol.

Julio Oroz ya estaba sentado al fondo de una hilera de mesas, cuando llegué. Se levantó para darme la mano. No me pasa a menudo, pero calculé la largura de su cuerpo echado sobre una mujer en el sofá del apartamento compartido.

Imaginé que era por haber estudiado tanto tiempo su fotografía en la solapa de un libro.

Hay personas que se quedan silenciosas y quietas y nos están llamando, y personas que palmean la espalda y sonríen y estrechan manos y besuquean y están con la cabeza en otra parte. Supe que Julio pertenecía al grupo de los mudos que gritan con todas sus fuerzas pero que no emiten ni un solo sonido ni hacen movimientos ni gesto alguno. Estatuas incandescentes que nadie ve por dentro. Tal vez por eso me quedaba yo ronca en su presencia. Porque la voz en esos casos no sirve para nada. Tartamudeé frases triviales de saludo con un súbito desfallecimiento del tono, pero fue Julio quien habló.

—No puedo empezar por el principio —dijo— porque nunca hay un principio. Creemos que sabemos dónde estamos y de pronto la tierra se hunde bajo nuestros pies. No ocurre nada en nuestras vidas, decimos, y cada vez que se abre la ventana y escuchamos voces que llegan de otros edificios, de otras ventanas, preferimos cerrar a cal y canto. Para qué saber lo que se cuece detrás de puertas ajenas, pensamos, para qué implicarnos, mejor que no ocurra nada, qué pereza. Pero de golpe, un día, creemos reconocer la sombra que se agita detrás de unos visillos. Alguien tiene la tentación de matarse, ¿y qué?, no estamos tan cerca como para poder detener la mano que aprieta el gatillo, ni tan lejos para ignorar el rostro crispado y los ojos ya muertos. Perdemos el tiempo buscando pretextos para asegurar que no hemos visto nada, que han tenido que ser imaginaciones. Unas horas más tarde suena el teléfono y nos hablan del funeral de un amigo. Murió solo. No había nadie allí para salvarle... Te preguntarás por qué te digo todo esto, si no te conozco, si nos hemos visto sólo una vez, unos minutos, en una galería de arte. Tú no sabes quién soy yo y yo no he sabido hasta hace muy poco quién eras tú. Eso es lo que tú y yo podríamos contar a todo el mundo, la explicación sencilla. Pero los dos sabemos que compartimos un secreto. Sabemos que nos acostamos en la misma cama en días diferentes y con personas a las que ni tú ni yo conocemos. Eso lo sabemos los dos, y también sabemos que yo tengo algo que te pertenece; por eso viniste a la exposición, por eso quisiste que nos presentasen en la galería, ¿no es cierto?

Acepté el juego cuando asentí con la cabeza y alcé los hombros. O puede que fuera al revés, primero alcé los hombros y luego asentí. Recuerdo que bebí el agua mineral fría que había traído el camarero: me pregunté si la nuez saliente de Julio sabría un poco salada si se pasase la lengua sobre ella, y le robé un cigarrillo con un gesto. Miré los nudillos de sus dedos cuando me dio fuego, en vez de mirar sus ojos que eran verdes, me pareció, y se clavaron en mí mientras siguió hablando.

—Freud dice que siempre dejamos un objeto olvidado para regresar al lugar del que no queremos irnos del todo. Un pañuelo de seda, un bastón, una bufanda de color albaricoque. Deseamos volver a ese lugar sin saber para qué, sin saber por qué. Eso, o el delincuente amateur que deja sus huellas por todas partes para ser cazado. Pulgarcito esparciendo regueros de pan a su paso. Buscamos un cierto orden en las cosas y, sin embargo, los cuervos se comen las miguitas y el caos se instaura por su cuenta. Nadie se hace responsable del descalabro. El bandido asegura impávido que él no robó, que él no afiló el cuchillo y lo clavó en la carne. El bandido, en lo más profundo de sí, piensa que su detención es injusta.

No es tan fácil aceptar la culpa. Por eso nuestros actos nos condenan más que nuestra razón. Las huellas delatoras, la bufanda, la carta olvidada. ¿Para qué querría alguien una carta de amor que no es suya? —Me miró un momento, pero supe que era una pregunta retórica y no respondí. Él siguió hablando—: Tú me has buscado a mí, pero ignoras qué interés puedo tener yo en recoger un objeto con tus huellas y en guardarlo en una bolsa esterilizada como hacen los policías. La prueba, acaso, de tu culpabilidad y la del hombre que ha escrito esas palabras. Ese hombre que se acuesta contigo a espaldas de su mujer, a espaldas de su mundo y de sus compañeros de trabajo, a espaldas, sobre todo, de sus hijos que esperan tranquilos a que su padre —ese hombre que a espaldas de todo el mundo abraza a una mujer desconocida en la cama de un apartamento escondido— les dé un beso antes de dormir. O puede ser que la mujer que se acuesta con el padre sea una amiga de la familia, una mujer de la que se conoce el nombre y el rostro y el rastro del perfume que deja al pasar (aunque el padre lo conoce mucho mejor, el padre tiene que ducharse varias veces para desprenderse de ese perfume que penetra en la piel como una chincheta en una suela), una visitante habitual de la casa que ha jugado con los niños muchas veces gastando bromas en el salón, mientras la madre acaba de preparar la cena antes de que los niños se retiren y dejen lugar a los mayores que ahora toman el aperitivo y que durante un momento consentirán que los niños estén con ellos un rato para saludar y decir buenas noches a los invitados. Así que tú te acuestas con ese hombre a espaldas de tu marido y tal vez de tus hijos, si es que los tienes. Porque estás casada, ¿verdad, Blanca?

Me sentía violenta. A él qué le importaba, por qué me

hacía avergonzar, por qué me preguntaba, yo sólo estaba allí para recuperar mi carta. ¿Qué quería de mí Oroz en aquella cafetería mientras los camareros circulaban inocentes ajenos a nosotros repartiendo batidos y tortitas con nata y sirope?

—Sí, estoy casada —le dije—. Pero no tengo niños.

Bebió un trago largo y sus ojos no se enfrentaron ahora a los míos. Me parece que tensó la mandíbula.

—Supongo que Ana te habrá contado lo de mi hija. Las mujeres habláis de muchas cosas. Mi hija murió en un accidente cuando tenía cinco meses. ¿Lo sabías?

No podía mentir.

—Ana lo mencionó vagamente. No tenemos mucha confianza. Ni siquiera sabe que voy a ese apartamento de vez en cuando. No importa cómo, pero supe que tú eras uno de los inquilinos del 4A. Pensé en Ana porque conoce a todo el mundo. Mentí para encontrarte. Se me ocurrió que podías saber algo de la carta que he perdido. La dejé en el sofá. Fue un acto estúpido, freudiano, como tú dices, pero necesito recuperarla.

Sé que mi tono resultó suplicante.

—Es cierto. Necesitas volver a recuperar el control de todas tus coartadas. Conozco esa sensación. Uno cree estar al descubierto cuando una pieza se sale de su sitio. Pero la vida es cabrona e incierta y cada poco tiempo nos descabala el dibujo del rompecabezas que acabábamos de componer como si no fuera a destruirse nunca. No sé con qué frecuencia ves al hombre que te ha escrito esa carta, sin firma, sin membrete. Sólo una rúbrica garabateada a pie de texto, acaso unas iniciales camufladas que únicamente tú conoces. Una carta que sólo un grafólogo experto podría comparar con otra y dictaminar que ambos remitentes son el mismo individuo y tal vez sacar a la luz la identidad que se esconde detrás de esos signos. Unas palabras que podría reconocer su mujer si hubiese leído muchas de sus cartas, aunque los matrimonios no se escriben apenas, a menos que pasen largas temporadas separados, y aun así, la gente prefiere telefonear. O puede que el corresponsal de esa carta sea descubierto por alguien que haya estudiado esa letra obsesivamente, por alguna razón, por algo que le incumbe, alguien que es capaz de reconocer un rasgo serpenteante en el trazado de la «o», y también un travesaño demasiado largo en cada «t», o a lo mejor es el gancho de la «m» mayúscula el que hace caer en la cuenta al observador atento que esa caligrafía pertenece al autor de esa otra carta que, por alguna razón, se conoce tan bien. Un hombre obsesivo y maniático, ese observador, empeñado en reconocer incluso el estilo de la escritura, una frase que se repite, una metáfora idéntica, la gente no tiene tantas cosas que decir, casi todo está ya dicho, a una amante se le pueden escribir palabras que ya se utilizaron en otra ocasión, acaso unos años antes, en la carta a una antigua novia, o a otra amante. Cuando se ha engañado una vez se puede volver a caer, las relaciones de los amantes se desgastan como las de los matrimonios, aunque a veces los amores furtivos duran más tiempo, sobre todo si los encuentros son esporádicos, uno se queda siempre con hambre en esos casos, no hay tiempo de hartarse, ocurre lo mismo que con el caviar o con otra exquisitez que se come únicamente de tanto en tanto. Quiero decir que la carta que sirvió para una amante podría servir para otra, basta con cambiar algunos detalles. No sé si me entiendes…

No, no le entendía. No podía entender ni una palabra.

Me gustaban su boca y los ojos cansados, y también el pelo flotante como si acabase de bajar de una avioneta y los músculos del cuello delgado, pero no le entendía.

—Necesito esa carta, Julio —protesté—. No hay ningún motivo para seguir adelante con esta historia.

—Todo a su tiempo —dijo él con frialdad.

—Necesito esa carta —repetí a piñón fijo como una demente.

Seguía ronca. Los labios secos y ganas de gritar, yo que soy incapaz de alzar el tono. De pura rabia recompuse el gesto y cobré poco a poco el dominio de la voz. Le hablé del respeto a la identidad ajena, y de la protección de la intimidad de terceras personas, de hilos de la vida que acaban embrollándolo todo, la carta ni siquiera era mía, mejor controlar las madejas antes de que los diferentes cabos se enreden y anuden en una maraña.

—Sí, claro —en su tono había una punta de burla—. Comprendo muy bien tus razones para querer recuperar esa misiva de amor, pero no acabas de entender por qué yo te he buscado a ti, por qué yo tengo interés en conservar esa carta, la carta del hombre con el que te acuestas en una ciudad que no es la tuya a espaldas de tu marido, la carta de un hombre que sin duda ha tenido otras amantes a las que ha podido escribir con esa misma letra. Seguramente temiste que tu carta pudiera servir para algún tipo de chantaje, aunque no parece probable. No está firmada, no hay ningún nombre o apellido comprometedor deslizado entre las frases. Y sin embargo, tenías miedo, todavía tienes miedo. Pensaste que en las ciudades pequeñas los azares están a la vuelta de la esquina, alguien podría reconocer la letra, acaso un compañero de trabajo de tu amante ocupa el apartamento otro día cualquiera, ese desconocido podría haber sustraído la carta comprometedora. O una mujer, quién te dice que esa mujer a la que se le ha ocurrido alquilar el 4A sólo por un día no es una antigua amante de tu corresponsal, o peor aún, podría tratarse de su propia esposa, en una ciudad pequeña esas cosas ocurren, las cartas de amor adúltero no se pueden dejar tiradas por ahí.

Pensé que Julio Oroz era uno de tantos sádicos. Era fácil imaginarlo en zapatillas, leyendo un libro, hundido en un sillón de orejas, pertrechado en su silencio. Un sordo ignorando la cháchara desesperada de su mujer.

—No sé qué pretendes, Oroz. Creo que estás chiflado. Haz lo que quieras con la carta. No merece la pena discutir.

Mi sequedad le pilló por sorpresa y se echó a reír.

—Es increíble —dijo—, acabas de poner voz de malvada de película en blanco y negro.

De puros nervios me eché a reír también.

—¿Cómo te las has arreglado para saber que yo era la destinataria de la carta?

Julio pidió otro JB al camarero antes de contestar. Me preguntó si yo quería más agua. Dije que no.

—No he tenido que hacer nada. A veces, sólo es cuestión de tiempo. Pensé que acaso tú me buscarías a mí. He estudiado atentamente el contenido de esa carta. Ese tipo está obsesionado por cómo le hablas en la cama. Además hay una alusión a la imposibilidad de veros más a menudo, a tu vida en Madrid, tan lejos de la suya. Cuando supe en la galería que doblabas anuncios y documentales, y que estabas de paso en la ciudad, pensé que podrías ser tú. Una especialista en voces: susurros publicitarios entre sábanas, seguro que es ella, pensé. Tenía que jugar de farol. No he estado seguro hasta esta mañana al hablar contigo. Una llamada extraña que has recibido con normalidad, como si la estuvieras esperando. Ni siquiera me has preguntado para qué quería verte.

Mis manos húmedas y la lengua pastosa. Supuse a Miguel frente al televisor. Yo estaba a solas con un sádico en el palacio de las tortitas con nata. El pelo flotante como si acabase de bajar de una avioneta y los músculos tensos del cuello delgado (¿quién sería la mujer que mordía ese cuello?) no me dejaban pensar con claridad. Y la boca, sobre todo la boca que no paraba y que obligaba a mis ojos a seguir los movimientos de los labios que, de haber sido besados en ese momento, sabrían a whisky y a tabaco negro. Hablé por hablar, sin esperanzas de salir del atolladero.

—Entiendo. Pero sigo sin saber por qué tienes tanto interés en una carta que no es tuya.

—Has dicho que debes proteger la identidad de tu amante, y lo comprendo, la cuestión es que yo necesito saber quién es el autor de esa carta porque tengo con él una cuenta pendiente.

Yo estaba empezando a impacientarme. Aquel tipo era un lunático y yo una trastornada por seguir participando en aquella conversación sin sentido.

—Todo esto es ridículo, Julio. Una película mala, eso es lo que pienso.

Me miró con dureza. También él parecía cansado del juego.

—De acuerdo. Voy a ser muy claro y quiero que lo entiendas, señorita de la voz de orgasmo. Ese tío es un cabrón y el responsable de la muerte de mi hija y de la locura de mi mujer. Conozco su letra porque tengo en mi poder una carta escrita hace dos años con idénticas características. Día tras día he observado con minuciosidad esos rasgos grafológicos, cada pequeño indicio contaba, no podía dejar de lado ningún detalle por minúsculo que fuera. Durante dos años he tratado de imaginar cómo sería ese hombre, pero no había muchas probabilidades de encontrar al individuo que me ha condenado a vivir una vida distinta de la planeada. Me había resignado a no saber quién es el tipo que ha destrozado para siempre la armonía de mi rompecabezas. He acabado por acostumbrarme a vivir con el sufrimiento de odiar a un desconocido. Doy puñetazos al aire, lucho contra el vacío igual que un ciego acosado por un enjambre de abejas. El zumbido constante y el aguijoneo del dolor. A oscuras. Es un sufrimiento difícil de definir. Avanza por todo el cuerpo como una especie de infección en la sangre. A veces ese dolor me produce un gran placer. Un placer agudo, extraño. ¿Has tocado alguna vez con la lengua un flemón? Uno regresa una y otra vez a la muela enferma porque al explorarla con la lengua nerviosa, al recibir el impacto nítido del punto dolorido, nos hacemos más conscientes de la sensación, y la sensación se nos revela como un instante de plenitud.

Siguió hablando del daño cristalizado. Yo podía ver cómo se posaba sobre él una nube de ceniza. La ceniza cubría por completo a Julio Oroz y sólo quedaba su cabeza parlante en el extremo de un volcán. Debajo de esa montaña apagada que le aprisionaba, en el interior de sus costillas, estaban las brasas. Las palabras de Oroz quemaban y le supe con boca de fuego, igual que el lanzallamas que Marta y yo habíamos visto hacía poco en el Retiro.

—Julio —le interrumpí—, no comprendo del todo… No sé qué decir. —Me miró como si me viera por primera vez.

—Siempre sufren los mismos, ¿lo sabías? Hay seres que provocan el sufrimiento de los demás, y otros que lo padecen. El hombre que se acuesta contigo pertenece al grupo de los hijos de puta. Más pronto o más tarde te hará daño. Ya se lo ha hecho a otros, un daño irremediable. Necesito echarme a la cara a ese individuo. ¿Lo entiendes? Por eso quiero que me digas de una vez por todas quién es el hombre que ha escrito esa carta.

13

Había varios bancos ocupados. La mujer de Julio estaba sentada en su lugar habitual del parque, junto a un templete decorativo que no parecía tener una función especial. Había otra mujer a su lado con una niña de unos cuatro años jugando en el césped. Desde el balcón, Julio se fijaba en la posición del cuerpo de Elena, que estaba sentada con descuido, puesto que creía que nadie la observaba. No podía saber que su marido la veía desde casa, porque a esas horas él tendría que estar en su puesto en la biblioteca; ella no tenía por qué saber que Julio había salido a media mañana con el pretexto de una cita médica. Había regresado a casa porque necesitaba estar solo, le pasaba casi todos los días, pero aquella mañana se le hacía imposible seguir frente al ordenador, rodeado de los compañeros del departamento.

Elena siempre se sentaba en el mismo banco. No fue difícil localizarla desde el ventanal. Tenía unas piernas bonitas, unas piernas que no se habían alterado después del nacimiento de la hija. Elena no era consciente de que tenía las piernas bonitas, eso era lo bueno, según Julio. Caminaba olvidada de sí, con pasos poco armónicos, de hecho se podía decir que era una mujer desgarbada, como si los movimientos de su cuerpo no consiguiesen estar sincronizados. Andaba mal, igual que algunas mujeres demasiado altas que han sido patosas en la adolescencia y arrastran desde entonces unos pasos desmañados. Elena caminaba de ese modo y sin embargo las piernas eran perfectas. Los transeúntes que se cruzaban con ella no percibían los gestos deslavazados de su cuerpo, porque toda la atención se concentraba en las extremidades. Eso ocurría cuando llevaba faldas, no exageradas pero lo bastante cortas para hacer que los hombres reparasen en aquellas piernas largas y suavemente dibujadas, de anuncio de medias. A Julio le gustaba mirarlas, todavía ahora, después de varios años de vivir juntos. Por eso Julio las observaba en aquel momento, presionados los muslos contra el extremo del banco, levemente separadas, la falda se habría subido, Julio no podía precisar tanto, pero pensó que acaso desde el banco de enfrente se adivinaría el pequeño triángulo blanco de las bragas. Julio comprobó que no había ningún hombre sentado en el banco que quedaba frente al de Elena. Sólo dos mujeres, una madre joven, o quizá era la niñera que había sacado al niño a pasear, y una abuela con su nieta. Elena estaba rodeada por otras mujeres en esa zona del parque. Un poco más lejos, junto al tobogán y los columpios, había algunos hombres mayores leyendo el periódico, jubilados seguramente. Pero cerca del banco de Elena no se veían hombres. Julio imaginó que todas aquellas mujeres con sus hijos o con sus nietos aprovechaban las horas del parque para escapar de sus rutinas, para no pensar en nada, para dejarse ir en el griterío de los chiquillos, olvidadas de sí mismas. Las mujeres se relajan cuando están solas entre ellas, había pensado Julio. No les importa que las faldas se suban, o que asome por la blusa el borde del sujetador. Parece que vigilan a los niños que juegan junto a ellas, pero no es cierto, tienen los ojos desenfocados, están en otro lugar.

Elena acunaba el coche de su hija de modo maquinal. No era probable que la niña llorase, a juzgar por la tranquilidad de Elena; acunaba el cochecito pero miraba hacia otro sitio, miraba hacia un claro de árboles donde unos niños correteaban jugando al escondite. Estuvo así durante un tiempo hasta que abrió el bolso con el gesto precipitado de quien de pronto recuerda algo. Julio no distinguía del todo bien, pero supuso que esos sobres que había sacado del bolso eran el correo que había recogido del buzón al salir de casa. Era ella quien se ocupaba del correo cuando bajaba para pasear a la niña, o cuando iba a la compra los días en que la asistenta se quedaba con la pequeña.

Desde su posición Julio no podía ver a la niña, sólo el coche del bebé y la colcha blanca. Ahora le dolía esa escena. Le envenenaba la idea de no haber bajado a estar con ellas. Pero le dio pereza bajar. Prefería seguir allí arriba, viendo a su mujer y a su hija desde lejos, como si no las hubiera visto nunca, observando los gestos que reconocía pero que ahora parecían cobrar un significado nuevo. Vio cómo Elena abría una de las cartas. Estuvo quieta mientras leía, y sólo con la mano seguía moviendo imperceptiblemente el cochecito. Unos segundos después la mujer que estaba junto a ella levantó la vista del libro y miró a Elena que había dejado caer la carta sobre el regazo.

Julio, mucho más tarde, sabría por la propia Elena que al acabar de leer la carta se le escapó un gemido. Desde el ventanal Julio no podía percibir con claridad las expresiones del rostro, pero advirtió algo raro en la posición corporal de su mujer. En ese momento, un hombre con dos perros pasó por delante del banco. Un instante después Julio vio que Elena se había levantado y con agitación atravesaba deprisa el camino, empujando el coche de la niña hacia la salida del parque. Julio tuvo la impresión de que algo anómalo ocurría. Pensó en bajar a su encuentro, pero se convenció de que eran aprensiones absurdas. Seguramente Elena había olvidado algo y regresaba a casa.

El hombre de los perros estaba saliendo del parque. La mujer del banco se había quedado mirando. Julio se dijo que no sucedía nada, algún asunto burocrático que Elena acababa de recordar. Al acercarse a la verja que rodeaba el parque, Elena miró hacia atrás. Julio no podía ver bien sus ojos porque, aunque estaba más cerca, ahora se había puesto gafas de sol. Pero no hacía sol. Por un momento la vio retroceder y caminar hacia el otro extremo como si buscase otra de las salidas del parque. La dejó de ver durante un momento. Pero luego la vio desandar el camino y dirigirse por el sendero hacia la puerta que quedaba justo enfrente de la casa.

Estaba concentrado en los movimientos que conocía, que había visto otras veces desde esa misma ventana cuando Elena volvía de paseo con la niña. No podía saber que había en el aire un latido de crispación. Intuía, sin embargo, que algo pasaba, pero no acertaba a saber qué. La vio mirar en dirección al paso de cebra, un poco más lejos, pero se situó en otro punto de la avenida, a Julio le extrañó, no era un lugar seguro para cruzar, los coches iban lanzados a pesar del parque cercano.

Elena miró a derecha y a izquierda. Julio recordó la desorientación que él traía siempre que volvía de algún viaje a Londres, cuando no sabía por qué lado iban a aparecer los coches. Su mujer miró también a los dos lados, con gestos bruscos. Pasado el tiempo Julio no podía explicar en qué momento vio venir a la furgoneta a toda velocidad. Pero lo presintió. Presintió el peligro en la boca del estómago. Quiso decir algo pero el cochecito ya había salido despedido y Elena se tiraba al suelo sobre las ruedas y el cuco para proteger a la niña. Julio bajó las escaleras a trompicones, gritando, golpeándose contra las paredes, no recordaba las palabras, sólo los alaridos de loco. Él no había oído desde arriba el grito de Elena pero se le había clavado en el cerebro el gesto de horror. No supo explicar nada al portero y corrió por la acera hasta la avenida aullando el nombre de su hija. Varios coches se habían detenido, el conductor de la furgoneta estaba desviando el tráfico agitando las manos, y empezaba a formarse un corro de curiosos. Cuando Julio llegó, su mujer estaba abrazada a la niña muerta envuelta en una toquilla. Sólo repetía: no puede ser, no puede ser.

Al parecer, Julio Oroz me contó los detalles del accidente en algún momento de nuestra cita en la cafetería de Gran Vía. Supongo que no dejé de mirar al cenicero o a la cajetilla de tabaco. No quería ver los ojos de un hombre que corre una y otra vez por un laberinto sin encontrar la salida. Creo que días más tarde llegué a pensar que de la boca de Julio no salió ni una palabra sobre esta escena. El caso es que pudo ocurrir de este modo. De este modo descubriría Julio, unas horas más tarde, una carta sin firma arrebujada en el bolso de su mujer. Una carta de despedida, una carta de un amante de hielo.

14

Pasé aquel domingo nerviosa, tratando de reconstruir mi encuentro con Oroz. Miguel comió con su madre y yo tuve la tentación de llamar a Álvaro a su casa, nunca lo había hecho, pero necesitaba hablar con él. Durante los últimos días me había dejado varios mensajes cifrados en el contestador, allí estaba un chico de película persiguiendo a una rana que nunca se convertiría en princesa, y la rana de voz de terciopelo, chapoteando en su charca, no le había devuelto las llamadas. Sabía que a él le acuciaba el hambre, y yo estaba sin ganas.

No siempre nos apetece ese queso tan rico que al principio significó una novedad. Los sabores nuevos con el tiempo pueden llegar a cansar, no conviene abusar, yo quería espaciar mis citas con Álvaro. Pero, ahora, después del encuentro con Julio, me urgía verle y me aterraba encontrarme con él, las dos cosas a la vez. No dejaba de ser absurdo. ¿Qué le iba a decir? Eres un criminal, te liaste con la mujer de Julio Oroz y cuando quisiste acabar con ella, del disgusto tuvo un impulso suicida en plena calle y ahora ha perdido a su hija y ha perdido la cabeza. ¿Cómo le iba a soltar eso a la cara?

Seguramente Álvaro, si es que Álvaro ha sido alguna vez el amante de Elena, ni siquiera sabrá que su carta de ruptura se convirtió en la ficha de dominó que se tambalea y provoca la hecatombe, pensaba yo. Además, los paranoicos ven al asesino en todas partes y no me quedaba más remedio que reconocer que Julio Oroz había resultado bastante paranoico.

Pero la paranoia, si quieren que les diga la verdad, es contagiosa. La mente de los paranoicos está llena de cuadros con ojos camuflados, de amenazas escritas entre líneas, de escaleras que crujen, de viandantes traicioneros y de mayordomos psicópatas. Puede que Julio Oroz no fuese más que un paranoico, pero a mí me empezaban a temblar las piernas cada vez que pensaba en llamar a Álvaro. Así que no llamé.

Al final acabó encontrándome una mañana sin la empalizada del contestador. Que cuándo iba, que tenía muchas ganas de verme, que había pasado un siglo desde la última vez. Yo también tengo ganas de verte, dije, y en realidad no mentía. El cuerpo tiene su propia memoria, y aunque yo no crea en calabazas que se transforman en carrozas de oro, le preguntabas a mi nuca, a mi cintura y a mis pechos y te decían que querían volver a sentir la lengua del príncipe encantado. En cuanto pueda iré, le decía. Te avisaré antes.

Yo tardaba en llamar, y cuando lo hacía siempre encontraba excusas para posponer mi viaje. Tengo cosas que resolver, Álvaro. Ha surgido un trabajo que requiere mucha concentración. Tendremos que esperar un poco. El silencio rencoroso de Álvaro a través del auricular se podía cortar con un cuchillo. No es pena por no verme, pensé, es simplemente la negativa, aunque sólo sea temporal, disuasoria, de una mujer que le niega algo. A Álvaro le parecía inconcebible que una mujer, por muy susurrante que resultase en la intimidad, descalabrase sus planes, sus propósitos.

El caso es que mis pretextos para no ir a verle eran ciertos. Por una parte, yo no quería presentarme en la ciudad del norte sin haber resuelto el asunto de la carta y estaba dispuesta a hacer una última intentona para negociar con Oroz y recuperar lo que era mío, zanjando la cuestión y convenciéndole de que todo lo demás eran aprensiones suyas.

Por otro lado, se encadenaron varios spots y me surgió un encargo inusual a través de Olga Navas, una compañera de oficio y amiga de la infancia.

Hacía un par de meses que no nos veíamos. Coincidimos en el estudio para grabar juntas uno de esos anuncios a dos voces. Era un trabajo entretenido: nos tocaba explorar el fastuoso mundo de las bayetas de cocina. Las imágenes eran las habituales: dos bayetas de colores danzaban en la cocina, dejando relucientes los azulejos. Olga era la amarillenta bayeta usada y yo, la rutilante bayeta nueva: azul, absorbente, de lo más atractiva. Mi voz tenía que ser chispeante, sexy, descarada, y la de Olga debía resultar quejosa, aburrida, pesada. Repetimos varias veces las tomas por divertirnos, hasta que encontramos el tono adecuado. La bayeta nueva cada vez más pizpireta y la bayeta vieja hecha unos zorros deprimiéndose por momentos. Salimos del estudio riéndonos de todo.

Olga es de mis pocas amigas íntimas en esta profesión. En realidad eso es lo que más me gusta de este oficio, navegas en solitario, trabajas la mayor parte del tiempo a solas con tu propia respiración, y en muy contadas ocasiones colaboras con alguien para una grabación que requiere dos, tres, o incluso cuatro voces; pero a la hora de la verdad no tienes jefe, ni compañeros de oficina, ni agente, ni horarios fijos. Raras veces te encuentras con las mismas personas para hacer los anuncios. No tienes que depender de nadie. Eres *la voz*. Nadie te pregunta en qué universidad has estudiado ni quiénes son tus padres o tus amistades. Da igual si te tiemblan las manos o si tienes un ojo marrón y el otro amarillo, porque lo único que tienes que hacer es encandilar a un micrófono con la vibración de tu garganta. Te reclaman directamente los estudios de grabación o las agencias de publicidad cuando ya te conocen de otras campañas y buscan una voz específica. Incluso impones tus propias tarifas dependiendo de tu cotización en el mercado. Olga y yo somos de las mejores, pero tenemos tesituras y coloraturas distintas. Mi timbre es más claro y sensual, casi nunca presto mi voz a amas de casa que tienden la colada familiar en el jardín o luchan contra la grasa de las vajillas. Olga, por el contrario, tiene una voz densa y muy adaptable, puede imitar voces de niños o ancianas cascarrabias. Pone voz, a menudo, a la suegra picajosa que aparece en algunos anuncios de productos de limpieza.

Por eso el trabajo del que quería hablarme tenía que ver con la simulación de voces. En realidad Olga es una magnífica imitadora de voces. Lo era ya desde pequeña, cuando jugábamos juntas en el pueblo de mi padre, donde ella veraneaba en la finca de su familia. Olga no llegó a salir con la pandilla de los veraneantes, ni conoció a Fredy, porque a los doce años dejó de ir a Sotoespino y empezó a pasar el mes de agosto en Dublín o en Londres. Y tampoco nos vimos de adultas en Madrid. De hecho nunca nos habíamos visto en Madrid, ni siquiera cuando éramos niñas y habíamos salido durante el verano. Nosotras vivíamos en un barrio obrero de las afueras, y Olga vivía, y sus padres siguen viviendo en la misma casa, en el barrio de Salamanca. Nos volvimos a encontrar hace cuatro años, en la cola de un cine, por casualidad, y a mi hermana y a mí nos costó un instante traer a la memoria el rostro pecoso de la amiga de nuestra infancia que nos había reconocido.

Olga había estudiado filología inglesa, daba clases de inglés en un colegio y se aburría. Le hablé de mi trabajo y la animé a que probara. Un día me llamó y la puse en contacto con unos estudios de grabación para que le hicieran unas pruebas. En poco tiempo se ha convertido en una de las mejores voces de esta profesión. Hace un año ha empezado a hacer doblaje de películas, pero todavía coincide conmigo en algunos anuncios.

De modo que nos conocemos desde que éramos muy pequeñas, nuestra amistad viene de cuando ella y Marta no tenían pecho todavía y se extrañaban de mis tetillas de cabra. Jugábamos con ella en su finca porque mi abuelo ayudaba en ocasiones al aparcero que se ocupaba de los cultivos y nos llevaba con él para que Olga, la única hija del dueño de la finca, tuviera compañía. Olga tenía un hermano, algo mayor, que a veces también venía con nosotras. El recuerdo que tengo de aquellos días es el de un tiempo feliz, Marta y yo adoptadas por una familia rica, protegidas de pronto por aquella enorme casa en penumbra, con muebles de caobas oscuras y cuadros misteriosos, y mimadas por la madre de Olga, una señora delgada de ojos acuáticos, alta, bien vestida, siempre caminando despacio y muy recta como una duquesa, que nos ofrecía zumos y bocadillos en bandejas de plata.

Cuando íbamos a la finca para bañarnos en la balsa que habían convertido en piscina, una doncella nos acompañaba al dormitorio de Olga y allí nos poníamos el traje de baño, cada una observando el cuerpo de las otras mientras Marta nos hablaba de los secretos de la vida y de perros que se apareaban por las esquinas. Sobrecogidas por aquel misterio de la carne que afectaba también a los mosquitos y a las lagartijas, dejábamos la ropa bien doblada sobre la cama y seguíamos a Olga que nos precedía por las escaleras talladas en las que veíamos sátiros y ninfas entrelazados, aunque puede que no fueran más que querubines inocentes. Nadie nos dijo nunca nada, pero bajábamos mudas y de puntillas para no romper el silencio de la casa. Sólo cuando llegábamos al jardín echábamos a correr hasta la piscina, que estaba mucho más lejos, en un lugar de la finca que nos pertenecía por entero.

El hermano de Olga inventaba juegos en los que invariablemente teníamos que desnudarnos. Íbamos a perecer en el cazo gigante de los comanches, pues venga, en pelota picada. Éramos amas de casa trogloditas perseguidas por una manada de dinosaurios, en cueros vivos. Las náufragas no llevan traje de baño, nos decía un día cuando nos arrastrábamos por las arenas ardientes de una isla desierta. Olga se encargaba de los efectos sonoros de las aventuras: era el viento ululante, el rugido de las bestias, y también las vocecillas de los personajes secundarios. Mi hermana Marta se desnudaba con toda tranquilidad delante de Santi y de los amigos de Santi que eran invitados a la finca de tanto en tanto. Se movía como un animal salvaje en medio del monte, y dejaba que, en cualquier momento, Olga y Santi explorasen los pliegues de su sexo como si fueran dos ginecólogos haciendo prácticas. Yo ahuecaba el tronco para disimular las tetas precoces que crecían cada vez más en mis pesadillas y de las que alguna vez se colgó Santi para mamar como un choto diciendo que era mi hijo pequeño y que no había comido en todo el día.

Al poco de volvernos a ver en Madrid, cuando empezamos a encontrarnos en los estudios de grabación, y a llamarnos de vez en cuando, Olga me invitó a su casa a tomar una copa. Me dijo que quería que supiera que vivía con una mujer. Somos pareja, aclaró.

—Me trae sin cuidado con quién comparte su cama la gente a la que quiero.

—Hay a quien le importa.

—Ya nadie se plantea eso —dije con desenfado—. Estamos al final del siglo xx. Nadie se mete en la vida privada de nadie. Nadie que esté vivo, quiero decir. Las momias de otro siglo pueden pensar lo que quieran. Si te pones a tiro siempre te meterán un cartucho en el cuerpo por algo. Algunos están deseando encontrar un chivo expiatorio, un chivito bien tierno que no se pueda defender para asar en la hoguera, un tonto del pueblo, una puta o un bicho raro al que apedrear en la plaza pública. Tiene que ver con pegar una patada al sendero por el que estamos obligados a arrastrarnos como orugas, en fila india, unos detrás de otros como si fuéramos clónicos. Y tú vas y le haces un corte de mangas al látigo, te sales de la fila, haces con tus muslos y tus dedos lo que te da la gana y te zambulles como una diosa sáfica en las playas con bandera roja. Que se jodan.

Nunca más hemos hablado de ello. Yo le pregunto por María como ella me pregunta a mí por Miguel. María y ella se acuestan, salen de vacaciones, van a trabajar, entran en coma sexual, se vuelven a poner en forma, comentan los libros que leen, se besan, se enzarzan sus manos y sus cuerpos en los días buenos, duermen en habitaciones separadas cuando les da la gana, hacen proyectos de futuro, cocinan, salen con otros amigos y amigas, beben vinos excelentes y van de compras juntas. Igual que otras muchas parejas del mundo occidental. Vete a saber si alguna de las dos tiene una amante. Puede que se vean en un apartamento a espaldas de su compañera, como yo me veo con Álvaro a espaldas de Miguel. Nunca le he hablado a Olga de Álvaro, ni ella me ha comentado nada sobre la existencia de una tercera en discordia. Tal vez María y Olga sean más fieles que yo y no necesiten probar nuevos sabores, o se esfuercen por ser sinceras entre ellas, por ajustar el deseo y sudar siempre juntas. Olga ha abandonado la fila de orugas y supongo que a su madre elegante se le pondrán los pelos de punta. Hay que tener coraje para contener la respiración, echar a correr delante de un cañón y dejar que te expulsen del paraíso por tomar por asalto un cuerpo prohibido.

Estoy de acuerdo: otra vez me he perdido en una escalera de caracol. ¿Dónde estábamos?

El anuncio de bayetas. Yo era la bayeta azul y pizpireta, ya lo he contado. Al finalizar la locución Olga dijo que quería hablarme de un trabajo que le habían encargado y que le era imposible llevar a cabo porque en esos días tenía que doblar una película. En realidad se trataba de un cliente privado con un capricho bastante morboso. Nada de líneas calientes, ni gargantas profundas, explicó Olga. Me pidió que hablase con el cliente y tomase la decisión con calma. El tipo estaba dispuesto a pagar a precio de oro, pero era un trabajo delicado. Percibí una punta de curiosidad en los ojos de Olga, intuí, también, que le parecía un reto interesante. Creo que me tentó la idea de perderme en la niebla y olvidarme por unos días de mis preocupaciones. Por eso le dije a Olga que iría a visitar al señor Villalonga, el joyero viudo que quería escuchar la voz de su mujer muerta.

15

En el fondo yo estaba haciendo tiempo para enfriarme por dentro y sepultar bajo un alud de zapatos gastados el recuerdo sabroso todavía de Álvaro, cruce de piernas de diplomático, su cuerpo desnudo en la oscuridad brillaba, vello satinado del pecho, o satinado el pecho, brillaba Álvaro Arriaga en lo oscuro, no sé por qué, unos bíceps de Bond, James Bond, Álvaro que se esfumaba saltando de mi cama como un muelle después de un concierto memorable de maullidos, graznidos y balidos a dos voces. Permítaseme añadir que también empecé a preguntarme qué clase de sangre correría por las venas de Julio Oroz. ¿Por qué su forma de hablar me perturbaba? Era muy enervante, como si unos dedos desconocidos hurgaran en mi maquinaria y equivocaran todos los cables de mi cerebro. Si cerraba los ojos, no se oía en mi cabeza sino la perorata de Oroz y se despertaba en mí el deseo de seguir escuchándole. Nunca había experimentado tal agonía. Pero, de pronto, el viudo Villalonga lo postergaba todo solicitando mi presencia e involucrándome en su historia so pretexto de un encargo que implicaba, en cierto modo, resucitar a su mujer.

—Desde aquí, desde este lugar veíamos la puesta de sol muchas tardes —dijo Villalonga, señalando el paisaje que se abrochaba como un cinturón de montañas en la lejanía.

Estábamos a treinta kilómetros de Madrid, en una urbanización vigilada por unos colosos de uniforme con perros asesinos. Yo nunca había visto una mansión tan inmensa, ni un jardín tan grande, ni un mayordomo tan disfrazado de mayordomo. En las películas, bueno, pero eso no cuenta. Villalonga era redondo, calvo, con ojillos de lince. Hablaba despacio, sin esperar ser interrumpido, más para sí mismo que para mí, creo que no llegaba a descifrar por qué había desaparecido de su vida su mujer, ponía empeño en recordar y repetía las frases como si estuviese en estado de trance, yo la única espectadora, invitada de piedra a una existencia ajena, hasta el punto que llegué a pensar que los dos nos habíamos equivocado de novela.

—Yo la conducía hasta aquí en su silla de ruedas, cubiertas las piernas con una manta de vicuña. Yo quise que fuera piel de vicuña; mandé que la enviasen desde Argentina, una piel muy cálida, un tacto generoso, de lo más suave.

Yo no tenía la más remota idea de cómo era la piel de vicuña. Las pieles de animales muertos me dan grima. Vi una película de una mujer que abandonaba a su marido, se liaba con un mafioso y asesinaba a media ciudad para asaltar una peletería. Pensé que era una cosa de locos. Villalonga seguía con su asunto:

—Todo me parecía poco para Eleanora. La traía hasta aquí por ese sendero por el que acabamos de pasar usted y yo. Mire: todavía se notan las marcas de las ruedas. Cuatro meses, ya. No puedo soportar este silencio. Ella era una mujer muy alegre, aunque con la enfermedad se había ido apagando un poco. Entiéndame, no se quejó jamás, no perdió la sonrisa ni siquiera en los últimos momentos, pero se había abatido sobre ella algo sombrío, cómo explicárselo, algo como una insensata fascinación por su propia decadencia, como si se dejase arrastrar por su estado con una elegancia malsana. Ella era así en todos los aspectos de la vida, se entregaba por completo a las cosas, y en cierto modo creo que también se entregó por completo a la enfermedad, aunque nunca lo diese a entender, su ánimo nunca decayó, al menos yo no la vi decaída jamás.

No me atrevía a interrumpir y caminaba callada junto al viudo con una libreta en la mano y los ojos fijos sobre la uniforme extensión de aquel césped, de idéntica altura, idéntico verdor, rasurado sin duda por un barbero cuidadoso que no permitía calvas ni penachos descuidados. Pensé que Marcos Villalonga tenía manos de tratante de ganado, a pesar del enorme solitario que lucía en el dedo anular, o tal vez precisamente por ese destello continuado en unas manos rudas, un destello que iluminaba el camino de su cuenta corriente.

—Por eso es tan importante para mí recuperar su voz, porque de pronto me vienen al pensamiento muchas de sus palabras y no quiero que con el tiempo acaben por borrarse, igual que la lluvia persistente embarra y confunde las huellas de los carros en el campo. De todas formas tengo la impresión de que algunas de sus palabras se han grabado a fuego dentro de mí, las escucho en mi cabeza, ¿sabe?, pero me gustaría cerrar los ojos y oír su voz en el exterior, como si Eleanora estuviera a mi lado. Son pequeñas frases, cosas ridículas que me decía a veces y que ahora cobran muchísima importancia para mí, y usted se preguntará por qué, y yo no sabré explicárselo. En este mismo lugar, por ejemplo, cuando en los últimos meses yo la traía hasta aquí para ver caer la tarde, siempre decía: «Esta puesta de sol no existe, Marcos, es una película que has mandado proyectar para mí.» Le gustaba gastarme esa broma, lo dijo muchas veces, o al menos así es como yo lo recuerdo, la memoria es tramposa, no soy del todo viejo, tengo sesenta y siete años y ya ve, fuerte como un roble, tengo todo lo que el dinero puede comprar, pero ya no tengo su voz, no sé si me entiende. Yo necesito aferrarme a sus palabras. Volver a escuchar algunas de las cosas que me dijo. Podría irme a vivir con mi hijo a Los Ángeles, embarcarme en un crucero, intentar olvidarla, concentrarme en las subastas de joyas, pero me perseguiría este vacío de su voz.

Villalonga hizo el gesto de espantar una nube de mosquitos, pero no había mosquitos, que yo viera no había mosquitos en ese momento. Imaginé que con ese gesto, Villalonga espantaba el silencio molesto y tumultuoso de vivir sin la presencia de su mujer.

Los ricos también lloran, así que era verdad. Allí estaba yo, paseando con el joyero Villalonga, a mil años luz de Miguel, de Arriaga, de Julio Oroz, concentrada en una vida que no era la mía (aunque en esos momentos la única vida que tenía era un puzzle desperdigado por un ventarrón traicionero), tratando de imaginar a una mujer a la que nunca había conocido, compartiendo los recuerdos de un iluso que desdeñaba la realidad, el hecho fatal de que Eleanora había callado para siempre.

—Si usted supiera reproducir su voz, si pudiera anotar las frases que yo le voy diciendo y devolvérmela a ella, yo le estaría muy agradecido. Ya sé que es un encargo raro, usted tiene que imitar la voz de alguien que ya no existe, la voz de una mujer a la que no ha oído jamás, y tampoco vio usted nunca la dulzura de su rostro cuando hablaba, eso es importante que usted lo entienda, siempre sonreía mientras pronunciaba las palabras, eso cambia por completo el tono de una voz, ¿se ha fijado alguna vez? Puedo enseñarle alguna fotografía. Le gustaba mucho retratarse, sobre todo en los viajes. Viajábamos a menudo, por mi trabajo y, a veces, también por placer. Le gustaban las ciudades con agua, con mar o con un lago, con río o incluso con canales. San Sebastián, Ginebra, Florencia, San Petersburgo; se sentía más a gusto en Amsterdam que en Venecia, ella decía eso cuando pasábamos una temporada en una de esas ciudades: «Me siento a gusto aquí.» Venecia, sin embargo, acabó por entristecerla. Un día dijo que había imaginado su funeral atravesando el puente Rialto. Era una especie de visión, no recuerdo si me dijo que lo había soñado o si simplemente lo imaginó. ¿Lo ve?, olvido los detalles. Es comprensible, claro, después de tantos años. El caso es que se había visto muerta en una góndola, rodeada de flores, deslizándose por los canales solitarios. No solía pensar en esas cosas, ya le he dicho que era una persona muy alegre, nunca hablaba de esas cosas, ni siquiera cuando supimos que su enfermedad era irreversible, pero en Venecia sí, Venecia la entristecía cada vez más, de modo que cuando íbamos a Italia nos quedábamos en Florencia, por la Galería de los Uffizi, y por el Arno, sobre todo. Decía que sentía la necesidad de ver correr el agua y, por esa razón, dábamos largos paseos por la orilla del Arno en Florencia o por la explanada del Neva en San Petersburgo, donde ella pasaba también muchas horas en el Ermitage. Había una obra, déjeme recordar, era un cuadro muy misterioso de Claude Monet, *El estanque de Montgeron*, creo que se llamaba, del que ella decía: «Si alguna vez desaparezco, si alguna vez te abandono sin decir una sola palabra y me pierdo por el mundo, búscame delante de este cuadro.» Yo voy a regresar un día a San Petersburgo, sólo por ver de nuevo ese cuadro que a ella le gustaba tanto. A usted le parecerá morboso, pero delante de *El estanque de Montgeron*, me gustaría volver a oír su voz. Creo que podríamos anotar lo que decía cuando admiraba la obra de Monet, le enseñaré una reproducción del cuadro, tal vez pueda hacerse una idea de la luz que había entonces en su voz.

Villalonga empezó a caminar hacia un banco de piedra. Me hizo sentar a su lado y se quedó un momento perdido en sus pensamientos, hasta que yo me impacienté y le pregunté si disponía de alguna grabación.

—Desde luego. Ya sé que una voz no se improvisa así como así. Le daré algunas cintas magnetofónicas, poca cosa, algunas frases sueltas, pero podrá hacerse una idea. Y también tengo películas de vídeo, grabaciones caseras, claro, fragmentos de conversaciones, algún comentario que ella hacía mientras sonreía a la cámara. Eleanora tenía una voz, no sé, un poco cansada, mi madre no entendió por qué me casé con una mujer extranjera. Era inglesa, no sé si se lo he dicho, pero aprendió rápidamente nuestro idioma. Tenía que haberla oído hablar en inglés, creo que también tengo unos poemas en inglés que grabó para nuestros nietos, usted sabrá idiomas, bueno no importa, yo necesito a Eleanora hablando en castellano, con ese suave acento que le digo. Llevábamos casados 42 años, Eleanora iba a cumplir 60, una dama hermosísima, incluso cuando sus piernas ya no le respondían.

Trataba de imaginar cuándo podría zafarme de Villalonga y regresar a Madrid. Creo que lo notó porque se puso de pie y me invitó a proseguir el paseo, esta vez en dirección a la casa.

Señoras y señores, no se ofusquen y exijan que vaya al grano, deben comprender que yo experimento cierto sosiego al transcribirles lo que sé de la peripecia de un personaje que no tiene nada que ver conmigo, aunque por un instante nos desviemos de mi historia. El joyero viudo es un lapso antes de volver a la ciudad del norte. Ustedes tal vez consideren que mi encuentro con Villalonga es un obstáculo más en los meandros de este relato; tal vez piensen que un escritor más experto hubiera pasado de largo: digresión, digresión, a la guillotina con las digresiones. Y si alguien tiene idea de cómo cargarse de un plumazo a Villalonga, que levante la mano.

Yo sabía que no se puede suplantar una voz, pero también sabía que Villalonga quería justo eso: llenar su tiempo, hacer encargos imposibles, tener un pretexto para resucitar a Eleanora. No discutió el precio. Me llevé las cintas y le dije que no necesitaba ver las películas. Villalonga me había enseñado fotografías de Eleanora. Le dije que le enviaría mi grabación por correo y le di los datos de mi cuenta bancaria.

Encontré a Miguel en casa con aspecto de tener una jauría de hienas sonrientes en la cara. Jugaba el Real Madrid contra el Atlético de Madrid. Me pidió que por favor le preparase la cena. Estaba excitadísimo. Cada vez que veía la expresión de Miguel ante uno de esos superpartidos me figuraba que tenía los nervios de un maníaco sexual a la espera de una estrella del cine porno. No era cosa de contarle mi encuentro con el viudo. ¿Para qué?

Los siguientes días traté de localizar a Julio Oroz en el teléfono que me había dado, pero no había nadie. Me dolía pensar en Álvaro como en un tenorio desalmado, rematando a sus amantes con cartas de cicuta. Le di vueltas y vueltas al asunto convertida en una colegiala histérica que no se quiere bajar del tiovivo. Me mareé y no saqué nada en claro.

No he sabido si al joyero Villalonga le convenció la cinta que le envié unos días antes de volver a la ciudad del norte. Me vino bien hacer de médium mientras me comía los pétalos de la margarita decidiendo si llamar a Álvaro o no llamar. Al final llamé.

16

El apartamento estaba muy templado cuando abrí la puerta con una bolsa de viaje y un paraguas. Yo llegaba del frío de la calle y de la lluvia de carreteras desangeladas. Miré el reloj y eran las cuatro de la tarde. Había comido en la cafetería de una estación de servicio. Pan reseco envuelto en una bolsa precintada que no abrí, un consomé para entonarme y una tortilla de jamón. Pedí un café porque el calor del coche y la música y los trazos idénticos del parabrisas sobre la monotonía del asfalto gris me adormilaban. Supe, mientras buscaba en el bolso una aspirina, que una punzada en la garganta me empezaba a rondar. Había otros viajeros frotándose las manos con esos gestos de destemplanza compartida que hace aflorar el mal tiempo. Desde el coche a la cafetería soplaba un aire helado que lanzaba la lluvia a la cara. Cuando me miré en el espejo del cuarto de baño descubrí unas imperceptibles líneas rojas en el borde de las pestañas y los ojos llorosos.

Una amante a punto de tener gripe. Una amante con fiebre en una casa que no es la suya con un hombre que no sabe arropar ni poner el termómetro ni bajar a la farmacia a por el jarabe de la tos. O al menos, un hombre que no sabe atender a su amante enferma, nunca lo ha hecho con ella, no es su papel, con la esposa sí, el amante está acostumbrado a la esposa debilitada, a la esposa griposa encogida como una niña chica, para la esposa el vaso de leche caliente con miel y la mano en la frente, para la esposa los mimos y la preocupación. A Miguel no le gusta verme enferma. Trata de disimularlo cuidándome con una dedicación inflexible. Que la habitación esté a la temperatura adecuada, que las medicinas se tomen a su hora, que la comida sea apetecible y vitamínica, que la fiebre no suba. Lo hace todo con una profesionalidad tenaz, desplegando sobre la mesilla recetas y remedios igual que un enfermero entregado. Pero si el malestar se prolonga, si no me curo de inmediato, lo veo impacientarse, como si aquello durase demasiado para sus fuerzas. Cuando no puede más se mete conmigo en la cama. El médico convertido de pronto en enfermo, reducido a la invalidez de su paciente afiebrada, contagiados los dos; los dos abrazados en medio de un mar de microbios.

Pensé en anular la cita con Álvaro. Pensé, también, en llamar a Julio Oroz para convocarle en el apartamento. Julio Oroz subiendo un caldo de la cafetería, colocando almohadas en el sofá, buscando mantas en los altillos de los armarios. Oroz leyendo un libro mientras yo cabeceo, vigilando de reojo mi respiración.

Cuando me desperté estaba tumbada en la cama con los botines y el chaquetón puestos. Tuve que bracear como una ciega hasta encender la lamparilla de noche. Durante casi tres horas había sido un rebujo sobre la colcha. Álvaro no podía tardar. A lo tonto, debatía conmigo misma sobre la conveniencia de confesarle toda la verdad. Pero la lluvia golpeando contra el cristal me disuadía. Mejor amarle por última vez, hace frío en la calle; total, ya estoy aquí. No es honesto, pensé, no se puede zancadillear y besar al mismo tiempo. Yo, Judas, que iba a traicionar también a Álvaro, acaso inocente, que ya había besado y engañado tantas veces a Miguel, tenía que ser franca. Me sumía luego en la duda. ¿Cómo iba a decirle que después de hablar con Julio Oroz sus brazos me parecían los de un asesino? Yo sabía de él algo comprometedor, un secreto que lo dejaba a la intemperie y ahuecaba todavía más su figura. ¿Cómo enlazarme con su lengua que ahora sabría amarga? Y sin embargo, pensaba, le estoy condenando sin juicio, sin pruebas concluyentes. Oroz podría estar equivocado. ¿En realidad qué tenía en su contra? Una carta. Indicios grafológicos, suposiciones, sospechas sin peso, nada. Mejor emborracharme como Yolanda la secretaria. Qué sería de los amantes sin alcohol, mejor beber y dejar que los acontecimientos me envuelvan en su ritmo. Ya veremos.

Me serví un Chivas antes de sacar las cuatro cosas de la bolsa. Lo bebí sin hielo, como lo toma Álvaro, a palo seco. Dejé, después, que el vapor de la ducha empañase el espejo y cuando el cuarto de baño estuvo caldeado como una sauna, me sumergí bajo la cascada de agua hirviendo y sacudí la cabeza como un perro. Nunca me maquillo, pero me empolvé despacio mientras apuraba el segundo vaso de whisky frente al espejo. Camisa blanca sin sujetador y los vaqueros limpios que había preparado sobre la cama. En condiciones normales le hubiera recibido descalza, pero me puse los botines y me serví otro dedo de whisky mientras esperaba en el sofá leyendo en voz alta el libro de Julio Oroz: «La locura nos ronda como una sombra. A nuestra espalda camina siempre el bulto mudo de un presentimiento que golpea como el tictac inexorable de un despertador de latón. Preferiría que mi tiempo lo marcase un silencioso reloj de arena. Los granos de arena que se deslizan y vuelven a resbalar una vez han cumplido su fragmento de tiempo, me hablan de una infinita rueda. Atrapada en su urna de cristal la arena promete una interminable repetición. El tictac, en cambio, nunca es el mismo, amenazante y escurridizo como la locura inadvertida que anuncia.»

Yo leía las páginas de Oroz y en la vitrina del aparador se reflejaban las formas desdibujadas de mi cara convertida en una máscara oriental. Bebí un trago largo. Una máscara blanca y quieta bastante mareada, los ojos negros y grandes de desconcierto y de khol, la boca perfilada y roja, como si una mujer japonesa hubiera estampado sus labios en los míos.

A pesar del alcohol, mis pensamientos seguían todavía una línea recta, demasiado claros para invitarme a saltarme renglones y a cometer torpezas. Fue entonces cuando Álvaro llamó al timbre y me besó mientras se quitaba la gabardina. No había paragüero, así que su paraguas negro se quedó colgado en el perchero de la entrada, junto al mío, también negro, líneas paralelas que nunca podrían encontrarse.

—Estás muy guapa —dijo distraído al tiempo que se acomodaba en el sofá y tentaba mis pechos por debajo de la blusa como si fueran un refugio seguro después de un día muy largo.

Me escabullí para lavarme los dientes y buscar un vaso y le dejé estudiar el libro de Oroz que yo había olvidado a propósito encima de la mesa.

—¿Conoces a Julio Oroz? —preguntó sin disimular su sorpresa.

—Me lo presentó Ana en una exposición. Me habló de su libro y se me ocurrió comprarlo al día siguiente. ¿Lo conoces tú?

Álvaro titubeó:

—En realidad no —dijo—. Bueno, alguna vez nos hemos visto, como todos aquí. No nos saludamos, si es eso lo que quieres saber.

Álvaro se había quitado la chaqueta y la corbata. ¿Quieren decirme qué puede hacer una mujer borracha sentada en un sofá junto a un hombre que conoce todas sus cavidades y que respira a su lado acariciando confiadamente su cuello? Los olores se buscan, ¿saben?, él llevaba la misma colonia de lobo marino saliendo victorioso de un maremoto, yo la mía de siempre, él la suele reconocer porque lo primero que hace es hundir su cabeza en mi pelo y besar mi nuca.

—¿Pero no sabes nada de él? —insistí tercamente, escapando de sus primeros besos.

—No —respondió cortante—. Lo único que sé es que es un tipo raro. Escribe cosas raras y se reúne con gente muy colgada en tugurios siniestros. Les acompaña un hedor a resentimiento que me saca de quicio. Una panda de fracasados. Y lo peor es que Oroz se cree un genio. Pero no entiendo por qué tenemos que hablar de ese tipo, Blanca. Hace semanas que no te veo, déjame tocarte. Hueles tan bien. Ya no podía más. Déjame comerte.

Yo luchaba. Les aseguro que luchaba manteniéndome quieta, dejando que él jugara con una mano a desabrochar los botones, mientras con la otra navegaba bajo la vela blanca de mi camisa acariciando sus presas; los pezones no sabían nada de mi lucha, se pusieron duros, se dejaron morder, yo no me movía, su cabeza sí, buceando en mi cuerpo, su boca también, su boca que se multiplicaba de un seno a otro, Álvaro parecía tener mil bocas succionadoras, niño insaciable aferrado a mis pechos mientras yo, inmóvil todavía, batallaba sin saber contra quién.

Recuerden que yo tenía fiebre y había bebido. Él, amante sin corazón, no lo notó. Lo que hubiese dado por un caldo, y sin embargo, llegué a medio vestir hasta la cama y le dejé hacer. Que estaba muy callada, dijo cuando se relajó satisfecho sobre mi cuerpo. Cierto, *la voz* no funcionaba, el magnetofón apagado: ¿dónde estaban los mensajes que le excitaban?, ¿los susurros incitándole a tragarse el mundo, a comerse mi cuerpo?

No fue un encuentro inspirado. No eran todavía las diez cuando Álvaro dijo de pronto que lo sentía muchísimo pero que tenía que dejarme antes que otros días. Había surgido un imprevisto de última hora. Su mujer daba una cena en casa. En realidad se le había olvidado por completo mencionarlo cuando acordamos nuestro encuentro y no se había atrevido a decírmelo nada más llegar. El khol que circundaba mi mirada atónita debía a esas alturas dibujar en mis párpados brochazos oscuros de tunanta. Gracias a que no había apenas luz (nos amábamos a oscuras, pero dejábamos el baño encendido y la puerta entreabierta para enfocar un rayo lunar hacia la noche de nuestros cuerpos), no pudo ver cómo tragué saliva, cómo torcí la boca y fruncí el entrecejo indignada.

Nunca he aprendido a montar una escena. El hijo de puta me acababa de rebanar el cuello de un zarpazo, dejándome paralizada y muda, igual que un conejito tamborilero falto de pilas. Me vestí completamente, me atusé el pelo de erizo y le acompañé hasta la puerta. Le despedí encogida por dentro, a punto de desplomarme más de rabia que de soledad.

Álvaro me miró con ojos de volcán apagado. De no tener tantas cosas que hacer el sábado, se disculpó, hubiera podido venir a verme antes de mi partida. Pero iba a ser imposible. Tenía un día complicado. Un día atroz.

Él me abofeteaba con una sonrisa amable, de acuerdo, yo también quería golpear. Congelé la voz para decirle que no importaba, que más valía así, que en realidad yo estaba decidida a poner punto final a nuestra historia. Esto ya no tenía sentido. Para eso había venido, incluso con gripe. Quería decírselo personalmente. Yo tampoco me había atrevido a mencionarlo antes. Yo también lo sentía. Lo nuestro se había acabado. Ya no habría más viajes míos desde Madrid. Eso era lo que había venido a decirle. Se acabó. *The End.*

Se quedó paralizado junto a un par de paraguas negros con un portafolios negro en la mano. Le faltaba un sombrero negro para convertirse en un personaje de un cuadro de Magritte. Ahora parecía desconcertado. Que yo estaba nerviosa, que ya lo discutiríamos otro día, que había sido una fatalidad. Su mujer y los invitados le esperaban, no podía quedarse más, seguro que yo estaba deprimida a causa de la gripe, se me pasaría, teníamos que hablar, ahora no era el momento, me llamaría a Madrid con calma.

Me encogí como un guiñapo y contemplé el aparador ovillada en el sofá. La animación del fin de semana en la pequeña ciudad se adivinaba en las luces de los coches que alcanzaba a ver desde la ventana. Supe que de un momento a otro me iba a derrumbar. Un café con leche y un coñac, pensé. Necesito un café con leche y una aspirina. Eso, salir a la calle y respirar. También podía telefonear a alguien desde la cafetería. Sólo se me ocurrió pensar en Julio Oroz.

Los camareros del turno de noche no me conocían. Me

instalé en la barra con el cuello del chaquetón subido hasta la barbilla y tosecillas breves que dibujaban una muralla en torno a mí. Sólo era cuestión de un remedio contra la gripe y un café con leche bien caliente con un chorrito de coñac. Que nadie se me acerque, gritaban mis ojos llorosos y el pañuelo estrujado entre mis dedos. Marqué el número de teléfono de Julio Oroz y una mujer (supuse que sería Elena) me dijo que no estaba.

—Necesito verle —confesé—, he venido desde Madrid para un asunto urgente. ¿Sabe dónde podría encontrarle?

—Hay un bar en el casco viejo al que suele ir —dijo la voz con indiferencia—, por la calle Calderería, me parece, el Submundo, o algo parecido.

A Elena le trae sin cuidado que otra mujer busque a su marido a altas horas de la noche, pensé. Me disculpé por molestar y di las gracias.

—¿Quiere dejar algún recado? —preguntó la voz.

—Soy Blanca. Dígale que ha llamado Blanca.

Colgué el teléfono y subí al apartamento para hacer tiempo. Ni siquiera eran las once. Los locales nocturnos no empezarían su ajetreo hasta medianoche. Me duché a conciencia. Quería arrancar de mi cuerpo las huellas de Álvaro. El café me había despejado pero temía sucumbir de un momento a otro. Me concentré en un maquillaje meticuloso. Cuando me pinto siempre parezco un mimo o una geisha, no sé por qué, uno de esos seres empolvados con talco que hacen de estatuas vivientes en las calles. Una máscara sin cicatrices, una muñeca rota sin sangre en las venas. Ésa era yo.

17

Oroz. Estaba dispuesta a buscarle toda la noche por tugurios infernales poblados por una fauna naufragada que navegaba a la deriva entre el alcohol y el hervor espeso del deseo que todo lo impregnaba. Ellas olfateaban la irrupción de un macho nuevo en cualquiera de los locales. Los titanes se desentendían aparentemente del género femenino discurseando entre ellos, rugidos de guerra, vozarrones ásperos, más copas, a pleno rendimiento las pulsiones genitales mientras no perdían de vista el paraíso de culos y tetas que parecían desbordarse en idas y venidas de una mesa a otra, del baño a la barra, de la barra al baño, del fondo del bar a la máquina de tabaco, del taburete a la puerta. ¿Por qué algunas chicas se agitan tanto cuando salen de marcha, como si estuvieran atacadas del baile de San Vito?

Me instalo por fin en la barra del Submundo rodeada de estos chicos del norte, melenudos y cabreados, con aspecto de ir a quemar un autobús de un momento a otro. Comprendo que esto es un nido de radicales y me asalta antes de hora el síndrome de Estocolmo porque pienso que estoy ante tíos en paro, marcados desde la cuna, resentidos sociales con razón, desesperados, sin expectativas, sin salida, con la droga como única aliada, confinados en el zulo de su propia violencia. El mucho alcohol me vuelve freudiana y me pongo a imaginar que serán folladores compulsivos, folladores llenos de furia, folladores que en el cuerpo de cualquier mujer quieren vengarse de sus madres babosas y de sus padres borrachos, violadores de aquí te pillo aquí te mato, lanzadores de chorros de esperma sin preservativo contra los cuerpos de algunas de estas chicas rapadas, suicidas, acostumbradas a ser violadas a trompazos desde el inicio de su adolescencia. Algunos de ellos hablan en euskera y me ignoran con el desprecio con que se ignora una mosca molesta.

Un barbudo con gafas de Trotski repara en mí:

—¿Qué te sirvo?

—Un whisky.

—¿Solo?

—Sin hielo y con agua. Un JB.

El local está atestado de gente joven, tipos mal vestidos que se mueven con ligereza, se enorgullecen del prominente paquete y ocultan cuerpos duros bajo la ropa sudada. Las chicas son flacas, con pantalones pegados a las piernas, miradas de piedra, y capaces de subir por un monte en bicicleta y bajar sin manos con los ojos cerrados. Entre tanto atleta sexual y muchachas ciclistas reparo en un gordo talludito con cazadora de cuero. Parece un marciano perdido en un concurso de cuerpos Danone.

Lo rodean chicas y chicos, a los que escucha paternalmente. Soba mejillas y palmea con familiaridad los hombros. Es evidente que le respetan por alguna razón, tiene aspecto de maestro, o de cura obrero, un hombre que ha aprendido a asentir en silencio, que sabe muy bien lo que se cuece en el Submundo. Por la edad, calculo que puede ser amigo de Julio. Sin darme cuenta le miro fijamente, hasta que él advierte mi insistencia.

Entonces el gordo se separa del grupo y se instala sin soltar su vaso en el taburete vecino. Descubro afabilidad en sus ojos sabios, en la boca infantil, en sus movimientos patosos de paquidermo bebedor y noctámbulo.

—¿Te molesta que me siente a tu lado?

Le digo que no.

—Tienes pinta de estar buscando a alguien. A lo mejor lo conozco.

Acepto el riesgo y me atrevo a mencionar el nombre que me abrirá la cueva de Alí Babá o me expulsará a la inhóspita noche:

—¿Conoces a Julio Oroz?

—¿Que si conozco a Oroz? Hemos ido juntos al colegio —dijo el gordo—. No tardará en venir. Viene todas las noches. ¿Eres amiga de Julio?

—En cierto modo.

—Me llamo Patxi Uzcudun —dijo con seriedad. Luego extendió su mano y estrechó la mía.

—Esto me recuerda las presentaciones en los cursos de idiomas —digo por hacer una gracia—. Me llamo Blanca y soy de Madrid.

—¿Te importa que te haga una pregunta, Blanca?

—Adelante.

—¿Qué hace una chica de Madrid en una ciudad como ésta?

Me pilla desprevenida. Improviso lo primero que se me ocurre, que resulta ser cierto, salvo que evito decir que me encamo con un amante hambriento en un apartamento de la ciudad.

—Hace unos meses trabajé aquí. Vengo de vez en cuando. Me gusta esta ciudad.

La cabeza de Uzcudun está un poco inclinada, extrañamente caída sobre el pecho, como si observase los botones de la camisa o tuviese mucho sueño. Sigue preguntando.

—¿A qué te dedicas?

No tengo ganas de contarle mi vida. Y por otra parte es complicado explicar que soy la voz de lujuria de los anuncios de la tele. Pero tengo que decir algo:

—Trabajo en la radio. En una ocasión grabé unos spots para Arriaga y Asociados.

Se le ensombrece el rostro.

—Pregúntale a Julio por Álvaro Arriaga. Fue compañero nuestro en el colegio. Se pasaba la vida compitiendo con Oroz. Oroz era más brillante, pero Álvaro tenía habilidad para manipular a la gente. Todavía la tiene. Un tipo listo, Álvaro. Se ha concentrado en hacer pasta. En fin. Tiene una facilidad especial para arrimarse al poder y sacar tajada.

Dejo de escuchar. Me lleno de veneno. Álvaro me ha mentido. Me ha dicho que apenas conocía a Julio. Embustero de mierda. Miro a mi alrededor. Veo los ojos salvajes de la clientela y me entran ganas de dar alaridos o de ponerme a correr delante de uno de estos orangutanes de cromañón. Tengo que hacer un esfuerzo para no gritar y aceptar el nuevo whisky que Uzcudun ha pedido para mí.

—Y tú, ¿a qué te dedicas, Uzcudun? —pregunto, aparentando mucho interés.

—Soy profesor en el instituto de un barrio industrial —dice Uzcudun alzando los hombros—. Profesor de literatura. Pero de lo que menos hablamos en clase es de literatura. En resumidas cuentas, trato de inculcarles algo de sensatez a los chicos que tienen la mala suerte de no tener futuro y crecer en bloques donde se multiplican los parados como hongos. Sus hermanos mayores incendian cabinas telefónicas en noches oscuras y algunos de sus amigos han aprendido química de tanto pincharse y de tanto fabricar cócteles molotov. Yo también crecí con ese olor a pólvora en las manos. Llegué a ser un experto en explosivos, pero un día cambié la metralla por la literatura. Debo de ser un caso raro. ¿Tú crees que esos chavales tienen ganas de leer a Baroja y hacer comentarios de texto?

—No, no lo creo.

—Están hartos de formar parte de una escoria a la que nadie tiene en cuenta. Y te aseguro que el primer día que incendian un autobús se sienten importantes. Alguien les necesita. Tienen una tarea que hacer. Muchos de estos que ves aquí están bailando sobre un polvorín a punto de estallar.

—¿Un polvorín?

—Se sienten víctimas, ¿entiendes? Necesitan una *descarga* contra un objetivo para sentirse mejor. Por eso se unen entre sí, como un solo cuerpo: contra la sociedad establecida, contra los que no piensan como ellos. Es lo que Elías Canetti llamaría la necesidad de ciertos grupos de convertirse en masa. La masa se siente fuerte frente al enemigo. Destruye casas y cosas, a ser posible con mucho estrépito.

—¿Con estrépito?

—Estoy de acuerdo con Canetti en que la masa sublima la violencia mediante el ruido; aspira a la demolición tumultuosa de puertas y cristales, se alía con el fuego devastador que crepita y ruge y no deja a su paso más que escombros. El símbolo de la destrucción es el gran estallido, ¿entiendes eso?

Cierro los ojos. En medio de mi delirio alcohólico veo cabinas incendiadas y edificios reducidos a cenizas. Veo la rabia acumulada disfrazada de ideología. Me concentro en esa rabia y pienso en nosotras, en mi hermana Marta y en mí, en las chicas de nuestro barrio que se tatuaron calaveras en el tobillo. Si yo hubiera sido negra, habría nacido en el Bronx, me digo. Si yo hubiera nacido en una ciudad del norte, llevaría la cabeza rapada y prendería fuego al mundo. Casi seguro.

Cuando abro los ojos Julio Oroz me está mirando con una sonrisa llena de curiosidad.

—¿Qué demonios haces aquí?

—Tengo fiebre y quería una copa.

Me acaban de colocar una pinza en la nariz y mi voz parece salir de un chiste de gangosos. Julio me pone una mano en la frente.

—Estás ardiendo. Te llevaré a casa.

Me despido de Uzcudun con besos y abrazos. De pronto me siento inclinada a querer a todo el mundo y le digo adiós al barbudo con gafas de Trotski. Aquí abajo, en el Submundo, tengo la sensación de estar en mi terreno. Arriba reina Álvaro Arriaga apoltronado en sus sillones de diseño con sus invitados poderosos y su esposa cornuda. Yo ya no soy la amante de Álvaro, pero habrá otras, pienso. Su esposa siempre servirá canapés de *foie* y vinos Gran Reserva con pasitos elegantes y el peso de unos cuernos descomunales.

¿A que no adivinan qué hizo Julio Oroz después de instalarme en el asiento del copiloto de mi propio coche y pedirme las llaves? Nunca lo adivinarían. Apenas dijo nada, no preguntó nada. Arrancó y condujo hasta una farmacia de guardia. Sugirió que esperase, y durante un momento no pude apartar la vista de sus pantalones de pana mientras se dirigía a la farmacia. Regresó con un termómetro, vitaminas, sprays nasales, pañuelos de papel, jarabe para los bronquios, inhaladores de eucalipto, caramelos de miel y limón. Me dijo que me olvidara de tomar más copas y que me iba a llevar derecha a la cama. Y lo decía en serio.

Subió conmigo al apartamento 4A y no se quedó tranquilo hasta que me vio en la cama tapada hasta el cuello. No hizo nada más. Nada de nada. Se sentó en el sofá del salón y estuvo leyendo su propio libro que yo había dejado abandonado en la mesita.

Yo dormí como un tronco en el dormitorio. Él debió dar cabezadas en el sofá. Por la mañana, cuando me vio duchada y vestida y con mejor aspecto, me pidió que le contara quién era mi amante. Le dije que estaba a punto de terminar con él, que ahora ya no tenía sentido.

—Tarde o temprano, lo sabré.

—Tal vez. Pero yo voy a ser una tumba —dije.

Salimos juntos del apartamento 4A. Ojalá Álvaro Arriaga pase ahora mismo por aquí y me vea con su compañero de colegio, pensé rencorosa. Julio se empeñó en invitarme a desayunar y me dijo que le gustaba más con la cara lavada. En el coche me dio un beso fugaz por la ventanilla; prometió llamar y amenazó con visitarme pronto en Madrid. Muy bien, de acuerdo. Álvaro acababa de pasar a la historia. Estuve segura cuando arranqué el coche y Julio se quedó en tierra viéndome partir como un aviador varado.

18

A los pocos días de mi regreso, mi hermana Marta se volvió a tropezar con el lanzallamas del Retiro. Una volatinera pelirroja recogía los bártulos de la actuación y él se las arregló para decirle a Marta que se llamaba Stanislav, que era ruso y que le gustaría verla otra vez. Marta dijo que se iba unos días de viaje con mi madre para descansar las dos juntas en una playa soleada, pero que podía llamarla en una semana. Marta le dio su tarjeta y el ruso le dijo adiós con esa mirada tan triste que tienen los rusos.

Mi madre y Marta pasearon por la orilla del mar y tomaron aperitivos en las terrazas de los chiringuitos, rodeadas de extranjeros colorados. Marta, tranquila, resignada, una visera dando un aire nuevo a su cara de santa; y ella, mi madre, silenciosa, agasajada y sorprendida, vigilando la expresión de Marta, rescatando de su memoria otras lejanas excursiones mediterráneas, observando distraída los movimientos a cámara lenta de una playa fuera de temporada.

Ahora me la imagino a mi madre sonriendo soñolienta mientras sacudía la arena de sus sandalias al volver a la explanada marítima de regreso al hotel, asombrada de la figura elástica de Marta, a quien a ratos tomaba por una enfermera cariñosa, a ratos por su hermana, y sólo a ratos la llamaba Marta y le hablaba de todo como si nunca hubiese estado enferma. Mi madre, cuerpo campesino engordado en la ciudad, mente de niña contemplando los puestos de collares y camisetas, glotona de paellas y aceitunas rellenas frente al mar, feliz lejos de su casa donde hay ruido de entrechocar de cazos en el patio y escasean el aire y el espacio para respirar hondo y mirar lejos.

Sé que las cosas se desarrollaron de esa manera porque Marta llamaba a Madrid y me contaba que cada día repetían exactamente el mismo itinerario porque a mamá le gustaba y porque, de ese modo, Marta podía relajarse también y dejarse llevar por la inercia. Veo a mi madre con su traje de florecillas malva y sus ojos adolescentes; unos ojos de emigrante asustada, ojos de alguien que estaba viendo crecer el trigo y se encontró en un laberinto de pasillos y escaleras en la torre de un barrio periférico de la gran ciudad. Seguramente, si Marta le hubiera acercado una caracola al oído, ella habría podido escuchar el rumor del viento sobre las eras de su pueblo.

Por raro que parezca, yo había terminado con Álvaro pero no estaba arrepentida de haber engañado a Miguel. Quiero decir que no tenía propósito de enmienda ni buenas intenciones ni nada de eso. Al contrario, Miguel me pesaba todavía más, ahora era una losa que yo arrastraba colgada del cuello, una losa de mármol que me impedía alzar el vuelo con un aviador. Porque, amigos, yo había empezado a darle vueltas y vueltas a la cabeza, y en el centro de mi torbellino flotaba Julio Oroz.

Además, a Miguel y a mí nos deprimía mirarnos a la cara. Cuando nos encontrábamos a la hora de la cena, el agujero negro de nuestra atmósfera irrespirable era un hecho que no podíamos ni mencionar ni olvidar. El deseo se extinguió al mismo tiempo que nuestras ganas de dar explicaciones. Sólo una noche Miguel se volvió hacia mi lado en la cama y me empezó a besar con desesperación. No pudimos seguir adelante porque se desmoronó en cuanto me sintió excitada. Humillado, dijo que quería leer en el sofá-cama del salón. Pensé que no serviría de nada pasarle la mano por el lomo. Dormir en habitaciones separadas nos relajó. A la tercera noche de presentir la respiración del otro a través del tabique empezamos a hablar de separarnos durante un tiempo. Miguel estaría bien en casa de su madre. Yo podía quedarme en nuestro piso. Era una solución temporal. Si recuperábamos la libertad, tal vez podríamos ver las cosas con más distancia.

El caso es que nos despedimos aguantando las lágrimas de cocodrilo igual que dos héroes obligados a luchar en campos de batalla enemigos. Miguel miró con nostalgia la pantalla gigante de su televisor y yo aseguré que ésta siempre sería su casa.

Yo no tenía la menor intención de empujar el río, pero cuando lanzas un barquito de papel a la corriente, una de dos, o se embala, o se queda empantanado para siempre entre los matorrales de la orilla. Y mi vida, convertida en una filigrana de papiroflexia, descendía por las aguas a toda vela como si a mí me tocara hacer surf sobre una tabla esquizofrénica.

Al cabo de una semana se me había olvidado el asunto de la carta de Álvaro y pensé que también se le habría olvidado a Julio Oroz. Me salió un trabajo de espuma capilar y un anuncio de margarina. Ya saben, familia blanca de clase acomodada de merienda campestre, en plan bucólico. Cuando me lo propongo en serio soy capaz de hablar con la voz de una madre planetaria. Al escucharme, la gente se figura que voy a llenar el mundo de niños felices devorando bocadillos untados con margarina. Entre unas cosas y otras me olvidé de la carta y me olvidé de Álvaro que no dio señales de vida en esos días. Yo esperaba una llamada de Julio. Esperaba que Julio preguntase cómo seguían mis bronquios. Esperaba que anunciase un inminente viaje a Madrid. Pero las cosas suceden siempre de otro modo. Julio volvió a la carga más obsesivo que nunca. Cuando se enteró de que Miguel ya no vivía en casa llamaba por las noches, sus frases nerviosas emergiendo de un pozo de alcohol.

Exigía una y otra vez el nombre de mi corresponsal. Me amenazaba con decírselo a mi marido, me hería a propósito para tirarme de la lengua, me acusaba de ser la cómplice de mi amante. Desbarraba, decía cosas incomprensibles. A veces hablaba como un predicador, otras como un profeta apocalíptico y la mayoría de las veces como un piloto borracho montado a horcajadas sobre un rayo. Yo no sabía con exactitud si era un loco furioso o si todo se trataba de una broma.

Le colgué el teléfono al cuarto día. A partir de entonces, metí la cabeza debajo de la almohada y le dejé enzarzarse con mi contestador automático.

19

Así fue como empecé a temer las llamadas de Julio Oroz convertidas en la pesadilla de mi contestador. Cuando llegaba a casa su presencia había colapsado el día con un atracón de recados: «No se puede ser inmune a lo trágico, Blanca, no me creo ni tu indiferencia ni tu ingenuidad. Si no me devuelves las llamadas es que estás asustada o eres una cobarde o las dos cosas…» «Cuando te abrases como a mí me quema el dolor entenderás por qué necesito hablar contigo…» «Mi pena es minúscula comparada con el destino de la humanidad. En mi peripecia de hoy, Elena me ha abandonado. Dice que no la escucho, que mi silencio la desestabiliza todavía más. ¿Y a mí, quién me escucha a mí? ¿Blanca, estás ahí?»

Yo empecé a impacientarme. Nunca me habían rondado los locos, no estaba acostumbrada. A mi hermana, sí, de siempre; Marta atrae la oscuridad desde sus brazos extendidos al mundo como si quisiera abrazar a un batallón de desposeídos y perturbados. Su belleza a corazón abierto hace pensar en las imágenes de algunas mártires serenas y acogedoras a la espera de desgraciados en las urnas de las iglesias. Siempre temo que unas flechas sangrantes acaben atravesando ese corazón a la intemperie. Pero ahora Marta acababa de volver de sus vacaciones y yo vivía cercada por la desesperación de Julio Oroz.

Tuve mucho trabajo en esos días. Una editorial alemana me contrató para grabar unos cursos de español. La voz tiene que ser muy nítida en esas audiciones, hay que articular con precisión. Se requieren muchas horas de morder un lápiz entre los dientes para que las palabras salgan con claridad. «Me llamo Lola y soy secretaria. He nacido en Valladolid. ¿Dónde has nacido tú, Pepe?» Llegaba a casa cansada de las aventuras de Lola. Lola en Toledo de excursión con su novio. Lola en la oficina. Lola de compras en el mercado. Lola en la carretera, con un pinchazo. Lola en el Museo del Prado con su amigo Pedro.

Yo dejaba pasar los recados de Oroz. Su soliloquio fragmentado surgía espectral del contestador cuando al regresar a casa escuchaba los avisos. Tengo que decir que a pesar de la aparente ansiedad de los recitados de Julio Oroz, había en ellos algo de juego, una teatralidad excesiva que me llevaba borrarlos con una sonrisa. Un martes por la noche, sin embargo, su voz consiguió intrigarme: «Tengo una nueva pista, Blanca. Saber quién escribió esa carta no me proporcionará más espacio vital, pero me sacará de la oquedad en que habito para enfrentarme a un nombre. Mi viejo compañero de colegio Álvaro Arriaga asegura haber trabajado contigo con motivo de una campaña electoral, pero sostiene que no te ha visto desde entonces. No te inquietes, no le he dicho qué estoy buscando; él cree que sólo quiero tu teléfono de Madrid y dice no tenerlo. Sé que Arriaga miente. ¿Hay alguna manera de encontrarte en casa?»

Álvaro no tardó en llamar. Creo que le excitaba la idea de

que otro hombre de su ciudad me persiguiera. Se alegraba de poder hablar conmigo, quería volver a verme, teníamos que encontrarnos, plantear las cosas de otra manera. Podíamos ir juntos a pasar un fin de semana a Francia. Lo intentó todo. Me tentó con posibles trabajos, me ofrecía algo mejor de lo que habíamos tenido hasta ahora (yo encarcelada, yo una reclusa de amor entre cuatro paredes), hablaba de regalarme más tiempo, de horizontes, de hoteles en playas exóticas. Nos queda todo por hacer, dijo. Sus señuelos me ponían en guardia, su oferta desmesurada me sonaba a hueca. Yo terca, yo incrédula, acostumbrada a escribir soñadoras cartas a los Reyes Magos y a recibir los modestos regalos de una familia sin rumbo ni ilusiones, no le quise escuchar.

Supe, sin embargo, que hay hombres caprichosos que abrillantan sus armas cuando se les escapa la pieza a cobrar. Les estimula el hecho de cazar, no la presa abatida y entregada. Cuanto más negaba yo, más insistía Álvaro, más urdía trampas y tendía hilos de miel hasta la guarida de la osezna. Yo era la pobre osezna acosada; aunque ya no me fiaba, había aprendido que al final del reguero de miel se oculta en muchos casos el peluche decapitado, la maniquí descoyuntada y abandonada para siempre. Una osezna entre rejas y alicaída no ofrece ningún aliciente para el cazador desalmado. Descubrí que Álvaro era de los que se enardecen con la indiferencia. A algunos les gusta saltar vallas. No hay obstáculos para los verdaderos ganadores. La estimulación del deseo masculino me parecía de pronto muy simple. Tú les dices que no quieres verlos, y ellos te persiguen medio histéricos; únicamente cuando tú no quieres nada de ellos, ellos lo quieren todo de ti. Y si tú quieres algo de ellos y se lo haces saber, ellos pierden todo el interés y ponen pies en polvorosa. No hay más que presionar los niveles de incertidumbre y su resorte sexual salta como un muelle. Hay hombres que buscan cariño y un poco de paz y hombres que no han abandonado la caverna ni la cachiporra erecta ni su afán de conquistar Evas a cualquier precio. Creo que Miguel pertenece al primer grupo y Álvaro al de los cazadores cavernícolas, por más que lo disimule con camisas de Armani.

Álvaro apelaba a los momentos compartidos, decía que era absurdo, aseguraba que habíamos sido felices, al menos él había sido feliz. Luego, conforme se iba sintiendo rechazado me pedía explicaciones sobre Oroz. Cuántas veces nos habíamos visto, qué me había dicho, por qué me buscaba. El tono ofendido envenenaba sus palabras, sacaba a la superficie de sus frases atisbos de resentimiento. Aquello empezaba a tener sentido. Si era cierto lo que sospechaba Oroz, si Álvaro había sido el amante de Elena, su mujer, no era de extrañar que estuviese nervioso al pensar que la madeja podría enredarse demasiado. Si además era cierto, como sostenía Uzcudun, que Álvaro había competido desde niño con Oroz, el hecho de que yo, su amante, pudiera preferir a Julio, explicaría la rabia que iba creciendo en Álvaro por segundos.

—Ten cuidado, Blanca —advirtió rencoroso—. Julio Oroz es un chantajista afectivo. Vomita su angustia a los ojos del mundo para atrapar a los demás. Despliega su caos mental como arma de seducción. —Yo me mantenía en silencio al otro lado del hilo. Álvaro quiso rematar su faena—. Y por si quieres saber algo más, su mujer no le aguanta; se la ha pegado montones de veces, nunca le ha podido aguantar.

Después hubo un silencio.

Imaginé que había dejado caer esa noticia para provocar-me, para despertar alguna reacción, o acaso para probarme, para saber si yo sospechaba algo. No hice ningún comentario y me despedí prometiendo llamar alguna vez. Con esa vaguedad: alguna vez. No me sentía triste, sino liberada. Álvaro mentiroso. Álvaro atrapado. Álvaro a punto de confesar por vanidad, por despecho. Seguro que Álvaro ha sido el amante de Elena, me convencí. Seguro que él escribió la carta envenenada. Me quedé de pronto hueca. Llega alguien con una cucharilla y empieza a vaciarnos por dentro, rebañando poco a poco los recuerdos, el pasado, las palabras que se perdieron, los paisajes que no tuvimos tiempo de soñar. Como un bote pegajoso de crema de chocolate con avellanas que un niño se ha comido a cucharadas, así me sentí. No era tristeza, era la inutilidad y el cansancio del bote vacío.

Todas esas noches me acosté pronto. Leía en la cama hasta que el sueño me vencía. Llamaba tía Leonor para decir que ella y mamá estaban bien. Mi madre tenía buen color, comía con apetito, hablaba un poco y había preguntado por mí. Yo no echaba de menos a Miguel, aunque nos manteníamos en contacto. Julio no tardó en venir a Madrid, persiguiendo a su mujer que le había dejado para refugiarse en casa de sus padres.

Me despertó el sonido del teléfono. Era medianoche y la voz de Oroz llegaba desde los ruidos de un bar.

—Estoy en Madrid, Blanca. Tengo que verte ahora mismo.

Si hubiera sido Álvaro Arriaga me hubiera negado a recibirle. Pero Julio Oroz se había ido metiendo en mi casa poco a poco. Desde que se fue Miguel, yo le esperaba, pero no lo supe hasta ese preciso momento cuando le di mi dirección. Yo estaba en pijama y tuve que vestirme. Cuando escuché el timbre del portero automático lo imaginé borracho sentado en mi sofá. Yo quería cerrar los ojos y escuchar a Julio Oroz.

Puede que no me crean, pero no era más que eso, quería que el borbotón de sus palabras me marease. No llegó a mirarme cuando entró, tan absorto estaba observando mis libros, que sin duda le parecerían pocos e inadecuados, y los sillones y la mesa del comedor y la televisión gigante para ver los partidos de Miguel. Se instaló en el sofá sin preguntar nada, como si ya conociera la casa, como si adivinase que allí me acurrucaba yo cada noche con un libro.

—Estoy aturdido, Blanca —dijo concentrado en el dibujo de la alfombra—. Llevo varios días sin pegar ojo. Doy vueltas y vueltas a las mismas ideas como un marinero tambaleante en pleno delirio alcohólico. Vértigo, eso es, tengo vértigo mental.

Nunca sé si habla en serio o en broma, así que moví la cabeza como se hace con los exagerados.

—Tú te crees que hablo por hablar —dijo—, pero mi cerebro está a punto de desintegrarse.

—Seguro que no es nada, Julio. Lo que pasa es que se te ha disparado la cabeza. Es la falta de sueño —me salió la voz empalagosa del teléfono de la esperanza.

—He venido a buscar a Elena, y ahora dice que no quiere volver, que prefiere quedarse con sus padres. Me enreda, ¿sabes? Me llama y me dice que se mata, que ya no le importa nada, y cuando vengo a por ella dice que bebo demasiado, que ya nunca seremos los mismos, que no puede vivir conmigo. La nuestra es una unión desquiciada. Lo que más me asombra es que no tenemos nada en común. O sí. Ella se compadece de mí y yo siento una piedad infinita por ella. Lo único que hacemos es compadecernos mutuamente. ¿Te aburro?… Tienes cara de dormida, a lo mejor te he sacado de la cama.

—No, no. Te estoy escuchando.

Se pasó la mano por los ojos y se reclinó en el asiento, tratando de ponerse cómodo. Yo me mantenía inmóvil a su lado.

—Hace un año que no mencionamos a nuestra hija, pero no dejo de pensar en ella.

Había bajado la voz y después siguió un largo silencio. Pensé que todo su cansancio se abatiría de golpe sobre él.

—Si quieres, puedo hacer café —dije.

—Escucha —dijo irritado—, lo que yo necesito es que te quedes ahí y te compadezcas de mí, como hace Elena, como hacen todos los demás. Todos en silencio, sin tocar el nervio en carne viva, como en una conflagración muda y universal. Uno trata de luchar contra la ponzoña que va creciendo por dentro. A veces me ahogo. Cuando volvía a casa los primeros días creía que Elena me estaría esperando con la niña. No ha pasado nada, pensaba, todo ha sido una pesadilla, Eva estará dormida en la cuna, me decía. Pero era mentira, yo sabía que me estaba mintiendo, en el ascensor ya imaginaba los ojos hundidos de Elena, el rostro devastado que no se atrevería a mirarme. A veces la encontraba en bata, no se había vestido en todo el día, decía que no tenía fuerzas. Algunas noches se despertaba aterrada, me preguntaba si no haría frío en el cementerio, cómo habíamos podido dejar a la niña sola debajo de la tierra, decía, se volvía loca entonces, aullaba entre mis brazos hasta que la zarandeaba y la obligaba a tomarse varios calmantes. Por la mañana estaba dopada, no se enteraba cuando yo me iba a la biblioteca.

Yo no podía resistir el soliloquio de Julio a palo seco. Le hice un gesto para levantarme y traer whisky. Él pidió también una copa y me miró con unos ojos espesos y doloridos, de buey.

—¿En qué piensas? —preguntó mientras yo fumaba mirando al techo.

—En nada —dije—. Ya no voy a volver al apartamento.

—¿Has terminado con ese tipo?

Asentí con la cabeza.

—Se acabó, sí. Se acabó todo.

Julio sonrió. Levantó mi barbilla para verme, todavía con una sonrisa triste, la mirada velada por el cansancio. Después siguió hablando.

—Algunos padres creen que los niños pequeños no se enteran de las cosas. Mi hija me empezó a observar enseguida con ojos de adulta. Me asustaba aquella mirada interrogante de Eva, como si supiera más de la cuenta. Yo la veía registrar mis gestos más insignificantes. ¿Qué pensaba mientras los mayores hacíamos gorgoritos y ella callaba? ¿Y si las mentes infantiles albergaran ya todo el saber y todo el sufrimiento de su vida futura? No sé si te has fijado en esos niños del tercer mundo que aparecen en los reportajes. Tienen los ojos heridos de los viejos. Son sentenciados a muerte, yo creo que lo intuyen, yo creo que conocen su sufrimiento de antemano.

—Yo también pienso que algunos niños preferirían no haber nacido —dije—. De poder elegir, algunos se quedarían en el limbo. No es fácil crecer en este mundo de pesadilla.

Entonces Julio se volvió hacia mí, bruscamente, como si una idea terrible se hubiera alzado dentro de su cabeza.

—Eso es lo que trató de explicarme aquel hombre.

Volvió a apetecerme su boca como el primer día en la cafetería de Gran Vía. Pensé que era por el cansancio y el alcohol, por el goteo lento de su cháchara a veces fragmentada e incomprensible.

—¿Qué hombre, Julio?

—El hombre del cementerio, el sepulturero, ¿no lo entiendes?

Les confieso que yo tenía miedo. Deseo y miedo al mismo tiempo, era una sensación fuerte y turbia. Julio Oroz loco, o Julio Oroz desnudándome en la cama, atenazando mis brazos, entrando en mí con la misma vehemencia a punto de estallar que encerraba su cerebro. Recuerdo que pensé: yo debo ofrecerme para el sacrificio, entregarle mi cuello para el asesinato o para el amor. Mantuve, sin embargo, la cordura.

—Perdona, Julio, no sé de qué me estás hablando.

Me asió con fuerza por los hombros y se quedó con su cara casi pegada a mi rostro.

—Repite lo que dijiste antes —dijo.

—¿Qué? —pregunté confundida.

—Que no es fácil crecer feliz en este mundo —dijo Julio.

—Hay que ser muy resistente para salir adelante. Es cierto —dije.

Se quedó pensativo. Me soltó sin mirarme y movió la cabeza.

—Entonces aquel hombre del cementerio tenía razón. Cavaba las tumbas, ayudó a colocar la lápida. Un enterrador, como en *Hamlet*. ¿Te das cuenta? ¿Has leído *Hamlet*?

Me entraron ganas de gritar, de verdad, ya sólo nos faltaba Shakespeare, qué pintaba aquí *Hamlet*, no, no lo había leído, ser o no ser, claro, como todo el mundo, y la calavera, creo que habíamos hablado de la obra en el instituto y en la tele hace mil años habían pasado una película en blanco y negro, con Laurence Olivier. La última no la había visto, la versión de Kenneth Branagh se me había escapado. *Ham-*

let, este tío está loco, pensé. Ser o no ser, claro, ¿quién no sabe eso?

—¿Qué fue lo que dijo aquel hombre? —pregunté intrigada.

—Había visto a la niña en el ataúd. Me dijo que no hubiera resistido. Me lo soltó así, simplemente, como si fuera su deber; se acercó, me tomó del brazo y me lo dijo: Ella se ha querido ir, señor, lo he visto en su semblante sereno, se ha despedido, no hubiera tenido fuerzas para aguantar todo esto. En ese momento hizo un gesto amplio con el brazo como si en aquel *todo* incluyera el cementerio y la ciudad a lo lejos y al cura que se disponía a hablar y al padre de Elena y a los pocos amigos que nos acompañaban, y abarcase también el mundo exterior y el futuro que la niña no llegaría a vivir.

Nos quedamos callados. Los ojos de Julio parecían ahora dos bolas de cristal. Pensé en bajarle los párpados como a un muerto para acabar con sus recuerdos.

—No pienses ahora en eso —le dije—, deberías dormir un poco. Te puedo hacer la cama en el sofá.

—No estoy mal. La niebla se ha disipado, en serio. No me había sentido tan despejado en mucho tiempo.

Me dijo que en el hospital vistieron a la niña con faldones blancos y sólo la recordaba más tarde en un ataúd pequeño de madera de pino. Él se tuvo que ocupar de todo. A su mujer se la llevaron a casa y esa tarde llegaron sus padres desde Madrid. Elena no se quiso meter en la cama, dijo Julio, se encogió en un rincón con los brazos protegiendo la cabeza como si presintiera más golpes y se quedó allí muchas horas acompañada por su madre. Le habían dado muchos tranquilizantes, pero de tanto en tanto se agitaba y sollozaba sin apartar las manos del rostro.

—Señor, su niña no hubiera resistido. Estará bien.

Confundía las palabras, pero recordaba muy bien el sentido. Más tarde pensó que no las había escuchado, creyó que fueron un invento de su imaginación, dijo Julio. Se había olvidado por completo del enterrador hasta esta noche. ¿Acaso no podía su hija haber desertado de la vida antes de tiempo? Algunos niños sobreviven después de caer de un cuarto piso, tienen voluntad de vivir, dijo Julio, pero Eva abandonó, al primer golpe tiró la toalla, entendió que estaba predestinada a la mala suerte y prefirió largarse de este mundo cuanto antes. Ahora lo veía claro. Él tenía a menudo la tentación de matarse. No era un movimiento desde la locura sino un impulso sereno, meditado. No lo llegaba a hacer por pereza, al final le daba tanta pereza provocar su muerte como seguir viviendo. Ahora lo veía claro: su hija había elegido la muerte porque había intuido que la vida le iba a provocar un gran malestar, como a él mismo. En el seno de su madre ya tuvo que notarlo. En el interior de mi mujer, dijo Julio, Eva debió de sentir que afuera encontraría amenazas y hostilidad.

Julio siguió hablando sin parar. Tras despotricar sobre la ciudad del norte, me habló de sus dudas respecto a la novela que estaba escribiendo. Sus libros deberían hurgar en las heridas, lo demás es vivir en el sopor, decía. En todas sus palabras había algo que arañaba, como si al golpearse a sí mismo pretendiese también hacerme daño a mí, o al mundo que no era justo y seguía girando sin cambiar de rumbo.

Al cabo de un buen rato se puso de pie titubeante, me levanté yo también y me alejé un poco, me miró desde su altura y concentrado y ausente a la vez avanzó hacia mí lentamente, como un caracol alucinado. De repente me obligó a sentarme, hizo un gesto nervioso y se movió hacia la ventana, parecía contenerse, luchaba consigo mismo igual que el doctor Jekyll frenando su metamorfosis en Mr. Hyde. Luego se calmó y volvió a sentarse; las bolas de cristal se habían humanizado y ahora parecían verme por primera vez. Éste es el momento en que me despedaza o me ama, pensé. Cuando empezó a besarme entre los almohadones supe que se había desatado un huracán de los que arrancan tejados y desploman rascacielos y hacen volar camiones enormes de costa a costa.

Acabamos en el suelo, destrozó la cremallera de mis vaqueros nuevos, rodamos los dos desnudos por la alfombra, tuvieron que golpearse nuestras cabezas contra las patas de mesas y sillones, no recuerdo, yo estaba semiinconsciente por el whisky y la irrealidad de su jugo cerebral destilado ante mis narices, él y yo seguíamos cayendo, besando, mordiendo, ataqué la nuez, el cuello deseado, un combate de boxeo entre dos ciegos, los ojos cerrados o la lámpara se estrelló contra el suelo, yo no veía nada, a mí qué me importaba. Oroz entero dentro de mi boca, embistiendo entero dentro de mi cuerpo, chupando las cuencas de mis ojos hasta horadarlas con la lengua igual que un gusano entra por los huecos de una calavera, ser o no ser, ahora sí he leído *Hamlet*, lo leí hace poco encadenada al sofá mientras esperaba su regreso, Oroz recuperando fuerzas aferrado a mis pechos como un ternero furioso, Oroz, un tifón arrasando mis defensas, yo con la cabeza debajo de la mesita del televisor, Oroz arrastrándome como un peso muerto hasta el otro extremo de la habitación para torear en los medios, yo mujer diana, él dardo certero clavado en mi centro.

Cuando abrí los ojos yo estaba contra el suelo y tenía los labios de Oroz en mi rabadilla. Recostado en mi espalda, medio dormido, con la boca expectante, a Julio Oroz se le había puesto cara de fraile joven, o mejor, de niño al que visten de fraile el día de su primera comunión. Le dije que prefería dormir sola y que él podía quedarse en el sofá. Lo hice a propósito, para endurecerme, para acostumbrarme a estar sin él porque sabía que en el itinerario de ciertos aviadores no está previsto detenerse dos veces en la misma pista de aterrizaje.

No le desperté por la mañana cuando me marché a una cita de trabajo. Dejé la cafetera y una taza en la mesa del comedor y escribí una nota de despedida. Sólo tenía que cerrar la puerta al salir.

20

Después de la visita de Oroz observé que mis movimientos eran mucho más lentos. Levántate, Blanca, por Dios bendito, deja de hacer sombras chinescas en las paredes, unos suspiros para tus admiradores, vamos, Blanca, salta de la cama, que diga algo la princesa de los gorgoritos, ¿quién se ha comido la lengüecilla de la muñeca parlanchina? Ya no me salía la voz concupiscente. Me costaba un esfuerzo sobrehumano llegar hasta el cuarto de baño. Permanecía allí, frente al espejo, asombrada de que mis ojos y mi boca fueran los mismos de siempre y no los de un fósil de mil años. Tras el desayuno me parecía imposible abandonar la mesa de la cocina, como si algo me obligase a mirar de modo obsesivo la bandeja de las magdalenas (yo, que sólo he leído a Proust a picotazos) y el azucarero y los azulejos blancos y amarillos del alicatado.

No entendía qué relación podía tener Oroz con mi súbito cansancio, no sabía por qué la idea de volver a verle me empujaba a atrincherarme en casa, oculta bajo tierra como un hilillo de agua subterránea. Sólo Oroz podía ser mi zahorí, se me ocurría, Oroz buscador de fuentes escondidas,

Oroz rama vibrante y agitada ante la proximidad de un pozo. Sí, pensé, mejor esperar en casa como un topo, observando el hueco que dejó en el sofá, porque si me pierdo en las calles, de él no quedará nada.

Marta que había regresado renovada de las vacaciones telefoneaba para invitarme a comer o a una sesión de cine. Yo inventaba mentiras para no ver a nadie. Tenía que terminar de sonorizar el curso de español, decía. Faltaban cuatro días de trabajo. Precisamente estaba a punto de salir para el estudio. Repetí la misma cantinela varias veces durante esos días. Se lo dije a Olga Navas, a Miguel, que llamaba para saber cómo me encontraba, a tía Leonor que contaba maravillas de la recuperación de mi madre después de los días en la playa, envolvía mis excusas en un tono tan convincente que casi llegué a creérmelas yo misma.

Pero no era cierto, ese trabajo se había terminado y de momento yo no tenía en mi agenda para esa semana más que las cuñas radiofónicas de unos grandes almacenes. Sabía que esas grabaciones me llevarían un par de mañanas, de modo que el resto del tiempo yo estaba libre. Libre para pasar las tardes junto al teléfono garabateando palabras sin mucho sentido, libre para dejar que mi voz en el contestador alejase de mi vida a los intrusos, libre para esperar los recados ansiosos de Julio Oroz. Pero Julio Oroz no dio señales de vida. Me salieron raíces en mi propia casa y me obligaba a hablarme en voz alta para saber que no estaba loca. Quería, sin embargo, perder la memoria. Quería convertirme en una piedra y que el tiempo puliese mis contornos y borrase las marcas de mi vida anterior. Casi lo conseguí.

Ya no había viernes de copas ni masajes en las plantas de los pies. Se habían quedado huérfanos mis muñones de mujer china. Me olvidé de las cenas en silencio con Miguel. Me olvidé de sus cosas todavía guardadas en los armarios. Me olvidé de que había tenido un marido. Me olvidé, también, de Álvaro Arriaga persiguiendo susurros de placer en nuestra celda. Y sin embargo fui incapaz de olvidar el cuerpo de Julio Oroz colisionando con el mío a una velocidad de vértigo como si fuéramos dos troncos dando tumbos por la ladera de una montaña.

No pasaba nada, y eso era lo peor. No me fío de los momentos de calma. Desde niña me mantuve alerta con esa mirada atormentada y vigilante que exhiben los perros que cuidan el rebaño. He comprobado que detrás de cada instante de aparente remanso, se agazapa una mala noticia que llega a galope para destrozar la frágil tranquilidad de un segundo de paz. Siempre ha sido así, de modo que no me sorprendí cuando, hace unos años, cuando todo parecía marchar sobre ruedas, Estrella, la compañera de mi padre, llamó para decir que papá había tenido un accidente. Afortunadamente no había sido nada, estaba ya en su casa, pero acababa de sufrir un fuerte shock y quería vernos a Marta y a mí.

Nunca he pensado demasiado en la relación entre Estrella y mi padre. Ella apareció en la vida de nuestro padre cuando mi madre se empezaba a convertir en un zombi. Mi madre fue perdiendo empuje a medida que pasaban los años, se disgregaba día a día sin ser capaz de distinguir lo que ocurría ante sus propios ojos. Se fue apartando de la vida y de las personas, sin odio ni resentimiento. Durante mi adolescencia yo veía que mi madre se desdibujaba pero le quedaba marcado en el rostro un gesto de perplejidad; entre las líneas del ceño, mi madre parecía llevar un signo de interrogación, quizá se preguntaba por qué no podía tocar el mundo con las manos. Estrella, en cambio, era una mujer organizadora y realista, con un cuerpo restallante dispuesto a la acción y buena disposición para mejorar el ánimo de un hombre que venía cansado de tragar kilómetros de ciudad en ciudad. Marta y yo lo hablábamos entonces. Le acogería en su nido como una hetaira hacendosa. Le prepararía un Martini con aceituna igual que había visto hacer en las películas y dejaría que los pechos firmes se desbordasen por el escote exagerado. Sabíamos que no le importaban la barba de varios días ni el olor a macho acorralado que desprendía la camisa arrugada después de un largo viaje ni la voz ronca ni las ganas de su hombre de tumbarse calzado sobre la colcha. Estrella había aprendido a compadecerse, a desatar con suavidad los cordones de los zapatos, a dejar el dormitorio a media luz y a esperar sentada en la salita, con los labios pintados. Mi padre hubiera hecho cualquier cosa por ella, pero nunca se aprovechó económicamente de él, por el contrario, le obligó a ocuparse de nuestros gastos y tuvo que sacarlo de apuros en varias ocasiones. Llamaba por teléfono para decirnos en qué ciudad se encontraba mi padre y para preguntar cómo estábamos. Teníamos que saber, decía, que si algo ocurría podíamos contar con ella. Creo que admiraba nuestras agallas y el hecho de que tan jóvenes hubiéramos aceptado la responsabilidad de una casa y los cuidados de una madre enajenada. Había elegido para la melena un tinte de walkiria, se hidrataba la piel con una crema que dejaba en el aire un denso olor a nardos, se contoneaba sobre los tacones y era fácil imaginar que ensayaba a solas bailes picantes para encandilar a mi padre; mucho más de lo que las carnes aturdidas de mi madre podían ofrecer.

El aspecto de mi padre cuando venía a vernos, lo decía

todo. Planchado, zapatos nuevos, el cinturón del pantalón en su sitio, los ojos brillantes. Hasta había adelgazado un poco. Desde entonces, si en alguna ocasión Marta y yo mencionábamos a Estrella, ya sabíamos que no había ninguna posibilidad de que mi padre regresara al destartalado hogar del que había huido para siempre.

Marta y yo conocíamos de sobra la casa de Estrella cuando papá tuvo el accidente, al menos la salita de estar atestada de adornos y baratijas, donde en varias ocasiones habíamos estado sentadas, sin hundirnos del todo en el sofá, como esas visitas que tienen prisa por marcharse. Cuando Estrella nos llamó alarmada, no nos detuvimos en la sala ni tuvimos tiempo de reparar en el brillo de los *bibelots*, horrorosos pero limpísimos, y pasamos directamente al dormitorio.

—Aquel cabrón pudo haberme matado —dijo mi padre todavía medio dormido como si la idea le hubiese rondado durante el sueño.

—Es cierto —añadió Estrella—. En el hospital dijeron que había sido un milagro. El doctor Almeida no ha visto más que magulladuras. Nos despachó diciendo que lo que necesita vuestro padre es mucho descanso. Así que los últimos tres días los ha pasado durmiendo, medio atontado, pero ahora dice que tiene vértigos, que se le va la cabeza. Yo lo que creo es que está todavía impresionado por el susto.

Se estaba haciendo de noche y Estrella encendió una lamparilla historiada con lágrimas, pastoras y capullos de porcelana; entonces mi padre le hizo un gesto para que saliera de la habitación.

—No me enteré de nada —dijo—. Escuché un chirrido y me encontré con las ruedas delanteras del camión a la altura de los ojos. No tuve tiempo de pensar y pegué un volantazo que impulsó mi coche fuera de la autovía. Di dos o tres vueltas por el campo. Podía oír los crujidos metálicos de la carrocería y el ruido de los cristales rotos. Me acojoné. Me llevé las manos a la cabeza y empecé a dar alaridos a pleno pulmón: «Voy a vivir, voy a vivir, por todos mis muertos, voy a vivir…» Grité así durante mucho tiempo. El coche daba vueltas y yo pegando aullidos como un loco. Luego perdí el conocimiento. Me salvó el *airbag*.

Me extrañaba estar allí en el dormitorio de mi padre. Nunca lo había visto en la cama, ni siquiera cuando vivía en nuestra casa. Se levantaba siempre el primero y en mi memoria no hay imágenes de mi padre enfermo o convaleciente. En los últimos años nos habíamos visto poco, un día o dos en Navidad, cuando nos llevaba a comer a Marta y a mí a una marisquería. De esas comidas estaban excluidos Estrella y Miguel, como si los tres, Marta, mi padre y yo, tuviéramos un negocio juntos, al margen de los otros.

—Es curioso —dijo Marta—, yo hubiera abandonado.

—¿Qué quieres decir? —preguntó mi padre.

—Los aullidos, papá, esas ganas de seguir viviendo. Yo no habría sido capaz. Me hubiera limitado a cerrar los ojos y a esperar un golpe definitivo.

—Maldita sea, eres hija mía —se indignó mi padre—, siempre has tenido arrestos. Nadie tiene derecho a andar por ahí dejándose aniquilar sin pegar cuatro patadas al puto destino.

—Será que no tengo tanto apego a la vida como tú —dijo Marta.

Mi padre se encogió de hombros y me miró a mí con gesto incrédulo. Creo que esperaba que yo mediara en su favor, alguna señal de complicidad, pero me mantuve al margen.

—De todos modos, uno nunca sabe cómo va a reaccionar

ante una situación así —resopló—. Se te pasan por la cabeza las ideas más peregrinas. Por eso quería veros. Le dije a Estrella que os llamase porque quería deciros algo que pensé cuando me llevaban al hospital. Ahora casi no lo recuerdo. Yo estaba inconsciente, pero mi cabeza seguía funcionando a toda máquina, era una sensación extraña. Creía que estaba muerto. Se acabó, tío, se acabó. Ya ves, me dije, uno se va al otro mundo sin despedirse de nadie, como un gilipollas. Y no sé por qué me acordé de vosotras dos cuando erais unas mocosas y me arrastrabais al equipo de música los domingos. A mí me gustaba volver a poner las cintas que escuchaba en el coche conduciendo solo por esas carreteras. Me hacía gracia que os volviera locas la voz de Marvin Gaye, como a mí, y veros bailar con Los Temptations. Jodidas niñas, pensaba. Si no llega a ser por mi manía del *soul*, yo me habría saltado la tapa de los sesos, por vuestra madre, no sé si me entendéis.

—No estoy segura —dijo Marta.

Mi padre señaló hacia una estantería donde había una fotografía enmarcada de Las Supremes con unos peinados muy cardados, labios entreabiertos y dientes blanquísimos.

—Seguí con el *soul* por vosotras, porque aunque erais tan pequeñas el veneno de aquella música ya se os había metido en el cuerpo. Yo os lo explicaba: es que los negros tienen la sangre caliente, nenas. Estaba contento de compartir algo con mis hijas, qué queréis que os diga, y por otro lado el resto de la semana me sentía muy solo por esos pueblos en los que no conocía a nadie, exceptuando a los empleados de las ferreterías, claro, que son gente bastante avinagrada. Es una vida muy solitaria. Si no fuera por la música uno se volvería loco. Incluso aunque ya estés acostumbrado. Estaba deseando volver a casa para veros. Lo malo era lo de tu madre. No había quien le arrancara un gesto cariñoso. Decía que si la manoseaba le daban arcadas. Para mí, que ya se estaba volviendo loca. El caso es que me convencí de que aquel camión me había mandado al otro barrio, porque vuestras caras eran las de entonces y se escuchaba *Baby call on me* de Wilson Pickett; por eso creí que había muerto y estaba en la gloria. Esto no está mal, pensé, que me pongan *Moonlight in Vermont* por Sam Cooke. Luego sentí un dolor muy fuerte en la cabeza y en el cuello y me pareció oír la voz de una enfermera diciendo que tenían que hacerme una cura.

Mi padre se llevó las manos a las sienes como si le volviera el dolor. Tenía barba de varios días con el mismo tono azulado de la carbonilla, y los cabellos veteados de gris, ahora apelmazados, le hacían parecer más viejo.

—A lo mejor no te conviene hacer esfuerzos para hablar —dijo Marta.

—Si no es nada —dijo mi padre, incorporándose un poco y atusándose el pelo—. Cuando todavía estaba medio inconsciente pensé en pedirle a la enfermera papel y lápiz para escribiros una carta. Por si me moría, ya podéis suponer. A uno se le ocurren esas cosas. A lo mejor mis hijas no entendieron por qué las abandoné, me dije, por qué me largué por las buenas de aquella casa que estaba acabando con mis neuronas. No sé muy bien si os dije alguna vez que había llegado al límite. No, seguro que no. Supongo que pensé que erais demasiado pequeñas. Simplemente fui desapareciendo, ¿no? Tenía prisa por esfumarme. Supongo que fue una cabronada. ¿Y qué otra cosa podía hacer? ¿A ver? ¿Estrangular a vuestra madre que llevaba tres años obligándome a dormir en el sofá? ¿Molerla a hostias cuando yo sabía que no regía? ¿Qué otra cosa podía hacer? A lo mejor todo esto a vosotras os trae sin cuidado, pero pensé que yo me iba a sentir mejor si os lo decía. Igual estas criaturas creen que soy un cabrón, pensé en el hospital. Esa idea me ha rondado por la cabeza muchas veces; lo pienso alguna vez cuando reconozco la voz de Blanca en los anuncios de la tele; igual yo no he sido capaz de hacerme entender.

—¿A qué te refieres? —pregunté yo.

—Nunca he tenido tiempo de explicar nada. Tampoco hubiera sabido hacerlo. Quizá si hubiera sido negro, con una de esas baladas que cantan unos tíos con gorguera sobre un tipo con mala suerte al que deja en la estacada una mujer con un culo magnífico…

—No es fácil explicar las cosas —le dije, acercándole el vaso de agua y acomodándolo mejor entre las almohadas.

—La vida es así —dijo él, aspirando a fondo una bocanada de aire—. Peor es estar muerto. Eso es lo que pensé cuando me desperté en el hospital y me dijeron que había sido un milagro.

Marta se inclinó hacia él y le arregló el embozo.

—Tenéis que disculparme. Todavía se me va la cabeza.

—No te preocupes, papá, ya nos vamos —dije.

—¿Necesitas algo? —preguntó Marta.

—Nada. Sólo quería veros. Estrella se las arregla bien.

No pasó de un susto, pero esa llamada de teléfono que te hace un nudo en los higadillos y las vísceras, llegó en uno de esos momentos de calma de los que desconfío. Por eso me mantenía alerta ante la electricidad invisible que flotaba en el aire después de marcharse Julio Oroz.

Pasada mi primera reacción, recuperé el pulso, volví a la vida normal y me lo tomé con calma. Ya volverá, me dije, y me dediqué a disfrutar de la espera como las novias de antes que hacían vainicas y punto de cruz hasta que de puro aburrimiento se les apagaba el fuego del infierno de la entrepierna y llegaban a la boda como malvas.

Y hablando de fuego, Marta se había empezado a ver con el lanzallamas ruso del Retiro.

—¿Por qué con el lanzallamas, Marta?

—Porque es la pera —contestó con ojos de vicio mi hermana—. Y además es un tragafuegos, no un lanzallamas.

—Tragallamas o apagaincendios, no saldrá bien.

—¿Por qué? Nunca se sabe. En Moscú era músico. Violinista.

Lo que nos faltaba, pensé, el violinista sobre el tejado.

—Creí que habías dicho que querías una temporada de tranquilidad —insistí.

Marta se extrañó de mis aprensiones. Dijo que yo estaba tensa por mis problemas con Miguel. Luego anunció que Stanislav era un verdadero genio en la cama y que ella se sentía como un stradivarius. Dijo también que no era culpa de Stanislav si no encontraba trabajo como concertista. Unas manos preciosas, manos de virtuoso. De hecho, todo lo del tragafuegos era de virtuoso. Marta se reía. Yo sabía que cuando empezaba así, no tenía remedio.

No le hablé entonces a mi hermana de Julio Oroz; pensé que ella ya tenía bastante con su colección de contorsionistas para añadir un funámbulo a nuestro circo sexual. En realidad, no le he hablado a Marta de Julio hasta hace unos días, cuando volví de Hendaya. Pero no me he atrevido a contarle toda la verdad. No le he contado a Marta lo que ocurrió un poco antes de mi viaje a Francia en una pensión de San Sebastián.

21

Aunque me costó algún tiempo acostumbrarme al silencio del televisor apagado por las noches, pensándolo ahora puedo decir que me gustaba estar sola, abrir en la cocina latas de espárragos y lavar con atención cogollos de lechuga para mis cenas frugales. De hecho, desde la visita de Oroz me pareció percibir que el destierro de Miguel había cobrado sentido. Era como si hubieran desaparecido diez años de mi vida, como si se los hubiera tragado la tierra y yo estuviera al inicio de algo nuevo y desconocido, no sabía bien qué. Sin embargo, me obligaba a mí misma a no desbocar mis pensamientos y me prohibía inventar necedades en compañía de un hombre medio desquiciado cuyo pelo flotaba como si acabase de bajar de una avioneta. Un hombre, en cualquier caso, que no había vuelto a dar señales de vida desde la noche en que colisionamos juntos al rodar desbocados por la ladera de una montaña. Trabajé con agujetas los días siguientes.

Los spots se sucedieron aunque yo caminara como una autómata. Me concentré en una pronunciación meticulosa. Repetía las palabras y las frases hasta encontrar el tono exacto. Si anuncias una laca o un champú, y si en las imágenes aparecen modelos rubias con cabellos de sirena, la voz tiene que sonar acariciadora pero clara, como si la sola idea de lavarse la cabeza con ese champú fuese lo único consolador de este perro mundo. Estoy acostumbrada a la publicidad de productos de belleza. Ya sé que esas semidiosas con nubes de oro por cabellera son un reclamo para ilusas que esperan convertirse en la muñeca Barbie después de un centrifugado capilar, pero, ¿qué quieren?, me gusta mi trabajo; disfruto arrancando nuevas sonoridades a unas frases llenas de tópicos. Consigo olvidarme de todo lo demás mientras le pongo voz de orgasmo a una Venus que agita a cámara lenta una brillante melena recién lavada.

Pero en esto me volví a tropezar con la pintora Mara Barbieri. Aunque en realidad fue ella la que me buscó a mí. Acababa de inaugurar una exposición en Madrid y Julio Oroz le había dado mi teléfono. Julio le había comentado que me interesaba su obra, a lo mejor me apetecía ver sus últimas instalaciones, sugirió. No supe qué decir, pero acordamos una cita dos días más tarde en una galería de la calle Claudio Coello. La verdad es que me traían sin cuidado Mara Barbieri y sus rebuscadas simbologías artísticas, lo único que me importaba era oírle articular en algún momento el nombre de Julio Oroz.

Mara Barbieri reapareció ante mí con su maquillaje pálido, su boca grande pintada de zarzamora, sus ojos asombrados y su aire enigmático. Tuve la sensación, nada más llegar a la galería y encontrar a la artista posando para un fotógrafo ante un descomunal montaje titulado *Fiebre de mercurio*, tuve la aguda sensación de ser un insecto insignificante al que Mara espantaba con una leve seña para que no interrumpiese la sesión fotográfica. Con ese mismo gesto Mara me indicaba que no molestara, que fuese viendo las obras del fondo de la sala y que esperase hasta que el fotógrafo hubiese terminado con ella.

La sensación de ser un microbio, bicho o insecto me asalta con especial intensidad cuando alguien me toma medidas desde lo alto del balcón de su importancia. Yo me quedo hundida en el fango, empantanada en las cloacas, convencida de que me examinan con el desprecio con que se observa un escarabajo patas arriba. Veo a menudo ese cruce de sables en el intercambio de miradas de los desconocidos. Soy más importante que tú, no sé quién eres pero para mí no eres nadie, yo soy más, dice una mirada a la otra. ¿No lo ves? Mi coche es más grande, mi ropa más cara, mi mujer está más buena que la tuya, declaran los ojos. La superioridad o el reconocimiento de los idénticos se debate en esos duelos. Ahí se decide el desprecio o la aceptación. Yo tengo todas las de perder, me quedo paralizada mientras los ojos miden y sopesan patrimonios y fuerzas. Muerdo el polvo enseguida, me agota la batalla antes de empezar. ¿Que usted piensa que soy un escarabajo hurgando en la basura? De acuerdo. Es demasiado cansado trepar a una torre de varios pisos para desde allí arriba sostener una mirada retadora.

Así que quedó claro: yo era un bichejo y Mara Barbieri la Callas del arte contemporáneo. Pero era inevitable preguntarse qué quería María Callas de un escarabajo. Fue en ese momento cuando se me encendió la bombilla. Algunas cosas se saben diez segundos antes de tener entre manos una evidencia. Con unos segundos de antelación supe que Mara Barbieri era la amante de Julio Oroz. Estuve segura de que ella era la mujer que se acostaba con Oroz un instante antes de que se diera la vuelta para despedir al fotógrafo y yo pudiera ver el pasador de ébano que recogía su melena. Entonces por mi mente cruzó a toda velocidad una imagen: aquella tarde en que yo espiaba a través de la mirilla del apartamento 4E los movimientos de la puerta del apartamento 4A y vi a una mujer de espaldas despidiéndose de Oroz en el ascensor. La lente deformante y la distancia no me permitieron ver más que la cabeza y la espalda de la mujer, pero recordaba con claridad el adorno que sujetaba el pelo. No me pasó inadvertido entonces, pero en la galería, al reparar en la extraña horquilla africana ensartada en el cabello recogido de Mara Barbieri, volvió a mí el recuerdo. Comprendí que la espalda de la amante de Julio Oroz era idéntica a la espalda de la pintora, al ver ahora aquella especie de moño atravesado por el pincho de ébano. La mujer que vi a través de la mirilla entrando en el ascensor después de haberse acostado con Oroz y Mara Barbieri eran una misma persona.

En algún lugar de mi interior bulleron a la vez varias sensaciones: la satisfacción y la intranquilidad de ponerle rostro a una sombra, y el placer reconfortante y victorioso de pensar que este escarabajo que era yo, el pequeño escarabajo patas arriba, se había revolcado con el hombre que se acostaba con Mara Barbieri.

Por fin Mara Barbieri reparó en mí y me invitó a sentarme con ella en el despacho de la directora de la galería, que en esos momentos había salido. Me escrutó con atención y me preguntó con su voz grave qué me había parecido su obra. Tuve que pensar deprisa, compuse una masa informe de palabras con las frases de Julio Oroz que recordaba haber leído en el catálogo y las solté con desenvoltura de experta.

—Planetas en miniatura —repitió lentamente Mara Barbieri—, planetas en miniatura observados con microscopio… *interesantísimo*… Julio escribió algo parecido: microcosmos, ¿recuerdas?, escenas nimias y triviales que pueden ser de máxima importancia. Creo que lo has captado, *gestos mínimos* al borde de lo patético. Me debato en el límite entre lo cruel y lo hermoso del universo cotidiano… Planetas en miniatura… qué interesante.

Descubrí que la gran diva de la vanguardia estaba en pleno ataque de María Callas y hasta me dio la impresión de que hablaba despacio para que yo pudiera tomar notas. Cada vez que oías hablar a Mara Barbieri, te figurabas que estaba recibiendo las palabras de un arsenal de genialidad celeste y por eso algunas ideas venían subrayadas con hilos de oro.

Yo sabía, sin embargo, que en cualquier momento entraría en materia. No tardó mucho en preguntarme si mi amistad con Julio Oroz venía de lejos. Me pilló desprevenida, pero no quise despejar sus dudas y esbocé una respuesta vaga, ni fu ni fa, el tiempo se nos escapa de las manos, con Julio nunca se sabe. Hacía un mes que ella no le veía, sólo hablaban por teléfono y lo había notado nervioso, más desquiciado que de costumbre, me dijo. Julio le había dicho que había hecho varios viajes a Madrid, y en alguna ocasión había mencionado mi nombre. Sabía que yo era una buena amiga y sólo quería estar segura de que él y Elena estaban bien, por eso se había atrevido a hablar conmigo. Por alguna razón daba por sentado que yo estaba al tanto de la relación entre ellos, o quiso ponerme al tanto, supongo que para ver si, de paso, desbarataba las aspiraciones de un escarabajo. Me pregunté si sabría algo de mis visitas al apartamento o si habría oído hablar de la carta que todavía seguía en manos de Oroz. Mara Barbieri, apoyando una mano en la pálida mejilla, abriendo mucho los asombrados ojos (esos ojos desmesurados y huecos que te recuerdan a la carta de ajuste de la tele), acabó reconociendo que, aunque habían estado muy unidos, ahora todo había acabado entre Julio y ella.

—Sabes —dijo bajando la voz hasta el tono reservado para las confidencias—, Julio y yo… bueno, lo nuestro ha sido únicamente una amistad profunda, él me comprende, no sé si lo entiendes, él me comprende de un modo *espiritual.*

—Sí, desde luego —convine por decir algo, sin atreverme a guardar silencio ante la caída de ojos que me interrogaba y me desenfocaba al mismo tiempo.

—Una compenetración intensa y creativa —dijo ella—. No sé por qué el sexo no puede ser creativo. La amistad no tiene por qué quitarle *intensidad* al sexo, ¿no crees? ¿Por qué un hombre y una mujer que son amigos no pueden tener una sexualidad creativa?

Mara Barbieri se llevó las manos a las sienes y entrecerró los ojos como si estuviera cansada de hacer al mundo esa pregunta.

—Es cierto, ¿por qué no? —contesté a la gallega.

—No hay necesidad de complicar las cosas. —Su voz era espesa, y pronunciaba las sílabas lentamente, como si cada una de sus palabras encerrase un misterio—. Nosotros nunca hemos estado enamorados, pero nos comunicábamos a un nivel muy profundo. Comunicación, ésa es la clave. Julio y yo hablábamos *muchísimo* de arte, de literatura. Nunca he ocultado que me fascina la inteligencia de Julio para ahondar en mi trabajo. Él sabe ver. Casi nadie sabe ver. La gente mira, pero muy pocos llegan a *ver.*

Mara estiró los brazos y entrelazó los dedos a la altura del pecho. Por lo que parecía dar a entender, ella y Julio montaban en torno a cada polvo coloquios culturales y mesas redondas de altos vuelos. Me pregunté si los debates eruditos tendrían lugar antes, después o durante el polvo.

—Entiendo —dije.

—Comunión entre artistas —confesó Mara Barbieri con una mirada soñadora—. En cierto modo los dos lo necesitábamos. Adoro a mis hijos y a mi marido, pero a los artistas nos agobia a veces la vida familiar. Además, yo intentaba ayudar a Julio. Elena nunca le ha entendido. Como aquella vez que leyó el borrador de una novela de Julio y le dijo: «Mira, Julio, no sé si te das cuenta pero todo esto es un galimatías; ésta es la obra de un alcohólico. Lo mejor que puedes hacer es olvidarte de la literatura.» Esto fue antes de que perdieran a la niña. Me lo contó el propio Julio. Dijo que la franqueza de Elena era afilada como una cuchilla de afeitar haciéndole heridas por todo el cuerpo. A mí me tocaba lamer esas heridas. Yo le devolvía la confianza en sí mismo. En ocasiones le dejaba que me infligiese pequeños castigos, porque descubrí que en mí se estaba vengando de la crueldad de Elena… ¿Ves ese cuadro? Se llama *Sacrificio*, la corona de espinas sobre un pubis inocente que espera ser atravesado por un falo furioso. Supe entonces que una amante es una especie de santa o de mártir, dispuesta a restaurar la identidad de un macho humillado por la mediocridad de su matrimonio.

Asentí sonriendo porque reconocía ese pensamiento y también porque acababa de comprobar mi miopía artística. Donde Mara Barbieri veía un «sacrificio» yo no había visto más que un estropajo metálico clavado en una superficie roja con un estoque taurino y rodeado por una alambrada de púas. Quedaba clara mi limitada visión ante los simbolismos de Mara Barbieri, pero también se demostraba que antes de retirarse de la escena la diva Barbieri estaba dispuesta a enredar un poco más la madeja, aunque sólo fuera midiendo sus fuerzas con un bichito recién llegado.

Ni ella ni yo sacamos nada más en limpio. Ninguna de las dos sabíamos a ciencia cierta en qué derroteros andaría en esos momentos el cerebro de Julio Oroz, ese aviador del precipicio.

22

Un día caminas por una calle cualquiera. Un psicópata que no te conoce de nada empieza a perseguirte sin ninguna razón especial. Te alcanza en una esquina y te da una paliza de muerte o te deja la cara marcada con una cicatriz. Son cosas que pasan. Los acontecimientos siniestros de la vida siempre nos sorprenden por la espalda. La mala suerte se abalanza sobre nosotros sin razón aparente, a menos que tengamos cierta predisposición para cruzarnos en el camino de los psicópatas. En cualquier caso, ya he dicho que nunca me fío de los momentos de calma y tampoco me extrañé cuando a Marta le ocurrió lo que le ocurrió justo cuando yo quería estar a solas para rumiar la desaparición de Oroz y vigilar la sonrisa que se encendía y se apagaba en mi cara como una bombilla dubitativa, según me diera por pensar que Julio iba a volver o que nunca regresaría.

Yo no esperaba a nadie un domingo antes de comer. Al abrir la puerta me encontré a Marta después de haber pasado por los colmillos de Drácula. Estaba pálida como una aparición. Entró sin darme un beso, sólo me pellizcó la mejilla.

—Tengo que beber un vaso de agua —dijo muy tensa.

—¿Te ocurre algo? No tienes buen aspecto.

—No, no tengo buen aspecto. Más bien estoy muerta. Comparto mi cama con un titiritero y cuando abro los ojos descubro que me la ha jugado con una volatinera pelirroja. Hay gente que se desliza por el carril de adelantamiento y otros que estamos cada dos por tres en la cuneta… Dame un vaso de agua, anda. Es mejor que me calle para que no te salpique la porquería.

—Vamos, Marta, suelta lo que sea —dije, y me preparé para lo peor.

—La vida es una mierda, es todo lo que te puedo decir por ahora. —Me dirigió una mirada desesperada—. Además, no me acuerdo de nada. Por la noche Stanislav y yo nos pusimos ciegos de hachís. Después nos acostamos. En algún momento tuvo que aparecer su cómplice, la pelirroja que hace monerías con él en el parque. Esta mañana me he despertado sin recordar nada y he tardado en darme cuenta de que habían desvalijado la casa.

Me quedé de piedra. Es curioso, el curso de los acontecimientos nos deja de piedra aunque en ocasiones dicho curso sea perfectamente coherente. Antes o después, le tenía que tocar a mi hermana. Siempre lo había pensado: cualquier día, alguien montará una hoguera en torno a Marta y le arrancará la cabellera. Allí estaba mi hermana llena de magulladuras morales después de ser atacada por los apaches. Parecía que se iba a quedar dormida acurrucada en el sillón con la cabeza desplomada sobre el pecho. Apoyé una mano cariñosa en su hombro.

—Marta. Por favor, di que estás bien.

—Estoy bien. Ahora sólo quiero estar aquí un rato tranquila. Además, tengo una especie de amnesia. No me preguntes lo que pasó, porque no lo recuerdo.

—No puedo creer que no te acuerdes de nada.

—No me acuerdo, Blanca. Quizá, con mucho esfuerzo podría recordar algunos detalles. Pero estoy demasiado cansada. Lo peor es que ella se reía de mí, eso lo recuerdo. Recuerdo el rostro de la volatinera entre una niebla espesa mientras alguien me impedía moverme de la cama.

—Hijos de puta. ¿Y luego?

—Luego traté de gritar y me taparon la boca con algo que olía a demonios. Creo que me desmayé, o al menos me quedé profundamente dormida. He dormido durante varias horas y cuando me desperté esta mañana no recordaba nada de la noche anterior. Me sentía fresca como una rosa y durante unos segundos pensé que era un domingo estupendo y que podía quedarme remoloneando en la cama. Después abrí los ojos y me di cuenta de que el armario estaba abierto con todos los cajones desparramados por el suelo.

—Tendrás que llamar a la policía.

—¿Para qué, Blanca? ¿Crees que me importa el equipo de música y el vídeo? Me trae sin cuidado el dinero que se han llevado y las cuatro baratijas de oro. Lo que me jode es la risa de la volatinera pelirroja. Era una risa vengativa, ¿sabes? Una de esas risas que no puedes sacarte de la cabeza.

—¿Qué vas a hacer?

—Tendrás que invitarme a comer.

—Quiero decir después. Podríamos buscarlos en el Retiro. A lo mejor siguen allí.

Marta sonrió con desgana. Daba la impresión de que reía con un gesto prestado, pero lo cierto es que esa sonrisa suya tan triste hacía que el día pareciera nublado, aunque el sol entraba por las ventanas.

—Ésos ya habrán desaparecido del mapa o estarán tragando millas con algún vehículo robado. Creo que entre sueños escuché el motor de una furgoneta.

—¿No puedes acordarte de nada más?

—Eso es prácticamente todo. Quizá si hiciese mucho esfuerzo lograría recordar otras cosas; lo que hablaban entre ellos, o incluso la mirada de Stanislav mientras me sujetaban a la cama. Pero lo doloroso es tener que recordarlo.

—Entiendo —dije.

—Piensas que siempre acabo con tíos basura, ¿no?

—No, no lo pienso. No eres más que una chica que apuesta por caballos maltrechos y nunca tiene suerte con los números de las rifas. Lo malo es que cuando no puedes más, empiezas a darte golpes en la cabeza contra los muros. Igual que ciertos locos. A otros les da por el alcohol o se meten un pico de heroína.

—Puede ser, pero ya estoy cansada de todo esto.

—Lo que me tranquiliza es que tienes ovarios para seguir apostando. Las cobardes se tiran desde la azotea de un rascacielos o se esconden bajo tierra de por vida.

Supe en ese momento que yo había envidiado a Marta desde niña porque a ella le ocurrían *cosas*. Para Marta los batacazos y los remolinos eran el reverso de la aventura. Una no puede sumergirse sin flotador en el Amazonas y esperar aguas tranquilas y aves exóticas revoloteando entre coros celestiales por el horizonte. Subidones de emoción y bajadas vertiginosas al infierno, más bien. Hasta ahora, después de un trompazo, Marta se sacudía el polvo del trasero y se levantaba con mirada inocente, como si no hubiera pasado nada. Pero por alguna extraña razón supe que mi hermana empezaba a sospechar que las pirañas y las cataratas de la vida no eran las de un parque de atracciones. A partir de este momento se protegerá más, pensé. Yo, en cambio, estaba a punto de experimentar cómo un tren a toda velocidad me pasaba por encima.

No hace falta que nadie me recuerde que yo me lo estaba buscando. Me había puesto a rastrear las huellas de un aviador desquiciado, o él las mías, ya no sé quién perseguía a quién, el caso es que ya no había vuelta atrás. Sé que no puedo esperar que me compadezcan por lo que ocurrió en San Sebastián. Pensarán que si alguien se convierte en una diana humana y se planta voluntariamente en el centro del tiroteo no tiene ninguna excusa. Lo único que les pido es que comprendan que hay un aburrimiento mortal, un aburrimiento más peligroso que las balas cruzadas. Esquivar los disparos tiene sus ventajas: el corazón te late más deprisa y el mundo se pone a girar a toda mecha. Yo estaba harta de tener la sangre espesa como puré de remolacha.

23

Hasta ahora no he tenido valor para recordar lo que ocurrió hace dos semanas en una pensión de San Sebastián. A lo mejor yo no voy a ser capaz de hablar nunca de lo que pasó en la habitación de aquella pensión, porque es demasiado humillante o porque la sensación se borró hace unos días en Hendaya, cuando he vuelto a reunirme con Julio Oroz y me he encerrado con él en una pecera frente al mar para oír doscientas veces una vieja cinta de Lou Reed.

No deberías haberlo hecho, me dijo mi hermana. Los tíos como Julio tarde o temprano se intentan saltar los sesos con una escopeta de cañones recortados, pero como tienen mala puntería, te acaban metiendo plomo en el culo si te encuentras a tiro y te dejan a la pata coja para los restos. Ya sé que Marta es la menos indicada para darme consejos, pero es que ahora asegura que se le han abierto los ojos después del incidente del lanzallamas y la chica de los volatines; dice mi hermana que está más que harta de saltimbanquis, ya no se fía de los contorsionistas, cuerpos de goma que se cuelan por las rendijas y salen por donde han entrado chupándote por dentro. Dice que quiere ponerle portones blindados al corazón. No es sólo por el hecho de que te desvalijen la casa o el alma; mi hermana está cansada de franquear el paso, de abrir piernas y puertas de par en par y comprobar que lo que quieren algunos profanadores de almas es arrancarte los dientes uno a uno para fabricarse a tu costa una dentadura reluciente de presentador de *show* de variedades. En cuanto te tienen como una bombilla fundida y sin dientes alzan el vuelo igual que Drácula después de un atracón de plasma.

Permanezco sentada en esta mesa con el rotulador rojo y no puedo ver el rostro del último borracho con el que nos cruzamos antes de entrar en aquel portal… pero seguro que hubo un borracho que miró la placa de la pensión Miramar. Yo ni siquiera había bajado el equipaje del coche. ¿Para qué? Llevaba un cepillo de dientes en el bolso y por la mañana tendría tiempo de buscar ropa limpia y cambiarme.

De repente me viene el recuerdo de un olor que presagiaba desgracias. Quiero decir que aquel olor te hacía envidiar a cualquiera que estuviera en otro sitio. Me refiero a ese olor que se mezcla con la certeza de que ya no se puede caer más bajo. No se sabe a ciencia cierta si las paredes grasientas y las moquetas llenas de lamparones atraen la mala suerte, pero yo estoy segura de que avisan del vértigo de ciertos huecos oscuros de escalera.

He puesto voz a muchos anuncios de perfumes: colonias para recién nacidos mulliditos y rubios, aromas salvajes para Ellos, fragancias con rosa de Marruecos, nenúfar y jacintos acuáticos para Ellas, ambientadores para el hogar que evocan el musgo fresco del amanecer, sin embargo, me parece que no es fácil describir un olor. ¿A qué huelen las pensiones baratas? ¿A qué olía en esa pensión del casco viejo de San Sebastián? Apuesto cualquier cosa a que Álvaro Arriaga no ha pisado jamás una pensión barata, ni siquiera de estudiante, ni siquiera cuando estudiaba en una universidad de niños ricos, él, hijo de un maestro pero con ambiciones, prefería cazar princesas con áticos de *Nuevo Estilo*, herederas bilingües que aprenden a lamer chocolatinas con morritos de lamer vergas y viceversa, ramilletes de espabiladas que estudian durante el día y por la noche ensayan posturas porno para levantársela a un príncipe de provecho. ¿A qué santo iba ir Álvaro Arriaga a una pensión? Los chicos no demasiado ricos que quieren llegar a la cumbre cuanto antes deben abandonar el olor a cocido de la infancia a toda pastilla, piernas para que os quiero, una boda por todo lo alto, una anoréxica con pedigrí, con capilla en la finca, a ser posible, ya aparecerá más adelante una asalariada con ganas de escalar posiciones o una madame Bovary fogosa que sepa follar como Dios manda. No, Álvaro no conocerá nunca ese tufo a moqueta sintética impregnada de col, espuma seca para alfombras, amoníaco, bigotes resecos de gamba, sexo y humedad, todo junto, ni se le habrá ocurrido jamás ducharse en un poliván con hilillos de herrumbre recorriendo los caminos de la miseria desde el grifo hasta el sumidero.

Un momento. Hay que encontrar cierto orden. No es justo que yo la emprenda precisamente ahora con Álvaro Arriaga, porque mientras yo me emborrachaba por las calles de San Sebastián con Julio Oroz, mientras Julio me arrastraba de bar en bar antes de hacerme perrerías en la pensión Miramar, Álvaro yacía como un *ecce homo* entre las sábanas blancas de una habitación blanca en una clínica blanca y reluciente donde las batas de enfermeras y doctores eran también de un blanco inmaculado.

Si yo hubiera leído aquellos días los periódicos de la ciudad del norte me habría enterado de que el reconocido profesional de la comunicación, Álvaro Arriaga, había sufrido un misterioso atentado que casi acaba con su vida. Pero yo no leía los periódicos de la ciudad del norte; no hablaban los periódicos del norte de un aviador demente ni de una chica tonta de Madrid que seguía con la sonrisa encendida en la cara por si él volvía.

Los asuntos feos, en cualquier caso, tienen caminos propios: corren de boca en boca, se deslizan por las ranuras de las puertas, te estallan en las manos en cartas traicioneras. Al final, más pronto o más tarde, siempre acabas enterándote de los asuntos feos.

Una noche en que estaba tratando de alejar de mi cabeza una persistente escena en la que Mara Barbieri desnuda en brazos de Julio Oroz iniciaba un simposio intelectual poscoito sobre la presencia del falo en el arte conceptual, recibí una llamada de Ana Iribar.

—Blanca, no te asustes —dijo, consiguiendo en el acto ponerme en guardia—. Tengo malas noticias.

En aquellos momentos sólo me preocupaba Julio Oroz, así que lo imaginé con la nariz partida en una película de mafiosos.

—Ana, ¿qué ha ocurrido?

—Se trata de Álvaro Arriaga. Pensé que deberías saberlo.

—Por Dios santo, ¿qué le ha ocurrido a Álvaro?

—Está en el hospital, pero ya está fuera de peligro. El viernes de madrugada unos encapuchados lanzaron cócteles molotov al paso de su coche. Ya sabes, esos artefactos con gasolina, pólvora y fragmentos de plomo que meten un ruido de mil diablos. Los explosivos consiguieron impactar en la luna del vehículo. De pronto fue un infierno: los cristales saltando en mil pedazos, el coche ardiendo; afortunadamente, Álvaro se las arregló como pudo para escapar de las llamas, pero tiene quemaduras graves y cortes en todo el cuerpo.

Me quedé callada al otro lado del hilo telefónico. Tuve una reacción primero de indignación y luego de pánico, porque inmediatamente pensé que Oroz había tenido algo que ver en el ataque y resultaba que, de alguna manera, yo era su cómplice.

—¿Se sabe quién puede haber sido? —pregunté.

—Se han barajado algunas hipótesis. No es la primera vez que los radicales se ensañan con gente como Álvaro, profesionales jóvenes, relacionados en cierto modo con los políticos locales, con dinero, nada complacientes con los violentos; pero yo creo que pensar en una agresión de ese tipo no tiene mucho sentido. Las cosas han cambiado mucho últimamente. Para mí que se la tenían jurada por otras razones.

—Es extraño —dije con cautela—. ¿A qué tipo de razones te refieres?

—Razones personales, no sé, resquemores que se incuban en las ciudades pequeñas, yo no creo que estemos hablando de un atentado terrorista. Además, la policía ha dicho que parece un trabajo de aficionados, que se les escapó vivito y coleando.

—¿Quieres decir que podrían haberlo matado?

—Iban a por él, desde luego, pero a lo mejor tuvieron escrúpulos en el último momento o, simplemente, pretendían darle un buen susto.

—¿Y nadie vio a los asaltantes?

—Eran las cuatro de la madrugada, Álvaro conducía solo de vuelta a casa después de tomar unas copas cuando el coche de los encapuchados le salió al paso. Los tipos lanzaron las bombas y luego huyeron a toda velocidad. Álvaro dice que le pareció ver a tres hombres con pasamontañas dentro de un coche blanco, y que uno de ellos era un individuo gordo con cazadora de cuero.

No me atreví a pedir más detalles, me disponía a borrarlo todo de mi mente; a borrar, también, el chispazo que me asaltó de pronto y se detuvo en mi cabeza igual que un fotograma congelado en una moviola: en un bar de la ciudad del norte, el gordo Patxi Uzcudun, el compañero de colegio de Julio, pedía un whisky para mí, hablándome de su pasada experiencia en explosivos. Patxi llevaba una cazadora de cuero.

Todavía fui capaz de hacer una pregunta de compromiso:

—¿Crees que debo llamarle al hospital?

—Yo le diré que he hablado contigo, si te parece. Puedes llamarle a casa más adelante. Estoy segura de que se restablecerá pronto.

—Gracias por avisarme, Ana, no dejes de tenerme informada.

24

Hay pocas cosas mejores que salir a la calle como un correcaminos cuando las paredes se te caen encima. Cuando me cansé de dar vueltas a la manzana andando muy deprisa para no pensar, me metí en el bar más desangelado que encontré. Quería una copa de vino rodeada de desconocidos, quería una horrorosa ración de boquerones fritos o de calamares, algo indigesto y con grasa, aún peor, quería provocar un cataclismo en mi estómago, tragar basura, no recordar, hablar del tiempo con un parroquiano que mordiese un palillo y tomarme dos Valium antes de dormir.

Bebí tres vasos de vino y una copa de coñac, que me repugna. Al volver a casa me tragué un par de Valium y caí redonda en el sofá.

Al día siguiente cuando me despertó el teléfono creí que no había mapas debajo de mis pies y que yo era la única superviviente de una glaciación. Tuve que mirar por la ventana, mientras descolgaba el auricular, para estar segura de que el mundo no había dejado de girar.

—¿Quién es? —dije, y descubrí que hablaba con ecos de espectro de ultratumba.

—¿Blanca, estás bien? Tu voz suena muy rara. Soy Julio Oroz.

La gente caminaba por las calles como todos los días, los coches se detenían ante los semáforos en rojo, del supermercado de enfrente salían mujeres cargadas de bultos, una detrás de otra como las porteadoras de víveres de un safari. Por la luz y el movimiento calculé que serían cerca de las doce. Yo era una momia en un frasco de formol. Me acordé de la mala noticia de la noche anterior y mi instinto me dijo que Julio Oroz me hundiría con él en las alcantarillas. Quise defenderme.

—Dime qué quieres, Julio, he dormido fatal y no tengo ganas de hablar con nadie.

—Necesito tu ayuda —dijo como si no se lo hubiera tragado la tierra después de arrancar la cremallera de mis vaqueros—. Quizá no debería haberte tocado a ti, Blanca, pero así es la vida. Vas a tener que echarme una mano.

—¿De qué estás hablando?

—¿Te han llegado noticias del accidente de tu amigo Arriaga?

—Algo he leído en los periódicos —mentí.

—No puedo explicarte nada por ahora, pero te aseguro que no es lo que tú piensas. Necesito hablar contigo. Quiero que nos veamos.

—Lo siento, Julio, lo único que yo quiero es volver a la cama.

—Escúchame, Blanca, mi vida se está desmoronando, tengo que verte.

—No estoy para ayudar a nadie en estos momentos; mi vida también se está desmoronando… ¿Desde dónde me llamas?

—Estoy en San Sebastián. Tienes que venir con el coche ahora mismo. Voy a viajar por Francia durante un par de semanas… Y ahí es donde intervienes tú —dijo—. Necesito que me prestes tu coche. En cierto modo, *todos* tenemos un problema.

Hijo de puta, pensé, está tratando de agarrarme por el cuello.

—Estás loco, Julio.

—Si no tardas mucho en salir, puedes llegar a San Sebastián a media tarde.

Tuve que aceptarlo: cada vez que olía la presencia de Julio Oroz se me arqueaba el lomo de gata ronroneante y se me hacía la boca agua. Así que acepté tragar kilómetros para ir a San Sebastián. Acepté, también, quedar con él en un bar de la parte vieja.

—Estaré en el Aralar, en la calle del Puerto, todo el mundo lo conoce. Pregunta a cualquiera. No me dejes colgado, Blanca. Esperaré lo que haga falta.

Empecé a pensar que estaba atrapada en una película. Más me valía echar a correr sin mirar atrás para esquivar las balas. Aunque sabía que al final una siempre corre en la dirección equivocada y se mete de cabeza en la boca del lobo. Bueno, hay veces que entran muchas ganas de tropezarse con el lobo. En algún lugar de San Sebastián me esperaba la boca de Julio Oroz y yo no estaba dispuesta a perdérmelo.

Ahora pienso que a lo mejor me puse a correr empujada por un impulso incontrolable porque quería saber qué era lo que sentía un asesino, si es que Julio Oroz era un asesino, o porque necesitaba meterme dentro de su piel y de su rabia y así explorar esas ansias de acabar con todo y abandonarme en otro cuerpo, en un cuerpo nervioso en el que anidaba el resquemor y los deseos de venganza. Quizá lo único que yo tenía en la cabeza era medir la magnitud del peligro que podía representar para mí estar con él en aquel momento. Sin embargo, una vocecilla tramposa se empeñaba en engañarme. Me convencí a mí misma de que debía ir a San Sebastián para suplicarle a Julio que dejara en paz a Álvaro. Veía una secuencia de melodrama, yo rogaba y él se negaba, pero lo que más me gustaba es que Oroz me miraba como mira Humphrey Bogart a Ingrid Bergman en *Casablanca*, y cuando yo ya me daba por vencida él me tomaba en sus brazos y me comía a besos antes de hacerme rugir de placer en la trastienda del bar Rick's.

Cuidado, me dije mientras preparaba el equipaje: si te empeñas en imaginar escenas cinematográficas es que algo va mal.

A trescientos kilómetros de Madrid pensé que estaba a punto de estropearlo todo. Mientras conducía por la Autovía del Norte imaginé que estaba acercándome a las arenas movedizas, igual que hicieron otras chicas de mi barrio, sólo que yo lo estaba haciendo con diez años de retraso y después de haber pisado tierra firme. Me pregunté si las vidas de aquellas chicas habrían descarrilado por amor. Si por amor las chicas guerreras de mi barrio se la habían jugado, acostándose con tipos con serpientes retorcidas tatuadas en el pecho y pinchazos mortales en los brazos, sabiendo que después de la excitación de los remolinos vienen los vapuleos de los rápidos y más tarde la caída vertiginosa por las cataratas.

Pero yo no había sido nunca una chica guerrera y de siempre me han aterrorizado las aguas turbulentas. Y la verdad es que apenas conocía a Julio Oroz, ese aviador demente. Aún estaba a tiempo de dar marcha atrás. Sólo tenía que detenerme en una gasolinera y telefonear a Miguel con voz de hija pródiga y balidos de oveja descarriada de vuelta al redil. Sólo tenía que hacer eso y desviarme en el primer cambio de sentido de regreso a Madrid. En tres horas estaría en casa con mi marido, sentados los dos en el sofá frente a un televisor descomunal.

Entonces lo supe. Supe que había dejado que Julio Oroz dislocase mis pasos porque estaba harta del tedio de coliflor al horno en que se había convertido mi vida con Miguel. Yo buscaba un electroshock, una descarga que despertase de nuevo las puntas sensibles de mis nervios desvitalizados, quería ser la mujer inmóvil clavada en la diana del lanzacuchillos, buscaba un orgasmo cósmico, unas uñas hincadas en la yugular hasta hacerme dar aullidos al amanecer. Sospechaba que Oroz ocultaba una bomba en la caja negra de su cerebro y yo quería jugar a desarmarla. Esta vez era yo la vampira dispuesta a reventar chupando la energía de la dínamo alojada en el interior de Julio Oroz.

Cuando te toca en la tómbola un amante como Álvaro Arriaga, músculos de acero, mandíbula de amo del universo, dedos de prestidigitador, voz de domador de mujeres y potencia sexual de Superman, crees que te han enchufado un botellón de oxígeno que aliviará la atmósfera asfixiante de tu pareja. Pero cuando pasan los meses y el juguete fornicador repite como un autómata los mismos gestos apasionados, idénticas frases engatusadoras, se sienta en el sillón de siempre y bebe el whisky contando batallas parecidas antes de reiniciar el ritual sexual correspondiente, te encuentras con que, de alguna manera, estás otra vez jugando a las casitas: la muñeca Barbie y su supernovio Ken en su nidito de amor.

Y lo que a mí me pedía el cuerpo era tirar los muebles por

la ventana, volver mi vida del revés y emprender un viaje a lo desconocido.

Al llegar a San Sebastián caía una lluvia fina y yo estaba cansada. Aparqué cerca del hotel Londres. Es la única parte de la ciudad que conozco bien y desde allí sabía orientarme hasta el barrio viejo. Además, quería asomarme a la playa de la Concha.

A mis pies, el mar era un líquido pesado que latía como un cerebro humano. Presentí corrientes interiores y fuerzas ocultas, pero la superficie permanecía tranquila, tal vez a la espera de algo, sólo con aquel gorgoteo de organismo vivo en constante ebullición. La tarde se apagaba a cámara lenta y estuve apoyada en la balaustrada hasta que reuní ánimos para adentrarme en las callejas dispuesta a enfrentarme a Julio Oroz.

—Parece que llevo un siglo aquí —dijo, dándome un beso precipitado que acertó en plena ceja—. He ido y venido a los bares de enfrente sin perder de vista esta puerta. Llevo ocho vinos, por lo menos.

Julio me explicó que algunos días las calles de esta zona de San Sebastián se vuelven laberínticas e impenetrables, defendidas por silencios y rostros indescifrables; nadie sabe qué piensa nadie, callejas que han sido escenario de batallas campales entre las fuerzas del orden y las desordenadas pandillas de incendiarios, amuralladas frente al exterior con pintadas que marcan el territorio de unos y disuaden a otros de internarse más entre sus muros. Pero aquella noche no percibí aire de amenaza y los bares estaban abarrotados de jóvenes que bebían e intercambiaban saludos con vozarrones cavernosos y apacibles.

Toda la noche me arrastró de bar en bar. Yo también bebía vino y escuchaba. Entre nosotros, varios palmos de distancia. Un abismo que no me atrevía a sortear. Ciertamente, se comporta como si yo le importara un bledo, pensaba yo bastante borracha y desanimada con ganas de chupar su nuez como aquel día en el palacio de las tortitas con nata de Madrid. Hablaba de todo y de nada, pero de pronto me dijo que había pensado quitarse de en medio por si a Álvaro se le ocurría relacionarle con el atentado. Álvaro podría sospechar de él, si, efectivamente, Arriaga hubiera sido el amante de su mujer. ¿Estarás de acuerdo conmigo?, me preguntaba. Pero me juraba que él no había tenido nada que ver con la agresión. Puesto que yo nunca había reconocido que Álvaro fuera mi amante, no tenía sentido putearle sin ninguna certeza, hubiera sido una cabronada, dijo. Yo no me fiaba. Le comenté que sospechaban de un tipo gordo con cazadora de cuero; le dije que su amigo Patxi Uzcudun estaba enterado de todos los vericuetos de los radicales de la ciudad, la gente lo respetaba, él mismo me había contado cosas de su etapa de incendiario.

Julio se puso serio.

—No menciones jamás a Uzcudun, ¿entendido? Olvida su nombre, ¿vale? No lo has conocido nunca. A Uzcudun, ni tocarlo.

Julio Oroz no quiere volver a mencionar el asunto. Insiste por última vez en que le conviene pasar a Francia por un tiempo, pero asegura que sus manos están limpias. Me dice que tengo que creerle y, al final, le creo. Ahora quiere emborracharse conmigo, charlar de otras cosas.

No sé durante cuánto tiempo estuvo Julio hablando de la dinamita que le bullía dentro, del vendaval que corría por sus venas, de los pasos que cambian de rumbo por culpa de una ficha de dominó, y de cómo los hombres acaban persiguiendo a las mujeres equivocadas. Me dijo que quería estallar, que quería disgregarse hasta la aniquilación, al diablo con la escritura, quería que su destrucción fuese su única novela. Me dijo que si en el amor no había paroxismo, el amor era una mierda. Yo seguía a duras penas la evolución de sus pensamientos pero casi todo el tiempo pensaba en su boca, en el instante preciso en que la inercia y el alcohol la fundieran con la mía. Me dijo que su amante (no mencionó el nombre de Mara Barbieri, pero yo sabía que estaba hablando de Mara Barbieri, la de los debates culturales antes, después o durante el polvo) estaba enamorada de sí misma: bastaba con abrillantar su ego para ponerla en ebullición. Desde lo de su hija, las mujeres para él eran puro trámite, pero yo le obsesionaba, no sabía por qué. A los doce años se hacía una pregunta: ¿por qué siempre hay alguien o algo que te acaba jodiendo la vida? Ahora tenía cuarenta y seguía haciéndose la misma pregunta. Por eso pensaba que el paso del tiempo era una inutilidad, ni siquiera servía para responder los tontos interrogantes de un niño.

A las dos de la mañana pude encajar algunas palabras. Le dije a Julio Oroz que nunca me habían dado una fiesta sorpresa y que algunas chicas de mi barrio estaban en Yeserías porque se enredaron en el descampado con chicos que llevaban escrito en la sangre, «mala jugada». Tíos flacos como Mick Jagger con bocas caníbales, y ahora esos chicos, si no se los ha tragado la noche, siguen vendiendo caballo ya sin dientes mientras ellas hacen cursos de peluquería y secretariado en la cárcel, por ver si pueden salir del agujero. Le dije que mi madre se había trasladado a Madrid desde un erial de La Mancha y que mi padre la encontró un domingo tomando Marie Brizard con hielo en un bar de la carretera. Mi madre nunca había oído hablar de Aretha Franklin, así que mi padre se la llevó al coche para que escuchase *Maybe I'm a fool*. A mi madre le dio por llorar al escuchar la voz aterciopelada de la negra Aretha y se fijó en las manos suaves de aquel viajante de ferretería. Unas semanas más tarde, después de haber llenado de música la cabeza de mi madre, mi padre tuvo que prometer una lavadora a plazos y una cocina alicatada hasta el techo. Sólo así mi madre consintió en abrir las piernas y cerrar los ojos. Y mi padre cumplió su promesa. Le dije a Julio que las mujeres a veces almacenamos sensaciones de jauría en la cabeza y él me dijo que le repugnaban los intelectuales por su complacencia. Refugiados en sus torres de marfil ignoraban el caos y la desesperación. Sin caos no hay pasión, me decía Julio Oroz unas cuantas copas más tarde.

A las cuatro de la madrugada entrábamos en el antro más siniestro de todos los muchos locales que habíamos pateado esa noche. Había unas cuantas mesas ocupadas y varios tipos con aspecto patibulario acodados en la barra. Julio saludó a un matón con cabeza rapada. Supuse que era el gorila del local. Nos instalamos en una esquina de la barra y un barman con aspecto de propietario nos sirvió dos cubalibres y desapareció por una oscuridad roja, que parecía conducir al infierno. Un poco más lejos, un tipo medio albino haciendo equilibrios en el taburete, no dejaba de observarnos.

Julio se acercó mucho para decirme que a aquellas horas no teníamos más remedio que alternar con lo peor de lo peor. Si alguno de ustedes me hubiese preguntado qué tal me sentía, lo más probable es que le hubiera contestado que en la gloria, los dos estábamos borrachos y tambaleantes y poco a poco nuestras manos se enredaban, brazos de pulpo tropezando en el aire.

De pronto el albino la tomó con nosotros:

—¿Qué tengo en la cara? —dijo—. A ver, tú, ¿qué tengo en la cara?

—¿Me está hablando a mí? —dijo Julio en voz alta dirigiéndose al tipo del pelo descolorido—. ¿Este sujeto me está hablando a mí?

—Sí, tío, va por ti, que ya me tienes harto. ¿Es que tengo monos en la cara?

—¿Y a éste qué le pasa? —dijo Julio alzando los hombros y buscando la mirada del que parecía el gorila encargado de que reinase la paz en aquel rebaño de zombis.

El del pelo descolorido volvió a la carga.

—Aquí no hay quien se tome una copa tranquilo, hay que joderse. ¿Es que no tienes otra cosa que hacer? Ya me estás mirando igual que la otra noche.

—¿De qué me está hablando, amigo? —dijo Julio irritado—, yo a usted no le he visto en toda mi puta vida.

—Dice que no me ha visto —gritó el hombre dirigiéndose al resto de los clientes—. Este tío es un berzas. Anoche vino con un cantamañanas y no me quitaron el ojo de encima, los muy maricones.

—Te voy a partir la cara —dijo Julio avanzando hacia él amenazadoramente—, ayer yo ni siquiera estaba en San Sebastián. Estás delirando.

El matón cabeza rapada cayó de pronto del cielo y se interpuso entre los dos, quitando leña al asunto.

—Hacía meses que no pisaba este local —se justificó Julio—, no he visto a este individuo en mi vida.

—A veces le entra la paranoia —dijo el matón con voz tranquila—. Anda, Sueco, es hora de irse a casa.

El que parecía el dueño del local salió de la cueva del infierno con una rubia peinada con moño de los sesenta y tapada con una hoja de parra prehistórica en forma de microfalda de cuero. El hombre la acomodó en una mesa con un guiño que prometía el regreso de James Bond. A continuación volvió a su puesto detrás de la barra y, retirando el vaso vacío, le dijo al Sueco:

—Por hoy se han acabado las copas. Vete a dormirla a casa.

—¿Qué es esa mierda de que no hay más copas? —se excitó el Sueco—. ¿Y ese tío? ¿Qué hace ese tío mirándome como un maricón? Lleva así desde ayer por la noche.

Julio de un salto ya tenía agarrado al Sueco de las solapas cuando el matón los separó de malos modos.

—Será mejor que se vayan también ustedes —nos dijo el matón.

Yo ya estaba arrastrando a Julio hacia la puerta mientras el albino se quedaba derrumbado sobre la barra con la mirada perdida.

—A mí no me echa nadie —le dijo Julio al dueño del local que ahora se sentaba en la mesa con la del moño—. Me voy porque no me gustan los borrachos, ¿entendido?

Durante unos minutos seguimos caminando dando tumbos, borrachos los dos, separados como dos peonzas rotando en diferente órbita. Yo pensaba: cuando lleguemos a la pensión me abrazará y veré las estrellas (no sabía hasta qué punto iba a ser cierto), y comeremos perdices y todo lo demás. Pero las pensiones que huelen a sexo y a humedad no presagian nada bueno.

¿Por qué les tengo que contar todo? ¿Por qué les tengo que decir que cuando llegamos a la pensión Julio Oroz se quedó dormido como un mazacote de madera y pasó así muchas horas? Un mazacote de madera al que me arrimé sin saber que un poco más tarde me iba a golpear con todas sus fuerzas. Te abrazas a un chico con expresión enternecedora, cierras los ojos y cuando los abres descubres que ese chico se ha convertido en un hijo de Satán. No me pegó literalmente, a ver si me entienden, pero me dejó molida, humillada, con moratones en el alma. Pueden ponerle música de ranchera o de tango. Fané y descangallá. Pero antes de llegar a ese punto, Julio Oroz, al despertar de su larga siesta al día siguiente me había hecho sentir como una carga de ropa limpia en una secadora. Me había sobado, agitado, calentado, centrifugado, mareado, transportado de un lado a otro en su avioneta voladora.

Entonces se me encendió el interruptor de *la voz*. Era la primera vez que me pasaba con Julio. Me puse a decirle a Julio Oroz cosas parecidas a las que le había dicho otras veces a Álvaro Arriaga. Y cuanto más hablaba yo más excitado se ponía él, aquello era la apoteosis. Parecíamos un catálogo de anuncios eróticos por palabras: beso negro, 69, estudiante viciosa, cubana exuberante, casada superinfiel, enfermera hambrienta, masaje mutuo, griego, francés, ampurdanés, ducha húngara, garganta profunda, esclava sumisa, gladiador opulento, mulato afrodisíaco, fresador superdotado, sultán insaciable. El delirio. Yo empezaba a recuperarme de tanta gimnasia porno cuando él me empezó a tratar con violencia. Me dijo que siguiera hablando con voz de zorra, me preguntó si eso era lo que le decía a Álvaro en la cama; estaba medio loco, me insultaba, me vapuleaba, me hacía daño con las manos y con el sexo, me empezó a penetrar a lo bestia, a medio asfixiarme mientras lo hacía, me tapaba la boca, no me dejaba gritar. Creo que durante unos segundos me desmayé o perdí la noción del tiempo. Cuando recobré el sentido de la realidad, Julio Oroz estaba eyaculando encima de mi cara con los ojos crueles y un terrible gesto de venganza.

Notas desde Hendaya

Deben creerme, Uzcudun no tuvo nada que ver con la caída de Álvaro Arriaga. Tampoco yo. Cualquiera pudo haberlo hecho. Todo ocurrió de forma previsible, acaso porque Arriaga había acumulado demasiados enemigos en la ciudad. Creo que él nunca fue consciente de ello; le cegaba su propio éxito.

Confío en que me crean. Permítaseme añadir que le estoy agradecido a Blanca por haberme buscado en esta madriguera después de lo ocurrido en San Sebastián. Cuando salí de aquella maldita pensión yo era un hombre enloquecido que acababa de arrojar a una ciénaga la única llave de su futuro. Sólo quedaba en mi chaqueta un vago olor a sexo y a moqueta húmeda y me dolía la cabeza. Blanca ya no me importaba. Álvaro y yo habíamos acabado nuestra vieja partida de ajedrez sobre su pequeño cuerpo ardiente y ahora ya no era asunto mío. Supe al dejar a Blanca que nunca podría volver a vivir con Elena. Me había quitado de encima a las dos mujeres que habían gozado con ese semental de Arriaga.

Cuando atravesé las callejas de la parte vieja para buscar el coche de Blanca, empecé a temblar. Eso ocurrió un poco antes de divisar la esquina del hotel Londres. En ese recorrido de sólo unos minutos mis piernas se empeñaron en quebrarse. Pensé en esos viejos que intentan ponerse en pie y les fallan las rodillas y se derrumban en un santiamén. No llovía, pero la calle estaba mojada y tuve la impresión de ir a resbalar si persistían la debilidad y los temblores.

Tuve que abrazarme a un semáforo. Cerré los ojos y me vi de nuevo eyaculando con violencia sobre el rostro de Blanca al tiempo que la zarandeaba. Así, con los ojos cerrados, mientras notaba las miradas de los transeúntes, su voz regresaba a mí a través de aquella queja en la que había más perplejidad que dolor: ¿por qué, Julio? ¿Por qué, precisamente yo?

No había desprecio por mí mismo en el impulso de dar la vuelta y regresar a la pensión, pero comprendí que era demasiado tarde para salvar a Blanca del recuerdo de aquella escena reciente. Mi bajeza me producía a la vez satisfacción y asco, pero necesitaba encontrar sosiego en su regazo. Me imaginaba entrando por la puerta con aire de cordero degollado. Ella abriría sus brazos, diría que sí a mi ruego de ducharnos juntos en aquel exiguo poliván, yo expiaría todos mis pecados al lavar su rostro con cuidado, igual que su hermana Marta había purificado a un vagabundo en la bañera de su casa, pobre Blanca, todavía quedarían restos pegajosos de mi esperma entre sus pestañas, déjame bañar tus pechos, le diría, mira cómo resbala por ellos el agua, mira cómo se desbordan entre mis manos. Yo, infame, secando su cabeza con una toalla barata, soplando el rosario de sus vértebras por ver si se convertían en alas, arañando los estratos de la tristeza que habría crecido en sus párpados hinchados. No regresé a la pensión, pero tampoco imaginé que cuatro días más tarde íbamos a abrazarnos frente al mar.

Al principio, no había proyectado quedarme en Hendaya, pero después lo pensé mejor cuando me hablaron del alquiler barato de un piso en el paseo marítimo. Cuando entré en la casa supe que había llegado a puerto seguro. Las habitaciones eran amplias y olía a alcanfor y también a la humedad salina del mar. A mis pies se extendía la playa. Algunos plásticos habían quedado atrapados entre las algas de la orilla. Esos plásticos eran como los desechos de mi pasado, pero subiría la marea y se los llevaría mar adentro. No quería recordar nada de las últimas horas y me las arreglé para convencerme de que ahora podría escribir mi novela. Siempre se empieza por lo más sencillo, así que nada más instalarme ordené unos cuadernos en blanco sobre una mesa y traté de mantener mi conciencia despierta durante tres días seguidos con sus noches. Escribí a mano, muy deprisa, a ratos escuchando una cinta de Lou Reed y a ratos en silencio.

Al cuarto día apareció Blanca y juntos destruimos todo lo que había escrito en uno de los cuadernos. Me dijo que empezara otra vez, que comiera a mis horas, que diera paseos al atardecer y que durmiera por las noches. Ahora estoy a punto de terminar otro cuaderno. Patxi Uzcudun vino el domingo a pasar el día y se interesó por los laberintos de mi historia.

Estoy sentado en una mecedora y escribo sobre las piernas. Puedo mecerme y escribir al mismo tiempo y es una sensación placentera, aunque no resisto demasiado tiempo sin marearme. Un día más enfrentado a la novela, un día más sin la presencia de Blanca y un día más que llueve mansamente. He recordado la visita de Uzcudun cuando he bajado a la playa esta mañana con un paraguas y he caminado hasta el monte, antes de comer. Los surfistas aparecen por la tarde, aunque llueva y haga demasiado frío para estas fechas;

hoy la humedad del ambiente me ha obligado a ver anochecer desde los ventanales. Las gentes del lugar se han acostumbrado a mi presencia, aunque me lanzan miradas más interrogantes que desconfiadas. Me parece que creen que tengo algo que esconder, que me refugio aquí porque me persigue alguien o he dejado un acontecimiento atroz a mis espaldas.

Después de irse Blanca, trasladé la mesa de trabajo hasta las puertas de la terraza y, mientras escribo, puedo ver la playa hasta más allá del casino acristalado. A lo lejos, si no hay demasiada niebla, distingo la forma compacta del monte y el faro en el extremo del espigón, inestable visto desde aquí, como si se pudiera partir por la mitad y caer al mar.

Patxi dedicó un par de horas a leer el manuscrito y se sorprendió al saber que Blanca había estado conmigo en Hendaya. No comprendía cómo demonios había podido perdonarme. Le dije a Uzcudun que los primeros días de nuestra estancia aquí, Blanca y yo, los dos juntos, nos asomábamos a la ventana del dormitorio para ver el mar. A los dos nos gustaba experimentar esta sensación de provisionalidad. En las noches claras, ahora que Blanca lleva algunos días en Madrid para grabar anuncios y solucionar sus asuntos con Miguel, me acerco al puerto por el gusto de escuchar los crujidos de las barcas al mecerse en el agua y pienso en ella. Eso no le extrañó tanto a Uzcudun como el hecho de que Blanca hubiera sido capaz de mirarme a la cara. Le dije que cuando llegó Blanca, yo apenas recordaba la escena de la pensión. Lo olvidé todo al escuchar su voz limpia y transparente. Pero justo antes, al poco de dejarla tirada e instalarme en Hendaya, no podía reconocer el sonido de sus frases.

—¿Tratabas de recordar su voz y no podías? —preguntó Uzcudun.

—Sólo oía los quejidos del último momento. En mis recuerdos su rostro emergía de entre las sábanas embadurnado de semen y llanto, la boca torcida en un gesto de incomprensión y desprecio. Quería balbucir algo pero no le salían las palabras y abría y cerraba unos labios indecisos y titubeantes que me hicieron pensar en las bocanadas agónicas de los pescados y de algunos ahogados. Me obligué a repasar cada una de nuestras conversaciones anteriores, pero no podía recomponer su voz, se habían desteñido los tonos y lo único que encontraba eran mis propios acentos y mi cháchara obsesiva. Llegué a creer que todo había sido fruto de mi imaginación. Pero, entonces, qué hacía yo escondido en Hendaya con un coche que no era mío y por qué guardaba en mi bolsillo un recorte de periódico que mencionaba el atentado sufrido por el brillante ejecutivo de comunicación, Álvaro Arriaga. Me decía a mí mismo: no tienes remedio, te has vuelto completamente loco, no hay salida para los tipos como tú. Por eso me empezó a obsesionar la idea de volver a ver a Blanca. Pensé que si ella había existido en realidad, yo podía desandar mis pasos y transformarme en un escritor de verdad.

—¿Llamaste a Blanca? —preguntó Uzcudun.

—Llamé a su casa. El marido me salió con el cuento de que Blanca se había ido a vivir a casa de su hermana. Advirtió que Blanca le había rogado que no diese su teléfono a nadie. Le dije que era urgente. Ella no me conoce, mentí, dígale que su coche ha aparecido en Hendaya. No dejé ninguna dirección, ningún número de teléfono, pero dos días más tarde el rostro triste de Blanca asomó por el bar donde suelo tomar la última copa. Aquí todo el mundo se conoce. No era difícil encontrar a un español alto que camina cabizbajo con una chaqueta de tweed y aspecto de meterse siempre en callejones sin salida.

Uzcudun me preguntó si cuando nos volvimos a encontrar percibí alguna aspereza en los dedos de Blanca. Me quedé en silencio, pensando y tratando de adivinar qué perseguían sus ojillos ahora achinados por la curiosidad. Finalmente, le respondí con otra pregunta.

—¿Por qué me iba a fijar en eso?

Uzcudun movió la cabeza.

—Sin embargo, es un dato importante —insistió. Trata de recordar si sus dedos estaban ásperos.

—Puede ser —le dije—, puede que estuvieran algo entumecidos.

—Una bolsa de viaje pequeña pero pesada —insinuó Uzcudun—. Tuvo que haber viajado en avión hasta San Sebastián sin facturar el equipaje. Estaba ansiosa por localizarte. Desde el aeropuerto tomó un taxi hasta Hendaya. Después anduvo por las calles a la deriva arrastrando la bolsa hasta que se le ocurrió dejarla en la consigna de la estación para seguir haciendo pesquisas. Cuando te encontró estaba cansada y sus dedos acusaban la reciente incomodidad del equipaje que seguía depositado en la estación.

—¿Cómo lo sabes? —pregunté asombrado.

—A veces los detalles insignificantes se mezclan en una constelación iluminadora. Basta con seguir los senderos que marca esa luz.

—De acuerdo —reconocí—, pero la multiplicidad de caminos inservibles es asombrosa. He llegado a pensar que todo esto eran delirios míos. ¿Quién me decía que no estaba metido en una pesadilla? ¿Qué tenía yo que ver con Julio Oroz? De no haber aparecido Blanca en Hendaya seguiría en la irresolución total, y aun así me sentía impulsado a seguir adelante por culpa de la inestabilidad de una ficha de dominó invisible que ni siquiera estoy seguro de que exista.

Uzcudun completó mi idea:

—Naturalmente, ya no sabías si dormías o no.

—Al subir con ella en el ascensor tuve la impresión de retroceder en el tiempo; al abrazar a Blanca creí que volvía a estar con Elena, mucho antes de todo, cuando todavía no nos habíamos casado y ella venía desde Madrid a encontrarse conmigo en un hotel de Zarautz.

—¿Y te despertaste abrazado a Blanca por la mañana? —me preguntó Uzcudun.

—Viéndola dormida y aferrada a mí como una niña pequeña sentí vergüenza por el modo en que la traté en San Sebastián. Tosió tres veces y me preocupé porque estaba desnuda y en estas fechas ya no encienden la calefacción. Cuando hice un nudo con mis piernas y las suyas pensaba más en calentar sus pies que en borrar mi ofensa. Me dormí de nuevo y soñé que Blanca no había existido nunca y que la que tosía a mi lado era una desconocida con la que había tropezado esa noche en un bar de Hendaya.

Uzcudun hizo un gesto de asentimiento, pero su mirada era enigmática, un poco teatral.

—Sin embargo el equipaje de Blanca seguía en la consigna de la estación, ¿no es cierto?

—Como ya te he contado, Blanca se quedó varios días. Los amores eternos me parecen atroces, de modo que no hay pruebas definitivas de que vaya a volver. Por otra parte, ignoro cuánto tiempo permaneceré aquí buscando un desenlace para mi novela.

Me apresuraré a agregar que Uzcudun me encontró nervioso y desmejorado y me convenció de que tengo que despertar de esta novela, poner el punto final definitivo. Quiero quitármela de encima, reconocí, pero tropiezo con esa inercia que tiende a mantenernos enredados dentro de un sueño.

Patxi paseó conmigo frente al mar, observando a los surfistas, como hacíamos Elena y yo en nuestras escapadas a Zarautz, fuera de temporada, antes de quedarse embarazada de Eva, y tomamos café en la pérgola del casino desde donde se divisa la bahía de Hendaya.

La sensatez de Uzcudun suele tranquilizar la virulencia de mis pensamientos. Tiene los dientes pequeños, infantiles, y vocaliza despacio, arrastrando las sílabas con la parsimonia del que está acostumbrado a no ser interrumpido; todo él se desplaza con lentitud de paquidermo, tan enorme como es. Dijo que en resumen mi novela le parecía de una satisfactoria pulcritud. Me reconoció un oído eficaz para ponerle voz y movimientos interiores a un personaje femenino. Junto a esa facilidad para suplantar a una mujer, estaban las imágenes del vagabundo y la escena final en la pensión, a las que se refirió con evidente frialdad. Se preguntaba si los episodios más imprecisos, los que apuro como de pasada y por los que me deslizo de un plumazo, no serían el resultado de una forma de pereza mental. Sin embargo tenía que admitir que la figura del escritor, tan parecido a mí, deambulando a la sombra de Ciorán, estaba puesta en pie con ironía y lirismo y la veía emparentada con el linaje de esos personajes extraviados que pueblan la literatura.

—Aunque en realidad —dijo Patxi— apenas hemos podido meternos en la cabeza de Julio Oroz.

—Es cierto —acepté—, pero recuerda que la historia la está contando Blanca, y además no hemos llegado todavía al final.

Uzcudun se quedó pensativo. Tenía la misma expresión de desconcierto que en el colegio cuando los otros chicos le humillaban. Creo que perdí la dimensión de la realidad durante un momento. Tuve una revelación instantánea: Álvaro Arriaga obligando a Uzcudun a tragar barro cuando éramos niños. Recordé la planta de mi zapato presionando el cuello de Álvaro arrodillado sobre la mole de carne del gordo para forzarle a liberar a Uzcudun, los pantalones de Patxi llenos de tierra cuando se levantó con los ojos llenos de lágrimas y la cara redonda congestionada mientras Arriaga se apartaba y me lanzaba una mirada tan llena de odio como la de Uzcudun al sentirse protegido había estado llena de gratitud.

—Es extraño —dijo Patxi—, siento la misma tristeza que me asalta cada vez que llego a la última estación de un viaje y tengo que bajarme del tren. Pero ahora entiendo algo, ésta no es tu novela, ésta es la novela de Blanca y por eso no sabes cómo va a terminar.

Es noche cerrada y ya no llegan ruidos desde la calle. Espero frente al mar que las cosas sucedan, como han sucedido siempre en mi vida, ajenas a mis maniobras inútiles, a mis intentos de controlar o modificar los acontecimientos. Al final me he dejado llevar. Soy culpable e inocente al mismo tiempo de todo cuanto ha ocurrido. ¿Pude haber salvado a Eva de morir antes de tiempo? Seguramente no. Tampoco pude evitar que Mara Barbieri me entregara su cuerpo en aquel apartamento que ella alquilaba. Veo las crestas blancas de espuma rompiendo en la oscuridad de la playa y pienso que mi vida ha seguido el curso incierto de las olas. En ese oleaje apareció la voz de Blanca. Yo no sé por qué la vibración de una mujer desconocida alteró mi pulso de esa manera y me condujo a esperarla en este lugar vacío, donde ya no hay fantasmas y donde tengo la impresión de poder convertirme en otro hombre. No me arrepiento de detestar a los tipos como Arriaga y tampoco pude evitar el amargo resentimiento, la venenosa bilis y el vómito de asco y desesperación con que pagué a Blanca en San Sebastián. Mis náuseas se habían acumulado durante mucho tiempo, no era nada contra Blanca, pero ella había despertado un resorte en mí y yo necesitaba expulsar los cuerpos extraños, la fetidez y el malestar que venían de más lejos.

Mientras estoy escondido en esta playa, esperando su regreso, porque ustedes tal vez desconfíen, pero yo sé que va a volver, me doy cuenta de que, después de todo, ésta podría ser una historia de amor. Ahora estoy seguro, aunque Blanca puso muchos peros a la posibilidad de un final feliz cuando me hizo destruir el primer cuaderno. Blanca es más dura, más descreída y más realista que yo. Incluso me amenazó con dar su propia versión de los hechos. Está bien, le dije, pero yo no me moveré de aquí hasta que oiga el relato contado por tu voz. De no haber existido Blanca, yo seguiría siendo un muerto viviente en una ciudad del norte.

Veo las olas a lo lejos y me siento renovado: la piel lustrosa y los pensamientos tranquilos. Pienso en el vagabundo recién bañado por la hermana de Blanca. No sabemos en qué dirección conduciría sus pasos. Pero se tuvo que sentir mucho mejor, estoy seguro. No tardaré en escuchar a Blanca, eso es algo que uno sabe, una certeza que crece y se instala como el faro que contemplo desde la ventana, en el espacio borroso de la incertidumbre. En cualquier caso, los caminos se mezclan de pronto en una encrucijada y en un recodo dos pasajeros desconocidos empiezan a respirar al mismo ritmo. Ahora sólo es cuestión de tiempo.

25

No puedo cerrar la puerta tranquilamente y decir: adiós, Miguel, quédate con tu televisor gigante, me espera en Hendaya el autor de *La cueva de los locos*, me voy, Miguel, te he engañado con un amante que encendía mi megafonía sexual, y después con un escritor llamado Julio Oroz, Oroz que se comportó como un cerdo en San Sebastián, ahora dirás que me gusta que me arrastren por los suelos, siempre has dicho eso de mi hermana Marta, nos falta un punto para la demencia, pensarás; puede ser, pero hace meses que me quedo helada a tu lado, dos témpanos, somos dos témpanos haciéndonos los dormidos, no tenemos nada más que decirnos, ya no cantamos en la ducha, ya no nos queda oxígeno para seguir respirando, ya no nos saben las bocas a caramelo de limón, quiero abrir los ojos por la mañana sin que me caiga encima esa mirada de víctima que gastas, como si yo tuviera la culpa de toda la tristeza del mundo, como si yo fuera la malvada de tu película, adiós, Miguel, que te vaya bonito.

No se puede. Debería ser mucho más fácil. Salir corriendo, cerrar la puerta a toda carrera y pillarle al perseguidor los dedos al dar un portazo. No se por qué tiene que ser complicado abandonar a Miguel mientras rellena una quiniela. Podría ser tan sencillo como consolar sus lágrimas de cocodrilo cuando su equipo pierde la liga: lo siento, amigo, no hay nada que hacer, tarde o temprano te recuperarás.

Quizá si Miguel hubiera encontrado en mi bolso una fotografía comprometedora. ¿Quién es este tío? ¿Por qué se pega a ti como una lapa? ¿Dónde está tomada esta foto? ¿Y cuándo has estado tú en Valencia o en Albacete o en Badajoz? Una fotografía delatora da mucho juego para una ruptura tajante, con reproches y lágrimas, con mucho aparato escénico: la fotografía se rompe en mil pedazos, el corazón se rompe en mil pedazos, la pareja, en un abrir y cerrar de ojos, se rompe en mil pedazos. Pero yo no me he retratado con Álvaro Arriaga ni con Julio Oroz, por eso no puedo esconder la fotografía de la deslealtad, ni dar explicaciones que no se me han pedido. ¿Y cómo se llama él? ¿Es más alto que yo? ¿Es más listo que yo? ¿La tiene más grande que yo? ¿Por qué coño se ríe en esta foto? ¿Os estabais riendo de mí? ¿Le has contado algo de mí? La esposa infiel y acorralada gimotea, moquea, lloriquea, se escaquea.

Pero Miguel no dispone de fotografías ni de cartas acusadoras, pregonando mi traición. Yo sólo le he dicho que me ahogo, que nos vemos borrosamente como dos transeúntes que se cruzan en la calle con trayectorias distintas: Miguel se sube a un autobús, yo levanto la mano con un gesto indeciso y paro un taxi. Le he dicho que nuestro silencio no es de resentimiento, ni de amargura, sino tal vez de impotencia y de telarañas sin quitar, por cansancio, por inercia, porque la araña vuelve a tejer sus redes en poquísimo tiempo. ¿Se han fijado alguna vez? Se limpian las telas de araña de las ventanas de una casa en el campo y al día siguiente han vuelto a aparecer, como el verdín resbaladizo en una pila de piedra, como las termitas en la madera, uno cree que ha conseguido acabar con su presencia, la telaraña desaparecida, el verdín restregado, las termitas aniquiladas, pero, al poco, sin darnos cuenta, vuelven a invadir la casa instalándose en nuestras vidas desde la nada.

Fui a Hendaya a por mi coche y a demostrarle a Julio Oroz que no le tenía miedo. Pensaba soltarle un discurso con voz de tango y recuperar mi dignidad cortándole la digestión con insultos rápidos y mortíferos como balas. Les aseguro que no estaba dispuesta a arrastrarme ante él. Después quería llevarme mi coche y olvidarme de su nombre para siempre. Pero cuando encontré a Oroz con cara de haber perdido sus pocas posesiones tras una riada, supe que mi sino era sacar del fango a los damnificados.

Estoy escribiendo nuestra novela, dice Oroz. ¿Nuestra novela?, será tu novela, le digo. Me hace leer uno de sus cuadernos de un tirón. Al principio todo me sonaba extraño pero luego comprendí que él necesitaba que la princesa-de-la-voz-de-orgasmo comiese perdices con él para justificar su vuelo de aviador errático que no tiene la más remota idea de dónde aterrizar. Miro el cuaderno de Oroz y luego le miro a él. Le digo que su final feliz es falso. Le digo que todos los finales felices son falsos. Le digo que yo no he terminado de contar mi historia, que tal vez mi historia no va a tener un desenlace definitivo. Te dejaré amarme durante unas cuantas noches y después regresaré a Madrid y me lo pensaré. Puse mi mejor voz de heroína de todos los cuentos para hacer semejante declaración. Permítanme que les diga la verdad, la primera noche prendimos una hoguera en la terraza para quemar el cuaderno y después organizamos un incendio con nuestros cuerpos en la cama. En medio de las llamas Julio me pidió esa noche, y las noches siguientes, que dejase a Miguel de una vez por todas.

Hoy había una gran jornada futbolística en televisión. Miguel estaba concentrado en la pantalla. Tenemos que hablar, le he dicho al tiempo que se escuchaba mi susurro más sensual en un anuncio que yo había grabado: *Apolo, el aroma de los hombres de hierro*. Se veían piernas musculosas en el vestuario de un gimnasio y torsos de mármol rociados con la dichosa colonia. *El aroma de los hombres que se comen el mundo*, musitaba mi voz pidiendo guerra, igual que había musitado tantas veces en la cama con Álvaro Arriaga. La siguiente imagen era la de un estadio abarrotado con una multitud vociferante. Yo sabía que había elegido un mal momento, pero lo he hecho a propósito; quería saber si nuestro naufragio podía competir con el partido del siglo. Tenemos que hablar, he insistido. Miguel me ha mirado sin verme. Ahora no, ha contestado con tajante frialdad.

He salido a la calle con una pequeña maleta. No he dicho adiós. Seguramente Miguel no me hubiera escuchado porque en ese momento había un griterío infernal en la pantalla. Ha sido fácil, después de todo. Sólo he tenido que cerrar la puerta.

Mi hermana me contempla preocupada mientras despliego estas páginas en el escritorio de su habitación de huéspedes. ¿Qué vas a hacer ahora?, me pregunta. No lo sé, Marta, pero me siento bien, estoy perdida y no estoy asustada, tal vez deba extraviarme entre la niebla para encontrarme, todavía tengo que acabar de escribir esta historia y un aviador sin rumbo está pensando en mi voz en mitad de la noche.

ESTE LIBRO HA SIDO IMPRESO
EN LOS TALLERES DE
LIMPERGRAF. MOGODA, 29
BARBERÀ DEL VALLÈS (BARCELONA)

LAO-TZU

TAO TE CHING

TRANSLATION OF THE
MA WANG TUI MANUSCRIPTS
BY D.C. LAU

EDITED AND INTRODUCED
BY SARAH ALLAN

EVERYMAN'S LIBRARY
Alfred A. Knopf New York London Toronto

158

THIS IS A BORZOI BOOK
PUBLISHED BY ALFRED A. KNOPF

First included in Everyman's Library, 1994 (US); 2017 (UK)
The English translation of the *Tao te ching* by D. C. Lau, using the traditional Wang
Pi text, was first published in 1963 by Penguin Books Ltd., England. A bilingual
edition with the 1963 translation and the Wang Pi text was published by The
Chinese University Press, Hong Kong with the addition of a second part consisting
of a translation of the text discovered in 1973 at Ma Wang Tui together with the
original text. A further edition in which the Ma Wang Tui translation was revised
was published by The Chinese University Press in 1989. The present translation is
the revised Ma Wang Tui translation of the 1989 edition.

© D. C. Lau 1963, 1982, 1989, 2001

This edition is licensed by The Chinese University Press of Hong Kong.

D. C. Lau's Appendices and Glossary were originally published in the 1963 edition
of the Wang Pi text and are included by kind permission of Penguin Books Ltd

Introduction, Bibliography and Chronology Copyright © 1994
by Everyman's Library
Typography by Peter B. Willberg
Sixteenth printing (US)

All rights reserved. Published in the United States by Alfred A. Knopf, a division of
Penguin Random House LLC, New York, and in Canada by Penguin Random
House Canada Limited, Toronto. Distributed by Penguin Random House LLC,
New York. Published in the United Kingdom by Everyman's Library, 50 Albemarle
Street, London W1S 4BD and distributed by Penguin Random House UK,
20 Vauxhall Bridge Road, London SW1V 2SA.

www.randomhouse.com/everymans
www.everymanslibrary.co.uk

ISBN: 978-0-679-43316-3 (US)
978-1-85715-158-9 (UK)

A CIP catalogue reference for this book is available from the
British Library

Library of Congress Cataloging-in-Publication Data
Lao-tzu.
[Tao te ching. English]
Tao te ching / Lao Tzu.
p.   cm.—(Everyman's library)
Includes bibliographical references.
ISBN 978-0-679-43316-3
I. Title.
BL1900.L26E5   1994   94-8353
299´.51482–dc20   CIP

Book design by Barbara de Wilde and Carol Devine Carson
Typeset in the UK by AccComputing, North Barrow, Somerset
Printed and bound in Germany by GGP Media GmbH, Pössneck

CONTENTS

COMPARATIVE TABLE

———

In the Ma Wang Tui manuscripts, the *Te Ching* precedes the *Tao Ching* and some sections are in a different order. Readers interested in comparing this translation of the Ma Wang Tui

MA WANG TUI	WANG PI	MA WANG TUI	WANG PI
TE CHING		TE CHING	
1	XXXVIII	23	LX
2	XXXIX	24	LXI
3	XLI	25	LXII
4	XL	26	LXIII
5	XLII	27	LXIV
6	XLIII	28	LXV
7	XLIV	29	LXVI
8	XLV	30	LXXX
9	XLVI	31	LXXXI
10	XLVII	32	LXVII
11	XLVIII	33	LXVIII
12	XLIX	34	LXIX
13	L	35	LXX
14	LI	36	LXXI
15	LII	37	LXXII
16	LIII	38	LXXIII
17	LIV	39	LXXIV
18	LV	40	LXXV
19	LVI	41	LXXVI
20	LVII	42	LXXVII
21	LVIII	43	LXXVIII
22	LIX	44	LXXIX

manuscripts with translations of the Wang Pi text may find the following table comparing chapter numbers useful.

MA WANG TUI	WANG PI	MA WANG TUI	WANG PI
TAO CHING		TAO CHING	
45	I	64	XX
46	II	65	XXI
47	III	66	XXIV
48	IV	67	XXII
49	V	68	XXIII
50	VI	69	XXV
51	VII	70	XXVI
52	VIII	71	XXVII
53	IX	72	XXVIII
54	X	73	XXIX
55	XI	74	XXX
56	XII	75	XXXI
57	XIII	76	XXXII
58	XIV	77	XXXIII
59	XV	78	XXXIV
60	XVI	79	XXXV
61	XVII	80	XXXVI
62	XVIII	81	XXXVII
63	XIX		

INTRODUCTION

The period from the fifth to third centuries BC was the golden age of Chinese philosophy. Politically, however, it was a time of increasingly vicious civil war, a period of Chinese history in which 'one hundred schools of thought contended', as numerous small states were defeated and taken over by their more powerful neighbours. The Chou Dynasty (*c.* 1100–222 BC) had been founded by an alliance of tribes. The Chou empire may never have been quite as vast as that of the previous dynasty, the Shang, but it covered much of the territory now designated as China, and the Chou rulers created a type of feudal system in which their relatives and allies had charge of various states. In 771 BC, however, rebellions and tribal incursions from the West forced the Chou rulers to move their capital eastward. From this time on, their power began to decline and that of the individual states to increase. The years from 722–481 BC are known as the Spring and Autumn Period, after the title of a history of the state of Lu, attributed to Confucius (551–479 BC). The following period during which Chou suzerainty ceased to even be acknowledged is called the Warring States (480–222 BC).

The Confucianists and the Taoists were only two of the many 'schools of thought' which contended, but they were the two which had the most long-lasting significance. Conceptually opposed in origin (and not entirely unitary as schools), they came to be regarded as two complementary aspects of human life in the later Chinese tradition: the public and the private; or the conformist and intellectual, as opposed to the natural and spontaneous. The Confucianists, whose major works were the *Analects* of Confucius, the *Mencius*, and the *Hsun-tzu*, provided the political and ethical foundations for the Chinese state and society until modern times; the Taoists, whose major works were the *Lao-tzu* and the *Chuang-tzu*, its creative and aesthetic impetus.

The philosophers spoke to the turmoil of their time. Confucius, and most other philosophers, saw the past as a golden age in which sage rulers handed down their power to virtuous men of their own choosing. Then, when the virtue of the ancients began to decline, came the period of the three dynasties – the Hsia, founded when the mythical Yu controlled the great flood; the Shang; and the Chou – in which rule was handed down hereditarily. They asked about the nature of political and social order and how it could be restored. The *Lao-tzu*, on the other hand, addressed those who sought to survive, though their initial position appeared to be one of weakness. It saw the activities of the sages as the cause of decline in the world and it did not look to the social order of the past for a model of behaviour, but to an intuitive understanding of the order of the natural world. Power lies with him who understands the principles of nature. And in nature, it is the soft and yielding, the passive and feminine, who survive when the hard and strong and active have given way.

Confucius (551–479 BC) was the first philosopher in ancient China; that is, he was the first thinker to form a school of followers who recorded his thoughts and transmitted them to posterity. Thus his philosophy forms the background against which the *Lao-tzu* was composed although no two works could be more radically different than Confucius' *Analects* and the *Lao-tzu*. Confucius was primarily concerned with ethics and political philosophy. The empire had already begun to disintegrate by his time and he looked back to an idealized conception of the early Chou Dynasty for a model which would bring peace to a troubled world. In this model, the empire was ruled by a sage king appointed by heaven on the basis of his virtue. The sage king appointed sage ministers who ruled according to the principles of benevolence (*ren*) and rectitude (*yi*), caring for and nurturing the people. In return, the people gave them their allegiance and recognized their right of sovereignty, loving them as a child loves his father and mother, for the ruler nourished and provided for them as a parent.

Confucius' philosophy was hierarchical and conservative, but it was also a radical reinterpretation of traditional religious ideas. The family provided the model for the state, which was based on the most primary of human emotions and relationships, the love between parents and their children.

Ancestral reverence became filial piety, a standard of ethical behaviour towards one's parents (and still, in performing the traditional ceremonies, towards one's ancestors). Although the ruler was appointed by heaven, heaven was a vague, impersonal force which would automatically appoint the man of true virtue. The Confucianists were specialists in ritual – and they were ridiculed by the Taoists for their love of archaic ceremony and the strange garments of antiquity, but ritual took on a new meaning, as a means of ordering relations between people in a chaotic world. The ideal of a 'gentleman' (*chun-tzu*, literally 'lord's son') was transformed from an hereditary class into a general standard of ethical behaviour.

The Confucian idea of the cosmos was one which was morally ordered, although there were no supernatural rewards or sanctions for individual behaviour. A man was good simply because it was the supreme expression of human being. He should study the ancients and learn to behave with benevolence and rectitude. Because the cosmos was ordered, a key to correcting the disorder which plagued his own time was the correction of names, i.e. the recognition of things as they truly were, so that the proper hierarchy could be re-established. A 'king' was not a 'king' unless he acted as a father and mother of the people; a 'gentleman' was not a 'gentleman' unless he behaved as such. Whatever position a man held, if he behaved immorally, he was a criminal and an outcast.

Confucius was a well-known historical figure, but we know almost nothing about the author of the *Lao-tzu*. The *Records of the Grand Historian (Shih chi)*, the compilation of which was finished in the early first century BC, records various conflicting accounts from which we know only that the history of the text was already lost. It includes one account that Lao-tzu was named Li Erh. However, no other early text refers to Li Erh, and Lao may be a surname. *Tzu* means 'master', so Lao-tzu could mean 'Master Lao'. The early texts speak of a certain Lao Tan, an older contemporary of Confucius (551–479 BC), whom he consulted on ritual matters and who, at least according to the Taoist Chuang-tzu, gave Confucius lessons in the futility of his attempts to strive for worldly success, calling him by his own name, as though he were a lowly student.

If this figure is the author, the text would date to the sixth century BC. However, there is reason for suspicion. The identification of the author of the *Lao-tzu* with someone to whom Confucius deferred in his most prized sphere, ritual, gives the Taoists precedence over the Confucians and there are many humorous stories in which Lao-tzu ridicules Confucius' pretensions and pomposity. Lao also means 'old' and so 'Lao-tzu' may simply mean 'Old Master'. There was a fashion in the late fourth to third centuries BC for giving texts this type of mysterious and anonymous authorship. Evidence for dating the text is still inconclusive, but modern scholarly opinion generally dates the text to this period on the basis of its language and ideas within the development of early Chinese thought.

Scholars generally agree that the text was addressed to the ruler of a small and weak state, but the nature of the text is also still in question. It is partly in prose and partly in verse – D.C. Lau has indented the verse sections in his translation – and includes some lines which appear in other texts as proverbs or common sayings. Some scholars, such as Lau, regard it as primarily an anthology of earlier writing; others, such as A.C. Graham, as primarily a long poem. Most agree, however, that it was not an entirely unified text, written by one hand at one time, but one that includes material which is earlier than its final date of compilation.*

The text may be called by its author, 'the *Lao-tzu*' – many early Chinese texts are named in this manner – or by the title *Tao te ching*. *Ching* means 'classic' and the term was applied to a canon of texts which were studied in the imperial academy and used for examinations. The *Tao te ching* was given this status in the Tang Dynasty (AD 618–907). It kept the title although it was not always so honoured in later dynasties. It is divided into two parts, the *Tao ching* and the *Te ching*. *Tao* is usually translated as the 'way' and it is the first word of the *Tao ching*; *te* is usually translated as 'virtue' or 'power' (following Arthur Waley), and it is the first important word in the *Te ching*. *Tao* gave Taoism its name and is discussed more

* For detailed discussions of the problem of authorship and the nature of the work, see Appendices 1 and 2 (by D. C. Lau).

frequently than *te* in the text, but both terms are significant.

The *Lao-tzu* does not mention Confucianism – or any other early school of thought – but many of its statements should be understood in the context of the other philosophical schools. It specifically rejects the value of the sages and their learning: 'Exterminate the sage, discard the wise; and the people will benefit a hundredfold' (63). And the specifically Confucian virtues of benevolence (*ren*) and rectitude (*yi*) and the rites (*li*), are designated as representing the beginning of the decline, the loss of the way which ensued when self-conscious virtues began to be cultivated: 'When the way was lost there was virtue; when virtue was lost there was benevolence; when benevolence was lost there was rectitude; when rectitude was lost there were the rites. Now the rites are the wearing thin of conscientiousness and good faith and the beginning of disorder' (1). The *Lao-tzu*'s point here is not, however simply to reject Confucianism *per se*, but to reject moralizing and the 'meddling' of the sage, which goes against the grain of the natural conduct of human affairs.

Tao, the 'way', is a common term in all early Chinese philosophical texts. The Confucianists, for example, speak of the 'way of a [true] king', the 'way of a sage' or even the 'way' of the archetypical historical villains. In the *Lao-tzu* the 'way' is a first principle, that which precedes and engenders all else: 'The way begets one; one begets two; two begets three, three begets the myriad creatures' (5). We are told again that the way is indescribable, something which is beyond the limitations which words would place upon it. It cannot be named because to name it would make it specific and: 'the way is shadowy, indistinct . . .' (65). Its most common metaphor, that which the *Lao-tzu* accepts as most like it, is water, and like water, it is indivisible.

In the *Lao-tzu*, the way takes the supreme position; in Confucianism and other early philosophical schools, this role was played by heaven. By the late Spring and Autumn and Warring States periods, heaven was an impersonal force, not a deity, that which was responsible for the morally ordered cosmos. Although the Confucianists spoke of heaven as 'appointing' the king, this mandate was awarded mechanically in reaction to virtue (or removed when the people were too oppressed). Even to Mo-tzu (*fl.* fifth century BC), the philosopher with the most interest in the supernatural, heaven had no personal identity. He argued that 'loving without discrimination', was the will of heaven, but his proof lay in a demonstration that this was the principle which would bring benefit to the largest number of people, not in any personal revelation. To understand heaven, the early philosophers agreed, one should study the patterns of ancient history.

The *Lao-tzu* is unique among the early philosophical texts in making no reference at all to previous dynasties or the archetypical historical figures who were the established currency of philosophical debate. Heaven appears in the *Lao-tzu* as the counterpart of earth, but both were preceded by the way. The way was not the way of a morally interested heaven, as it sometimes appears in the Confucian texts, but a spontaneous natural order, 'that which is naturally so': 'Man models himself on earth, earth on heaven, heaven on the way, and the way on that which is naturally so' (69). Rather than studying the patterns of ancient history to understand the order of heaven, the true sage of the *Lao-tzu* cleared his mind and intuitively grasped the movements of nature.

The counterpart of *tao*, the way, is *te. Te*, 'virtue', is also a common term in Confucianism and other philosophical schools. In the *Lao-tzu*, it may be used derogatorily to refer to the moral value, 'virtue', as cultivated by the sage. The *Lao-tzu* continually stresses the feminine aspects of the *tao* as a first principle, but when *tao* is paired with *te*, *te* takes the female role, 'The way gives them life and virtue rears them' (14). As the counterpart of the way, *te* is the specific as opposed to the general. It is that which is incipient in something, its nature or virtue. Thus, it is at its most intense before it is developed: 'One who possesses virtue in abundance is comparable to a new-born babe' (18). In man, it may suggest a kind of charismatic power, and the Chinese scholar Qiu Xigui and the Russian, Vassili Kryukov, have both suggested recently that its history and early usage are comparable to that of the term *mana* in Polynesia.

Dualism is an important aspect of the *Lao-tzu* and it is

continually used to break down conventional preconceptions. The terms *yin* and *yang* are only used once in the text, but the relationship of the pairs is that which was later expressed in terms of *yin/yang* theory, i.e. complementary pairs of opposites which mutually require one another: 'Something and Nothing producing each other; the difficult and the easy complementing each other; the long and short off-setting each other ... These are in accordance with what is constant. Hence the sage dwells in the deed that consists in taking no action and practises the teaching that uses no words' (46).

The concept of 'taking no action' (*wu wei*) is a critical one in the *Lao-tzu* and its meaning has been much discussed by scholars. The 'action' which is to be avoided is that which is deliberate, conscious, thought out, rather than spontaneous accord with the patterns of nature. Water, which takes no conscious action, but overcomes the strongest obstacle, is an important metaphor in understanding the meaning of this term: 'The most submissive thing in the world can ride roughshod over the most unyielding in the world – that which is without substance entering that which has no gaps. That is why I know the benefit of taking no action' (6). *Wu wei* is often translated as 'doing nothing', but the negative (*wu*) modifies the 'doing'; it is not that one does nothing, but that there is no 'action' which is not spontaneous.

The *Lao-tzu*'s cosmos is patterned according to natural laws, and the true sage who 'dwells in the deed which consists in taking no action', behaves according to the patterns which are 'naturally so'. The Taoist cosmos is not, however, morally ordered like that of the Confucians. 'Heaven and earth are ruthless; they treat the myriad creatures as straw dogs. The sage is ruthless; he treats the people as straw dogs' (49). 'Straw dogs' are traditionally interpreted as straw figures used in the sacrificial rites and then discarded. Lau's translation of 'ruthless' here is, perhaps, misleading. More literally, 'Heaven and earth are not benevolent', that is, nature is not morally ordered, but indifferent, and the true sage should also be indifferent, not guided by artificially created moral values such as 'benevolence'.

In presenting its pairs, the *Lao-tzu* continually stresses the superior value of that which is normally regarded as inferior: the low rather than the high, nothing rather than something – 'Knead clay in order to make a vessel. Make the nothing therein appropriate, and you will have the use of the clay vessel' (55). Most strikingly, the female is always presented as superior to the male – 'Know the male, but keep to the role of the female' (72). The role of the female is to submit passively, but ultimately it is she who is productive whereas the male wears himself out with his exertions (both in the sexual act itself and in his striving for success in the world): 'In the intercourse of the world, the female always gets the better of the male by stillness' (24). It is the female who in her submissiveness represents the ideal of 'taking no action' and the female (associated with water and valleys) who is the ultimate source: 'The spirit of the valley never dies; this is called the dark female. The entry into the dark female is called the root of heaven and earth. Tenuous, it seems as if it were there, yet use will never exhaust it' (50).

The role of the male – or the Confucian sage – is one of 'acting with ulterior motives'; that of the female, to 'take no action'. Submissiveness does not, however, imply the acceptance of defeat, but has a positive strategic value: 'The most submissive thing in the world can ride roughshod over the most unyielding' – water may overcome stone, as we have already seen. 'He who is fearless in being bold will meet with his death; he who is fearless in being timid will stay alive' (38); 'One who is good at overcoming his adversary does not join issue with him' (33). This aspect of the *Lao-tzu*, will, of course, be well known to those who practise any type of martial arts and it became an essential part of later Chinese works on military strategy, such as the *Sun-tzu*.

*

No Chinese work has been translated into English as many times as the *Lao-tzu*. Possibly, no work in any language has as many different English renderings. There are many reasons why this text has been translated so often: It speaks of the ineffable in a secular manner, taking the natural world for its imagery, so that its message seems to transcend time and place. The classical Chinese in which it is written is richly ambiguous so that many interpretations of individual lines are often possible. The original language is also so distant from modern English that no translation can fully reflect its meaning. No translation is ever definitive, however accurate; other possibilities always remain.

The nature of the text and the problems in translation can perhaps best be approached by looking at a few lines of the original Chinese in some detail, together with some translations. The Chinese characters for the first four lines of the *Tao ching* are given in Figure 1a (p. xxiii). This version of the text is the most common of the various editions transmitted from antiquity. Figure 1b (p. xxiii) is the version of the text found on the silk manuscripts excavated at Ma Wang Tui in 1973. The modern pronunciation of each character is written below it. Classical Chinese was largely monosyllabic and so each character represents a word. Grammar was contained in the word order and the addition of grammatical particles rather than by changes in word form. Characters are sometimes useful in understanding the etymology of a word, as, for example, are Latin or Greek origins in English, but they were already highly conventionalized representations, containing both semantic and phonetic elements, not pictographs as sometimes supposed.

Let us first look at the text associated with the commentator Wang Pi. The following are three translations of the Chinese text reproduced in Figure 1a (p. xxiii):

D. C. Lau (1963):

> The way that can be spoken of is not the constant way;
> The name that can be named is not the constant name.
> The nameless was the beginning of heaven and earth;
> The named was the mother of the myriad creatures.

Arthur Waley (*The Way and its Power*, 1939):

The Way that can be told is not an Unvarying Way;
The names that can be named are not the unvarying names.
It was from the Nameless that Heaven and Earth sprang.
The named is by the mother that rears the ten thousand creatures,
    each after its own kind.

Rhett Y. W. Young and Roger Ames, based on the interpretation of Ch'en Ku-ying (*Lao-tzu: Text, Notes and Comments*,
Chinese Materials Center, 1981):

> The Tao which can be spoken of is not the eternal Tao:
> The name which can be named is not the eternal Name.
> 'Non-being' names this beginning of Heaven and Earth;
> 'Being' names the mother of the myriad things.

The first character, *tao*, left untranslated by Young and
Ames, is rendered as the 'Way' by Waley and Lau. It is, of
course, a key term, that from which the Taoists derive their
name, but, as the text tells us, it is ineffable. 'Way' is the
conventional English translation, and the Chinese word is
similar in that it may suggest either a physical course – the
way from here to there – or a metaphorical one – the way in
which we conduct ourselves. The Confucianists usually
employed the term in this sense; speaking, for example, of the
way of a true king or the way of a sage. However, to the
Taoists, it was also a first principle, the natural order (which
the Confucianists called 'Heaven') – the way of all the things
in the cosmos and that which precedes and generates them.
The character itself consists of a head element, which was
probably a phonetic indicator, and a semantic element which
refers to movement.

The second character, *k'o*, is a grammatical particle which
also indicates that the following is a verb in the passive sense.
It is the source of the 'can be ... -ed' in all three translations.

The third character, *tao*, is the same as the first, but we
know from the preceding *k'o* that it should be taken as a verb
here, the '*tao* [which] can be *taoed*'. *Tao*, as a verb, may mean
to 'speak of' or 'tell'. The ancient Chinese commentaries agree
that it has this meaning here and it makes a pun. It has,
however, caused disquiet among some translators, who would
prefer a verb more closely linked to the meaning of the noun,
especially since they are written with the same character.
Thus, for example, Victor Mair translates this line as 'the
ways' – classical Chinese nouns do not indicate number, so *tao*
may be either singular or plural – 'which can be walked'.
Unfortunately, however, *tao* is not used to mean 'to walk' in

Figure 1*

a)

道可道非常道
tao k'o tao fei ch'ang tao

名可名非常名
ming k'o ming fei ch'ang ming

無名天地之始
wu ming t'ian ti chih shih

有名萬物之母
yu ming wan wu chih mu

b)

道可道也非亙道也
tao k'o tao ye fei heng tao ye

名可名也非亙名也
ming k'o ming ye fei heng ming ye

无名萬物之始也
wu ming wan wu chih shih ye

有名萬物之母也
yu ming wan wu chih mu ye

*Calligraphy by Roderick Whitfield

xxiii

classical Chinese texts, although it may mean 'to lead' or 'guide' (a homonym, usually written with the addition of a hand element). The cleverest rendering of this line is, perhaps, that hit upon by the non-specialist, Alan Watts: 'The course which can be discoursed.'

The next character, *fei*, is again a grammatical particle, a negative copula: A *fei* B means A is not B. (Chinese has no verb 'to be' equivalent to the English copula or to the existential usage of the English verb.)

Ch'ang modifies the *tao* which follows it. Our three translations are 'constant', 'unvarying' and 'eternal'. 'Eternal' is particularly misleading because it brings to mind 'eternity' and is associated with our own ideas of a transcendent reality which are absent from ancient Chinese thought. The *tao* may go on and on, but there is no concept of 'forever' in the absolute sense in early China. Furthermore, although the ineffable *tao* is, in a sense, constant or invariant, such constancy encompasses all the regular changes of the natural order. Classical Chinese is also devoid of articles, such as 'the' or 'a', so Waley renders the line as 'not *an* unvarying way' rather than '*the* unvarying way'.

The second line is identical to the first except that it concerns *ming*, rather than *tao*. *Ming* means 'name' and, as a verb, 'to name'; thus 'the name that can be named is not the constant name' (Lau). This line has a further philosophical significance beyond the simple recognition of the impermanence of language. The Confucianists argued that names should be rectified; by recognizing things for what they were and calling them by the correct name, order could be restored in the world. Mencius (fourth century BC and probably roughly contemporary to the *Lao-tzu*) argued, for example, that a 'king' was one who acted as such, and only such a person deserved obeisance; those who held the position but did not fulfill the role, should not be so named, or recognized. On the other hand, if one acted as a 'king' – were a 'father and mother to the people' – one could unify the whole empire and the people would give their allegiance to the 'king' rather than to the 'outcasts' who claimed to be king.

Lao-tzu, however, perceived that all of these names and the

positions to which they were attached were ephemeral. Indeed, the recognition of the artificiality of language and the futility of striving for success are two of the major themes in the text. In our own conceptual scheme (which is closely tied to both its Judeo-Christian religious origins and the philosophical tradition of ancient Greece, as well as its Indo-European linguistic origins), opposites, such as black and white, good and bad, high and low, are usually understood as antagonistic. In the Chinese tradition, however, opposites are normally conceived of as polarities or complementary pairs: black implies white, the concept of good requires bad. And, as the *Lao-tzu* is never tired of telling us, he who reaches great heights will inevitably fall to great depths. The seed becomes a plant, fruits and 'returns to its root'. The names which we give to things will inevitably cease to represent reality, they are not the 'constant names' or the indivisible *tao*.

The question of names is continued in the third and fourth lines. *Wu*, the first character in the third line, is another negative and it is usually understood as modifying the following character, *ming*; thus, *wu ming* means 'nameless'. The third character in this line, *t'ien*, means 'heaven' or 'sky' and *ti* means 'earth'. 'Heaven and earth' is the conventional way of referring to the world in general, the cosmos in its various manifestations. *Chih* is a grammatical particle which indicates that 'heaven and earth' modify the next character, *shih*: 'beginning', 'source'. Two nouns placed together in classical Chinese are usually a copula, i.e. A B means 'A is (or was) B'. Thus, Lau's translation: 'The nameless was the beginning of heaven and earth.'

The fourth line begins with *yu*, the opposite of the negative *wu*. *Yu-ming* means 'having a name' or, 'the named', in Lau's and Waley's translations. *Wan* means 'ten thousand' and is used as a general term similar to 'myriad'. *Wu* is sometimes translated as 'creatures' and sometimes as 'things'. In fact, in classical Chinese, it does not refer to objects, but includes all living or animate things, plants as well as animals, a category for which there is no ready equivalent in English, which distinguishes men and other 'creatures' in a radical manner from plant life. From the nameless, then, sprang heaven and earth, but the named or the giving of names gave birth to the myriad different (i.e. differentiated) things.

Young and Ames' translation (following Ch'en Ku-ying) of these two lines is quite different. According to one traditional commentary, *wu* and *yu* should be taken as nouns in this line and *ming* as a verb. Thus, *wu* names (*ming*) heaven and earth's beginning and *yu* names the mother of the myriad living things. But what are *wu* and *yu*? As I have already noted, there is no classical Chinese verb which is strictly equivalent to the English verb to 'be' as a copula or in its existential sense, and the translation 'Non-being' and 'Being', with their connotations of transcendence, are misleading, even if one accepts the grammar. *Yu* means to 'have' as a verb, it is that which is there, something; *wu* is the negative form of *yu*, to 'not have', that which is not there, nothing. According to the *Lao-tzu*, from that which is not there comes that which is there. And that which is there will become that which is not there. This refers to a natural cycle. *Wu* is not a transcendent plane nor an absolute reality; nor is it in exclusive opposition to *yu*, for we are told again that 'some thing' implies its absence, and its absence, the thing itself.

Another reason for different translations is the great number of variant versions of the original text. The work is relatively short (around five thousand characters) and it must have been memorized and then recorded by different people at different times, often with slight variations. In copying the text, people occasionally made errors. They also compared different manuscripts, making their own emendations, so that there are now hundreds of extant editions. Most of these differences are minor, but, as we have already seen, the text is already rich in ambiguity. Some of the extant copies are over one thousand years old, including stone engravings from the Tang Dynasty (AD 618–907). There are also some earlier fragmentary manuscripts still extant, including one partial manuscript which is dated to the equivalent of AD 279.

Most versions of the *Lao-tzu* can be grouped together as editions associated with one of the main commentary traditions. That usually translated into English is the Wang Pi edition; i.e. the edition associated with the commentary written by Wang Pi (AD 226–49). The other main commentary tradition is that of Ho-shang Kung (probably written in the Eastern Han, i.e. AD 25–220). Wang Pi's commentary is favoured by Western scholars because it is more interesting philosophically, whereas the Ho-shang Kung commentary is associated with popular religious beliefs and cosmology and so-called 'religious Taoism'. In 1973, however, archaeologists unearthed two copies of this text written on silk from a Han Dynasty (206 BC–AD 220) tomb, at Ma Wang Tui, near Changsha, in Hunan Province. The tomb in which they were placed was that of the son of a man called Li Ts'ang, the Marquis of Tai and prime minister of the small state which was centred in Changsha. It included over fifty items of text written on silk or on slips of bamboo or wood. An inventory slip (to record the grave goods buried with the deceased) tells us that the burial took place on the equivalent of 4 April 168 BC.

People were forbidden to write the characters in the names of deceased emperors, and these tabooed characters are one means of dating a text. Of the two copies from Ma Wang Tui, Copy A observed no Han Dynasty taboos at all and so we may surmise that it was written before the death of the first Han emperor in 195 BC. Copy B observed the taboos on the founder's name, but not those of his successor and so it must have been copied between 195 and 180 BC. The two copies are not identical, but they are very close, and most scholars regard them as representatives of a single textual tradition. Their primary importance is that they include many grammatical particles which are absent from later versions and these often help to clarify the text. There are also a few important substantive differences. For example, the phrase *wu wei er wu pu wei*, literally 'taking no action, there is no not acting', which has caused much puzzlement and debate, does not occur in the excavated texts at all. Unfortunately, the Ma Wang Tui manuscripts contain not only differences but some obvious errors in copying and they are not the definitive answer to all textual problems. They do represent, however, an important advance in our knowledge of the original text.

Let us look, for example, at the four lines we have already

discussed as they appear in the Ma Wang Tui text. The Chinese is given in Figure 1b. The characters here are written in the style of the excavated text, whereas those in Figure 1a are written in a modern form. The primary difference from the Wang Pi edition we have already looked at (Figure 1a) is the addition of a grammatical particle *ye*. In the first line, this occurs after *tao k'o tao* and after *fei ch'ang tao*. *Ye* indicates a copula; A B, as we have noted, may mean A is B. The addition of the grammatical particle makes the grammar more explicit, eliminating ambiguity: A B *ye* means A is B, so the way *is* what can be spoken; and *fei* B *ye* means [it] is not B (the constant way), as before. Thus, D. C. Lau, in his revised translation based on the Ma Wang Tui manuscripts – the translation which we include here – now translates this line and the following one as:

> The way can be spoken of, but it will not be the constant way;
> The name can be named, but it will not be the constant name.

The effect of the discovery of the Ma Wang Tui text, in this line at least, is to reduce the number of possible interpretations. Another difference in the Ma Wang Tui version is that it has *heng*, where the later versions have *ch'ang*. The meaning is very similar (although 'eternal' is even less likely as a translation); the difference is that when *heng* was tabooed under the reign of the Han emperor Wen (reigned 179–156 BC), whose personal name was Liu Heng, *ch'ang* was substituted for it.

The addition of the final particle *ye* at the end of the third and fourth lines has a similar effect of clarifying the grammar. It clearly suggests a copula in which *wu ming* and *yu ming* act as nouns, making Ch'en Ku-ying's interpretation unlikely to be correct. In the third and fourth lines of the Ma Wang Tui version, *wan wu*, 'myriad creatures', is repeated:

> The nameless was the beginning of the myriad creatures;
> The named was the mother of the myriad creatures.

Whether the 'heaven and earth' of the Wang Pi version in the third line is still correct is a matter of debate: some scholars have suggested that 'myriad creatures' was copied inadvertently. Or, the point may be that the named gave birth to the distinctions whereas the nameless was the beginning of the creatures themselves.

Traditionally, the *Tao ching* was placed before the *Te ching*. Both copies from Ma Wang Tui, on the other hand, place the *Te ching* before the *Tao ching* and that is the order adopted here. The traditional order in which the Classic of the Way comes before that of Virtue means that the text begins with the most general and it tends to stress the cosmological, rather than the socio-political. The 'way' is emphasized, rather than good government and individual behaviour, although both sections include important chapters on both themes. Which order is correct is uncertain. Some scholars have suggested that the placement of the Classic of Virtue first was a device of the Legalist school of philosophers, rather than the original order, to emphasize the political potential of the text as they interpreted it, but the evidence is inconclusive. The text can be read in either manner and many readers may still find that they prefer to begin with the *Tao ching*.

Another distinction of the Ma Wang Tui copies is that they are not divided up into chapters. Traditionally, the text had eighty-one chapters. This division seems to have been made around the first century BC and probably reflects ancient Chinese numerology. The number nine was the number of the divisions of the earth (a square with nine parts) and also the number of the fullness of *yang* in the *yin/yang* cosmology which was attached to the *Yi ching* (*Classic of Changes*). Magically, nine, nine times, was a particularly powerful number. There is, however, still some uncertainty about where some of the chapters begin and end, and the order of some of the passages in the Ma Wang Tui copies is different from that in the Wang Pi edition. However, traditional chapter divisions have been retained for ease of reference. Some parts of the *Lao-tzu* are in prose and some in verse. In D. C. Lau's translation the rhymed passages have been indented.

Although the *Lao-tzu* tells us that the way that can be spoken of is not the constant way, it also states: 'My words are very easy to understand and very easy to put into practice, yet amongst men there is no one who is able to understand them and there is no one who is able to put them into practice' (35).

According to A.C. Graham, the 'Taoist relaxes the body, calms the mind, loosens the grip of categories made habitual by naming, frees the current of thought for more fluid differentiations and assimilations, and instead of pondering choices lets his problems solve themselves as inclination spontaneously finds its own direction, which is the Way.'

The power of the *Lao-tzu*'s imagery and, ultimately, the simplicity of its message seem to be able to overcome the problems of language and of distance in time and place, so that at the end of the twentieth century, this has become one of the most influential of texts, cherished by people in all walks of life throughout the world, some with the most superficial of understandings, others with a more profound one, none perhaps truly able to 'put the words into practice', but many finding them valuable nevertheless.

Sarah Allan

SELECT BIBLIOGRAPHY

OTHER IMPORTANT TRANSLATIONS

CHAN, WING-TSIT, *The Way of Lao Tzu*, Bobbs-Merrill, Indianapolis, 1963.

CH'EN KU-YING, *Lao-tzu: Text, Notes and Comments*, trans. Rhett Y. W. Young and Roger Ames, Chinese Materials Center, San Francisco, 1981. Includes a translation of the text with notes on the interpretation and original commentaries, as well as Ch'en Ku-ying's own commentary.

DUYVENDAK, J. J. L., *Tao Te Ching: The Book of the Way and Its Virtue*, John Murray, London, 1954.

HENRICKS, ROBERT G., *Lao-tzu Te-tao Ching: A New Translation based on the Recently Discovered Ma-wang-tui Texts*, The Bodley Head, London, 1990. Includes original Chinese text and scholarly commentary.

LAU, D. C., *Lao Tzu: Tao Te Ching*, Penguin Books, 1963. Translation of the edition associated with Wang Pi's commentary.

—, *Chinese Classics: Tao Te Ching*, Chinese University Press, Hong Kong, 1982. Includes translations of both the Wang Pi and Ma Wang Tui editions, and the original Chinese texts.

LIN, PAUL J., *A Translation of Lao Tzu's Tao Te Ching and Wang Pi's Commentary*, Michigan Papers in Chinese Studies, Center for Chinese Studies, University of Michigan Press, Ann Arbor, 1977.

MAIR, VICTOR, *Tao Te Ching*, Bantam Books, New York, 1990.

WALEY, ARTHUR, *The Way and its Power: A Study of the Tao Te Ching and its Place in Chinese Thought*, George Allen and Unwin, London, 1934.

GENERAL WORKS ON THE LAO TZU AND TAOISM

CHAN, ALAN K. L., *Two Visions of the Way: A Study of the Wang Pi and the Ho-shang Kung Commentaries on the Lao-tzu*, State University of New York Press, Albany, 1991.

CREEL, H. G., *What is Taoism? And Other Studies in Chinese Cultural History*, University of Chicago Press, Chicago, Ill., 1970.

KALTENMARK, MAX, *Lao Tzu and Taoism*, translated from the French by Roger Greaves. Stanford University Press, Stanford, Calif., 1970.

LAFARGUE, MICHAEL, *The Tao of the Tao Te Ching*, State University of New York Press, Albany, 1992.

MASPERO, HENRI, *Taoism and Chinese Religion*, translated from the French by Frank A. Kierman, Jr, University of Massachusetts Press, Amherst, 1981.

RUMP, ARIANE, in collaboration with Wing-tsit Chan, *Commentary on the Lao Tzu by Wang Pi*. Monographs of the Society for Asian and Comparative Philosophy, no. 6, University of Hawaii Press, Honolulu.

RELATED WORKS ON CHINESE PHILOSOPHY AND BACK-GROUND READING

ALLAN, SARAH, *The Heir and the Sage: Dynastic Legend in Ancient China*, Chinese Materials Center, San Francisco, 1981.

—, *The Shape of the Turtle: Myth, Art and Cosmos in Early China*, State University of New York Press, Albany, 1991.

AMES, ROGER, *The Art of Rulership*, University of Hawaii Press, Honolulu, 1983.

CHAN, WING-TSIT, *Source Book of Chinese Philosophy*, Princeton University Press, Princeton, NJ, 1963, reprint 1973.

FINGARETTE, HERBERT, *Confucius: The Secular as Sacred*, Harper Torchbooks, New York, 1972.

FUNG YU-LAN, *A History of Chinese Philosophy*, trans. Derk Bodde, Princeton University Press, Princeton, NJ, 1953.

—, *A Short History of Chinese Philosophy*, trans. Derk Bodde, Macmillan, New York, 1958.

GRAHAM, A. C., trans., *The Book of Lieh-tzu*, John Murray, London, 1960.

—, trans., *Chuang Tzu: The Inner Chapters*, George Allen & Unwin, London, 1981.

—, *Disputers of the Tao: Philosophy and Philosophical Argument in Ancient China*, Open Court, La Salle, Ill., 1989. The most important recent history of Chinese philosophy.

—, *Studies in Chinese Philosophy and Philosophical Literature*, State University of New York Press, Albany, 1990.

—, *Yin-Yang and the Nature of Correlative Thinking*, Institute of East Asian Philosophies, Singapore, 1986.

HALL, DAVID, and AMES, ROGER, *Thinking Through Confucius*, State University of New York Press, New York, 1987.

HANSEN, CHAD, *Language and Logic in Ancient China*, University of Michigan Press, Ann Arbor, 1983.

KNOBLOCK, JOHN, *Xunzi: A Translation and Study of the Complete Works*, Stanford University Press, Stanford, Calif., volume 1 (1988), volume 2 (1990), volume 3 (1992).

LAU, D. C., trans., *The Analects of Confucius*, Penguin Classics, Harmondsworth, 1979.

—, trans., *Mencius*, Penguin Classics, Harmondsworth, 1970.

SELECT BIBLIOGRAPHY

MOTE, FREDERICK W., *Intellectual Foundations of China*, Alfred A. Knopf, New York, 1989.

MUNRO, DONALD J., *The Concept of Man in Early China*, University of Michigan Press, Ann Arbor, 1977.

NEEDHAM, JOSEPH, *Science and Civilization in China*, volume 2: *History of Scientific Thought*, Cambridge University Press, Cambridge, 1956, reprint 1972.

RICKETT, W. ALLYN, trans., *Guanzi*, Princeton University Press, Princeton, NJ, 1985.

ROSEMONT, HENRY, JR, ed., *Chinese Texts and Philosophical Contexts*, Open Court, La Salle, Ill., 1990.

SCHWARTZ, BENJAMIN I., *The World of Thought in Ancient China*, Harvard University Press, Cambridge, Mass., 1985.

VANDERMEERSCH, LEON, *La Formation de legisme*, Ecole Française d'Extrême Orient, Paris, 1965.

WALEY, ARTHUR, *Three Ways of Thought in Ancient China*, Allen & Unwin, London, 1939.

WELCH, HOLMES, and SEIDEL, ANNA, eds., *Facets of Taoism*, Yale University Press, New Haven, Conn., 1979.

CHRONOLOGY

Hsia Dynasty (not authenticated)

Shang Dynasty: *c.* 1700–1100 BC

Chou Dynasty: *c.* 1100–222 BC

    Eastern Chou: 770–256 BC

        The Spring and Autumn Period: 722–481 BC
            Confucius (551–479 BC)

        The Warring States Period: 480–222 BC
            Mo-tzu, *fl.* fifth century BC
            Mencius, *fl.* fourth century BC
            Lao-tzu, possibly fourth century BC?
            Chuang-tzu, middle of fourth to beginning of third century BC
            Hsun-tzu, latter half of fourth to middle of third century BC
            Han fei-tzu, d. 233 BC

Ch'in Dynasty: 221–207 BC

Western Han Dynasty: 206 BC–AD 8
        Burial of the Ma Wang Tui manuscripts 4 April 168 BC
        The *Huai nan-tzu*, compiled *c.* 140 BC
        The *Records of the Grand Historian* (*Shih chi*), completed by Ssu-ma
            Ch'ien, *c.* 90 BC

Hsin Dynasty (Wang Mang): AD 9–23

Eastern Han Dynasty: AD 25–220
        Ho-Shang Kung (Commentator to the *Lao-tzu*)

Three Kingdoms Period: AD 220–80
        Wang Pi (Commentator to the *Lao-tzu*), AD 226–49

TE CHING

I

The man of superior virtue is not virtuous and that is why he has virtue. The man of inferior virtue does not lapse from virtue and that is why he has no virtue. The man of superior virtue resorts to no action, nor has he any ulterior motive for action. The man of superior benevolence acts but has no ulterior motive for his action. The man of superior rectitude acts and has an ulterior motive for his action as well. The man superior in the observance of the rites acts, but when no one responds to his action rolls up his sleeves and resorts to dragging by force.

Hence when the way was lost there was virtue; when virtue was lost there was benevolence; when benevolence was lost there was rectitude; when rectitude was lost there were the rites.

> Now the rites are the wearing thin of conscientiousness
> and good faith
> And the beginning of disorder;
> Foreknowledge is the flowery embellishment of the way
> And the beginning of folly.

Hence a great man abides in the thick not in the thin, in the fruit not in the flower.

Hence he discards the one and takes the other.

2

Of old, these came to possess the One:

Heaven possessed the One and became thereby limpid;
Earth possessed the One and became thereby settled;
Gods possessed the One and became thereby potent;
The valley possessed the One and became thereby full;
Lords and princes possessed the One and became there-
by leaders of the empire.

But when this is pushed to the utmost,

It will mean that not knowing when to stop in being
limpid heaven will split;
It will mean that not knowing when to stop in being
settled earth will sink;
It will mean that not knowing when to stop in being
potent gods will get spent;
It will mean that not knowing when to stop in being
full the valley will run dry;
It will mean that not knowing when to stop in being
noble the high lords and princes will fall.

Hence it is necessarily the case that the noble has as its root
the humble and the high has as its foundation the low.
Now this is why lords and princes refer to themselves as
'solitary', 'desolate' and 'hapless'. This is the humble as root,
is it not?

Thus the highest renown is without renown.
Hence wishing not to be one among many like jade,
Nor to be aloof like stone.

3

When the best student is told about the way,
It is barely within his power to practise it;
When the average student is told about the way,
It seems to him one moment there and gone the next;
When the worst student is told about the way,
He laughs out loud at it.
If he did not laugh at it
It would not have been good enough to be the way.
Hence the *Chien yen* has it:
The way that is bright seems dull;
The way that leads forward seems to slip backwards;
The way that is even seems rough.
The highest virtue is like the valley;
The sheerest whiteness seems sullied;
Ample virtue seems deficient;
Vigorous virtue seems indolent;
Unadorned genuineness seems soiled.
The big square has no corners;
The big vessel is the last to be completed;
The big note is rarefied in sound;
The big image has no shape.
The way, being ample, is nameless.
It is the way alone that is good at beginning and at completing.

4

Reversal is the movement of the way;
Weakness is the use of the way.
The creatures in the world are born from Something, and
Something from Nothing.

5

The way begets one; one begets two; two begets three, three begets the myriad creatures.

The myriad creatures carry on their backs the *yin* and hold in their arms the *yang*, taking the *ch'i* in between as harmony.

The only names detested by the world are 'solitary', 'desolate' and 'hapless', yet princes and lords use them to name themselves.

Thus a thing is sometimes added to by being diminished and diminished by being added to.

Thus what others teach I also, after due consideration, teach others.

Thus as the violent do not come to a natural end, I take this as my preceptor.

6

The most submissive thing in the world can ride roughshod over the most unyielding in the world—that which is without substance entering that which has no gaps.

That is why I know the benefit of taking no action. The teaching that uses no words, the benefit of taking no action, these are beyond the understanding of all but a very few in the world.

7

Your name or your person,
Which is dearer?
Your person or your goods,
Which is worth more?
Gain or loss,
Which is a greater bane?
Excessive stinginess
Is sure to lead to great expense;
Too much store
Is sure to end in immense loss.
Knowing contentment
You will suffer no humiliation;
Knowing when to stop
You will be free from danger;
You will thereby endure.

8

Great perfection seems chipped,
Yet use will not wear it out;
Great fullness seems empty,
Yet use will not drain it;
Great straightness seems bent;
Great skill seems awkward;
Great surplus seems deficient;
Great eloquence seems tongue-tied.
Restlessness overcomes the cold; stillness overcomes the heat.
Limpid and still,
One can be a leader in the empire.

9

When the way prevails in the empire, fleet-footed horses are relegated to providing manure for the fields; when the way does not prevail in the empire, war-horses breed on the border.

> There is no crime greater than being desirable;
> There is no disaster greater than not being content;
> There is no misfortune more painful than being
>   covetous:

Hence in knowing the sufficiency of being content, one will constantly have sufficient.

10

By not setting foot outside the door
One knows the whole world;
By not looking out of the window
One knows the way of heaven.
The further one goes
The less one knows.
Hence the sage knows without having to stir,
Identifies without having to see [it],
Accomplishes without having to do it.

11

One who pursues learning makes gains every day; one who gets to hear about the way makes losses every day. One loses and loses until one takes no action. One takes no action nor does one have any ulterior motive for action. If your wish is to gain the empire you should constantly refrain from meddling. By the time you meddle, you are not equal to the task of gaining the empire.

I 2

The sage is constantly without a mind of his own. He takes as his own the mind of the people.

Treat as good those who are good. Treat as good also those who are not good. By doing so you gain in goodness. Have faith in those who are of good faith. Have faith also in those who lack good faith. By so doing you gain in good faith.

The sage in his attempt to distract the empire, seeks urgently to muddle it. The people all have something to which to attach their eyes and ears, and the sage treats them all like babies.

13

When going one way means life and going the other means death, three in ten will be comrades of life, three in ten will be comrades of death, and the people who move into the realm of death through valuing life will also number three in ten. Now why is this so? Because they value life. I have heard it said, one who is good at holding on to life does not try to avoid the rhinoceros or the tiger when travelling on highland nor does he arm himself with armour and weapon when charging into an army. There is nowhere for the rhinoceros to pitch its horn; there is nowhere for the tiger to land its claws; there is nowhere for the weapon to lodge its blade. Why is this so? Because there are no fatal spots on him.

I 4

The way gives them life
And virtue rears them;
Things take shape
And vessels are formed.

Hence the myriad creatures all revere the way and honour virtue. The way in being revered, and virtue in being honoured are constantly so of themselves without anyone bestowing nobility on them.

The way gives them life and rears them,
Brings them up and accomplishes them,
Brings them to fruition and maturity,
Feeds and shelters them.
It gives them life without claiming to possess them;
It benefits them yet exacts no gratitude for this;
It is the steward yet exercises no authority over them.
Such is called dark virtue.

15

The world had that from which it began
And this is taken as the mother of the world.
After you have got the mother
You can in turn know the son.
After you have known the son
Go back to abiding by the mother,
And to the end of your days you will not meet with danger.
Block the openings,
Shut the doors,
And all your life you will not run dry.
Unblock the openings,
Add to your affairs,
And to the end of your days you will be beyond help.
To see the small is called discernment;
To abide by the submissive is called strength.
Use the light
But give up the discernment.
Bring not misfortune upon yourself.
This is known as following the norm.

16

Were I possessed of the least knowledge, my only fear, when I walk on the great way, would be paths that lead astray. The great way is very smooth, yet the people prefer mountain paths.

> The court is clean swept,
> The fields are overgrown with weeds,
> The granaries are empty;
> Yet there are those dressed in fineries,
> With sharp swords at their sides,
> Filled with food and possessed of excessive wealth.
> This is known as being a bandit chief.
> A bandit chief is, indeed, a far cry from the way.

17

What a man has firmly planted cannot be pulled up;
What a man has tightly embraced will not slip loose;
Through this the offering made by descendants will
   never come to an end.
Cultivate it in your person
And its virtue will be genuine;
Cultivate it in the family
And there will be virtue to spare;
Cultivate it in the hamlet
And its virtue will endure;
Cultivate it in the state
And its virtue will abound;
Cultivate it in the empire
And its virtue will be pervasive.
Hence look at the person through the person; look at the
family through the family; look at the hamlet through the
hamlet; look at the state through the state, look at the empire
through the empire. How do I know that the empire is like
that? By means of this.

18

One who possesses virtue in abundance is comparable to a
new-born babe:

> Poisonous insects and snakes will not sting it;
> Predatory birds and ferocious animals will not pounce
>   on it;
> Its bones are weak and its sinews supple yet its hold is
>   firm.
> It does not know of the union of male and female yet its
>   male member will stir:

This is because its virility is at its height.

> It howls all day without having to struggle for breath:

This is because its harmony is at its height.

> To know harmony is called the norm;
> To know the norm is called discernment.
> To try to add to one's vitality is called ill-omened;
> For the mind to dictate to one's *ch'i* is called violent.
> A creature old in its prime
> Is known as being contrary to the way.
> That which is contrary to the way will come to an early
>   end.

19

One who knows does not say it; one who says does not know it.

> Block the openings,
> Shut the doors,
> Soften the glare,
> Follow along old wheel tracks;
> Blunt the point,
> Untangle the knots.

This is known as dark identity.

Thus you cannot get close to it, nor can you keep it at arm's length; you cannot bestow benefit on it, nor can you do it harm; you cannot ennoble it, nor can you debase it.

Hence it is the most valued in the empire.

20

Govern the state by being straightforward; wage war by
being crafty; but win the empire by not being meddlesome.
How do I know that it is like that? By means of this.

> Now the more taboos there are in the empire
> The poorer the people;
> The more keen instruments the people have
> The more benighted the state;
> The more knowledge men have
> The further novelties multiply;
> The more prominent the laws
> The more thieves and bandits there are.

Hence in the words of the sage,

> I take no action
> And the people are transformed of themselves;
> I prefer stillness
> And the people are rectified of themselves;
> I am not meddlesome
> And the people are rich of themselves;
> I desire not to desire
> And the people become like the uncarved block of
> themselves.

21

When the government is muddled,
The people are dull;
When the government misses nothing,
The state is decisive.
It is on disaster that good fortune perches;
It is beneath good fortune that disaster crouches.
Who knows the limit? Does the straightforward not exist?
But the straightforward changes once again into the crafty,
and the good changes once again into the monstrous. Indeed,
it is long since men were perplexed.

Hence square-edged but does not scrape,
Having corners but does not jab,
Spread out but does not encroach on others,
Shining but does not dazzle.

22

In ruling over men and in serving heaven, there is nothing
    like being sparing.
It is because a man is sparing
That he can follow the way from the start;
Following the way from the start is what is called accumulat-
    ing an abundance of virtue;
Accumulating an abundance of virtue he overcomes every-
    thing he meets;
When he overcomes everything he meets, no one will know
    his limit;
When no one knows his limit
He can possess a state.
When he possesses the mother of a state
He can then endure.
This is called the way of deep roots and firm stems by which
    one lives to see a good many more days.

23

Governing a large state is like boiling a small fish.
When the empire is ruled in accordance with the way, the
spirits are not potent. Or, rather, it is not that they are not
potent, but that in their potency they do not harm men. It is
not only they who, in their potency, do not harm men, the
sage, too, does not harm them. Now as neither does any
harm, each attributes the merit to the other.

24

A large state is the lower reaches of a river—the female of the world. In the intercourse of the world, the female always gets the better of the male by stillness. It is because of her stillness that it is fitting for her to take the lower position.

> Hence the large state, by taking the lower position, annexes the small state;
> The small state, by taking the lower position, is annexed by the large state.
> Thus the one, by taking the lower position, annexes;
> The other, by taking the lower position, is annexed.
> Thus all that the large state wants is to take the other under its wing;
> All that the small state wants is to have its services accepted by the other.
> Now if they both get their desire,
> It is fitting that the large should take the lower position.

25

The way is the reservoir towards which the myriad creatures
gravitate:

> It is the treasure of the good man
> And that by which the bad is protected.
> Beautiful words can be used for bartering;
> Honoured behaviour can put a man above others.

Even if a man is not good, why should he be abandoned?
Thus when the emperor is set up and the three ministers are
appointed, rather than jade disks followed by a team of four
horses better offer this without stirring from one's seat. Why
was this valued in antiquity? Was it not said that by means of
it one got what one sought and escaped the consequences
when one transgressed.

Hence it is the most valued in the empire.

26

Do that which consists in taking no action; pursue that which is not meddlesome; savour that which has no flavour.

Make the small big and the few many; do good to him who has done you an injury.

Lay plans for the accomplishment of the difficult while it is still easy; make something big by starting with it when small. The difficult in the world must of necessity have its beginning in the easy; the big in the world must of necessity have its beginning in the small. Hence it is because the sage never attempts to be great that he succeeds in becoming great.

Now one who makes promises rashly rarely keeps good faith; one who is in the habit of considering things easy will find himself beset with difficulties.

Hence even the sage does not underestimate the difficulty of things.

That is why in the end there are no difficulties for him.

27

It is easy to maintain a situation while it is still secure;
It is easy to deal with a situation before symptoms
    develop;
It is easy to break a thing when it is yet brittle;
It is easy to disperse a thing when it is yet minute.
Deal with a thing while it is still nothing;
Keep a thing in order before disorder sets in.
A tree that can fill a man's embrace
Grows from a downy tip;
A terrace nine storeys high
Rises from hodfuls of earth;
A height of a thousand yards
Starts from underneath one's feet.
He who does anything will ruin it; he who holds will lose it.
Hence the sage, because he does nothing, never ruins any-
thing; and, because he does not hold, loses nothing.
In their enterprises the people constantly ruin them when on
the verge of success.
Thus it is said,
    Be as careful at the end as at the beginning
    And there will be no ruined enterprises.
    Hence the sage desires not to desire
    And does not value goods that are hard to come by;
    Learns not to learn
    And turns back where the multitude has overshot the
        mark;
    Is able to help the myriad creatures to be natural and yet
        dare not do it.

28

Of old those who practised the way did not use it to enlighten the people but to hoodwink them. Now the reason why the people are difficult to govern is that they are too clever.

> Thus to understand a state through knowledge
> Will be to the detriment of the state;
> And to understand a state through ignorance
> Will be to the good of the state.

Be constantly aware that these two are models.

> Constantly to be aware of the models
> Is known as dark virtue.
> Dark virtue is profound and far-reaching,
> But when things turn back it turns back with them.

Only then does it go completely with the stream.

29

The reason why the River and the Sea are able to be king of the hundred valleys is that they are good at humbling themselves before them. Hence they are able to be king of the hundred valleys.

>   Hence the sage, in desiring to rule over the people,
>   Of necessity, in his words, humbles himself before them,
>   And, in desiring to lead the people,
>   Of necessity, in his person, follows behind them.

Thus the sage takes his place in front of the people yet they do not find him an obstruction, takes his place over the people yet they do not find him a burden. The whole empire supports him joyfully without ever tiring of doing so.

Is it not because he is without contention that no one in the empire is in a position to contend with him?

30

Reduce the size and population of the state. Ensure that even though there are tools ten times or a hundred times better than those of other men the people will not use them; ensure also that they will look on death as a grave matter and give migration a wide berth.

They have ships and carts but will not go on them; they have armour and weapons but will have no occasion to make a show of them.

Bring it about that the people will return to the use of the knotted rope,

> Will find relish in their food,
> And beauty in their clothes,
> Will be happy in the way they live
> And be content in their abode.

Though adjoining states are within sight of one another, and the sound of dogs barking and cocks crowing in one state can be heard in another, yet the people of one state will grow old and die without having had any dealings with those of another.

3 I

Truthful words are not beautiful; beautiful words are not truthful.

He who knows has no wide learning; he who has wide learning does not know.

He who is good does not have much; he who has much is not good.

The sage has no hoard. Having bestowed all he has on others, he has yet more; having given all he has to others, he is richer still.

Hence the way of heaven does not harm but benefits; the way of man does not contend but is bountiful.

3 2

The whole world says that I am vast, vast and resemble nothing. It is because I resemble nothing that I am able to be vast. If I resembled anything, I would, long before now, have become small.

> Now I constantly have three treasures
> Which I hold and cherish.
> The first is known as compassion,
> The second is known as frugality,
> The third is known as not daring to take the lead in the empire;
> Being compassionate I am able to be courageous;
> Being frugal, I am able to be extensive;
> Not daring to take the lead in the empire I am able to be lord over the complete vessels.

Now to forsake my compassion for courage, to forsake my frugality for expansion, to give up my position in the rear for the lead, is sure to end in death.

Through compassion, I can triumph in war and be impregnable in defence.

When heaven sets up something, it keeps it, as it were, behind ramparts of compassion.

33

One who is good at being a warrior does not appear
  formidable;
One who is good at fighting is never roused in anger;
One who is good at overcoming his adversary does not join
  issue with him;
One who is good at employing others humbles himself
  before them.
This is known as the virtue of non-contention;
This is known as making use of the efforts of others;
This is known as the limit that is as old as heaven.

34

There is a saying about strategy,
> I dare not play the host but play the guest,
> I do not advance an inch but retreat a foot instead.

This is known as
> Marching forward when there is no road,
> Rolling up one's sleeves when there is no arm,
> Taking hold of a weapon when there is no weapon,
> And dragging one's adversary by force when there is no
> adversary.

There is no disaster greater than being without an equal. Being without an equal nearly cost me my treasure. Thus when the two sides raising arms against each other are evenly matched, it is the one that is sorrow-stricken that wins.

35

My words are very easy to understand and very easy to put into practice, yet amongst men there is no one who is able to understand them and there is no one who is able to put them into practice.
Words have an ancestor and affairs have a sovereign.
It is because men are ignorant that they fail to understand me.

　　When those who understand me are few,

　　Then I shall be highly valued.

Hence the sage, while clad in homespun, conceals on his person a piece of priceless jade.

36

To know yet to think that one does not know is the
   best;
Not to know yet to think that one knows will put one
   in difficulty.
That the sage meets with no difficulty is because he is alive to
difficulty. That is why he meets with no difficulty.

37

When the people are not overawed by what is awesome,
then some awful visitation is about to descend upon them.
Do not constrict their living space; do not press down on
their means of livelihood. It is because you do not press down
on them that they will not weary of the burden.
Hence the sage knows himself but does not display himself,
treasures himself but does not exalt himself.
Hence he discards the one and takes the other.

3 8

He who is fearless in being bold will meet with his death;
He who is fearless in being timid will stay alive.
Of the two, one leads to good, the other to harm.
Of heaven's hates,
Who knows the reason?
The way of heaven
     Is good at overcoming though it does not fight,
     Is good at responding though it does not speak,
     Attracts though it does not summon,
     Is good at laying plans though it appears slack.
The net of heaven is cast wide. Its mesh may be coarse, but it
lets nothing slip through.

39

If the common people are constantly unafraid of death, why intimidate them with killing? If the people were constantly afraid of death, and I were able to arrest and put to death those who innovate, then who would dare? If the people are constantly afraid of death, then there will constantly be an executioner. Now to kill on behalf of the executioner is what is described as chopping wood on behalf of the master carpenter. Now of those who chop wood on behalf of the master carpenter, few will escape hurting their own hands instead.

40

That men are hungry
Is because too many live off the taxes.
That is why they are hungry.
That the people are not in good order
Is because those in authority have ulterior motives for
their actions.
That is why they are not in good order.
That the common people treat death lightly
Is because they set too much store by life.
That is why they treat death lightly.
It is precisely the man that has no use for life who is wiser
than him that values life.

41

A man is supple and weak when alive, but hard and stiff when dead. The myriad creatures and grass and trees are pliant and fragile when alive, but dried and shrivelled when dead. Thus it is said, the hard and the strong are the comrades of death; the supple and the weak are the comrades of life.

    Hence a weapon that is strong will not vanquish;
    A tree that is strong will come to its end;
    Thus the strong and big takes the lower position;
    The supple and weak takes the upper position.

42

The way of heaven is like one who stretches a bow:
>The high he presses down,
>The low he lifts up;
>The excessive he takes from,
>The deficient he makes good.

Thus it is the way of heaven to take from what has in excess in order to augment what is deficient. The way of man is otherwise. It takes from what is deficient in order to offer to what has in excess. Now who is there that is able, when he has in excess, to take therefrom to offer to heaven? Perhaps only he who has the way.

>Hence the sage benefits them yet exacts no gratitude,
>Accomplishes his task yet claims no merit.

It is to that extent that he dislikes being considered better than other men.

43

In the world there is nothing more submissive and weak than water. Yet for attacking that which is unyielding and strong nothing can take precedence over it. This is because there is nothing that can take its place.

> The weak overcomes the unbending,
> And the submissive overcomes the strong,
> This everyone in the world knows yet no one can put it into practice.

Hence in the words of the sage,

> One who takes on himself the abuse hurled against the state
> Is called a ruler worthy of offering sacrifices to the gods of earth and millet;
> One who takes on himself the calamities of the state
> Is called a king worthy of dominion over the entire empire.

Straightforward words seem paradoxical.

44

When peace is made between great enemies,
Some enmity is bound to remain undispelled.
How can this be considered perfect?
Hence the sage takes the left-hand tally, but does not use it to
exact payment from others.
Hence the man of virtue takes charge of the tally;
The man without virtue takes charge of exaction.
It is the way of heaven to have no favourites:
It is constantly on the side of the good man.

TAO CHING

45

The way can be spoken of,
But it will not be the constant way;
The name can be named,
But it will not be the constant name.
The nameless was the beginning of the myriad creatures;
The named was the mother of the myriad creatures.
Hence constantly rid yourself of desires in order to observe
  its subtlety;
But constantly allow yourself to have desires in order to
  observe what it is after.
These two have the same origin but differ in name.
  They are both called dark,
  Darkness upon darkness
  The gateway to all that is subtle.

46

The whole world knows the beautiful as the beautiful, and
this is only the ugly; it knows the good as the good and this
is, indeed, the bad.

> Something and Nothing producing each other;
> The difficult and the easy complementing each other;
> The long and the short off-setting each other;
> The high and the low filling out each other;
> Note and sound harmonizing with each other;
> Before and after following each other—

These are in accordance with what is constant.

Hence the sage dwells in the deed that consists in taking no
action and practises the teaching that uses no words.

> It makes the myriad creatures without being their
>   initiator,
> It benefits them without exacting any gratitude for this;
> It accomplishes its task without claiming any merit for
>   this.
> It is because it lays no claim to merit
> That its merit never deserts it.

47

Not to honour men of excellence will keep the people from contention; not to value goods that are hard to come by will keep the people from theft; not to display what is desirable will keep the people from being unsettled.

Hence in his rule, the sage empties their minds but fills their bellies, weakens their purpose but strengthens their bones. He constantly keeps the people innocent of knowledge and free from desire, and causes the clever not to dare.

He simply takes no action and everything is in order.

48

The way is empty, yet when used there is something that
  does not make it full.
Deep, it is like the ancestor of the myriad creatures.
Blunt the sharpness;
Untangle the knots;
Soften the glare;
Follow along old wheel tracks.
Darkly visible, it only seems as if it were there.
I know not whose son it is.
It images the forefather of God.

49

Heaven and earth are ruthless; they treat the myriad creatures
as straw dogs. The sage is ruthless; he treats the people as
straw dogs.
Is not the space between heaven and earth like a bellows?
  It is empty without being exhausted;
  The more it works the more comes out.
  To hear much will lead only to a dead end.
  Better to hold fast to what is within.

50

The spirit of the valley never dies;
This is called the dark female.
The entry into the dark female
Is called the root of heaven and earth.
Tenuous, it seems as if it were there,
Yet use will never exhaust it.

51

Heaven and earth are enduring. The reason why heaven and earth can be enduring is that they do not give themselves life. Hence they are able to be long-lived.

> Hence the sage puts his person back and it comes to the fore,
>
> Treats his person as extraneous and it is preserved.

Is it not because he is without thought of self that he is able to accomplish his private ends?

52

That which is most good is like water. It is because water is not only good at benefiting the myriad creatures but also vies to dwell in the place detested by the multitude that it comes close to the way.

In a dwelling it is the site that is valued;
In quality of mind it is depth that is valued;
In giving it is being like heaven that is valued;
In speech it is good faith that is valued;
In government it is order that is valued;
In affairs it is ability that is valued;
In action it is timeliness that is valued.

It is because it does not contend that it is never at fault.

53

Rather than fill it to the brim by keeping it upright
Better to have stopped in time;
Hammer it to a point
And the sharpness cannot be preserved always;
There may be gold and jade filling the chamber
But there is none who can keep them safe.
To be overbearing when one has position and wealth
Is to bring calamity upon oneself.
To retire when the task is accomplished
Is the way of heaven.

54

When carrying on your head your perplexed bodily soul can
    you hold in your arms the One
And not let go?
In concentrating your breath can you become as supple
As a babe?
Can you polish your dark mirror
And leave no blemish?
In loving the people and bringing life to the state
Are you capable of not resorting to knowledge?
When the gates of heaven open and shut
Are you capable of keeping to the role of the female?
When your discernment penetrates the four quarters
Are you capable of not resorting to knowledge?
It gives them life and rears them.
It gives them life without claiming to possess them;
It is the steward yet exercises no authority over them.
Such is called dark virtue.

55

Thirty spokes
Share one hub.
Make the nothing therein appropriate, and you will have the use of the cart. Knead clay in order to make a vessel. Make the nothing therein appropriate, and you will have the use of the clay vessel. Cut out doors and windows in order to make a room. Make the nothing therein appropriate, and you will have the use of the room.

Thus we gain by making it Something, but we have the use by making it Nothing.

56

The five colours make man's eyes blind.
Riding and hunting
Make his mind go wild with excitement;
Goods hard to come by
Serve to hinder his progress.
The five tastes injure man's palate;
The five notes make man's ears deaf.
Hence in his rule, the sage is
    For the belly,
    Not for the eye.
Thus he discards the one and takes the other.

57

Favour and disgrace are like being startled;
Honour is a great trouble like your body.

What is meant by saying that favour and disgrace are like being startled? Favour being that which when bestowed on a subject serves to startle as much as when withdrawn, this is what is meant by saying that favour and disgrace are like being startled. What is meant by saying that honour is a great trouble like your body? The reason I have great trouble is that I have a body. When I no longer have a body, what trouble have I?

Hence he who values putting his person in order more than putting the empire in order can be given the custody of the empire. He who grudges using his person for putting the empire in order can be entrusted with the empire.

58

Look at it and you do not see it, this you call minute;
Listen to it and you do not hear it, this you call rarefied;
Feel for it and you do not get hold of it, this you call intangible.
The three cannot be fathomed
And so they are confused and looked upon as one.
Of the One,

>   Its upper part is not dazzling;
>   Its lower part is not indistinct.
>   Dimly visible, it cannot be named,
>   And returns to that which is without substance.
>   This is called the shape that has no shape,
>   The image that is without substance.
>   This is called indistinct and shadowy.
>   Follow behind it and you will not see its rear;
>   Go up to it and you will not see its head.
>   Hold fast to the way of today
>   In order to keep in control today's realm.
>   To know thereby the beginning of antiquity
>   Is called the thread running through the way.

59

Of old he who was well versed in the way
Was minutely subtle, mysteriously comprehending,
And too profound to be known.
It is because he could not be known
That he can only be given a makeshift description:
    Tentative, as if wading through water in winter,
    Hesitant, as if in fear of his neighbours;
    Formal like a guest;
    Falling apart like thawing ice;
    Thick like the uncarved block;
    Murky like muddy water,
    Immense like a valley.
    The muddy, being stilled, slowly becomes limpid,
    The settled, being stirred, slowly comes to life.
    He who treasures this way
    Desires not to be full.
    It is because he desires not to be full
    That he is able to be worn and incomplete.

60

I attain the utmost emptiness;
I keep to extreme stillness.
The myriad creatures all rise together
And I watch thereby their return.
The teeming creatures
All return to their separate roots.
Returning to one's roots is known as stillness.
Stillness is what is called returning to one's destiny.
Returning to one's destiny is normal.
Knowledge of the normal is discernment.
Not to know the normal is to be without basis.
To innovate without basis bodes ill.
To know the normal is to be tolerant.
Tolerance leads to impartiality,
Impartiality to kingliness,
Kingliness to heaven,
Heaven to the way,
The way to perpetuity,
And to the end of one's days one will meet with no danger.

61

The best of all rulers is but a shadowy presence to his subjects.
    Next comes the ruler they love and praise;
    Next comes one they fear;
    Last comes one they treat with impertinence.
Only when there is not enough faith is there a lack of faith.
    Hesitant, he does not utter words lightly.
    When his task is accomplished and his work done
    The people all say, 'It happened to us naturally.'

62

Thus when the great way falls into disuse
There are benevolence and rectitude;
When cleverness emerges
There is great hypocrisy;
When the six relations are at variance
There are the filial;
When the state is benighted
There are true subjects.

63

Exterminate the sage, discard the wise,
And the people will benefit a hundredfold;
Exterminate benevolence, discard rectitude,
And the people will return to being filial;
Exterminate ingenuity, discard profit,
And there will be no more thieves and bandits.
Concerning these three sayings,

It is thought that the text leaves yet something to be
desired

And there should, therefore, be something to which it is
attached:

Exhibit the unadorned and embrace the uncarved
block,

Have little thought of self and as few desires as possible.

64

Exterminate learning and there will no longer be worries.
Between yea and nay
How much difference is there?
Between the beautiful and the ugly
How great is the distance?
He whom others fear
Ought also to fear others.
Waxing, it has not reached its limit.
The multitude are joyous
As if partaking of the *t'ai lao* offering
While going on a terrace in spring.
I alone am inactive and reveal no signs,
Like a baby that has not yet learned to smile,
Listless as though with no home to go back to.
The multitude all have more than enough.
I alone am in want.
Mine is the mind of a fool—how blank!
Vulgar men are clear.
I alone am drowsy.
Vulgar men miss nothing.
I alone am muddled.
Unbounded, like the sea;
Limitless, as if there is nowhere to stop.
The multitude all have a purpose.
I alone am foolish and uncouth.
I want to be different from all others
In valuing being fed by the mother.

65

In his every movement a man of great virtue
Follows the way and the way only.
As a thing the way is
Shadowy, indistinct.
Indistinct and shadowy,
Yet within it is an image;
Shadowy and indistinct,
Yet within it is a substance.
Dim and dark,
Yet within it is an essence.
This essence is quite genuine,
And within it is something that can be tested.
From the present back to antiquity
Its name never deserted it.
By means of it one goes along with the fathers of the multitude. How do I know that the fathers of the multitude are like that? By means of this.

66

He who blows cannot stand.
He who displays himself is not conspicuous;
He who shows himself is not manifest;
He who boasts of himself will have no merit;
He who brags about himself will not endure.
From the point of view of the way these are 'excessive food
and excrescent conduct'. As there are things that detest these,
a man of ambition does not abide therein.

67

Bowed down then whole;
Warped then true;
Hollow then full;
Worn then new;
A little then benefited;
A lot then perplexed.

Hence the sage grasps the One and is the shepherd of the empire.

He does not display himself, and so is conspicuous;
He does not show himself, and so is manifest;
He does not boast of himself, and so has merit;
He does not brag about it, and so is able to endure.

It is because he does not contend that no one is in a position to contend with him.

The way the ancients had it, 'Whole through being bowed down', is as true a saying as can be. Truly, it enables one to hand it back whole.

68

    To use words but rarely
    Is to be natural.
A gusty wind cannot last all morning, and a violent down-pour cannot last all day. Who is it that produces these? Heaven and earth. If even heaven and earth cannot make them go on for long, much less can man.

Hence in his pursuit, a man of the way conforms to the way; a man of virtue conforms to virtue; a man of loss conforms to loss. To him who conforms to virtue the way gives virtue; to him who conforms to loss the way gives loss.

69

There is a thing confusedly formed,
Born before heaven and earth.
Silent and void
It stands alone and does not change,
Goes round and does not weary.
It is capable of being the mother of heaven and earth.
As yet I do not know its name.
I style it 'the way'.
I give it the makeshift name of 'great'.
Being great, it is described as receding,
Receding, it is described as far away,
Being far away, it is described as turning back.
The way is great; heaven is great; earth is great, and the king
is great.
Within the realm there are four greats and the king counts as
one.
Man models himself on earth,
Earth on heaven,
Heaven on the way,
And the way on that which is naturally so.

70

The heavy is the root of the light;
The still is the lord of the restless.
Hence the gentleman travels all day without ever letting his
heavily laden carts out of sight. Only when he is at leisure
behind a ring of watch towers is he above worries. How,
then, should a king with ten thousand chariots make light of
his person in the eyes of the empire?
If light, then the root is lost;
If restless, then the lord is lost.

7 1

One who is good at travelling leaves no wheel tracks;
One who is good at speech has no flaws;
One who is good at reckoning uses no counting rods;
One who is good at shutting uses neither bolt nor lock
    yet what he has shut cannot be opened;
One who is good at tying uses no cords yet what he has
    tied cannot be undone.

Hence the sage is always good at saving people, and so abandons no one; nor does he abandon any useful material where things are concerned.

This is called following one's discernment.

Hence the good man is the teacher of the good man
While the bad man is the material for the good man.
Not to value the teacher
Nor to love the material
May, perhaps, be clever, but it betrays great
    bewilderment.

This is called the subtle and the essential.

72

Know the male
But keep to the role of the female
And be a ravine to the empire.
If you are a ravine to the empire,
The constant virtue will not desert you.
When the constant virtue does not desert you,
You will again return to being a babe.
Know the white
But keep to the role of the sullied.
And be a valley to the empire.
If you are a valley to the empire,
The constant virtue will be sufficient.
When the constant virtue is sufficient,
You will again return to being the uncarved block.
Know the white
But keep to the role of the black
And be a model to the empire.
If you are a model to the empire,
The constant virtue will not deviate.
When the constant virtue does not deviate,
You will again return to the infinite.
When the uncarved block shatters it becomes vessels. When
the sage is employed he becomes the chief of the officials.
Now the greatest cutting
Never severs.

73

Whoever takes the empire and puts it in order I see will find there is no stop to it. Now the empire is a sacred vessel. It is not a thing that can be put in order. He who puts it in order will ruin it; he who holds will lose it.

　　Some things go forward and some follow behind;
　　Some blow hot and some blow cold;
　　Some are strengthened and some suffer setback;
　　Some are banked up and some are pulled down.
Hence the sage avoids excess, arrogance and extravagance.

74

When assisting the ruler of men according to the way, one does not become the strongest in the empire by means of arms. This is something which is liable to rebound. Over the place where troops have encamped brambles will grow.

One who is good is simply resolute and should not thereby become strong. He should be resolute but must not be arrogant; he should be resolute but must not brag about it; he should be resolute but must not boast of it. The resolute is what one abides in when there is no choice. This is known as being resolute without being strong.

A creature old in its prime
Is known as being contrary to the way.
That which is contrary to the way will come to an early end.

75

Arms are instruments of ill omen. There are things that detest them. Hence a man of ambition does not abide therein. The gentleman gives precedence to the left when at home, but to the right when he goes to war. Thus arms are not the instruments of the gentleman. Arms are instruments of ill omen. When one has no alternative but to use them, it is best to do so without relish. One should not glorify them. If one glorifies them this is to exult in the killing of men. Now one who exults in the killing of men will not have his way in the empire.

Hence in celebrations precedence is given to the left; in funerals precedence is given to the right. Hence a lieutenant's place is on the left; the general's place is on the right. That is to say it is funeral rites that are observed. When men are killed in great numbers, one should look on them with sorrow. When one is victorious in war, this calls for the observance of funeral rites.

76

The way is constantly nameless.
Though the uncarved block is small
No one in the world dare treat it as a subject.
Should lords and princes be able to hold fast to it
The myriad creatures will submit of their own accord,
Heaven and earth will unite and send down sweet dew,
And the people will be equitable though no one so
  decrees.
Then only when it is cut are there names.
Once there are names
One should know it was time to stop.
Knowing when to stop is the way to be free from
  danger.
The way in distracting the empire is similar to the case of a
small valley in relation to the River and the Sea.

77

He who knows others is clever;
He who knows himself has discernment.
He who overcomes others has force;
He who overcomes himself has strength.
He who knows contentment is rich;
He who perseveres in action has purpose.
Not to lose one's station is to endure;
Not to be forgotten when dead is long lived.

78

The way is broad, reaching left as well as right.
Having accomplished the task and having done the
work it does not assume the name of owner.
The myriad creatures turn to it yet it does not act as their
master. Thus in so far as it is constantly without desire it can
be named amongst the small; but in so far as it does not act
as their master when the myriad creatures turn to it, it can
be named amongst the great. Hence the sage succeeds in
becoming great because he makes no attempt to be great. It is
for this reason that he succeeds in becoming great.

79

Have in your grasp the great image
And the empire will come to you.
Coming to you and meeting with no harm
It will be safe and sound.
Music and food,
For them the wayfarer stops.
Hence the way, in coming out with words, says,
    Insipid, it has no flavour,
    There is not enough of it, when looked at, to be visible,
    Nor is there enough of it, when listened to, to be
       audible.
    Yet use cannot exhaust it.

80

If you would have a thing shrink,
You must first stretch it;
If you would have a thing weakened,
You must first strengthen it;
If you would desert a thing,
You must first be its ally.
If you would take from a thing,
You must first give to it.
This is called faint enlightenment:
The submissive and weak will overcome the unyielding and
    strong.
The fish must not be allowed to leave the deep;
The instruments of power in a state must not be revealed to
    others.

81

The way is constantly nameless,
But should lords and princes be able to hold fast to it,
The myriad creatures will be transformed of their own
accord.
After they are transformed should they desire to rise
I shall press them down with the weight of the nameless
uncarved block.
When they are pressed down with the weight of the nameless
uncarved block,
They will not desire;
When they do not desire and are still,
Heaven and earth will be proper of their own accord.

APPENDICES

APPENDIX 1*
The Problem of Authorship

The most difficult problem in dealing with the history of Chinese thought in the ancient period is how to establish the approximate dates of the various philosophers and philosophical works so that a rough chronological order may be decided on, which is essential to an understanding of the historical development. For instance, given two philosophical works, A and B, the way the thought contained in them is interpreted if A is earlier than B often has to be radically changed if it is shown that B is, in fact, earlier than A. The interpretation of the *Lao tzu* is a case in point. This depends on whether we accept the traditional view that it was written by Lao Tzu who was an older contemporary of Confucius and so was a work of the sixth century BC, or the view favoured by a great number of modern scholars which would place the work in the late fourth or early third century BC. For this reason it is vital to our task of correctly interpreting the thought in the *Lao tzu* to examine the soundness of the traditional view.†

The traditional view is based on the fact that a meeting was supposed to have taken place between Confucius and Lao Tzu, and the earliest historical work that contains an account of such a meeting is the *Shih chi*. In both the biography of Lao Tzu and that of Confucius in this work, the account begins with Confucius going to Chou to put questions to Lao Tzu concerning the rites, but in the actual account nothing further is said about the rites. All that takes

*Both this Appendix and the following one were originally written by D. C. Lau for his translation of the Wang Pi text published in 1963. [ed.]
†A chronological table is provided on page xxxv.

place is a lecture from Lao Tzu on the kind of behaviour to be avoided. This seems to show that Ssu-ma Ch'ien must have used two distinct sources, one concerning Confucius receiving instruction in the rites which, as we shall see, is of Confucianist origin, and the other concerning the censure of Confucius by Lao Tzu which is of Taoist origin. Although we no longer have the sources that Ssu-ma Ch'ien used, fortunately we have accounts concerning the meeting in two extant works. On the one hand, we have in the *Chuang tzu* accounts of the meeting and of the censure of Confucius by Lao Tzu. On the other, in the *Li chi* (*Records of Rites*), a Confucianist work compiled in the first century BC, we have four instances of Confucius recalling what he learned about the rites from Lao Tzu, though there is no account of the actual meeting.

In the *Chuang tzu* there are several versions of the story, and though these all differ considerably from those in the *Shih chi*, they are, as is the case with the *Shih chi* accounts, of Taoist origin. The *Li chi* passages concern the rites only, but, as the *Shih chi* does no more than mention the rites, they serve to give us some idea of the nature of the points of rites involved and the kind of sources the *Shih chi* might have used. Because both the *Shih chi* and the *Li chi* are of comparatively late date, and the *Li chi* does not contain an account of the actual meeting between the two, far more weight has been attached to the *Chuang tzu*, and it is upon the accounts in the *Chuang tzu* that the traditionalists' case rests. It is argued that as accounts of the encounter between Lao Tzu and Confucius are to be found in the *Chuang tzu*, the story, at least, of such an encounter must have existed at the time of Chuang Tzu, and the man Lao Tzu must have existed before Chuang Tzu, and the book *Lao tzu* must have been written, even if the story is untrue, before the end of the fourth century BC, but as early as the sixth century if the story is true. Needless to say, this argument is highly unsatisfactory, as it rests on the simple but questionable assumption that the *Chuang tzu* was written by Chuang Tzu and the *Lao tzu* by Lao Tzu, with no more grounds than that these books are traditionally thought to have been named after their authors. It is further argued that as accounts are found in the *Chuang tzu* it follows that Chuang Tzu knew of Lao Tzu, and from this it is concluded that the book *Lao tzu* must have existed in the time of Chuang Tzu. Moreover, it is assumed that if the story was current in Chuang Tzu's time, even if this was no more than a story, it established the priority in time of Lao Tzu over Chuang Tzu. This is to ignore the possibility that Lao Tzu might not have been a historical personage at all.

Let us take the assumption that the *Lao tzu* was written by Lao Tzu and the *Chuang tzu* by Chuang Tzu. This is an exceedingly questionable assumption and has to be carefully examined. In order to do this, we must make a digression and say something about the way books were compiled in ancient China.

The earliest works, as is well known, are collections of the sayings of particular thinkers which must have undergone more than once the process of compilation in the hands of disciples and their disciples in turn, and so on. These works came, at some time or other, to be known by the name of the thinkers in question. Practically all ancient philosophical works are so named with the exception of the collection of sayings by Confucius which was known as the *Lun yü*.

Within the same work, another principle of compilation seemed to have operated as well. Passages that have something in common, a common topic or a common interlocutor, for instance, are placed together. It is not clear at what date this principle came to be adopted, but we can find examples of this in the *Analects of Confucius* and in the

Mencius. For instance, in Book 4 of the *Analects*, sections 1 to 6 all deal with 'benevolence', and sections 18 to 21 with 'filial conduct', while in the *Mencius* Book 5 Part 1 consists solely of answers given by Mencius to questions expressing doubt over accepted traditions concerning sage kings. This principle was not only followed but explicitly stated by Liu Hsiang at the end of the first century BC when he edited the *Shuo yüan* and the *Hsin hsü*. Each of these two works are divided into a number of books, and each book comprises passages concerning a common topic. (Indeed this principle survived in the compilation of encyclopedias ['*lei shu*'] in later times.) One suspects that parts of the *Chuang tzu*, for instance, were compiled on this principle as well, though this fact has been obscured by subsequent re-editing. We can still see that the chapter *Jang wang* (Abdication) consists of a number of stories concerning the abdication of the various legendary sage kings, though some extraneous matter has been introduced, while at the same time some of the abdication stories have found their way to other chapters.

In the case of stories, there are some instances where editors have not only placed those that are of the same kind together but have even included variant versions of the same story. These may be slightly different stories about the same characters or similar stories about different characters. This practice can be most clearly seen in, for instance, the *Han fei tzu*, particularly in chapters 30 to 35, where variant versions are often introduced by the formula 'one version has it'.

It is obvious, if books were compiled on such a principle, that material from alien sources and possibly of a considerably later date might easily find its way into a work in spite of the fact that the work is named after a particular thinker and indeed represents in the main the thought of that thinker or at least his school. There are reasons for thinking that this happened more often with works of the later part of the

Warring States period, say, from the beginning of the third century BC, than with works of the preceding period. Earlier works, viz. the *Analects of Confucius* and the *Mencius*, not only consist of sayings by a particular philosopher, but these are invariably introduced by the formula 'Master So-and-So said' or simply 'The Master said' in the case of the *Analects*, and although passages with a common topic are placed together they remain distinctly separate sayings. Furthermore, the formula, though it can obviously never guarantee the authenticity of a saying, nevertheless serves as a sign that the saying was at one time accepted as a saying of the Master, thus rendering it difficult, if not impossible, for alien material to have been incorporated *by accident*.

Again, most of the passages consist of serious discussions about moral and political problems. The occasional story is used only to illustrate a point under discussion. The impression one gets in reading these works is that the sayings were taken down by disciples to whom the memory of the Master was sacred. The result is that these sayings truly reflect both the thought and the style of the man. We feel we are listening to the individual voice of a thinker whose thought exhibits a high degree of unity. There is bound to be material which was probably of a later date, but even this is still material belonging to the same school, though it may belong to a tradition somewhat further removed from the Master. In the case of Mencius, we are probably fortunate in having only a version of his works with all books of a doubtful nature removed by the editor of the third century AD. Confucius is a more complicated case, because at a very early stage he became known as a sage and so attracted the attribution of apocryphal sayings and the invention of apocryphal stories. But even the inclusion of these, because they are invented deliberately, is quite different from the inclusion of totally alien material by accident.

All this was changed in the case of later works like the *Chuang tzu* and the *Hsün tzu*. These works no longer consist of a series of short sayings introduced by the formula 'Master So-and-So said'. In fact the name of the thinker after whom the work is known figures but rarely. In the *Chuang tzu*, Chuang Tzu's name appears far less frequently than those of the legendary kings Yao and Shun and even that of Confucius. In the *Hsün tzu*, which is a work of considerable length, Hsün Tzu's name occurs in no more than half a dozen or so passages where actual conversations in which Hsün Tzu took part are recorded. Moreover, short sayings have given way to much longer passages, which are often couched in the deceptive form of a continuous exposition. It is only when one examines these passages carefully that one realizes that they are very often actually compiled out of shorter units which are only loosely connected and sometimes not connected at all. This lack of connection is often disguised by the appearance of connecting words like *ku* (therefore) and *shih yi* (hence). This is a point to which we shall return.

In this respect, the first thirty-five chapters of the *Mo tzu* stand half way between the *Analects* and the *Mencius* on the one hand, and the later works on the other. These chapters in the *Mo tzu* seem to contain continuous exposition, though, in fact, they consist of independent units which have been put together. These shorter units are often of such generality that they can be used equally in a number of contexts. But in one respect the *Mo tzu* is still akin to the *Analects* and the *Mencius*. The formula 'Master So-and-So said' is still to be found, at least at the beginning of each chapter. This, together with the distinctive style of Mohist writing, is to a certain extent a reassurance that the material, though it underwent subsequent editing, is more or less homogeneous and belongs to the same school. In the case of the later works we no longer have such reassurance, particularly where the text is corrupt. The *Chuang tzu*, with which we are immediately concerned, is a case in point. The state of the text is exceedingly corrupt, and it would be over-sanguine not to expect a good deal of alien material to have found its way into such a work. In some chapters there are parts, for instance the end of chapters 23 and 26, which give the impression that not only extraneous matter has been incorporated but that the text has been compiled from broken bamboo slips★ so fragmentary in nature as to make no sense whatsoever as they stand.

There is one other feature of these later works. In some of them, there is an increasing tendency to use stories for the sake of the moral in them. These stories are no longer used in the context of an actual argument as in the earlier works, but are entirely independent. In such cases, it is difficult to find any marks of authorship or of origin, particularly when slightly different versions of the same story sometimes occur in more than one work.

It is possible that if a detailed study were made of such stories they could be grouped into categories according to their form. But a discussion of this problem will take us too far afield. The category that has special relevance for our immediate purpose is what may be called the illustrative story. An illustrative story is a story which is told for its point, and this is the only factor which matters and which remains constant while other factors may vary from version to version. These include the identity of the characters other

---

★Bamboo was the common writing material in ancient China. It was cut into narrow slips on which columns of characters were written. These slips were then strung together by cords to form a book which was in effect like a curtain that has been turned sideways. It often happens that the cords rotted with time and that some of the slips got broken at the ends as well. In that case, an editor might have to put together, to the best of his ability, a bundle of loose and at times broken slips. It is not surprising that some of these broken slips found their way into the wrong books.

than the main character, the location of the story and so on. We shall return to this point.

To go back to the works of the latter part of the Warring States period. Because of the features that we have seen, unless there are strong reasons, it is never safe to assume that any such work was actually written by a particular thinker or even that the whole work represents a single tradition in a closely-knit school. It is far safer to assume that it is an anthology which passed through the hands of a compiler or of a series of compilers, in the course of time. The judgement of the compilers need not always be sound, and the fact that passages are placed together need not have very much to do with their contents. Although in the majority of cases such passages deal with a common topic, it sometimes happens that these have nothing more in common than one or more catchwords and the point made in each passage is quite different.

I hope enough has been said to show that it is not safe to assume that the *Chuang tzu* was written by Chuang Tzu simply because such an attribution is traditional. If that is so, we cannot assume, because Lao Tzu is mentioned in the *Chuang tzu*, that Chuang Tzu must have known of him. In fact what we are entitled to is simply the tautological statement that the parts of the *Chuang tzu* which contain stories about Lao Tzu must have been written at a time when the stories were already current. All we have done is to exchange the problem about the date of Lao Tzu for the problem about the date of the parts of the *Chuang tzu* which contain stories about Lao Tzu, and even then, what we can hope to settle, assuming for argument's sake that we can come to any definite conclusions about the date of these parts of the *Chuang tzu*, is the date of the currency of the stories, not the date of Lao Tzu the man.

Although the mere fact that stories concerning Lao Tzu

are to be found in the *Chuang tzu* does not entitle us to answer the question, 'did Chuang Tzu know of Lao Tzu?' it is nevertheless an interesting question and one that we ought to ask. One of the strongest arguments against the traditionalists' case for placing Lao Tzu in the sixth century BC is the fact that Mencius, in spite of his strong sense of mission against heterodox schools, attacks Yang Chu and Mo Tzu but does not mention Lao Tzu. Not only does he not mention Lao Tzu explicitly, but he never even shows any awareness of any of the views we associate with Lao Tzu. The traditionalists' answer often takes the form that, although Mencius did not mention Lao Tzu, Chuang Tzu certainly did. We have seen that the force of the argument depends on whether by 'Chuang Tzu' is meant the work or the man. If the work is meant the fact is undeniable but proves nothing. But if the man is meant, then the question is an interesting one and should be examined.

In order to answer this question, we have to re-formulate it and ask: in passages in the *Chuang tzu* where Chuang Tzu figures in a serious philosophical discussion does he ever mention, or, in general, show any signs that he knows of Lao Tzu? The answer to this is no. It may be said that in the passages where Chuang Tzu figures, perhaps there is no reason for him to mention Lao Tzu. This may be true of some of these passages, but there is one passage where Chuang Tzu's silence on the point is, to say the least, surprising. In chapter 24 there is a conversation between Chuang Tzu and his friend, the famous sophist, Hui Shih. Chuang Tzu said, 'Ju, Mo, Yang, and Ping are four. Together with you I will make five.' If we leave on one side Ping whose identity is certainly not relevant to our question, we can see only three schools of thought, viz. Ju, i.e. the Confucian school, Mo, i.e. the school of Mo Tzu, and Yang, i.e. the school of Yang Chu are named by Chuang Tzu. Why did Chuang Tzu not mention Lao Tzu and his school, particularly as, according to the traditionalist view, Chuang Tzu was the second great Taoist thinker who carried on the teachings of the school founded by Lao Tzu? This silence seems to go some way in providing evidence to show that Chuang Tzu was not aware either of Lao Tzu or of his school or, at least, not as a prominent school of thought dating from the time of Confucius.

Although we can proceed no further with the problem as far as the *Chuang tzu* is concerned, there is one piece of evidence which is relevant. In chapter 3 of the *Mo tzu*, Mo Tzu was said to have been moved by the sight of silk coming out the colour of the dye. This was taken as a moral the application of which could be extended to the state and the individual. When the king of a state is influenced by good ministers, that state will be well governed. When an individual is influenced by good teachers and friends, he will be a good man. Examples are given in each case. Now this chapter is to be found also in the *Lü shih ch'un ch'iu* (chüan 3, pt 4), and the two versions are in fact identical up to the end of the section about the 'dyeing' of states. The final section about individuals is quite different. In the *Mo tzu* version three examples only are given of individuals who came under the influence of good men, viz. Tuan-kan Mu, Ch'in Ku-li and Fu Yüeh. Tuan-kan Mu was a Confucian and Ch'in Ku-li a well-known disciple of Mo Tzu's, both of the fifth century BC (Fu Yüeh was an ancient figure and does not concern us). In the *Lü shih ch'un ch'iu*, however, the list is augmented, and at the head of this list of illustrious individuals is Confucius who was said to have come under the good influence of, amongst others, Lao Tzu. It seems that between the time the *Mo tzu* chapter assumed its present form and the time it was incorporated, in its modified form, into the *Lü shih ch'un ch'iu*, the story of Confucius receiving instruction from Lao Tzu must have become so well known that in revising the list the editors of the *Lü shih ch'un ch'iu* placed Confucius at the head of it. As we know roughly the date of composition of the *Lü shih ch'un ch'iu*, if we could determine approximately the *terminus a quo* of the *Mo tzu* chapter we can determine the period in which the story gained currency. This we are fortunately in a position to do. The *Mo tzu* chapter mentions the death of King K'ang of Sung which took place in 286 BC. Thus we can say that the chapter could not have been completed in its present form before that date, although there is no reason to doubt the authenticity of the saying attributed to Mo Tzu in the opening section. We can say, then, that it must have been within the period of the forty years or so between 286 and 240 BC that the story of the encounter between Confucius and Lao Tzu became widely known and accepted.

We can sum up our somewhat lengthy discussion so far of the problem of whether Lao Tzu was a historical figure who lived in the sixth century BC, in this way. Not only did Mencius show no signs of awareness of Lao Tzu and his school, Chuang Tzu who lived probably well on into the third century BC showed no knowledge of Lao Tzu either. This is surprising in the case of Mencius for he was such a staunch supporter of the Confucian philosophy and was tireless in his attacks on heterodox views, and it is equally surprising in the case of Chuang Tzu for, according to the traditionalist account, he was the successor to Lao Tzu in the Taoist school of thought. We have seen that it was not until the second half of the third century BC that the story of an encounter between Lao Tzu and Confucius became widely known. And it is solely on this story that the traditionalists' case for Lao Tzu being an older contemporary of Confucius is founded.

Apart from the late date of the story of the encounter,

there is another reason for looking upon it with suspicion as evidence of the date of Lao Tzu. When we examine this story we can see that it is, in fact, an illustrative story. It is, therefore, highly precarious to take the events contained in it as historical, particularly where the events concern only the variable factors. In our story, the point is the discomfiture of Confucius in the hands of some hermit or other. The identity of the hermit, the location of the incident and the way the discomfiture is brought about are all variable factors. It is interesting to note that the accounts in the *Shih chi* are not in fact very close to the accounts about the encounter between Lao Tzu and Confucius in the *Chuang tzu*, but resemble, in some features, rather more closely the account in the same work (chapter 26) of a meeting between Lao Lai Tzu—one of the persons with whom Lao Tzu is identified in his biography—and Confucius. This illustrates the point that the identity of the interlocutor is of little importance. Stories of this kind are to be found in more than one work, and one suspects that these originated with schools other than the Confucianist, in many cases probably Taoist. But some of these stories came to be accepted even by Confucianist circles at a fairly early date, as a few of them are to be found even in the *Analects of Confucius*.* If we look upon these stories as forming a genre which must have been popular from fairly early times, then the fact that in a few of these the hermit happens to be Lao Tzu loses any historical significance it might have had they been unique. That a few illustrative stories of probably a late date are to be found in the *Chuang tzu* is hardly sufficient evidence on which to rest the whole case for the historicity, let alone the early date, of Lao Tzu.

We cannot leave the present topic without taking at least a cursory glance at the passages in the *Li chi*. As we have seen,

*See the stories about the madman Chieh Yü of Ch'u, the tillers Ch'ang Chü and Chieh Ni, and the Old Man with the Basket (Book 18, sections 5 to 7).

in these passages Confucius merely recounts what he heard from Lao Tzu when he was with him. The Lao Tzu here is not a hermit who held Taoist views but an elderly gentleman well versed in the rites, as what Confucius learned from him concerned the finer points in their observance. The *Li chi* is a compilation of the first century BC, and as we do not know from what sources these accounts were derived we can do no more than speculate about their date. My conjecture is that these were later in date than the stories in the Taoist tradition, and constituted a move on the part of the Confucians to counter the successful attempts by Taoists to make Confucius a figure of ridicule. Instead of denying flatly that Confucius ever met Lao Tzu, or alternately, that Lao Tzu was a historical figure, they transformed him into an elderly gentleman well versed in the rites and so, in effect, turned him into a good Confucian. This was a very shrewd move, as it is far easier to change the nature of a widely accepted tradition than to discredit it altogether. That the move was successful can be seen from the fact that by the time Ssu-ma Ch'ien came to write the biographies of Lao Tzu and Confucius, he made use of Confucianist sources as well as the Taoist.

There is another tradition which is to be found in the biography of Lao Tzu in the *Shih chi*. This concerns his westward journey through the Pass and the writing of a work in two books at the request of the Keeper of the Pass (*kuan ling yin*). This story has no direct bearing on the date of Lao Tzu, but, nevertheless, it repays closer examination. Now at some time or other, after the story had gained wide acceptance, Kuan Yin* (the Keeper of the Pass) came to be

---

*Kuan Yin, the Keeper of the Pass, is not to be confused with Kuan Yin, the bodhisattva in Chinese Buddhism. There is no connection whatsoever between the two other than the accidental fact that their names, though totally different in Chinese, come out the same in romanized spelling.

regarded as a philosopher in his own right, accredited with
not only philosophical views but a philosophical work as
well. It is interesting that Kuan Yin is mentioned in the *Lü
shih ch'un ch'iu* (chüan 17, pt 7) as valuing 'limpidity'. He is
also mentioned in the final chapter of the *Chuang tzu* which is
a sort of general account of ancient Chinese thought and is
considered by most scholars to be later in date than the main
body of the work. In the *Chuang tzu*, Kuan Yin is mentioned
in only one other chapter, chapter 19, but, again, there are
some reasons for thinking that this chapter may be late as
well. The *Hsün tzu*, for instance, mentions Lao Tzu's views
once but not Kuan Yin, although, curiously enough, the
notion of 'limpidity' figures prominently in a theory of the
mind in chapter 21. This would seem to show that it was
after the composition of the relevant parts of the *Hsün tzu*
that Kuan Yin became an individual with a distinct identity.

Finally, there is one piece of evidence which is of some
interest to us. In the *Yang chu* chapter of the *Lieh tzu*, there is
recorded a conversation between Yang Chu and Ch'in Ku-li
which ends with Ch'in Ku-li saying, 'If one were to ask Lao
Tan and Kuan Yin about your opinion they would agree
with you and if one were to ask the Great Yü and Mo Ti
about mine, they would agree with me.' It is true, most
scholars agree that the *Lieh tzu* is a late compilation, but
much of the material in it is early and there is no reason to
think that this story was an invention by the compiler. The
point that concerns us is the apparent Mohist origin of the
story. It seems hardly likely to be a pure coincidence that not
only the tradition that Confucius received instruction from
Lao Tzu had something to do with the Mohist school, but
the name of Kuan Yin was also coupled with that of Lao Tzu
in the words attributed to a well-known Mohist.

The tentative conclusion we have arrived at concerning
Lao Tzu the man is this. There is no certain evidence that he

was a historical figure. What is certain is that there are two stories about him, and concerning these there are two points worth noting. Firstly, both stories have something to do with the Mohist school; and secondly, both came to be widely known in the forty years or so before the compilation of the *Lü shih ch'un ch'iu* in 240 BC. That in the *Lü shih ch'un ch'iu* the stories are taken for granted may be due to the fact that there probably was a Mohist among the editors. All this, and indeed my whole account of Lao Tzu, is speculative, but when there is so little that is certain there is not only room but need for speculation.

APPENDIX 2*
The Nature of the Work

In the latter part of the Warring States period philosophical works no longer consisted of recorded sayings explicitly attributed to a particular thinker. The *Lao tzu* is no exception. Neither Lao Tzu nor the name of any other person appears in the work. That it is attributed to Lao Tzu is purely a matter of tradition.

Another feature of the works of this period is the increasing use of rhyming passages. In the case of the *Lao tzu* these amount to considerably more than half of the whole work. Such passages must have been meant to be learned by rote with the meaning explained at length in an oral commentary. Hence the cryptic nature of most of the sayings. As these rhyming passages were handed on orally, there probably was no one authoritative form nor one unique interpretation for them. They were common property to followers of various schools sharing a common tendency in thought.

There was, presumably, no one standard collection of such sayings either. This is confirmed by a cursory glance at the bibliographical chapter of the *Han shu*. Besides a work called *Lao lai tzu*, named after one of the figures with whom Lao Tzu was identified in the *Shih chi* biography, there are two works with titles that are interesting. These are the *Lao ch'eng tzu* and the *Cheng chang che*. Now *Lao ch'eng tzu* literally means 'the old man with mature wisdom' while *Cheng chang che* means 'the elder from the state of Cheng'. If we remem-

*As this Appendix was originally written by D. C. Lau for his translation of the Wang Pi text (1963), citations that follow differ slightly from the current translation of the Ma Wang Tui text. (See table on pages x–xi to compare the two versions.) Lau had also divided the text into sections, the numbers of which are included here in parentheses. [ed.]

ber that *Lao tzu* literally means 'the old man' we cannot help being impressed by the similarity of the titles of the three works. As far as I am aware, we have no extant quotations from the *Lao ch'eng tzu*, but fortunately for us there are preserved three quotations from the *Cheng chang che* in the *Han fei tzu* (twice in chapter 34 and once in chapter 37), and these bear a singular resemblance to the *Lao tzu*. We can only conclude that in that period there were a number of works which were Taoist in content, appearing under various titles all of which meant 'old man' or 'elder', and the important point for us is that the *Lao tzu* was only one of these works. It so happened that Lao Tzu was also one of the hermits that figured in the illustrative stories about Confucius. The two facts reinforced each other so that the *Lao tzu* was able to survive as the sole representative of this genre of literature, and, by the last quarter of the third century BC, the work was firmly associated with Lao Tzu, the man who was said to have instructed Confucius in the rites.

Not only were there other collections similar to the *Lao tzu*, but the *Lao tzu* itself probably did not exist in a definitive form until a later period. In this respect, it is interesting to note that in the *Huai nan tzu*, particularly in chapter 12, which uses stories taken from various works as pegs for hanging quotations from the *Lao tzu*, the text explicitly quoted as sayings of Lao Tzu is practically identical with our present text. On the other hand in the *Chieh Lao* (Explanations of Lao) and *Yü Lao* (Illustrations of Lao) chapters in the *Han fei tzu* where quotations are never introduced by 'Lao Tzu said', though in a few cases by 'the Book said', the text is close to, but not identical with, the present text, and quotations attributed to Lao Tzu in the final chapter of the *Chuang tzu*, though in most cases recognizable as such, differ considerably from the present text. It seems then that the text was still in a fluid state in the second half of the third century BC or even later, but by the middle of the second century BC, at the latest, the text already assumed a form very much like the present one. It is possible that this happened in the early years of the Western Han Dynasty. There is some reason to believe that in that period there were already specialist 'professors' (*po shih*) devoted to the study of individual ancient works, including the so-called philosophers (*chu tzu*), as distinct from the classics (*ching*). If that is the case, then the *Lao tzu* which was held in great esteem in court circles was almost certain to have its *po shih*. This would cause the text to become standardized and would also account for the fact that the text used by the editors of the *Huai nan tzu* was already, to all intents and purposes, identical with the present text.

It follows from what we have said about ancient Chinese works that they are best looked upon as anthologies. At best the material contained in such works consists of sayings of a particular thinker, often augmented by later material belonging to the same school. At worst the material is no more than a collection of passages with only a common tendency in thought. A careful reading of the *Lao tzu* cannot but leave us with the impression that it is not only an anthology but an anthology of the second kind. There are various features which give rise to such an impression.

Many chapters fall into sections having, at times, little or no connection with one another. In the compilation of works of the latter part of the Warring States period one of the principles was the placing together of passages about the same topic which sometimes meant no more than passages having one or more catchwords in common. Whether this results in the putting together of passages which are relevant to one another depends on the purpose of the compiler which may be simply to facilitate memorization. This is true of the *Lao tzu*. If we do not bear this in mind and insist on treating chapters as organic wholes we run the risk of distorting the meaning. Two examples will make clear the kind of thing I have in mind. In chapter V we have

> Heaven and earth are ruthless, and treat the myriad creatures as straw dogs; the sage is ruthless, and treats the people as straw dogs. (14)

This is followed by

> Is not the space between heaven and earth like a bellows?
> It is empty without being exhausted:
> The more it works the more comes out. (15)

It is a different point that is made in each passage. In the first passage, the point is that heaven and earth are unfeeling, while in the second it is that they are inexhaustible though empty. There is no connection between the two passages other than the fact that they are both about 'heaven and earth'.

Again, in chapter LXIV we find

> Whoever does anything to it will ruin it; whoever lays hold of it will lose it. Therefore the sage, because he does nothing, never ruins anything; and, because he does not lay hold of anything, loses nothing. (154a)

This is followed by

> In their enterprises the people
> Always ruin them when on the verge of success.
> Be as careful at the end as at the beginning
> And there will be no ruined enterprises. (155)

Here we can see that the two passages have been placed together because they both deal with how things come to be ruined and how this can be avoided. But beyond this the point made in each passage is, once again, quite different. In the first passage, the sage avoids failure by not doing anything, while in the second the common people are exhorted to avoid failure when on the verge of success by being as careful at the end as at the beginning. In the one case, action is condemned as the cause of failure, because true success lies in not taking any action at all. In the other, it is assumed that success can be achieved through action, provided that one can be careful throughout the duration of the action. The two points of view are not simply unconnected; they are inconsistent.

Since passages which are placed together in the same chapter are very often unconnected or even inconsistent, many scholars in the past have felt dissatisfaction with the existing arrangement of the text, and some have even attempted to have the text rearranged. As these attempts seem to me to be based on mistaken assumptions, I have chosen to deal with the problem by a different method.★

In the *Lao tzu* the same passage is often to be found in different chapters. As the work is so short it is exceedingly unlikely that a single author should be so much given to repeating himself, but if we look upon the work as an anthology it is easier to see how this could have happened. Although in some cases one gets the impression that a passage which occurs more than once fits better into one context than into another, in other cases it seems to fit equally well into the different contexts. This confirms the suggestion I made earlier regarding the probability that these passages existed as independent sayings with no fixed contexts. Again, in some cases it is clear that what is found in more than one chapter is really the same passage in a slightly different form. Incidentally, the recurrence of the same passage in different contexts often helps the reader to understand a text which, generally speaking, offers so little contextual aid.

A few illustrative examples will make this clear. In chapter XVII we find

> When there is not enough faith, there is lack of good faith. (40)

This is found also in chapter XXIII (53). In neither case is this

★This refers to the further subdivision of the text into sections in the translation of the Wang Pi text. [ed.]

passage connected with its context. In fact it has more affinity
with the passage in chapter XLIX which says

> Those who are of good faith I have faith in. Those who are lacking in good
> faith I also have faith in. In so doing I gain in good faith. (111)

We can see here that what is advocated is that we should
extend our faith to even those who lack good faith. This is
because by so doing we have some hopes of transforming
them into men of good faith, whereas placing no faith in
them will serve only to confirm them in their bad ways.
Hence in a way the lack of good faith is the result of the lack
of faith.

In contrast to the passage that does not seem to belong to
any context, there is the passage which seems to belong to
more than one. In chapter IV we have

> Blunt the sharpness;
> Untangle the knots;
> Soften the glare;
> Let your wheels move only along old ruts. (12)

In chapter LII we have

> Block the openings,
> Shut the doors,
> And all your life you will not run dry.
> Unblock the openings,
> Add to your troubles,
> And to the end of your days you will be beyond salvation. (118)

Yet in chapter LVI we find

> Block the openings;
> Shut the doors.
> Blunt the sharpness;
> Untangle the knots;
> Soften the glare;
> Let your wheels move only along old ruts. (129)

Faced with this, one's first reaction is to think that sections 12
and 118 are independent passages and that section 129 is a
conflation of the two. This is probably the case, but one

cannot be absolutely sure because sections 12 and 118 happen to share the same rhyme, and the two opening lines of section 12, moreover, happen to consist, like the lines in section 118, of three characters each.

We have seen that in chapter LXIV there is the passage

> Whoever does anything to it will ruin it; whoever lays hold of it will lose it. (154)

> Therefore the sage, because he does nothing, never ruins anything; and, because he does not lay hold of anything, loses nothing. (154a)

This passage does not have any connection with either what follows or what goes before. Section 154 appears again in chapter XXIX:

> Whoever takes the empire and wishes to do anything to it I see will have no respite. The empire is a sacred vessel and nothing should be done to it. Whoever does anything to it will ruin it; whoever lays hold of it will lose it. (66)

Here a different context is given to the opening sentence. Whether this is, in any sense, the original context it is impossible to say, but it is at least more helpful to the understanding of the sentence than the obvious conclusion that 'the sage, because he does nothing, never ruins anything, and, because he does not lay hold of anything, loses nothing'.

Then there are cases where we find slightly different formulations of what is essentially the same passage. In chapter XXII we find

> He does not show himself, and so is conspicuous;
> He does not consider himself right, and so is illustrious;
> He does not brag, and so has merit;
> He does not boast, and so endures. (50b)

In chapter XXIV there is this,

> He who shows himself is not conspicuous;
> He who considers himself right is not illustrious;
> He who brags will have no merit;
> He who boasts will not endure. (55)

It is obvious that these two passages are simply the positive and negative ways of saying the same thing.

Take another case. In chapter LXX we find

> My words are very easy to understand and very easy to put into practice, yet no one in the world can understand them or put them into practice. (170)

In chapter LXXVIII we have

> That the weak overcomes the strong,
> And the submissive overcomes the hard,
> Everyone in the world knows yet no one can put this knowledge into
>   practice. (187)

Here we have not only a different formulation of the same saying, but also an apparent difference in substance. In section 170 it is said that '*no one* in the world can understand', while in section 187 it is said that '*everyone* in the world knows'. The difference, however, is more apparent than real. What the sage says is really very easy to understand, and in a sense everyone understands it, but it is because the truth is so simple and easy to understand that the clever people tend to find it ridiculous. But the difference between those who understand and those who do not is unimportant, because they are alike in their inability to act on the moral contained in the words. This seems to show that the same saying, in the process of oral transmission, assumed slightly different forms in different contexts while retaining essentially the same moral.

The work then is an anthology, compiled by more than one hand, and there are at least three ways in which the existing material has been dealt with. Firstly, two or more pre-existing passages are joined together. This is too common to need examples. Secondly, a pre-existing passage is followed by a passage of exposition. A good example is section 30 and 30a in chapter XIII. Thirdly, a pre-existing passage is preceded by a passage of exposition. Section 191 in chapter LXXIX is an example. In cases of the last two types, it frequently happens that the pre-existing passage is in rhyme, while the exposition that is added is in prose, but it also sometimes happens that the exposition added is so contrived as to rhyme with the original passage. Section 7a is a particularly interesting example, because, by rhyming *chü* with *ch'ü*, the editor was in fact revealing that he pronounced *ch'ü* in a way different from the way it was pronounced when section 7 was composed.

In all these cases, the clue to the editing lies often in the use of connectives like *ku* (therefore, thus) and *shih yi* (hence). Naturally, these words are often used in their proper function as links in a consecutive argument, but more often they are to be found precisely where the logical link is weakest. A careful reading of the texts of the latter part of the Warring States period with an eye to the continuity of argument will confirm the impression that these words were used to connect passages which have in fact little or no connection. There is one clear example of these words being deliberately put to such a use in the *Huai nan tzu*. Chapter 12 of this work consists of a collection of stories each culminating in a quotation from the *Lao tzu*. The quotations in most cases are from a single chapter of the existing text, but in three cases the quotations are from two different chapters. Instead of having the quotation from each chapter preceded by the formula 'Lao Tzu said', a single formula serves to introduce both quotations which are separated by the word *ku*. It seems that the editors of the *Huai nan tzu* were still aware of the editorial function of such words and used them as an indication to the reader that the two parts of the same quotation were in fact from different chapters of the *Lao tzu*.

One type of editorial comment stands out very clearly. There are certain set formulae that are used more than once.

For instance, chapters XII, XXXVIII, and LXXII all end with the line

> Therefore he discards the one and takes the other.

Again, chapters XXI and LIV and the opening section in chapter LVII all end with the line

> How do I know that ... is (or are) like that? By means of this.

On the question of the date of the work it is not possible to arrive at an exact answer. As we have seen, there is reason to believe that there were similar collections in the Warring States attributed to other wise old men, and that there were probably different versions of the *Lao tzu* at one time, though by the beginning of the Han Dynasty the text was already very much the same as the text we have at present. It also seems to be clear that the text must have existed for some time before then, for we find a highly esoteric interpretation in the *Chieh Lao* chapter in the *Han fei tzu* which was probably somewhat earlier than the *Huai nan tzu*, as the text quoted in it from the *Lao tzu* diverges to a greater extent from our present text. As to how long a period is needed for a tradition of esoteric interpretation to grow up, this is a question to which there is no ready answer.

Taking all factors into account, I am inclined to the hypothesis that some form of the *Lao tzu* existed by the beginning of the third century BC at the latest. This is supported to a certain extent by the fact that in the *Lao tzu* are to be found many ideas which were associated with a number of thinkers of the second half of the fourth and the first quarter of the third century BC. The general impression one gains in reading the *Lao tzu* is that it was the product of this same golden period which produced so many great thinkers many of whom congregated at Chi Hsia in the state of Ch'i during the second half of the fourth century BC. This does not, of course, mean that the *Lao tzu* does not contain some material which is much earlier than this period. It has, for instance, been often pointed out that the line

> Do good to him who has done you an injury,

in chapter LXIII was already treated as a common saying in the *Analects of Confucius* (14.36). Again, a passage very similar to section 79 in chapter XXXVI is attributed in both the *Han fei tzu* and the *Chan kuo ts'e* to a work called the *Book of Chou* and quoted as from a poem in the *Lü shih ch'un ch'iu*. In a work of this nature it is not surprising that it should contain material that ranges over a wide period of time.

GLOSSARY*

BOOK OF CHANGES. Although this is numbered among the Thirteen Confucian Classics, it was, in its basic text, originally no more than a manual for divination by the method of the hexagrams. A hexagram, which is made up of two trigrams, is a figure consisting of six lines, one placed above another. As there are two kinds of lines, the broken and the continuous, the total number of possible hexagrams is sixty-four. There is a text on each hexagram which explains the prognosticatory significance both of the hexagram as a whole and the individual lines. But from very early times, attempts were made to read a philosophical significance into this system. This is the purpose of some of the commentaries, commonly known as 'the ten wings'. The broken line is taken to represent the *yin* and the continuous the *yang*, and the *yin* and the *yang* are looked upon as the basic forces in the universe which wax and wane alternately and relative to each other, thus giving rise to a cyclic process of change. An obvious instance of this process is the four seasons. In summer the *yang* force is at its highest and the *yin* at its lowest while in autumn the *yang* is on the decline and the *yin* on the rise. In winter the state of affairs is the reverse of that in summer, and that in spring the reverse of that in autumn.

BOOK OF HISTORY. Also one of the Thirteen Confucian Classics. This is the earliest extant collection of historical documents. The present text consists of 58 chapters. Of these 33 chapters which are equivalent to 28 of the so-called 'modern script' text are considered genuine while the rest are very late forgeries compiled out of ancient material. The

*This Glossary was originally prepared by D. C. Lau for his translation of the Wang Pi text, 1963. [ed.]

period of history covered ranges from Yao who was one of the legendary kings to the Chou Dynasty.

BOOK OF ODES. Another of the Thirteen Confucian Classics. It is the earliest collection of poems, some three hundred in all, that were composed in the five centuries or so before the time of Confucius. The work is divided into three parts, the *feng*, the *ya*, and the *sung*. The *feng* consists of folk songs of the various states; the *ya* consists of songs sung at court during banquets and entertainment of guests; and the *sung* consists of songs in praise of imperial ancestors sung on sacrificial occasions.

CHAN KUO TS'E (*The Stratagems of the Warring States*). In the Warring States period there was a large class of political adventurers who travelled from one state to another offering advice to the rulers. This work is a collection of such stratagems arranged under the various states, which has come down to us in a version edited by Liu Hsiang. It is not certain when the work was first compiled, but there is a view that this was done at the beginning of the Han Dynasty.

CHI HSIA. In the Warring States period wandering scholars and political advisers attained a much higher status than in the preceding period, and it became fashionable for feudal lords to gather them at their courts. One of the most famous of such gatherings was at Chi Hsia in the state of Ch'i. The Chi gate was the western gate of the capital of Ch'i, and Chi Hsia simply means 'under the Chi gate'. The scholars gathered there for discussions and it is said that an academy was built there for that purpose. Chi Hsia was at the height of its fame under King Wei (356-320 BC) and King Hsüan (319-301 BC), though it probably began before then and certainly was revived at the time of King Hsiang (283-265 BC) when Hsün Tzu was the most senior among the scholars. Many of the brilliant thinkers of the period were at one time or another at Chi Hsia. It is interesting to note that, though he was in Ch'i during the time of King Hsüan, Mencius never was numbered amongst the scholars of Chi Hsia.

CHOU. The name of the Dynasty which lasted from 1027 to 256 BC, with its capital transferred to Loyang in 770. By the Spring and Autumn period, however, the Chou emperor was no more than the titular head of the empire and his territory was no bigger than that of a minor state. It was to Loyang that Confucius was supposed to have gone to seek the instruction of Lao Tzu.

CONFUCIUS (551–479 BC). Confucius was brought up in humble circumstances but was, from an early age, known for his learning. Though he had hoped to attain a position of political influence, he never succeeded in realizing this ambition and his life was spent in teaching. The importance of Confucius lies in his being the first great teacher as well as philosopher. In denying no one acceptance as a disciple provided that he was genuinely eager to learn, he probably did more than anyone in preventing education from becoming the exclusive privilege of the aristocracy. He was the first philosopher to whom a collection of sayings is attributed which is, on the whole, reliable. This is the *Lun yü* or the *Analects of Confucius* as it is commonly known in English.

CHUANG TZU. We know very little about Chuang Tzu. According to the *Shih chi*, his given name was Chou and he was a contemporary of King Hui (369–319 BC) of Wei and King Hsüan of Ch'i. It is also said that his thought was derived from that of Lao Tzu. The *Chuang tzu* is certainly a very mixed collection. Some of the earliest chapters probably represent the thought of Chuang Tzu while the later chapters probably belong to the Ch'in or even the early Han period. Although Chuang Tzu is always mentioned with Lao Tzu as the other great Taoist thinker, the thought in the more

representative parts of the *Chuang tzu* differs considerably
from that of the *Lao tzu*. Two points in the thought of the
Chuang tzu are particularly interesting. Firstly, judgements
about right and wrong are said to be always made from some
point of view, so that not only are different judgements made
concerning the same things from different points of view but
also it is impossible to decide on the relative merits of these
different standpoints. As a solution, the *Chuang tzu* suggests a
higher point of view which is impartial in its attitude
towards all the possible points of view. These are treated as
equally valid or, if you like, equally invalid. It follows that
life is desirable and death undesirable only from the point of
view of the living. How then does one know that the reverse
is not the case from the point of view of the dead? The result
is the position that there is no reason to prefer one view to
another. Secondly, the *Chuang tzu* shows great interest in the
problem of whether there is something which is in effective
control over mental activities such as sense-perception. This
'mind' or 'soul' which is the elusive sovereign of the body
seems to be thought of as a counterpart to the '*tao*' which is
the equally elusive sovereign of the universe.

HAN FEI TZU. Han Fei Tzu was a member of the royal
house of the state of Han. He was said to have studied under
Hsün Tzu at the same time as Li Ssu who subsequently
became the prime minister of Ch'in. When Han was on the
verge of collapse in the face of the attack by Ch'in, Han Fei
was sent as envoy to Ch'in. Though the king of Ch'in was
pleased with him, he was said to have died as a result of the
machinations of Li Ssu, who was jealous of his superior
talent. In his thought Han Fei combined the teachings of a
number of schools to form the system known as Legalist
thought. It combined 'the methods of dealing with the
subjects' advocated by Shen Pu-hai, 'the rule of law' advo-

cated by Lord Shang and 'the exploitation of the vantage position of the ruler' advocated by Shen Tao. Some Taoist ideas are also given a Legalist interpretation.

HAN SHU. Pan Piao began the *Han shu* but died before he could complete it. His son Pan Ku carried on and all but finished the work. It covered the history of the Western Han Dynasty to Wang Mang. The bibliographical chapter of the *Han shu* is of the greatest interest and importance to students of ancient Chinese literature. Most of the ancient works came down to posterity through the recension of Liu Hsiang who was entrusted with the task of editing the books in the Imperial library. His son Liu Hsin (d. AD 23) made a catalogue of these books under the title of the *Ch'i lüeh* (*The Seven Summaries*). This is no longer extant, but fortunately we have the *Han shu* bibliographical chapter which was based on the *Ch'i lüeh* and it is to this chapter that we owe most of our information about the books in the ancient period.

HSÜN TZU. After Mencius, the most important name in the Confucian school. From the *Hsün tzu* we can see that the most important points in his teaching are these. Human nature is evil. This means that if men were to follow the dictates of their nature, the result can only be conflict and disorder. As a solution to this problem the sage kings invented morality. Since morality has no basis in his nature, the only way of making man moral is by sheer habituation. Hsün Tzu draws a clear distinction between what pertains to heaven and what pertains to man. Under the influence of the Taoists, heaven in the *Hsün tzu* became no more than Nature in its regularity, which is no longer looked upon as having a moral purpose. The greatest contribution of Hsün Tzu lies in his realization that if heaven is nothing but the regular workings of Nature man should no longer model his way of life on Nature but should work out his own salvation. Hence the importance of the clear understanding of the difference between 'heaven' and 'man'.

HUAI NAN TZU. Liu An, a grandson of the first emperor of the Han Dynasty, was made Prince of Huai Nan in 164 BC, ten years after his father, who held the same title, starved himself to death on being banished by Emperor Wen for his part in an unsuccessful rebellion. Liu An, following in the footsteps of his father, cast covetous eyes on the Imperial throne and when his plot came to light committed suicide (in 122 BC) rather than face the death sentence. The *Huai nan tzu* was compiled by scholars he gathered around him at his court. Its value and that of the *Lü shih ch'un ch'iu* before it cannot be put too high. When most ancient Chinese works are of uncertain date, these two stand out as landmarks of certainty. Moreover, the views of earlier thinkers whose works are no longer extant are often incorporated in these two works. In this respect, the *Huai nan tzu* is even more important than its predecessor, which it surpasses in philosophical interest. This rich mine of information has, however, scarcely been tapped.

KUAN TZU. A work attributed to Kuan Chung, the most illustrious statesman in the Spring and Autumn period through whose efforts Duke Huan of Ch'i (685–643 BC) became the acknowledged leader of the feudal lords, but in fact a collection of heterogeneous materials which vary widely in nature as well as in date.

LIEH TZU. Lieh Tzu is a rather nebulous figure, and the present work named after him is a late compilation, though the compiler made use of a great deal of material which was genuinely early. The argument from the existence of Lieh Tzu who is himself problematical to that of Lao Tzu is of no value at all.

Lü SHIH CH'UN CH'IU. A work compiled by the scholars in the service of Lü Pu-wei, the prime minister of Ch'in from 249 to 237 BC, with a postface dated 240 BC. It was meant to be a compendium of all knowledge that mattered and is therefore a useful source for the views of schools of thought whose representative works are no longer extant.

MENCIUS. The most illustrious thinker in the Confucian school. Like Confucius, he spent many years travelling in different states trying to persuade rulers to follow his philosophy but met with little success. He is best known for his theory that human nature is good. This means that man is born with the ability to distinguish between right and wrong, naturally approves of the former and disapproves of the latter and feels ashamed when he fails to do what is his duty. This aimed, on the one hand, at countering the theory current in his day that human nature consists merely of appetites and, on the other, at re-interpreting the traditional view subscribed to by the Confucian that morality was decreed by heaven. Mencius successfully broke down the rigid distinction and opposition between human nature and heavenly decree. Morality is as much part of human nature as appetites, and appetites are as much part of heavenly decree as morality. Another of the views of Mencius is worth noting. The function of the ruler is the furtherance of the good of the people. If a ruler tyrannizes over the people he is no longer a ruler but just 'a fellow' and the people have the right to revolution.

MO TZU. We know very little about Mo Tzu. From the *Shih chi* we learn only that his given name was Ti and his surname was Mo, that he was an officer of the state of Sung and was, according to one view, contemporary with, but according to another later than, Confucius. The most basic tenet of his teachings is 'love without discrimination' which is the 'will of heaven'. He was an extreme utilitarian. Everything that is of no obvious utility to the people is to be given up. This includes war, elaborate burial, prolonged mourning, and the performance of music. He was a considerable mechanic and was able to devise tools of defensive warfare. One extremely interesting part of the *Mo tzu* is the six chapters devoted to the discussion of topics of a scientific and logical nature. These probably belonged to a later period but there is no doubt that they were the work of the Mohist school. Unfortunately, the text, through centuries of neglect, is exceedingly corrupt.

THE PASS. In the story of the westward journey of Lao Tzu the Pass he was supposed to have gone through has been variously identified as the Han Ku Pass and the San Pass, but it is most probably the former which is to the south of Ling Pao Hsien in the modern province of Honan.

SHIH CHI. Ssu-ma Ch'ien succeeded his father as official Historian in 108 BC at the age of thirty-eight, and devoted himself to the preparation of material for the writing of a general history of China, as this was the unrealized ambition of his father. This resulted in the *Shih chi* which he finished about 90 BC after he had suffered the most humiliating punishment at the hands of Emperor Wu in 98 BC. This work has exercised tremendous influence on subsequent historiography. It set the pattern for all the later so-called 'official histories'. The *Shih chi* consists mainly of biographies, though it contains a number of tables and there are chapters on various general topics like 'rites', 'the calendar', 'astronomy', 'irrigation', and 'public finance'. He drew on a large number of works, archives of his own office and oral tradition which he diligently collected in his travels. In cases where he was able to judge he chose what he believed to be reliable. But he did not reject what was no more than doubtful where he had no grounds for choice. This would account for the inclusion of so much legend in the biography of Lao Tzu.

SUNG K'ENG. The only thing we know for certain about Sung K'eng's views is to be found in the *Hsün tzu*. He is there represented as saying that man does not by nature desire a great deal. As strife is the result of covetousness, if only men could be brought to realize that they do not in fact desire a great deal, there would be no strife. He also believes that there is no disgrace in being insulted. People fight because they feel disgraced, and if they could realize that there is no disgrace in being insulted, they would not be inclined to fight. These views seem rather paradoxical, but these might not have been presented in their best light by the *Hsün tzu* which is critical of them. At any rate, they do show that there is some affinity between the views of Sung K'eng and the austere and pacifist views held by the Mohists.

TAOISM. The English term 'Taoism' is ambiguous. It is used to translate both the Chinese term '*tao chia* (the school of the *tao*)' and '*tao chiao* (the Taoist religion)'. In the present work, Taoism is used only in the former sense, though the more popular schools of Taoist thought in the early Han probably had considerable affinity with the views of the later devotees of the Taoist religion which came into being towards the end of the Eastern Han.

TE. *Te* means 'virtue', and seems to be related to its homophone meaning 'to get'. In its Taoist usage, *te* refers to the virtue of a thing (which is what it 'gets' from the *tao*). In other words, *te* is the nature of a thing, because it is in virtue of its *te* that a thing is what it is. But in the *Lao tzu* the term is not a particularly important one and is often used in its more conventional senses, of which it has several. Firstly, it means 'moral virtue'; secondly, it means 'bounty'; thirdly, it means 'to be grateful' or 'to be conscious that others ought to be grateful to oneself'.

T'IEN. This term means both 'heaven' and the 'skies'. Because of this, there is a tendency in Chinese thought not to distinguish the two.

WANG PI (AD 226-49). A brilliant thinker who, in spite of the fact that he died at the early age of twenty-three, has exercised tremendous influence on subsequent thought. He has left a commentary on the *Book of Changes* and one on the *Lao tzu*. In the former he gave a philosophical, rather than numerological, interpretation, and this commentary of his was accepted into the corpus of 'official commentaries' on the Confucian classes in T'ang times. His commentary on the *Lao tzu* is equally important because it is the earliest extant philosophical commentary on the work. He is also responsible for the tendency to find an affinity between the two works.

YIN, YANG. It is probable that the two terms originally meant 'sunless' and 'sunny'. For instance, the southern side of a mountain is *yang* and the northern side *yin*, while the southern side of a river is *yin* and the northern side *yang*. Then they came to mean 'female' and 'male'. Finally, they became general terms for the fundamental and opposite forces or principles of nature. In the commentaries on the *Book of Changes*, *yang* was used to describe the continuous, and *yin*, the broken, line in a hexagram. The fact that *yin* and *yang* became important philosophical terms is not unconnected with the fact that the *Book of Changes* was transformed at the same time from a manual for divination to a work of profound philosophical significance.

ABOUT THE TRANSLATOR

D. C. LAU, who died in 2010, was the twentieth century's foremost translator of the Chinese classics into English. He also wrote extensively on Chinese philosophy and philosophical texts. Besides the *Lao-tzu: Tao te ching* he also translated the *Analects* of Confucius and the *Mencius*. He was Professor of Chinese at the School of Oriental and African Studies, University of London, before becoming Professor of Chinese Language and Literature at the Chinese University of Hong Kong in 1978.

ABOUT THE INTRODUCER

SARAH ALLAN is Burlington Northern Foundation Professor of Asian Studies at Dartmouth College. Previously she taught Classical Chinese and Chinese Philosophy at the School of Oriental and African Studies, University of London. Her books include: *The Heir and the Sage: Dynastic Legend in Early China*; *The Shape of the Turtle: Myth, Art and Cosmos in Early China* and *The Way of Water and Sprouts of Virtue*.

This book is set in BEMBO which was cut
by the punch-cutter Francesco Griffo
for the Venetian printer-publisher
Aldus Manutius in early 1495
and first used in a pamphlet
by a young scholar
named Pietro
Bembo.